STUDIES IN

AFRICAN AMERICAN HISTORY AND CULTURE

edited by

GRAHAM HODGES
COLGATE UNIVERSITY

A GARLAND SERIES

"WE WANT JOBS"

A HISTORY OF AFFIRMATIVE ACTION

ROBERT J. WEISS

GARLAND PUBLISHING, INC.
NEW YORK & LONDON / 1997

Library of Congress Cataloging-in-Publication Data

Weiss, Robert J., 1954–
    "We want jobs" : a history of affirmative action / Robert J.
Weiss.
        p.   cm. — (Studies in African American history and
culture)
    Includes bibliographical references and index.
    ISBN 0-8153-2750-1 (alk. paper)
    1. Affirmative action programs—United States—History.
I. Title. II. Series.
HF5549.5.A34W44 1997
331.13'3'0973—dc21

                                                          96-30018

Printed on acid-free, 250-year-life paper
Manufactured in the United States of America

Dedication

This book is dedicated in loving memory to my father, George P. Weiss.

Contents

Introduction

This monograph is a study of equal employment opportunity, with special emphasis on the development of affirmative action. It examines the evolution of public policies designed to eradicate and overcome the effects of economic discrimination in the United States. The narrative focuses primarily on the period after 1960, although the first two chapters provide background information dating back to the nineteenth century.

Because this topic is potentially so broad, I had to narrow the focus of the study. It is therefore important to understand which issues the book does and does not address. To begin with, the monograph focuses on the issue of *jobs*. Its major focus is the struggle by African Americans to secure a permanent and equitable foothold in U.S. industries and labor unions. Related issues such as housing and busing, although examined briefly, are not explored in any detail. Moreover, this book does not deal with the subject of education, because the problems and enforcement mechanisms involved in education differed somewhat from those affecting industries and unions. Moreover, the study focuses primarily on the actions of the federal government, although a brief analysis of state policies is included for the sake of context. Finally, the study addresses the question of *race* discrimination. To the extent that the African-American struggle for economic justice overlapped with those of other groups—females, Latinos, Native Americans, Asian Americans—these groups have been incorporated into the narrative. Detailed analysis of goals and strategies, however, is reserved for African Americans.

The central theme of this book is the rejection by civil rights groups of gradualism in favor of rapid, concrete gains and the coalescence of an opposition to this process. This study argues that civil rights groups spearheaded the drive for civil rights legislation and subsequently relied on the courts and the federal bureaucracy to implement progressively broader affirmative action policies. The failure to achieve more than token progress toward equal employment opportunity prior to the 1960s convinced most civil rights groups of the inadequacy of vague promises of nondiscrimination. Consequently, by the early 1960s, while most white liberals argued for legislation to ensure simple nondiscrimination, civil rights groups such as CORE and the NAACP already were espousing concrete affirmative actions, including numerical goals and modification of traditional business practices.

The phrase *affirmative action* is vague and often misunderstood. Affirmative action is frequently equated with quotas. In fact, quotas represent only the most extreme form of affirmative action. Affirmative action can best be defined as any policy or practice designed to overcome the effects of past discrimination. According to economist Barbara Bergmann, affirmative action has three basic objectives: (1) to overcome discrimination; (2) to increase diversity within the labor force; and (3) to reduce poverty among groups historically victimized by discrimination. Proponents of affirmative action recognized that the mere prohibition of employment discrimination was not sufficient to negate the effects of more than three centuries of slavery and second-class citizenship. They argued that African Americans required, and were entitled to, special assistance until they could compete with whites on an equal basis.

To acknowledge the need for affirmative action was one thing, however, and to achieve a consensus on appropriate policies was another. In a March 1973 article in *Fortune*, Daniel Seligman proposed a four-tier classification of antidiscrimination policies: (1) simple nondiscrimination; (2) "pure" affirmative action, that is, policies such as job training and remedial education designed to increase the pool of qualified minority workers; (3) goals and timetables, which are *flexible* numerical hiring targets; and (4) fixed, rigid quotas. As the demands of civil rights leaders increasingly moved toward the latter stages, many individuals and groups who had sympathized with the more moderate goals of the movement joined in opposition to this new "extremism." The result was the shattering of the liberal-labor-civil rights coalition that had emerged during the New Deal.

The issue of job discrimination was a central feature of the civil rights movement throughout the twentieth century. Job discrimination victimized African Americans from *all* classes and regions of the country—North as well as South—and defied simplistic solutions. The key political milestones in the struggle against job discrimination were the passage of the Civil Rights Act of 1964 and the issuing of executive orders by presidents Kennedy, Johnson, and Nixon mandating "affirmative action" by federal contractors. These actions enabled civil rights groups—with the assistance of public interest lawyers, federal judges, and sympathetic bureaucrats—to incorporate many of their definitions and proposals regarding job discrimination into the federal equal employment apparatus. As the complexities and magnitude of job discrimination increasingly revealed themselves in the course of the 1960s and early 1970s, many liberal politicians who had underestimated the scope of the problem and were poorly prepared to address the issue of *systemic* discrimination came to accept the necessity of affirmative action as defined by civil rights activists. Moreover, the existence of legal and bureaucratic mechanisms to challenge the racial policies of employers and unions enabled civil rights groups to pursue their economic goals without engaging in the protracted processes of building coalitions and compromising objectives that were necessary to pass civil rights laws. By the 1970s, advocates of affirmative action generally had come to define their objectives as the attainment of proportional representation by African Americans in employment and union membership throughout the economy within a limited time span. Underlying this goal was the assumption that in the absence of discrimination African Americans would have achieved proportional representation in most or all segments of the U.S. economy.

As the concept of affirmative action broadened, so did the opposition to its implementation. This opposition was motivated by racial, economic, and ideological factors. Employers objected to the surrender of a degree of autonomy in hiring and promotion procedures and criticized what they defined as a modification of the merit system. Labor unions, entrusted with protecting the jobs of their members, felt threatened by the movement of black workers into traditionally white areas of employment. Some liberals who clung to the vision of a color-blind society rejected the color-consciousness inherent in affirmative action. Many writers and intellectuals recounted the historical use of quotas to limit the participation of Jews in a number of U.S. institutions. Conservatives who opposed even the most basic civil rights reforms could not accept the philosophy of affirmative action. Underlying some of this opposition, of course, was continued racial prejudice.

One critical factor in crystallizing this opposition to affirmative action was the economic downturn of the 1970s and 1980s. Affirmative action was introduced to the U.S. economy during a period of rapid economic growth. The expansion of the economic "pie" enabled black workers to progress without substantially displacing white workers. By 1970, however, this economic surge had been replaced by "stagflation" and recession, which transformed the arena in which the affirmative action conflict was conducted. In the absence of sustained growth, the U.S. economy became more of a "zero-sum game" in which black advancement was more likely to occur at the expense of white workers. This situation was especially troublesome for labor unions, which, already experiencing a decline in membership, sought to protect their members' jobs while being pressured by the government and civil rights groups to admit nonwhites. The struggle over increasingly scarce resources exacerbated existing racial tensions within the labor force.

The same economic forces, however, that intensified white opposition to affirmative action worked to increase black demands for compensatory treatment. As was true in previous economic recessions, black workers, concentrated in less-skilled, blue-collar occupations and lacking seniority status in most fields, disproportionately lost their jobs. Determined to avoid a recurrence of "last hired, first fired," black groups advocated affirmative action, including proportional hiring, modification of seniority arrangements, and back pay, as a defense against the effects of the economic downturn. The result was a fundamental conflict of interest between white and black workers, a struggle complicated by racial animosities.

Compounding all these difficulties were the inadequate enforcement efforts of federal antidiscrimination agencies. The period following 1960 witnessed a proliferation of executive orders, civil rights laws, and bureaucratic regulations requiring nondiscrimination and affirmative action by employers and unions. The federal government established an imposing apparatus to ensure union and business compliance with nondiscrimination regulations regarding testing, interviews, educational requirements, seniority arrangements, wage scales, promotions, and a number of related practices. Several large companies, including AT&T and the major steel producers, entered into compacts with federal agencies that provided for back pay and increased opportunities for minority and female workers. Employers throughout the nation implemented affirmative action plans and hired affirmative action officers to oversee them.

Despite these developments, affirmative action remained a paper compliance program in many areas. Employers and unions often devoted greater energy and resources to circumventing affirmative action regulations than they did toward implementing them. The preeminent federal equal employment opportunity agencies—the Equal Employment Opportunity Commission (EEOC) and the Office of Federal Contract Compliance (OFCC)—were understaffed, poorly financed, and overburdened and lacked adequate enforcement powers. By the mid-1970s, for example, the EEOC's backlog exceeded 125,000 cases. The time and expenses involved in pursuing bureaucratic relief, coupled with the uncertainty of success, discouraged many workers from filing complaints. The philosophy of "voluntary compliance" often prevented government officials from pressuring companies into adhering to the law. The very concept of affirmative action remained vague and difficult to define. How did one measure "underutilization" or identify "good faith efforts?" This confusion and uncertainty impeded effective enforcement of equal opportunity laws. For most civil rights groups, the legacy of federal antidiscrimination efforts was unfulfilled promises. While these groups criticized federal activities as inadequate, many businesses and labor unions denounced these same actions as excessive. As opposition to affirmative action broadened, the movement increasingly became a minority one, pursued by women's and minority groups such as NOW and the NAACP. Opposition to affirmative action has become a staple of the conservative movement that has emerged since the early 1970s. At the same time, the questions of job discrimination and the plight of African-American workers remain unresolved to this day.

Acknowledgments

This monograph grew out of my Ph.D. dissertation, which was submitted to the Department of History at New York University in 1985. I therefore would like once again to express my gratitude to those individuals at NYU who guided me through the dissertation process. First and foremost, I wish to acknowledge the support and contributions of my dissertation adviser, the late Albert U. Romasco. The other members of my dissertation committee were David M. Reimers, Thomas H. Bender, Daniel J. Walkowitz, and the late Vincent P. Carosso. In addition, Irwin Unger read and contributed to the manuscript. Among those who were especially supportive during my graduate studies were Carl E. Prince, Frederick C. Schult, and the late John W. Wilkes. I am also grateful to Deborah Truhan, formerly of the NYU Center for Latin American and Caribbean Studies, who critiqued and proofread the manuscript.

A special note of gratitude to those who agreed to be interviewed for this monograph and thereby contributed information I could not otherwise have acquired: James Haughton, Herbert Hill, James MacNamara, Leon Panetta, and Robert C. Weaver.

The incentive to expand and publish the work was provided by Garland Publishers. I wish to express my appreciation to my editors at Garland for their support: Robert McKenzie, Michael Galligan, and Kristi Long. I also wish to thank Mollie Quasebarth for formatting and proofreading the manuscript.

The challenge to expand the dissertation into a book was made easier by the encouragement of many friends and colleagues, whose names are too numerous to list. I would be remiss, however, in failing to mention Robert Tomes of St. John's University, on whose advice and support—moral and academic—I came to rely as I was completing the project.

Finally, a very special thank you to my family for their encouragement and support throughout these long years.

"We Want Jobs"

I

Discrimination and Protest: An Overview

Economic discrimination has been an inherent feature of race relations in the United States since the first blacks arrived in the North American colonies in 1619. It was widespread in the North as well as the South and, as late as 1960, relegated blacks to a vastly inferior position within the U.S. economy. The desire for equal employment opportunity was a major feature of the civil rights movement of the post-World War II era.

Under slavery, blacks were generally confined to agricultural and domestic work. Some slaves, however, primarily urban slaves, acquired valuable artisanal skills, especially in the construction trades. According to one study of six southern cities, over 20 percent of urban slaves worked as artisans, usually as masons, blacksmiths, carpenters, and painters. In fact, of the 120,000 southern artisans recorded in a census of 1865, about 100,000 were black.[1]

The abolition of slavery generated some immediate gains for southern blacks. During the period 1859-1879, the material income of blacks on large plantations increased by 30 percent, and work hours declined by approximately 33 percent. The share of agricultural income received by former plantation slaves increased 150 percent.[2] Following these initial gains, African Americans experienced little economic improvement for the remainder of the nineteenth century. One crucial factor impeding black progress was the failure of Reconstruction to distribute land to the former slaves, thereby relegating most blacks to the relatively powerless and vulnerable status of sharecroppers or tenant farmers. Denied the opportunity to succeed as yeoman farmers, many African Americans turned to southern industries, which expanded rapidly in the latter half of the nineteenth century, to escape their plight. Unfortunately, the rise of southern industry coincided with the emergence of the post-Reconstruction "Jim Crow" system. Southern blacks, therefore, were unable to take advantage of the economic resurgence of the South to improve their socioeconomic status to any significant degree.

From its inception, southern industry adopted a "rigid color line," restricting African Americans to lower-paying, less skilled "Negro jobs."[3] This system became formalized over time, varying from industry to industry. The most extreme form of discrimination was outright exclusion. This practice was rare, however, because African Americans represented a valuable pool of cheap labor. More common was the adoption of separate lines of progression: hierarchical successions of jobs within a given industry. In the Jim Crow system, blacks entered into a line of progression that led at best to a semiskilled or higher-level unskilled job. In contrast, white lines of progression often led to white-collar work. Other discriminatory practices included segregated departments and separate bargaining units, including, eventually, separate union locals for African-American workers.[4]

Each industry developed a unique system, depending on the nature of the work involved. In the construction trades, where black workers had attained a foothold by 1865, whites replaced skilled black workers after the war. Because the "modern" construction crafts—electricians and plumbers, for example—emerged during the Jim Crow years, black construction workers were excluded from these occupations and confined to the less skilled "trowel trades," such as plasterers, bricklayers, and unskilled laborers. A more extreme situation developed in the textile industry. Although slaves had been active in the production of textiles before the Civil War, most blacks were displaced from the industry during the postbellum years. Although African Americans continued to be well represented among unskilled construction workers, as late as 1940 they constituted only 2 percent of the entire textile labor force.[5]

The tobacco industry, which also had relied heavily on slave labor, continued to hire African Americans after the war but segregated them physically as well as occupationally in less skilled, lower-paying departments. This system rigidified following the invention of the tobacco machine in 1884: White women served as machine operatives; white men performed as set-up men, mechanics, supervisors, and general white-collar workers; blacks held less skilled jobs in the stemming and processing departments. Conditions in the latter departments were so unhealthy that black women often wore handkerchiefs over their mouths to protect themselves from the tobacco dust. Reinforcing this system were separate lines of progression and separate union locals, both of which were incorporated into collective bargaining agreements when the industry unionized in the 1930s.[6]

The pulp and paper industry, which is concentrated in the South, evolved similarly to the tobacco industry. The paper companies denied

African Americans access to skilled jobs in the paper mills and confined them to the most unpleasant and physically demanding tasks. Whereas the companies often hired whites with the idea of promoting them to better positions, they hired blacks solely as unskilled laborers. As with the tobacco industry, the paper industry and unions formalized these arrangements through separate lines of progression and segregated union locals.[7]

Economic discrimination permeated all southern industries and formed one component of a larger network of racial oppression, enforced ruthlessly and often violently. Belief in black inferiority was reflected in such Jim Crow practices as separate locker rooms, drinking fountains, and toilets in public facilities and workplaces. The concentration of African Americans in the least-skilled occupations not only reinforced a system of social and political subordination, but it also rendered black workers vulnerable to displacement resulting from mechanization. In both the tobacco and paper industries, for example, the percentage of African-American workers declined throughout much of the twentieth century. These discriminatory job patterns, combined with the desire to escape the oppressive environment of the South and secure some measure of opportunity, generated a large-scale black migration to the North.[8]

The "Great Migration" of southern blacks to northern cities began in the late nineteenth century and intensified with the labor shortages precipitated by World War I. As late as 1890, some 90 percent of all African Americans lived in the South; by 1960, that number was 60 percent.[9] Unfortunately, the expectations of a "promised land" in the North proved illusory. Although African Americans achieved a certain degree of political freedom in the North, economic discrimination was as much a reality there as in the South. Excluded from the most desirable occupations, African Americans often settled for employment as domestic and service workers. In industrial cities such as Detroit, Chicago, Cleveland, and Pittsburgh black workers were confined to semiskilled and unskilled occupations. In many cases black workers first entered northern industries as strikebreakers.

Compounding the difficulties of northern blacks was the hostility of labor unions and immigrants who perceived blacks not only as inferior but also as economic rivals. Management's liberal use of African Americans as strikebreakers intensified these hostilities. Economic tensions between white and black workers contributed significantly to the race riots of the World War I era in such cities as Chicago and East St. Louis. White union members played a major role in these riots. Exploited by management and despised by white workers, blacks who migrated from the South also were coolly received by established northern blacks, who often regarded the newcomers as dirty, obsequious towards whites, and ill prepared for urban life.[10]

Business practices in northern cities closely paralleled those of the South. In white-collar and service industries such as supermarkets, department stores, and the drug industry, African Americans were virtually invisible until World War II and remained underrepresented thereafter. Those who found employment generally occupied the less skilled, lower-paying positions. Large numbers of African Americans entered the meat-packing and automobile industries, but often in unskilled or custodial capacities. The one notable exception was Henry Ford's River Rouge plant, which hired blacks for most blue-collar jobs, including supervisory positions. Even Ford, however, refused to hire African Americans in plants located outside Detroit, except as janitors.[11]

The steel industry was both a major employer of black labor and a major perpetrator of racial discrimination. Compelled to hire African Americans by the labor shortages engendered by two world wars, the steel companies generally confined blacks to unskilled blast furnace jobs, which contained "a great deal of the hot, dirty, heavy work which Negroes were thought to be eminently qualified to perform."[12] Preferential treatment accorded to white workers and separate lines of progression contributed to the pattern of discriminatory hiring and promotions. Consequently, by the early 1960s African Americans constituted more than 25 percent of the unskilled workers in the steel industry but less than one-tenth of 1 percent of the white-collar workers. This situation prompted one federal judge to characterize one Bethlehem Steel plant as a "microcosm of classic job discrimination in the North."[13]

The existence of discriminatory job patterns throughout the nation indicated, among other things, that northern and southern employers shared attitudes regarding minority hiring. Many employers perceived blacks as less intelligent, less reliable, and, in general, less desirable as employees than whites. Those holding such views considered unskilled labor to be the "natural" profession of black workers. As the changing circumstances of the twentieth century rendered such explicitly racist views less acceptable, the more common rationalization for discriminatory hiring patterns became the perceived lack of "qualified" minority job candidates. Employers cited the inferior quality of black education, lower scores on standardized tests, "attitude problems," and a host of other factors (for which they disclaimed responsibility) as the true culprits. These arguments denied the existence of intentional discrimination in business as well as the need for antidiscrimination legislation or policies. In one study of personnel managers conducted in the mid-1960s, for example, more than one-half of the respondents agreed that African Americans were primarily responsible for their inferior job position. The prevalence of such attitudes contributed to the relative absence of on-the-job training programs for African-American workers, because such efforts were deemed useless and unprofitable given the "inferior" quality of black labor.

Given the relative absence of vocational and educational opportunities for blacks, it is probable that African-American employees and job candidates sometimes possessed inferior job skills and training. The nation's racial hiring patterns, however, revealed a pervasive denial of opportunity to all but a handful of African Americans, regardless of qualifications.

Employers also feared the adverse reactions of white employees, customers, and community residents that they assumed would follow integration. Consequently, throughout the twentieth century blacks were unable to attain sales positions, where they would have to sell to white customers, or supervisory positions, which would require giving orders to white employees. Similarly, northern firms with plants in the South commonly acquiesced in local Jim Crow standards. Most business people denied any responsibility to serve as leaders in the movement for economic justice.[14]

Government employment exhibited many of the same discriminatory practices as private business. The federal government hired African Americans throughout the twentieth century but generally excluded them from the higher policymaking levels. A similar pattern emerged in state and local governments, where African Americans were overrepresented in "common laborer and general service worker" positions. Both federal and state governments assigned minority personnel most often to social welfare departments whose clientele included many "disadvantaged" persons. African Americans seldom found employment in agencies that dealt with financial or administrative affairs or in law enforcement agencies, including the Justice Department and local police and fire departments.[15]

Besides being victimized by discriminatory employers, African-American workers throughout this period had to contend with the ambiguous policies of labor unions. Organized labor was both a major proponent of civil rights laws and a major practitioner of racial discrimination. The racial policies of labor unions varied from organization to organization. During the nineteenth century, the short-lived National Labor Union, comprised of skilled craft workers, denied membership to blacks, preferring a separate black union. The Knights of Labor, seeking to organize craft and industrial workers, opened their organization to African Americans, although confining them to separate locals. The eventually unsuccessful Industrial Workers of the World (IWW), in their pursuit of "one big union," admitted African Americans into integrated locals. As socialists, IWW leaders refused to recognize race discrimination as a problem separate from class discrimination but instead felt that the plight of black Americans would be alleviated with the liberation of the working class.[16]

Of greater historical significance was the relationship between African Americans and the American Federation of Labor (AFL). Almost from its beginning in 1886, the AFL adopted an official policy of opposition to racial discrimination. A resolution of 1890 affirmed that the federation "looks with disfavor upon trade unions having provisions which exclude from membership persons on account of race or color."[17] Unfortunately, the AFL seldom transformed such noble sentiments into action. AFL craft unions retained a high degree of autonomy and received little pressure from the national office to modify their racial policies. Equally important, Samuel Gompers and the national leadership, giving highest priority to increasing membership roles, argued that offending unions could be reformed *after* they joined the federation. Thus, many unions, including the building trades unions, the Seafarers International Union, the Machinists, the Boilermakers, and the Carmen became AFL affiliates despite exclusionist policies, rendering the 1890 resolution "a forlorn wish in the face of the impossible."[18]

Exclusionist tactics ranged from explicit provisions in union constitutions to informal arrangements within locals. A clear illustration of the philosophy of the AFL leadership was the following pronouncement of William Green, who succeeded Gompers in 1924: "While it (AFL) endorses without reservation the policy of nondiscrimination in employment, the executive council takes strong exception to the compulsory imposition upon unions of this or any other policy interfering with the self-government of labor organizations." Clearly, labor autonomy was paramount; civil rights were secondary.[19]

One notable exception to the racial apathy and prejudice of the AFL was the United Mine Workers (UMW). Founded in 1890, the UMW organized black and white miners and elected blacks to local, regional, and state union offices. Richard L. Davis, the most prominent black member of the UMW, was elected to the union's Executive Board in 1896 and 1897. The union's progressive racial policies evolved in part from the extensive presence of African-American workers within the mines. By 1900, for example, 24 percent of the nation's bituminous coal miners were African-American. In addition, the admission of African Americans into the union prevented their acting as strikebreakers, a common practice in mining disputes at that time. Although some discrimination survived within the union, the UMW's racial legacy outshone that of most AFL unions.[20]

African Americans were more responsive to the industrial union philosophy espoused by the Congress of Industrial Organizations (CIO) during the 1930s and 1940s than they had been to the AFL. Cooperation between African Americans and the CIO developed for many reasons. CIO organizers properly considered African-American support to be vital to the successful organizing of basic industries that employed black workers, such as steel and automobiles. Moreover, the CIO, locked in fierce competition with the AFL, saw an opportunity to expand its membership by capitalizing on black disillusionment with craft unionism. The more progressive racial policies of the CIO also reflected the influence of the Communist Party within the organization. Indeed, the most racially progressive unions, including the Transportation Workers Union, the National Miners Union, the Mine, Mill, and Smelter Workers, and the United Packinghouse Workers of America, were those unions in which the Communists were influential. In addition, African Americans and CIO organizers shared an ideological bond: Both embraced the emerging liberal precept that government should intervene to assist the powerless and disadvantaged in society.

The CIO designed strategies specifically to attract African-American workers, including the hiring of African-American organizers, donations and formal pledges of support to the National Association for the Advancement of Colored People (NAACP), and the creation in 1942 of a Committee to Abolish Racial Discrimination. The overall racial record of the CIO was, however, an uneven one. Although many locals, especially in northern cities, implemented progressive racial policies, some CIO locals—often but not always located in the South—remained bastions of racism. Concerned primarily with organizing workers, CIO affiliates frequently were unable or unwilling to promote racial progress in unionized industries.[21]

Among the more progressive CIO unions were the United Automobile Workers (UAW), the United Packinghouse Workers of America (UPWA), and the International Union of Electrical, Radio and Machine Workers of America (IUE). The UAW, which became a major force through its organizing drives of the 1930s and the 1940s, made a special effort to include African-American workers. This was especially true at the Ford River Rouge plant, where decades of paternalistic treatment by Henry Ford had made black workers reluctant to support the union that Ford bitterly opposed. At River Rouge, Ford employed African Americans in all phases of production, paid them decent wages, and "fashioned a close alliance with the leadership of the black community," including the local ministers, the Detroit Urban League, and the Detroit chapter of the NAACP.[22] As a result, most black auto workers refused to participate in the sit-down strikes and reversed their position only after intensive lobbying efforts by black unionists, Communist activists, and NAACP Executive Secretary Walter White. Following the accreditation of the UAW at River Rouge in 1941, "the Ford Company retreated from its concern with black philanthropy, and blacks began looking to the UAW for help in achieving better job opportunities."[23] The UAW responded to these developments by donating money to the NAACP, campaigning for a national fair employment bill, establishing a Fair Practices Department, and conducting "civil rights educational programs among its locals."[24] UAW President Walter Reuther became a member of the NAACP Board of Directors.

These positive developments, however, were marred by continued complaints of discrimination within the union. Local 988 in Memphis, for example, maintained segregated rest rooms as late as 1960. Despite the liberal philosophy of the UAW leadership, the rank-and-file often resisted racial progress, especially if it threatened their own status or economic security. The union's inability to solve its racial problems contributed to a growing African-American militancy within its ranks during the 1950s. Black automobile workers established an independent caucus, the Trade Union Leadership Conference, within the UAW and demanded a special vice-presidency for blacks. These racial divisions escalated into open rebellion by militant African-American automobile workers in the late 1960s.[25]

No CIO union was more responsive to civil rights initiatives than the UPWA. Composed largely of "remnants" of leftist packinghouse worker organizations of the 1920s, the UPWA claimed a sizeable Communist presence, although it was never a Communist-dominated union. Struggling to organize a work force that was 25 percent black, the UPWA made attacks against racial discrimination an essential feature of organizing drives in the North and South. In a move that prefigured the affirmative action settlements of later decades, the UPWA included in their collective bargaining agreement with Swift and Company in Chicago a clause mandating proportional hiring of African Americans based on the city's African-American population. Other UPWA activities included striking to protest racial discrimination, assisting in NAACP registration drives, and conducting a school at the Highlander Folk Center in Tennessee, a major training site for civil rights activists. The union pursued these policies despite violent attacks by the Ku Klux Klan and other racist groups.[26]

Another CIO union with an impressive civil rights record was the IUE. An industrial union as opposed to the craft-oriented, AFL-affiliated International Brotherhood of Electrical Workers (IBEW), the IUE under James B. Carey displaced the Communist-dominated United Electrical, Radio, and Machine Workers of America (UE)—also a racially progressive union within the CIO—in 1949. The IUE collaborated with the NAACP on unionization/integration drives, demands for civil rights legislation, and other activities.[27]

Unfortunately, the racist policies of other CIO affiliates often overshadowed the accomplishments of the progressive unions. Many southern CIO locals maintained segregated union halls and facilities. Workers in steel and other industries often participated in Ku Klux Klan activities, and the Klan conducted meetings in CIO halls. (The same was true of AFL unions in the paper industry and building trades.) In the mid-1960s, the Imperial Wizard of the Georgia Klan was a member of the Atlanta UAW local. Racist workers, in collaboration with the Klan and White Citizens Councils, spearheaded the opposition to integration in the South in the 1950s and the 1960s.[28]

The International Union of Teamsters, Chauffeurs and Longshoremen, expelled from the AFL-CIO in 1957, also engaged in discriminatory behavior. Although African Americans found employment in warehouse and local driving jobs, they were not hired as "over-the-road" drivers, the most sought-after position. This discriminatory practice arose from the unwillingness of white drivers to spend an extended period of time on the road with black drivers. As one driver explained: "When a man is black, I don't care to live cheek-to-cheek with him for a couple of days in a truck." The President of a Teamsters local was even more explicit: "Would you like to climb into a bunk bed that a nigger just got out of?"[29]

The AFL-CIO merger of 1955 was a milestone in U.S. labor history. The consolidation of the power of "big labor," juxtaposed with the effects of Cold War policies, generated a conservatism within the labor movement. Although many organizing battles remained to be fought—primarily in the South—organized labor by the 1950s was more concerned with maintaining hard-fought gains than with undertaking new crusades. According to historian Harvey Levenstein, by the 1950s, "the American labor's mainstream became the most politically conservative of any in the Western industrial world."[30] The purging of Communists and other leftists from CIO unions, a symbol of this new conservatism, eliminated many advocates of racial justice from the AFL-CIO.

The AFL-CIO's position regarding job discrimination was a familiar one: national support for a policy of nondiscrimination, but widespread violations by locals throughout the nation. On the national level, the official merger of the two unions was accompanied by a formal pledge to abolish racial discrimination within the organization. The new union created a Civil Rights Department, and AFL-CIO President George Meany publicly called on all locals to include a nondiscrimination clause in collective bargaining agreements. By the early 1960s, some progress along these lines was evident. Most exclusionist unions had abandoned their "whites only" policies, and some of the most blatant forms of discrimination—segregated facilities, for example—were beginning to disappear. (These advances, as will be demonstrated later, also reflected growing black militancy and government pressures.) Symbolic of this emerging labor-civil rights alliance were such activities as AFL-CIO endorsement of the *Brown v. Board of Education* school desegregation decision of 1954, its public advocacy of federal legislation prohibiting employment discrimination, and the participation of thousands of AFL-CIO members in the August 1963 March on Washington.

Unfortunately, the AFL-CIO often demonstrated greater enthusiasm for combating discrimination within society at large than with addressing the problem within its own unions. The national union was unable and unwilling to enforce nondiscrimination forcefully and effectively. Despite Meany's call for nondiscrimination clauses in union-management agreements, as late as 1961 only one-fifth of major collective bargaining agreements contained such provisions. In addition, many of these antidiscrimination agreements were, in the words of an AFL-CIO official, "paper programs that mean nothing." Even in situations in which the union leadership sincerely desired racial progress, hostility and noncooperation by rank-and-file workers prevented implementation of antidiscrimination policies. Despite evidence of widespread union discrimination, the AFL-CIO failed to expel a single affiliate for such behavior. The AFL-CIO antidiscrimination effort was, in the words of one critic, "piecemeal and inadequate."[31]

Employer discrimination and union discrimination often were interrelated and mutually reinforcing. Many forms of job discrimination became codified in collective bargaining agreements in steel, paper, tobacco, and other industries.

Nowhere were union and employer discrimination more closely interrelated than in the construction industry. Although African Americans were a major source of skilled construction labor in the South, they were displaced from their positions and excluded from the emerging construction crafts during the Jim Crow era. During the twentieth century, the industry developed a system that reserved the skilled crafts—plumbers and pipefitters, sheet metal workers, elevator constructors, asbestos workers and electricians—for whites, while confining blacks to the "trowel trades"— bricklayers, plasterers, roofers, and unskilled laborers. Within the twentieth century construction industry, the construction company functioned primarily as a contractor, directly hiring only workers in the "basic trades," such as bricklayers and laborers. Skilled labor was provided through agreements with the craft unions, which workers to construction projects through the union hiring hall. Thus, the unions, through the hiring hall (the constitutionality of which was upheld in 1961) determined *who* worked on *which* projects. Given the strength of the unions and the fluctuating and seasonal nature of employment within the industry, the hiring hall occupied a vital position in the life of a construction worker, providing companionship and stability as well as jobs. Thus, the building trades unions formed "a tight-knit social group," reluctant to extend membership to outsiders.[32]

In addition to assigning work, the building trades unions historically controlled entry into the construction crafts. The "standard" mode of entry—apprenticeship—although subject to general regulation by the Bureau of Apprenticeship and Training within the Department of Labor, was administered on a day-to-day basis by the unions or by union/employer joint apprenticeship committees (JACs). In this manner, the unions effectively controlled the supply of skilled labor while excluding particular groups from membership. This power enabled the building trades unions to implement a policy of "planned scarcity" that inflated wage rates by "manipulating the supply of available workers."[33] Not surprisingly, the unions tenaciously defended this prerogative against all outside incursions.

The apprenticeship system became fairly standardized throughout the construction industry. Normally, an apprenticeship program lasted three to five years. Entrance requirements varied in particulars but generally included age restrictions, usually 18-26 years; educational requirements, generally a high school diploma; written and oral examinations; and sometimes contacts or sponsors within the union. These requirements served to limit the accessibility of apprenticeship programs to African Americans, who had a much higher high school dropout rate and lacked union contacts. African Americans were less likely to perform well on a written construction test that asked such "relevant" questions as: "_____ is to phlegmatic as vivacious is to _____"; or to pass an oral exam administered by white examiners that measured such highly subjective personal attributes as "attitude" and "work habits." Even if an apprentice completed the program, he or she did not automatically receive union membership. Unions sometimes demanded work experience, which the hiring hall could render impossible through its control over job referrals. Also, many unions required recommendations or endorsements by union members, a stipulation few African Americans could meet. [34]

Despite the esteemed position of apprenticeship within the construction industry, many building trades union members never served an apprenticeship. Some members were nonunion workers who eventually received union membership, and many others were admitted directly to construction work, learned the craft through on-the-job training, and received union cards. Not surprisingly, this system—like many apprenticeship programs—was nepotistic. The building trades were "father-and-son" trades where male friends and relatives of union members received priority and privileges. As Peter Schoemann, President of the Plumbers Union in the 1960s declared: "Sponsorship and favoritism are phenomena of American political and business life. Indeed, one may wonder whether they are not necessarily inherent in a free democratic society."[35] In addition, particular ethnic groups—for example, the Irish and Italians in New York City—sometimes dominated particular crafts or even entire segments of the industry within a city. Consequently, individuals with union contacts were notified of openings in apprenticeship programs, were allowed to accumulate on-the-job training, and generally were welcomed into the closely knit society of the construction unions. Union membership became so important that during "boom" periods, unions in large cities imported out-of-town union labor rather than refer local nonunion workers.

Maintained from decade to decade, this system became a self-perpetuating mechanism for excluding African Americans from skilled construction work. Union officials cited the reluctance of black workers to apply for "white" positions as evidence that blacks preferred unskilled labor to the skilled crafts. As one construction official explained: "The people that do the cement finishing in most cases are colored. I mean, they just like that work for some reason." Another union official stated that, "Jews and colored folks don't want to do plumbing work because it is too hard." [36]

Although the full effects of discrimination cannot be measured by numbers, an examination of employment statistics provides some indication of the status of African Americans around the middle of the twentieth century. Within the construction industry, as late as the 1960s, African Americans were virtually invisible in the skilled crafts, despite the fact that the construction industry was concentrated in urban areas that contained sizeable minority populations. African Americans, for example, constituted less than 2 percent of construction union membership in Pittsburgh in the late 1960s and were less than 1 percent of union plumbers and electricians in Philadelphia. In Cleveland, the pipefitters union had 1,600 members of whom *one* was black, and the Iron Workers, with 1,800 members, had one black apprentice. In Washington, D.C., a city more than 70 percent nonwhite, the glaziers, painters and sheet metal workers had no black apprentices. Hearings conducted in San Francisco revealed that black representation in several unions, including sheet metal workers and plumbers, was below 1 percent. The 1950 Census revealed only 2,190 black apprentices in the entire nation; a decade later, the number had increased to 2,191! It is not surprising, therefore, that the construction industry became a major target of black protests after 1960.[37]

The overall employment picture throughout the U.S. economy was no brighter. According to the 1950 Census, nearly 10 percent of whites but only 2 percent of blacks were employed as "managers and officials"; for sales workers, the respective numbers were 13.2 percent and 1.3 percent. That same year, 14.6 percent of blacks but only 1.2 percent of whites were listed as "private household" employees. Ten years later, blacks still represented less than 1 percent of the nation's architects, engineers, and accountants. By the mid 1960s, although 57 percent of all female workers and 37 percent of all male workers held white-collar jobs, the numbers for African Americans were 28 percent and 7 percent, respectively. In the tobacco and railroad industries, African Americans represented less than 1 percent of all white-collar workers. Following the Korean War, black unemployment rates consistently were double those of whites. The legacy of racial inequality had permeated every aspect of economic life in America.[38]

Where there is oppression, there is protest. Racial protest in this nation dates to the slave era. Prior to the 1950s and 1960s, however, most black protests were limited in size and in the scope of their demands. Unable to make racial issues a high priority within the federal government, civil rights activists achieved mostly token or small-scale victories during these years despite continuous pressure on the political system.

Racial protests during slavery most frequently consisted of isolated personal acts such as sabotage and arson. The abolition of slavery and the post-1910 Great Migration to the North enabled African Americans to substitute organized activities for sporadic acts of protest. Civil rights activists gravitated toward two key organizations, the NAACP and the National Urban League, formed in 1909 and 1911, and reflecting the philosophies of W.E.B. DuBois and Booker T. Washington, respectively. The NAACP and the Urban League battled discrimination in employment and other areas through a variety of strategies ranging from private discussions with businessmen to public demonstrations. By the 1920s the NAACP was orchestrating boycotts against institutions in African-American neighborhoods, especially chain stores like Woolworth's and Walgreens, that refused to hire African Americans. These activities intensified with the coming of the Depression, which devastated black workers even more so than whites. The "Jobs-for-Negroes Campaign" materialized in 35 cities, including St. Louis, Baltimore, Pittsburgh, and Cleveland, rallying black support for boycotts and pickets under the motto "Don't Buy Where You Can't Work." Much of the leadership for this movement emanated from community groups such as the Illinois Civil Association in Chicago and the Citizens League for Fair Play in Harlem, with the active support of the black clergy and the black press.

The jobs campaign claimed some successes. Chicago blacks secured some jobs in South Side stores and restaurants, and New York protests resulted in increased hiring in the city's mass transportation system and at the 1939 World's Fair. Proponents of this new activism achieved a major victory in 1938 when the Supreme Court upheld the right of African Americans to picket employers who practiced hiring discrimination. This decision helped clear the way for renewed picketing and boycotts during the 1940s, often directed against defense industries. The 1940s also witnessed the creation (in 1942) of another direct-action organization, the Congress of Racial Equality (CORE).[39]

Participants in the struggle against economic injustice faced the problems of defining discrimination and devising standards by which it—and racial progress—could be measured. Slowly but inevitably, civil rights proponents came to use numbers to indicate the status of African Americans within particular industries. Although the phrase "affirmative action" was not formally applied to the civil rights movement until 1945, the implementation of numerical formulas dates at least to the immediate post-World War I era. Disturbed by the disproportionate layoffs of blacks in most U.S. industries following the war, a group of black ministers requested that Henry Ford not follow that pattern in his River Rouge plant. Ford promised to maintain a proportion of black workers at River Rouge equal to the proportion of blacks in the Detroit population.

Because this arrangement was considered unique and most likely was intended as a buffer against unionization, it would be a mistake to characterize it as a precedent. Nevertheless, the idea of proportional representation had been implemented and later would be pursued by other groups. The UPWA-Swift accord described earlier provided for black employment based on the black population of Chicago. During the 1930s, the Harlem Section of the Communist Party proposed that white employees be transferred from Harlem retail stores and black workers be hired until the latter comprised 50 percent of the stores' work force.

The most controversial incident involving proportional hiring during the Depression occurred in Harlem in 1934. A group known as the "Picket Committee of the Citizens League for Fair Play," which had broken from the original Citizens League, visited various business establishments in Harlem, threatening them with pickets and boycotts if they did not hire a certain percentage of African Americans. One of their targets, the A.S. Beck Shoe Corporation, located on 125th Street, refused to comply. Soon after, the committee initiated a picketing campaign, carrying signs reading, "A.S. Beck does not employ 50 per cent negroes. Stay Out. Do not buy here." At one point, a picket physically restrained a customer from entering the store, leading to a disturbance in which the police arrested two pickets for disorderly conduct.

A.S. Beck successfully appealed to the New York Supreme Court for an injunction against the pickets. The court, while conceding "an understandable desire on the part of some of the negroes in this community that the stores in their neighborhood where they spend their money, should employ a percentage of negro help," nevertheless ruled against the pickets. In addition to "irreparably injuring the plaintiff's business," the protests, in the eyes of the judge, could lead to similar activities by other racial and ethnic groups. The court also claimed that hostile reactions to such activities could precipitate "race riots and race reprisals." Significantly, many community leaders, as well as the local press, did not support the activities of the Picket Committee.[40]

A similar case materialized in California after World War II and involved the Richmond branch of the Lucky Stores supermarket chain. This particular store, located near a large housing project, served a clientele that was nearly 50 percent African American. An African-American group called the Progressive Citizens of California, which included Louis Richardson of the Richmond NAACP, claimed that many qualified black clerks were available and demanded that blacks be hired to fill all vacancies until the proportion of black employees reflected the percentage of black patronage of the store. When negotiations broke down, blacks picketed the store for three days in May 1947. Lucky Stores procured an injunction against the pickets. Several African Americans who defied the injunction were arrested and convicted on contempt charges. One of the protestors, John Hughes, appealed the convictions and won a preliminary victory when the California

Court of Appeals voided the injunction. The court ruled that picketing was an acceptable means of fighting discrimination and that charges of "reverse discrimination" were meaningless in a state that did not have an antidiscrimination law. When the California Supreme Court, in response to an appeal by Lucky Stores, overturned this decision, Hughes appealed to the U.S. Supreme Court.

The Hughes case created a dilemma for the national headquarters of the NAACP, which had not been consulted regarding the initial suit and had problems reconciling a "quota" system with its official position of nondiscrimination. Ultimately, the NAACP filed an *amicus curiae* brief based on the general issue freedom of speech, but it emphasized that "the NAACP is opposed to proportional hiring or proportional firing and quotas in general."[41] In 1950, the Supreme Court ruled that picketing for proportional hiring constituted a form of discrimination and therefore was *not* protected by the Fourteenth Amendment.[42]

The *A.S. Beck* and *Hughes* decisions tempered, but did not check, the protest movement. Demonstrations involving CORE, the NAACP, the Urban League, and, beginning in 1957, the Southern Christian Leadership Conference (SCLC) continued throughout the 1950s. Among the targets were the Automobile Club of New York, an A&P supermarket in St. Louis, and a Philco plant in Philadelphia. Protestors generally demanded that black workers be hired and/or promoted, but they avoided references to numerical hiring targets. These activities continued into the 1960s, when racial protests shattered the Jim Crow system forever.[43]

African Americans also agitated against discrimination in labor unions at the same time that they tried to use the labor movement as a vehicle for economic advancement. The most important African-American trade union figure of the twentieth century was A. Phillip Randolph, who organized the Brotherhood of Sleeping Car Porters (BSCP) in 1925 and pressured the AFL leadership to abolish racism within its affiliates. After the BSCP received an AFL charter in 1929, Randolph was able to address union officials directly, especially during AFL conventions. African Americans were more responsive to the overtures of the CIO and participated in several CIO union drives during the Depression and World War II. Significantly, African-American spokespersons were among the leading opponents of Section 7A of the National Industrial Recovery Act of 1933 and the National Labor Relations Act of 1935. Revered as labor's "bill of rights" by white workers, these laws were rejected by black leaders out of fear that organized labor would use its newly won power to consolidate its exclusionist system and remove black laborers from union shops.[44]

World War II, which created many job opportunities for blacks, also generated a major controversy between black and white workers over one of labor's most cherished practices: seniority. Because African Americans were forced to battle their way into defense industries during the war (an issue to be discussed in more detail in the next chapter), they were victimized after the war by the policy of "last hired, first fired." To rectify this situation, Local 252 of the United Electrical, Radio, and Machine Workers (UE), a Communist Party-affiliated union, proposed a system of "superseniority" in which black and white workers would be placed on separate seniority lists and laid off in equal proportion to each other. As with proportional hiring, the NAACP found this philosophy too extreme. As one official stated: "We cannot 'plump' for a quota system without, by implication, encouraging its concomitant—segregation."[45] There were, however, additional underlying reasons for NAACP opposition to "superseniority." The NAACP was aware of the political affiliation of the UE, and, with the onset of Cold War politics, sought to divorce itself from the "Communist inspired proposal."[46] Furthermore, African-American leaders feared an outbreak of antiblack sentiments among white unionists if this proposal were adopted. NAACP rejection of "superseniority" temporarily defused the controversy, although the seniority question reemerged as one of the most volatile civil rights issues of the 1970s and 1980s.[47]

The growing black militancy of the 1950s, coupled with the increasing conservatism of organized labor, created an almost contradictory situation in which the two groups quarreled regularly over the question of union discrimination at the same time that they cooperated at the national level in support of liberal political candidates and civil rights legislation. The AFL-CIO took an important step by appointing A. Phillip Randolph to its Executive Council; he remained, however, "a lonely, unheeded figure" within the organization.[48] His rising to speak at a convention often served as a signal for white unionists to vacate the auditorium. Randolph's charges of racist union practices so irritated Meany and other officials that the AFL-CIO Executive Council officially censured him in 1961, holding him responsible for "the gap that has developed between organized labor and the Negro community."[49] The union ultimately allowed the motion to die, however, and effected a rapprochement of sorts the following year.[50]

The NAACP became more active against union discrimination during the 1950s and early 1960s. Occasionally, cooperative efforts between the NAACP and organized labor produced positive results. In 1957, for example, the AFL-CIO, in response to NAACP complaints and an order from the Cleveland Community Relations Board, threatened to revoke the charter of Local 38 of the International Brotherhood of Electrical Workers if the union refused to abandon its exclusionist practices. Shortly thereafter, the union admitted three black mechanics.

Even this type of modest success, unfortunately, was the exception rather than the rule. Union officials generally reacted to NAACP complaints with indifference, if not outright hostility. In 1958, NAACP Labor Secretary Herbert Hill submitted a detailed series of charges, including affidavits by victims of discrimination, to the Civil Rights Department of the AFL-CIO. Among those accused were plumbers, paper mill workers, railway workers, and communications workers. AFL-CIO spokesmen denied the charges, emphasizing instead their record of support for civil rights causes. Hill subsequently leveled charges against, and aided a congressional investigation into, the racial policies of the International Ladies Garment Workers Union. Although these particular charges were withdrawn in 1963, conflicts between white unionists and blacks intensified throughout the 1960s.[51]

Black unionists themselves were active, sometimes establishing independent unions like the BSCP, and other times organizing black caucuses within white unions, including the United Steelworkers of America, the American Federation of Teachers, and the United Automobile Workers. Many of these caucuses merged into the Negro American Labor Council (NALC), organized in 1960 with Randolph as president. An all-black organization dedicated to improving the position of blacks within business and labor, the NALC symbolized the growing alienation of black workers from the white union structure. Although unable to initiate extensive reforms within the labor movement, the NALC played a pivotal role in organizing the 1963 March on Washington.[52]

The growing militancy of African-American workers by the beginning of the 1960s was a product of the limited success achieved in the field of equal opportunity up to that time. The absence of real progress reflected the limitations of civil rights strategies during these years. Black jobs protests generally were limited in scope, focusing on a particular store or industrial plant and, in the wake of the *A.S. Beck* and *Hughes* rulings, accepting unspecified assurances of future nondiscrimination. Any successes generated by these strategies were piecemeal and restricted to individual employers. Moreover, the leading civil rights organizations, especially the NAACP and the Urban League, were primarily middle- and upper-class organizations with limited grassroots support. Alonzo Hamby's description of NAACP activities during these years as "carried on by the black elite and its white allies in distant court rooms and legislative offices" was equally applicable to the Urban League.[53] The inability of civil rights groups to generate widespread grassroots activism severely hampered the struggle for equal employment opportunity.

By the end of the 1950s, however, the civil rights movement slowly but irrevocably began to move in new directions. When the police arrested Rosa Parks in December 1955 for refusing to surrender her seat on a Montgomery, Alabama, bus, the city's African-American population responded with a boycott of the public transportation system. Working-class blacks as well as the middle and upper classes participated in this movement, demonstrating a previously unrealized capacity for sustained mass protest. (Significantly, the question of jobs was fundamental to this protest, since protestors' demands included the hiring of African-American bus drivers.) The successful boycott produced a new, all-black organization, the Southern Christian Leadership Conference (SCLC), and the civil rights movement's most important leader, Martin Luther King, Jr. A "charismatic leader who could . . . mobilize blacks of all classes," King helped to usher in an era of direct mass action, that augmented, but did not replace, such traditional strategies as boycotts and legal suits.[54]

King's initial strategy has been characterized as "converting" his opponents.[55] Following the Montgomery episode, King described nonviolence as "the method which seeks to implement the just law by appealing to the consciences of the great decent majority who through blindness, fear, pride, or irrationality have allowed their consciences to sleep."[56] Such a strategy offered at best a limited threat to deeply rooted traditions of job discrimination in the United States. With the coming of the 1960s, however, a new generation of African Americans redirected their energies from appealing to dormant consciences to demanding equality. The Student Nonviolent Coordinating Committee (SNCC), which evolved from the February 1960 sit-ins at Greensboro, North Carolina, spearheaded this movement. CORE, the SCLC, and many local and regional civil rights groups quickly followed suit. In the 1960s, this heightened activism shattered American complacency and pressured the political system to address—belatedly—its massive racial problems. Conversely, the absence of this grassroots militancy prior to the 1960s contributed greatly to the paucity of reform generated in the area of economic discrimination.[57]

NOTES

1. Herbert Hill, *Black Labor and the American Legal System* (Washington, DC, Bureau of National Affairs, 1977), p. 9; Richard L. Rowan and Lester Rubin, *Opening the Skilled Construction Trades to Blacks* (Philadelphia: University of Pennsylvania Press, 1972), p. 10; and Roger L. Ransom and Richard Sutch, *One Kind of Freedom: The Economic Consequences of Emancipation* (New York: Cambridge University Press, 1977), pp. 31-34.

2. Ransom and Sutch, *One Kind of Freedom*, pp. 4-7.

3. Quotes from Donald Dewey, "Negro Employment in Southern Industry," *The Journal of Political Economy* 60 (August, 1952): 280; and Alfred Blumrosen, *Black Employment and the Law* (New Brunswick, NJ: Rutgers University Press, 1971), p. 167.

4. Blumrosen, *Black Employment*, p. 167.

5. Construction information from Hill, *Black Labor*, p. 14; Mark W. Kruman, "Quotas for Blacks: The Public Works Administration and the Black Construction Worker," *Labor History* 16 (Winter, 1975): 38; and George Strauss and Sidney Ingerman, "Public Policy and Discrimination in Apprenticeship," *The Hastings Law Journal* 16 (1964-65): 288. Textiles from Richard L. Rowan, *The Negro in the Textile Industry* (Philadelphia: University of Pennsylvania Press, 1970), pp. 1-54; Gary Becker, *The Economics of Discrimination*, 2nd Ed. (Chicago: University of Chicago Press, 1971), p. 89; and Gunnar Myrdal, *An American Dilemma* (New York: Harper and Row Publishers, 1944, 1962), p. 1110.

6. Herbert R. Northrup, *The Negro in the Tobacco Industry* (Philadelphia: University of Pennsylvania Press, 1970), especially pp. 1-25; and *Quarles v. Phillip Morris, Inc.*, 279 F.Supp. 505, especially pp. 505-510.

7. Herbert R. Northrup, *The Negro in the Paper Industry* (Philadelphia: University of Pennsylvania Press, 1969), pp. 1-45; *Local 189, United Papermakers and Paperworkers, AFL-CIO v. U.S.*, 416 F.2d 983; *Hicks v. Crown Zellerbach Corporation*, 319 F.Supp. 318 *et seq.*; *Albermarle Paper Company v. Moody*, 95 S.Ct. 2362; and NAACP Press Release of September 17, 1965, NAACP Files, U.S. Library of Congress, Group III, Series B, #362.

8. Northrup, *Paper Industry*, pp. 32-34; and Northrup, *Tobacco Industry*, pp. 26-31.

9. William Harris, *The Harder We Run: Black Workers Since the Civil War* (New York: Oxford University Press, 1982), p. 52.

10. For statistics regarding black employment in the North, especially domestic service, *see* Harris, *The Harder We Run*, p. 59; and U.S. Commission on Civil Rights, *Twenty Years After Brown:Equality of Economic Opportunity* (Washington, DC: U.S. Government Printing Office, 1975), pp. 30-32. For references to the black proletariat *see* Harris, p. 59; Allan Spear, *Black Chicago* (Chicago: University of Chicago Press, 1967), p. 155; and Kenneth L. Kusmer, *A Ghetto Takes Shape: Black Cleveland, 1870-1930* (Chicago: University of Chicago Press, 1976), p. 70. For strikebreakers, *see* Kusmer, p. 70; Spear, p. 36; Harris, pp. 41-43 & 55; and Robert C. Weaver, *Negro Labor: A National Problem* (New York: Harcourt, Brace and Co., 1946), pp. 6-7. For unions and immigrants, *see* Myrdal, *American Dilemma*, pp. 292-294; Spear, pp. 34 & 163-164; Kusmer, pp. 66-67; and Harris, chapters 2-3. For riots *see* Spear, p. 202; F. Ray Marshall, *The Negro and Organized Labor* (New York: John Wiley and Sons; Inc., 1965), p. 22; and Nancy J. Weiss, *The National Urban League 1910-1940* (New York: Oxford University Press, 1974), pp. 206-207. On reaction of northern blacks to southern immigrants, *see* Harris, p. 54; Kusmer, p. 215; and Gilbert Osofsky, *Harlem: The Making of a Ghetto* (New York: Harper and Row, Publishers, 1963, 1966), pp. 43-44.

11. For retail industry, *see* Gordon F. Bloom, F. Marion Fletcher, and Charles R. Perry, *Negro Employment in Retail Trade* (Philadelphia: University of Pennsylvania Press, 1972). For drug manufacturing, *see* F. Marion Fletcher, *The Negro in the Drug Manufacturing Industry* (Philadelphia: University of Pennsylvania Press, 1970), especially statistics pp. 30-31. For meat-packing and automobiles *see* Harris, *The Harder We Run*, pp. 61-62; Kuniko Fujita, *Black Workers' Struggles in Detroit's Auto Industry, 1935-1975* (Saratoga, CA: Century Twenty One Publishing, 1980), pp. 11-13; and August Meier and Elliot Rudwich, *Black Detroit and the Rise of the UAW* (New York: Oxford University Press, 1979), pp. 5-8.

12. Richard L. Rowan, *The Negro in the Steel Industry* (Philadelphia: The University of Pennsylvania Press, 1968); pp. 28-29.

13. Quote from *United States v. Bethlehem Steel Corporation*, 446 F.2d 655. Other information *ibid.*, pp. 652-655; *Whitfield v. United Steelworkers of America*, 263 F.2d 547, ff.; NAACP Press Release of September 17, 1965, in NAACP Files, U.S. Library of Congress, Group III, Series B, #362; and Rowan, *Steel Industry*, especially pp. 1-77.

14. For a thorough discussion of business attitudes, *see* Steven M. Gelber, *Black Men and Businessmen: The Growing Awareness of A Social*

Responsibility (Port Washington, NY: National University Publications, Kennikat Press, 1974) especially pp. 4-88 & 126. *See also* F. Ray Marshall, *The Negro Worker* (New York: Random House, 1967), pp. 115-116; Dwight D. Vines, "The Impact of Title VII of the 1964 Civil Rights Law on Personnel Policies and Practices" (Ph.D. dissertation, University of Colorado, 1967), pp. 129-167; Earl J. Reeves, "Making Equality of Employment Opportunity a Reality in the Federal Service," *Public Administration Review* 30 (January-February, 1970): 45; Charles E. Silberman, "The Businessman and the Negro," *Fortune* 68 (September, 1963): 184; Northrup, *Paper Industry* p. 35; Harris, *The Harder We Run*, p. 187; Rowan, *Steel Industry*, pp. 92-93, and Marshall, *Organized Labor*, pp. 138-139.

15. Quote from U.S. Commission on Civil Rights, *For All the People . . . by All the People: A Report on Equal Opportunity in State and Local Government Employment* (Washington, DC: U.S. Government Printing Office, 1969), p. 1. Other information *ibid.*, pp. 1-16; *Hearings before the Subcommittee on Civil and Constitutional Rights of the Committee on the Judiciary House of Representatives, 95th Congress, 72nd Session, on GAO Report on the EEO Action Programs at the Department of Justice* (Washington, DC: U.S. Government Printing Office, 1978), especially pp. 1, 4, 599 & 646; and David H. Rosenbloom, *Federal Equal Employment Opportunity* (New York, Praeger Publishers, 1977), pp. 5-13.

16. NLU from Malik Simba, "The Black Laborer, the Black Legal Experience, and United States Supreme Court with Emphasis on the Neo-concept of Equal Employment," (Ph.D. dissertation, University of Minnesota, 1977), p. 108; and Harris, *The Harder We Run*, pp. 25-26. Knights of Labor from Harris, pp. 26-28. IWW in Harris, pp. 48-50; and Simba, p. 100.

17. Quote from Simba, *Equal Employment*, p. 114.

18. *Ibid.*

19. Green quoted in Hill, *Black Labor*, p. 376. Other information from Herbert Hill, "Race and Ethnicity in Organized Labor: The Historical Sources of Resistance to Affirmative Action," *The Journal of Intergroup Relations* 12 (Winter, 1984): 19-24; Marshall, *Negro Worker*, pp. 17-19; Simba, Equal Employment, p. 114; and Marshall, *Organized Labor*, pp. 15-16.

20. Herbert G. Gutman, "Black Coal Miners and the American Labor Movement," in *Work, Culture and Society in Industrializing America* (New York: Random House, Vintage Books, 1976), pp. 121-208; Hill, "Race and Ethnicity," p. 20; and Harris, *The Harder We Run*, pp. 43-44.

21. Letter from James B. Carey to Channing Tobias, March 11, 1953, NAACP Files, U.S. Library of Congress, Series A Group II, #349; Marshall, *Negro Worker*, pp. 24-25; Harris, *The Harder We Run*, pp. 114-115; Phillip S. Foner, *Organized Labor and the Black Worker, 1619-1981* (New York: International Publishers, 1981), p. 292; Harvey A. Levenstein, *Communism, Anticommunism and the CIO* (Westport, CT: Greenwood Press, 1981), especially p. 332; Meier and Rudwick, *Black Detroit*, pp. 26-27 & 109-110; John Frederick Martin, *Civil Rights and the Crisis of Liberalism: The Democratic Party, 1945-1976* (Boulder, CO: Westview Press, 1979), p. 52; and Roderick N. Ryon, "An Ambiguous Legacy: Baltimore Blacks and the CIO, 1936-1941," *The Journal of Negro History* 65 (Winter, 1980): 29-30, especially.

22. Meier and Rudwick, *Black Detroit*, p. 16.

23. *Ibid.*, p. 108.

24. Hill, *Black Labor*, p. 261.

25. Memorandum from Jewish Labor Committee, December 18, 1953, NAACP Files, U.S. Library of Congress, Group II, Series A, # 264; Harry Fleischman, "Part Report of Union Race Relations Progress 1955-1960," p. 3, NAACP Files, Group III, Series B, #363; NAACP Files, Group III, Series B, #142; Marshall, *Negro Worker*, pp. 24-27; Marshall, *Organized Labor*, pp. 40-41; Fujita, *Black Workers' Struggles*, pp. 18-31; Harris, *The Harder We Run*, p. 139; Meier and Rudwick, *Black Detroit*; and Levenstein, *CIO*, pp. 315-316.

26. Russell Lasley to Walter White, July 3, 1951, NAACP Files, Group II, Series A, #349; UPWA Memo, *ibid.*; Harvey Sitkoff, *A New Deal for Blacks* (New York: Oxford University Press, 1978, 1981), p. 184; Marshall, *Organized Labor*, pp. 179-182; Hill, *Black Labor*, p. 260; Levenstein, *CIO*, p. 69.

27. Herbert Hill to Robert Clarke, April 3, 1952, NAACP Files, Group II, Section A, #328; IUE Memorandum, July 31-August 1, 1953, *ibid.*; IUE *Civil Rights Bulletin*, January, 1957, p. 2, NAACP Files, Group III, Series B, #133; James Trenz to Herbert Hill, Jan. 10, 1956, *ibid.*; *UE News*, February 17, 1958, NAACP Files, Group III, Series B, #142; Brooklyn NAACP Memo, October 9, 1965, NAACP Filest Group III, Series A, #88; and Levenstein, *CIO*, pp. 59-62 & 298-301.

28. William Evans to Walter White, March 14, 1941, NAACPFiles, Group II, Series A, #344; NAACP Memorandum, May 11, 1953, NAACP Files, Group II, Series A, #119; Herbert Hill to Walter White, May, 1953, *ibid.*; Hill to White, September 16, 1953, *ibid.*; Herbert Hill, *Racism within Organized Labor* (Published by NAACP in 1961), pp. 3-4; Marshall,

Negro Worker, pp. 47-49; Marshall, *Organized Labor*, p. 190; Harris, *The Harder We Run*, pp. 137-138; and Foner, *Black Worker*, p. 292.

29. Quotes and information from *Wall Street Journal*, March 31, 1966, pp. 1&8; U.S. Commission on Civil Rights, *The Challenge Ahead: Equal Opportunity in Referral Unions* (Washington, DC: U.S. Government Printing Office, 1976), pp. 98-100; and F. Marion Fletcher and Gordon F. Bloom, "The Negro in the Supermarket Industry," in Bloom, Fletcher, and Perry, eds., *Retail Trade*, p. 140.

30. Levenstein, *CIO*, p. 331.

31. Quotes from Joseph C. Goulden, *Meany* (New York: Atheneum Press, 1972), p. 318; and Hill, *Racism*, p. 1. For merger *see* Hill, *Racism*, p. 1; Hill, "The Racial Practices of Organized Labor," in *The Negro and the American Labor Movement*, ed. Julius Jacobson (Garden City, NY: Anchor-Doubleday and Co., Inc., 1968), p. 287; Harris, *The Harder We Run*, p 140; and Levenstein, *CIO*, pp. 330ff. For AFL-CIO Civil Rights Department *see* Memorandum from Herbert Hill to Boris Shiskin, NAACP Files, Group III, Series B, #139, of December 4, 1958; and Harris, p. 165. For civil rights progress, *see Report of the Labor Secretary*, March, 1957, *ibid.*; Leon E. Lunden, *Antidiscrimination Provisions in Major Contracts 1961*, Department of Labor Bulletin No. 1336 (Washington, DC: U.S. Government Printing Office, 1962), p. 1; Benjamin Wolkinson, *Blacks, Unions and the EEOC* (Lexington, MA: Lexington Books, DC Heath and Company, 1973), p. 9; *Chicago Defender*, June 29, 1963, p 1; Rowan, *Steel Industry*, p. 101; Foner, *Black Worker*, pp. 330 & 349; and Goulden, *Meany*, pp. 309 & 319.

For racial problems see testimony of George Meany in *Hearings before Subcommittee #5 of the Committee on the Judiciary, House of Representatives, 88th Congress, 1st Session, on Miscellaneous Proposals Regarding the Civil Rights of Persons within the Jurisdiction of the United States* (Washington, DC: U.S. Government Printing Office, 1963), pp. 1765-1766; and *before the Subcommittee on Labor and Public Welfare, U.S. Senate, 88th Congress, 1st Session* (Washington, DC: U.S. Government Printing Office, 1963), p. 152; Thomas O'Hanlon, "The Case Against the Unions," *Fortune* 77 (January, 1968): 171; *Wall Street Journal*, August 3, 1964, p. 1; Lunden, p. 1; Meier and Rudwich, *Black Detroit*, pp. 110, 221, and Chapter 5, generally.

32. Quote from Strauss and Ingerman, "Apprenticeship," p. 302. Also, U.S. Department of Labor, *Weekly News Digest*, Nov. 19, 1964, p. 2; Advisory Committees to the U.S. Commission on Civil Rights, *Report on Apprenticeship* (Washington, DC: U.S. Government Printing Office, 1964),

pp. 113-115; Daniel Quinn Mills, *Industrial Relations and Manpower in Construction* (Cambridge, MA: MIT Press, 1972), p. 14; Irwin Dubinsky, *Reform in Trade Union Discrimination in the Construction Industry* (New York: Praeger Publishers, 1973), p. 27; and Strauss and Ingerman, p. 297.

33. Frances Reissman Cousens, *Public Civil Rights Agencies and Fair Employment: Promise vs. Performance* (New York: Frederick A. Praeger, Publishers, 1969), p. 67.

34. Interview with James Haughton, April 4, 1984; Memorandum in the United States District Court for the Eastern District of Pennsylvania for *Taylor v. Department of Labor*, December 7, 1982, p. 11; *Local 53 of the International Association of Heat and Frost Insulators and Asbestos Workers v. Volger*, 407 F.2d 1048-1050; Dennis A. Derryck, *The Construction Industry: A Black Perspective* (Joint Center for Political Studies, 1972), pp. 12-13; Rowan and Rubin, *Opening the Construction Trades*, p. 23; O'Hanlon, "Case Against the Unions," p. 173; Strauss and Ingerman, "Apprenticeship," p. 292; Civil Rights Commission, *Challenge Ahead*, pp. 63 & 81; Dubinsky, *Trade Union Discrimination*, pp 29-31; and F. Ray Marshall and Vernon M. Briggs, Jr., *The Negro and Apprenticeship* (Baltimore: John Hopkins University Press, 1967), especially pp. 1-49.

35. Schoeman quoted in Marshall, *Organized Labor*, p. 234.

36. Quotes from U.S. Equal Employment Opportunity Commission, *The First Decade* (Washington, DC: U.S. EEOC, 1974), p. 23; and testimony of Herbert Hill before NYC Commission on Human Rights, September 26, 1966, in NAACP Files, Group III, Series B, #363, p. 9. *See also* Oscar A. Ornati and Edward Gilbin, "The High Cost of Discrimination," *Business Horizons* 18 (February, 1975): 38; and Diana Balmori, *Hispanic Immigrants in the Construction Industry: New York City, 1960-1982*, New York University Center for Latin American and Caribbean Studies Occasional Papers No. 38, May 1983, pp. 29-38.

37. Statistics from U.S. Commission on Civil Rights, *Hearings in San Francisco* (Washington, DC: U.S. Government Printing Office, 1967), pp. 323-326; *Hearings in Cleveland* (1967), p. 443; U.S. Department of Labor, Manpower Administration, *Negroes in Apprenticeship* (Washington, DC: U.S. Government Printing Office, 1967), p. 7; Rowan and Rubin, *Opening the Construction Trades*, pp. 29 & 32; and *The New York Times*, September 16, 1969, p. 35; December 23, 1969, p. 30.

38. U.S. Equal Employment Opportunity Commission, *Equal Employment Opportunity Report #1* (Washington, DC: U.S. EEOC, 1966), pp. 3 & Al; Civil Rights Commission, *Twenty Years After Brown*, pp. 30-32; U.S. Department of Labor, Bureau of Labor Statistics, *Handbook of*

Labor Statistics, Bulletin #2715 (Washington, DC: U.S. Government Printing Office, 1983), p. 63. One theory explains the relationship between black and white workers in terms of a conflict between the "mainstream" working class (whites) and "marginal" working class (blacks). The former are "culturally heterogenous" and "belong to a dominant racial group," while the latter "belong to a subordinate racial or ethnic group which is usually proletarianized and highly segregated." Although both are workers, the dominant group seeks to defend its privileges against the marginal group. For a discussion of this theory, *see* John C. Leggett, *Class Race, and Labor: Working-Class Consciousness in Detroit* (New York: Oxford University Press, 1968, 1971), especially pp. 14-15. Quotes from pp. 14-15.

39. For slave protests, *see* Herbert Aptheker, *American Negro Slave Revolts* (New York: International Publishers, 1963); appropriate chapters of John W. Blassingame, *The Slave Community: Plantation Life in the Antebellum South*, Rev. Ed. (New York: Oxford University Press, 1979); and Eugene D. Genovese, *Roll, Jordan, Roll: The World that the Slaves Made* (New York: Vintage Books, 1974, 1976).

For twentieth century, *see* August Meier and Elliot Rudwick, *CORE* (New York: Oxford University Press, 1973), pp. 8 & 27-29; Edgar A. Toppin, *A Biographical History of Blacks in American since 1528* (New York: David McCay Co., Inc., 1969, 1971), p. 389; Mark D. Naison, "The Communist Party in Harlem 1928-1936," (Ph.D. dissertation, Columbia University, 1976), pp. 86ff.; Henry Lee Moon, "The Black Boycott," *The Crisis* 73 (May, 1966): 249-250; Sitkoff, *New Deal*, p. 263; Simba, "Black Laborer," pp. 219-220; Weiss, *National Urban League*, pp. 1-67; Dorothy K. Newmann et al., *Protest, Politics, and Prosperity* (New York: Pantheon Books, 1978), pp. 12-13; Rio Ottley, *New World A-Coming* (Cambridge, MA: The Riverside Press, 1943), pp. 113-116 & 228-229; and Ryon, "Blacks and CIO," p. 22.

40. Ford arrangement from Fujita, *Black Workers' Struggles*, pp. 15-16; and Myrdal, *Dilemma*, p. 1121. UPWA from Sitkoff, *New Deal*, p. 184. Communist Party from Naison, "Communist Party," pp. 198-199. A.S. Beck from *A.S. Beck Shoe Corporation v. Johnson*, 153 Misc. 363.

41. Thurgood Marshall Memo, October 26, 1949, NAACP Files, Group II, Series B, #121.

42. *Hughes v. Superior Court of California in and for County of Contra Costa*, 70 S.Ct. 718; *Hughes v. Superior Court in and for Contra Costa County*, 186 P.2d 756; Pertinent information in NAACP Files, Group II, Series B, #121; and Earl M. Curry, Jr., "Employment Equality in a Color-Blind Society," *Akron Law Review 5* (Spring, 1972): 171-175.

43. *CORE-lator,* #67, February, 1956, pp. 1-2; #72, February, 1958, p. 4; #74, Fall, 1958, p. 1; # 96, June, 1962, pp. 3-4; Newmann, *Protest,* p. 51; Meier and Rudwick, *CORE,* pp. 59-60 & 93.

44. John B. Kirby, *Black Americans in the Roosevelt Era* (Knoxville, TN: University of Tennessee Press, 1980), p. 41; Raymond Wolters, *Negroes and the Great Depression* (Westport, CT: Greenwood Publishing Corporation, 1970), Chapter 7; and Harris, *The Harder We Run,* pp. 80-90 & 110-115.

45. Leslie Perry to Walter White, September 22, 1944, NAACP Files, Group II, Series A, #622.

46. *Labor Reports* VI (August, 1949): 1, in *ibid.*

47. For documents relating to "superseniority" *see* materials in NAACP Files, Group II, Series A, #622. Also, personal interview with Herbert Hill, 1984.

48. Goulden, *Meany,* p. 308.

49. Quote from Lester A. Sobel, ed., *Civil Rights, 1960-1966* (New York: Facts on File, 1967), p. 99.

50. *Ibid.*; Goulden, Meany, p. 308; Hill in Jacobson, *American Labor Movement,* p. 288; Marshall, *Negro Worker,* p. 37.

51. Herbert Hill, "The ILGWU Today - The Decay of a Labor Union," Reprint from *New Politics; Report on the Labor Secretary,* September 3, 1957, NAACP Files, Group III, Series B, #139; *Report of the Labor Secretary,* April, 1957, *ibid.*; Memo from Herbert Hill to Borish Shiskin, December 4, 1958, *ibid.*; Marshall, *Organized Labor,* pp. 58-60; and Marshall, *Negro Worker,* pp. 37-39.

52. Thomas R. Brooks, *Toil and Trouble: A History of American Labor,* 2nd Ed. (New York: Delacorte Press, 1971), p. 324; Haughton Interview; Fujita, *Black Workers' Struggles,* pp. 38 & 52; Harris, *The Harder We Run,* pp. 140 & 162; Sobel, *Civil Rights,* p. 100; and Meier and Rudwick, *Black Detroit,* Chapter 5, especially pp. 219-220.

53. Alonzo L. Hamby, *Liberalism and Its Challengers: FDR to Reagan* (New York: Oxford University Press, 1985), p. 141.

54. *Ibid.,* p. 142.

55. Bo Wimark, "Nonviolent Methods and the American Civil Rights Movement 1955-1965," *Journal of Peace Research* XI (1974): 126.

56. King quoted in David L. Lewis, *King: A Critical Biography* (Baltimore: Penguin Books, Inc., 1970, 1971), p. 85.

57. Montgomery in *ibid.,* Chapter 3; and Hamby, *Liberalism,* pp. 151-155. Strategies from Hamby, pp. 155, ff.; Lewis, p. 85; and Wimark, "Nonviolent Methods."

II

Too Little, Too Late: the Federal Government and Job Discrimination from Roosevelt to Eisenhower

In addition to relying on their own efforts, proponents of equal employment opportunity have worked to involve the federal government in this struggle. This process was a long and arduous one that initially bore little fruit. Currently a crucial element in the struggle against discrimination, the federal government for much of the twentieth century was apathetic, if not hostile, toward the plight of African Americans. Prior to Franklin Roosevelt's New Deal, African Americans wielded little political power and were unable to secure any meaningful reforms or concessions from a succession of administrations. During the New Deal-World War II years, northern blacks became stalwarts within the Democratic coalition and no longer could be ignored by the Democratic Party, or by the political system in general. Black political influence, however, was limited by the continued disfranchisement of southern blacks, the absence of large-scale grassroots protests during the 1940s and 1950s, and the disproportionate power of the southern Democratic congressional bloc, especially within the Senate. Prior to 1960, therefore, federal civil rights activities were largely token and cosmetic. Not until the racial situation exploded during the 1960s did the government accord a high priority to civil rights issues.

Government initiatives towards African Americans throughout the first three decades of this century were largely symbolic. Theodore Roosevelt invited Booker T. Washington to the White House; years later, Herbert Hoover extended a similar courtesy to Robert Morton of the Tuskegee Institute. Hoover also created a scandal by inviting the wife of African-American congressman Oscar de Priest of Chicago to a social tea at the White House. These actions offered little consolation to African Americans, especially in light of the government's generally negative racial policies during these years. Of far greater significance was the government's refusal to address such basic issues as violation of constitutional rights, disfranchisement, and economic discrimination.[1]

Ironically, even those administrations designated by historians as "Progressive" exhibited negative racial attitudes. The first "Progressive" president, Theodore Roosevelt, appointed some African Americans to federal offices. At the same time, he refused NAACP requests to issue public statements against discrimination and disfranchisement. In 1906, following a violent incident in Brownsville, Texas, Roosevelt dishonorably discharged all three companies of the black 25th U.S. Infantry—including six Medal of Honor winners—stationed at nearby Fort Brown. Despite congressional protests led by Ohio Senator J.B. Foraker, and despite convincing evidence of the soldiers' innocence, Roosevelt refused to commission an inquiry into the affair or to restore the troops' pensions. In 1912, the nominating convention of Roosevelt's Progressive Party refused to seat southern black delegates.

In November 1912, Woodrow Wilson, a Democrat who championed states' rights and maintained that segregation "worked to their (blacks') advantage," won the presidency.[2] Wilson rejected civil rights activist Oswald Garrison Villard's proposed National Race Commission to investigate U.S. race relations and refused to appoint African Americans to public offices. He approved proposals by Postmaster General Albert Burleson and Treasury Secretary William McAdoo to segregate their respective departments, although protests from northern Democrats and liberal-progressive groups later forced him to terminate this practice. Wilson also refused to act against the revived Ku Klux Klan, even when it murdered African-American veterans after World War I.[3]

The demise of the Progressive movement during World War I and the Republican ascendancy of 1921 offered little relief to African Americans. Warren Harding, who captured the African-American vote in 1920, opposed in theory economic and political discrimination—but *not* social segregation—but made no significant efforts to implement these views. To his credit, he requested an antilynching law, which passed the House of Representatives in January 1922 but was killed by a southern Senate filibuster. Harding appointed few African Americans to government offices, however, and he approved the elimination of southern blacks from the Republican Party in an attempt to create an all-white southern Republican Party. Harding's successors, Calvin Coolidge and Herbert Hoover, "re-instituted the customary do-nothing policy towards Negroes."[4] Hoover "condemned lynching publicly but sponsored no legislation against it."[5] Hoover continued the drive for a Republican resurgence in the South by purging southern blacks from the party and abolishing the black division of the Republican National Committee. In addition, he nominated for the Supreme Court John Parker, a North Carolina judge, who, in 1920, had argued that North Carolina blacks were not qualified to participate in state politics. The Senate, pressured by civil rights and labor groups, refused his nomination by a 41-39 vote. Despite this dismal Republican record, African-American voters remained loyal to the "party of Lincoln" in 1932, while the Democratic candidate, Franklin D. Roosevelt, pursued southern white votes.[6]

By 1932, however, forces were at work that transformed the nature of African-American participation in the political system. The Great Migration relocated millions of blacks from the South—where they had been disfranchised around the turn of the century—to northern cities, where they formed sizeable voting blocs. In 1929, Oscar de Priest of Chicago became the first African American to sit in the House of Representatives since the beginning of the century. Long before Franklin Roosevelt assumed the presidency, local politicians like Mayor William Thompson of Chicago had realized the political advantages of granting concessions, albeit "largely formal and ceremonial," to African-American voters.[7] As African Americans became more active politically, they exhibited greater independence from party affiliation. Democratic Mayor James Walker, for example, courted and received votes of New York blacks. In addition, the maturation of the Urban League and especially the NAACP provided northern blacks with valuable political leadership.

The final element responsible for rechanneling African-American political activity was the Depression itself. The Depression devastated black Americans even more than white Americans. The heavy industries that suffered the greatest losses, such as steel, automobiles, and construction, were the same industries in which black workers were concentrated. Not only were blacks disproportionately laid off in these industries, but they also were displaced by whites from traditional "Negro jobs" such as garbage collecting and streetcleaning. Consequently, according to Robert Weaver, "almost a half of the skilled Negro males in the nation were displaced from their usual types of employment during the period from 1930 to 1936."[8] Unemployment among urban blacks often exceeded 50 percent. The very extent of the black employment nightmare made it inevitable that blacks would receive some benefit from New Deal programs, even if this was not a major objective of the Roosevelt administration.[9]

The New Deal, especially in its initial phases, achieved few civil rights successes. Housing projects constructed by the Federal Housing Authority and the Tennessee Valley Authority generally excluded African Americans.

Subsidizing policies established by the Agricultural Adjustment Act uprooted African-American sharecroppers and tenant farmers. Because the majority of African Americans were farmers or domestic workers, they did not receive social security benefits. Segregation was widespread in the Civilian Conservation Corps and the Civil Works Administration. Conscious of southern Democratic power, Roosevelt refused to endorse antilynching bills or to intervene against the decimation of the Southern Tenant Farmers Union.

There was, however, a positive side to this picture. In moves designed to appease northern liberals and attract black votes, Roosevelt brought many black and white civil rights proponents into his administration, including Will Alexander of the Farm Security Administration (FSA), Mary McLeod Bethune of the National Youth Administration (NYA), and Secretary of the Interior Harold Ickes. Judicial appointments included the liberal Felix Frankfurter, a former NAACP official who became a Supreme Court justice in 1939, and the first African-American federal judge, William Hastie of the NAACP. Some New Deal programs bore the imprint of these liberal appointments. Under Alexander, blacks received a proportional share of FSA loans, and monies from the Federal Theater Project were awarded to all-black theater companies.[10]

The most significant civil rights progress occurred within the Department of the Interior. It was here that the first federal "affirmative action" program (although the phrase was never used) for African Americans was developed in conjunction with the Public Works Administration (PWA). Created in 1933 by Title II of the National Industrial Recovery Act, the PWA was designed to relieve unemployment through massive construction projects for housing, schools, courthouses, hospitals, and other public buildings. The PWA was located within the Interior Department under the supervision of Secretary Harold Ickes. Former president of the Chicago NAACP and a personal friend of NAACP Executive Secretary Walter White, Ickes brought several important African Americans into Interior, including William Hastie and Robert Weaver. In 1934, Weaver replaced Clark Foreman as Ickes's Advisor on Negro Affairs. Determined to eliminate racism within the programs under his authority, Ickes ordered that "there be no discrimination exercised against any person because of color or religious affiliation" on PWA projects.[11]

Unfortunately, Ickes' proposal, while well intentioned, accomplished little. Lacking any concrete definition or criteria for "discrimination," the order was too vague to be enforced effectively. Moreover, the displacement of African-American workers, which was a *fait accompli* by 1933, meant that a policy of simple nondiscrimination, even if enforced, at best would freeze African Americans into highly inferior positions. As Robert Weaver observed, "experience has shown that a simple nondiscrimination clause was not enough."[12]

Pressured by White, Weaver, and by African-American job protests throughout the nation's cities, Ickes sought a more effective, result-oriented program and found it in the PWA Housing Division. Designed to construct low-income housing for urban blacks, the Housing Division offered an ideal opportunity to tap the still-extensive supply of black construction labor. Rather than issue a general nondiscrimination directive, William Hastie suggested that employment statistics be used as *prima facie* evidence of discrimination or nondiscrimination. Weaver concurred, and he proposed that all PWA housing contracts include a "minimum percentage clause" in which contractors agreed to direct a specified proportion of their payroll to African-American workers. Failure to achieve the stated percentages would be interpreted as evidence of discrimination. Thus, the onus was on employers to prove nondiscrimination, rather than worker to prove discrimination. The percentages would be derived from the number of African Americans in the labor force of each locality as recorded in the 1930 census. Approved by Ickes, the plan became a standard feature of all PWA housing projects.

The first PWA project, in Atlanta, included a clause affirming that "the failure of the Contractor to pay to Negro skilled labor at least 12 percent of the total amount paid in any one month under the Contract for all skilled labor (irrespective of individual trades) shall be considered *prima facie* evidence of discrimination by the Contractor."[13] The Atlanta contract served as a prototype for subsequent projects in ninety-five cities. Weaver's office examined monthly payroll reports for compliance. The Urban League assisted the PWA in locating qualified black workers. In some instances where the supply of black union labor was inadequate to meet the requirements, contractors were required to hire nonunion workers. Not surprisingly the building trades unions adamantly opposed the program and cooperated only under pressure from the Department of Labor. Although most black spokespersons supported the plan, some, including the *Amsterdam News*, were hostile, arguing that "minimum" quotas easily could become "maximum" quotas. In 1937, the government transferred the program to the newly created United States Housing Authority.[14]

The PWA-USHA program, although unquestionably innovative for its time, was not as "radical" as it might appear on paper. To begin with, the program was designed specifically for a sector of the economy in which

African-American labor already was concentrated; job training and upgrading of skills were *not* part of this program. Moreover, PWA construction jobs were temporary and did not lead to union membership. Although African Americans ostensibly were to be hired for all phases of construction, contractors who claimed that no African Americans with particular skills were available could substitute a "blanket quota" for the entire project. Consequently, African Americans, as usual, were concentrated in the trowel trades and underrepresented in the skilled crafts. Perhaps most fundamentally, as even Weaver admitted, the minimum percentage clauses "were frankly a device to regain lost ground: they were not designed to open new types of employment."[15] The paramount goal of the PWA program was to provide temporary relief for African-American workers by restoring them to their pre-Depression status in the construction industry. The government neither intended, nor undertook, any long-range restructuring of the construction industry.

Given the limited objectives of the Housing Division, the program was successful. By the end of 1940, African Americans had received 13 percent of the USHA payroll. Among skilled workers, however, they received only 5-6 percent of the payroll, demonstrating their overrepresentation in the less-skilled trades. Significantly, however, even the lower numbers exceeded the African-American percentage of skilled artisans as recorded by the 1930 census. Thus, the PWA-USHA housing program stands as one of the notable—and unfortunately one of the few—civil rights successes of the New Deal. Unfortunately, the program was short-lived. With the approach of World War II, Congress severed funding for public housing, and the minimum percentage clause policy drifted into insignificance.[16]

As the United States moved from the New Deal to World War II, African Americans increasingly focused their job demands on defense industries. The patterns in these industries reflected those of the economy as a whole. African Americans either were excluded, as in the aircraft industry, or were restricted to unskilled jobs, as in shipbuilding. Nationwide protests organized by the NAACP and a more militant Urban League achieved some results—in 1940, for example, the Civil Service Commission issued a directive prohibiting racial discrimination in federal employment—but their primary objective, the elimination of discrimination in defense industries, remained elusive. The government applied some pressure on AFL and CIO unions to reform their policies, but compliance was negligible. As one labor leader stated: "Organized labor has been called upon to make many sacrifices for defense and has made them gladly, but this (admission of Negroes) is asking too much."[17]

Frustrated and impatient, African-American leaders resorted to direct mass action, organizing the March on Washington Committee to prepare for a mass demonstration in the nation's capital scheduled for July 1, 1941. As the projected size of the demonstration approached 100,000 people, a disconcerted Roosevelt requested, through such "intermediaries" as Eleanor Roosevelt and New York City Mayor Fiorello LaGuardia, that Randolph cancel the March. These efforts proved unsuccessful, and, with the deadline rapidly approaching, the president personally met with committee leaders on June 18th. When the committee members remained adamant regarding the march, Roosevelt responded one week later by issuing Executive Order 8802, establishing the Fair Employment Practices Committee. Executive Order 8802 ordered that all training and vocational programs for jobs in defense industries be "administered without discrimination because of race, creed, color, or national origin." To enforce these directives, a Fair Employment Practices Committee (FEPC) was created within the Office of Production Management to "receive and investigate complaints of discrimination" and "take appropriate steps to redress grievances which it finds to be valid."[18]

As would be so often true of federal civil rights initiatives, Roosevelt's executive order appeared more imposing on paper than it really was. The order contained no definition of "discrimination," and the FEPC, although authorized to investigate charges and issue "directives," was allocated no direct enforcement power. Maintaining that the order prohibited "discrimination against white as well as against colored employees," the FEPC rejected any suggestions of proportional hiring.[19] The committee members were to serve on a part-time basis "without compensation."[20] The Committee's budget for the first year totaled only $80,000. A year after its creation, the FEPC was transferred to the War Manpower Commission, a government agency preoccupied with the success of the war effort and "indifferent and sometimes hostile to the problems of job discrimination." The committee's transfer reduced its influence and its access to the White House.[21]

The apparently cursory treatment accorded the FEPC by the White House dismayed and outraged African-American leaders. The NAACP and other groups proposed not only that the committee be reorganized but also that Cabinet agencies be empowered to withhold money from contractors that practiced discrimination. When Paul McNutt, head of the War Manpower Commission, postponed hearings into discrimination within the railroad industry, mass resignations from the FEPC followed. Responding to heightened pressure from liberal and civil rights groups, Roosevelt in May

1943 issued Executive Order 9346, which restored the FEPC as an independent agency within the Office of Production Management, answerable directly to the president. Committee members were increased in number and were awarded salaries. Perhaps more important, the executive order was expanded to include *all* government contractors, not just defense industries.[22]

The FEPC opened a new conduit for equal employment efforts. Rather than appeal directly to employers or unions, African Americans for the first time could file complaints with a government agency. African-American workers capitalized on this unprecedented opportunity. By 1946, African-American individuals and groups, especially the NAACP, had filed over 14,000 complaints with the FEPC against employers and unions. The committee itself estimated that 80 percent of the complaints it received had been filed by African Americans, with Jews and Mexican Americans accounting for most of the remaining 20 percent. The targets ranged from the construction industry to the building trades unions. The committee boasted some concrete accomplishments, including the successful resolution of five thousand complaints.

Perhaps its most dramatic moments occurred in Philadelphia in 1944, when white employees of the Philadelphia Transportation Company staged an illegal strike to protest the hiring of black workers following FEPC pressure. Only after Roosevelt ordered federal troops into the city to take command of the trains and buses and arrest the strike leaders did the strikers agree to return to their jobs. Although Roosevelt's primary concern in this affair undoubtedly was the disruption of wartime production, his actions secured job benefits for African-American workers. The FEPC also claimed much credit for a substantial increase in African-American employment in defense industries during the war years. Lockheed, for example, which had only 40 African-American employees in 1941, claimed three thousand by 1944. These accomplishments must be viewed in perspective, however. African-American employment in defense industries, although facilitated by the FEPC, resulted primarily from a dire labor shortage and was therefore a temporary phenomenon. In addition, the failure to grant enforcement powers to the FEPC allowed unions and employers to disregard FEPC directives. In the South especially, federal agencies continued to conduct business with their regular contractors, despite evidence of racial discrimination. The overriding goal of efficient wartime production completely overshadowed that of antidiscrimination.[23]

Not surprisingly, the FEPC fostered numerous enemies, inside and outside the government. Business and labor leaders defied its directives.

White workers in defense plants struck on numerous occasions to protest the introduction of black workers. In Congress, the southern conservative bloc tried to destroy the committee by terminating its funding. Representative Martin Dies of the House Committee on Un-American Activities typically agitated against the "Communist influence" within the FEPC.[24] Although liberal representatives were able to preserve the committee during the war years, the death of Roosevelt and the end of the war removed the most pressing justification for the existence of the FEPC. Unable to overcome a southern filibuster, FEPC supporters agreed to a massive reduction in funding in 1945, allocated specifically for "liquidating its affairs."[25]

In 1946, the FEPC issued its final report, containing observations that would affect civil rights strategies for the next two decades. First, the committee pointed out that most wartime employment gains for African Americans had occurred in occupations and industries slated for the greatest postwar contraction. The combination of contraction and discrimination, it warned, would erase whatever progress African Americans had achieved during the war. The committee also maintained that the tenuous nature of its own existence stemmed from the fact that it was the product of an executive order rather than an act of Congress. The committee's proposed solution to this problem was a permanent FEPC based on law rather than on presidential proclamation. Finally, the FEPC asserted what became gospel for all future antidiscrimination agencies: "The majority of all discrimination cases can be settled by formal negotiation."[26] Having offered these final recommendations, the FEPC officially ceased to exist in June 1946. The battle for a permanent FEPC, however, was just beginning.[27]

The arduous and often virulent confrontations over funding for the FEPC convinced many representatives of the need for an FEPC law. The struggle for FEPC legislation began in 1942 when Representative Vito Marcantonio of New York introduced a fair employment bill into the House, and it continued throughout the war years. As FEPC bills languished in Congress, a support network evolved that included liberal politicians, religious and labor groups, and civil rights organizations. In 1944, these groups formed the National Council for a Permanent FEPC, which lobbied extensively for a fair employment law. That same year, the Republican Party tried to upstage its Democratic rivals, and to reclaim the African-American vote that it had lost to Roosevelt, when the Republican National Convention officially endorsed a permanent FEPC. The bill died in Congress, however, when Truman refused to intervene against a southern filibuster. Also contributing to the defeat of the bill was the opposition of the AFL, which did not endorse such legislation until after 1947.[28]

In 1948, Truman included in his civil rights message to Congress a request for civil rights legislation, including an FEPC provision. Two years later, Representative Adam Clayton Powell, Jr., of New York introduced a bill providing for an FEPC empowered to investigate charges of discrimination and to enforce its rulings. Fearing that this bill was too extreme for Congress, the House substituted a measure by Representative Samuel McConnell, Jr., of Pennsylvania, which replaced the power to enforce decisions with the power to recommend solutions. Endorsed by the CIO, NAACP, American Jewish Congress, and Americans for Democratic Action, among others, the bill passed the House but, like its predecessors, met its death at the hands of a southern filibuster. By the time Representative Franklin D. Roosevelt, Jr., introduced an FEPC bill in 1954, its list of supporters included the National Conference of Christians and Jews, the American Civil Liberties Union, B'nai B'rith, the CIO, and the National Board of the YMCA and the YWCA. By then, many of these groups had joined forces in an umbrella organization known as the Leadership Conference on Civil Rights (LCCR). Even their combined strength, however, was insufficient to overcome a southern filibuster and White House indifference. Despite the determined actions of its proponents, a fair employment law remained an elusive dream until the passage of the 1964 Civil Rights Act. The one consolation for civil rights activists was the emergence of a labor-liberal-civil rights coalition, embodied by the LCCR, that fought incessantly for civil rights laws throughout the 1950s and early 1960s.[29]

Rebuffed in their efforts to secure passage of a national law, civil rights leaders took some solace in the passage of numerous state FEPC laws. The first such law, the Ives-Quinn Act, went into effect in New York in 1945. The Ives-Quinn Act issued directives against discrimination by employers with more than four employees and by labor unions, to be enforced by the newly created State Commission Against Discrimination, later renamed the State Commission on Human Rights. The New York commission had greater power than Roosevelt's FEPC, being authorized to investigate charges of discrimination submitted by workers and to issue cease-and desist orders if such charges were confirmed. If the offending party failed to comply with a commission ruling, the commission then would be required to seek a court order in support of its directives. Not until 1965, however, was the commission empowered to initiate its own investigations. Significantly, when the commission found discrimination, it was authorized to compel offending parties to "take such affirmative action, including (but not limited to) hiring, reinstatement or upgrading of employees, with or without back pay, restoration to membership in any respondent labor organization."[30] This language was adopted from the National Labor Relations Act, which empowered the NLRB to mandate "affirmative action including reinstatement of employees with or without back pay."[31] The NLRA and Ives-Quinn both acknowledged that outlawing discriminatory behavior, directed against union members or minority groups, would be of limited value unless it was accompanied by specific remedial activities on behalf of the victims. It should be noted, however, that the New York law defined "affirmative action" in terms of concrete steps in response to individual acts of discrimination. "Affirmative action" in 1945 did *not* refer to class action suits or proportional hiring. Nevertheless, the government of New York had confirmed the inadequacy of simple nondiscrimination in promoting equal employment opportunity for nonwhites. The idea that affirmative action was vital to effective antidiscrimination efforts eventually became a basic tenet of civil rights ideology.

The enactment of the New York FEPC bill, followed quickly by the passage of similar bills in New Jersey and Indiana, signaled the beginning of a new phase in the civil rights movement. By 1963, some 25 states had passed FEPC laws of varying strength and effectiveness. Some states imitated the New York model of delegating cease-and-desist authority to the antidiscrimination agency; others, such as Wisconsin, passed laws without any enforcement mechanism. In some states the antidiscrimination agency actually relied on voluntary workers. In contrast, states such as Ohio, Connecticut, and Massachusetts allowed their FEPC boards to file their own complaints rather than wait for aggrieved parties to submit charges. Regardless of the relative strength or weakness of the various laws, however, most state FEPCs adopted the same general approach. An individual filed a complaint, which was then investigated by the state antidiscrimination agency. If the agency found probable cause, it usually arranged a conference with the employer or union in hopes of achieving a voluntary solution. Only when such conciliatory efforts failed did the commission resort to more stringent measures—for example, public hearings, cease-and-desist orders, and court rulings.

The effectiveness of the state laws is difficult to measure. On the one hand, most state agencies claimed a high rate of successful conciliation. On the other hand, the number of charges filed with the state agencies was rather low. Ignorant of the existence of these laws, fearful of retaliation, and uncertain of the time and expenses involved, minority groups did not make extensive use of state FEPCs. The agencies themselves were hampered by the difficulty of proving discrimination; an employer, after all, could simply claim that few qualified minorities applied for jobs. Perhaps the best conclusion is that state FEPC's assisted many *individuals* but did not alter general racial hiring patterns in any dramatic way.[32]

Business and other conservative groups organized and lobbied against state FEPC laws. Businesses feared government intervention in their affairs, especially the imposition of hiring quotas. The New York Assembly approved the Ives-Quinn Act only after a dire warning from the New York Chamber of Commerce that the bill would "attract an undesirable element from outside the State and it might give rise to a burning resentment leading to possible race riots, pogroms, and other evils." A conservative opponent denounced a California FEPC bill of 1947 as the work of "Communists, fellow travelers, parlor pinks, left wingers and radicals of all hues."[33] During the 1950s, business representatives often proposed voluntary action plans as alternatives to antidiscrimination legislation. As one individual has observed: "Impending FEPC legislation had an uncanny ability to stimulate moral commitment."[34]

Whatever their effectiveness, state laws were no substitute for federal action, especially since the southern states, which practiced the most extreme forms of discrimination, generally failed to enact such laws. Despite mounting pressure for a national FEPC law during the Truman and Eisenhower years, both administrations resorted to executive orders, thereby avoiding bitter congressional battles. Truman's first concrete act regarding equal employment opportunity was his issuing of Executive Order 9980 on July 26, 1948. Truman's order created a Fair Employment Board within the Civil Service Commission to ensure "fair employment throughout the Federal establishment, without discrimination because of race, color, religion, or national origin."[35] (That same day, Truman issued Executive Order 9981, which outlawed segregation in the armed forces.) This board, which included George Meany of the AFL and James Carey of the CIO, could investigate charges of discrimination and suggest remedies, but it had no enforcement powers. A second executive order of December 3, 1951, created the Committee on Government Contract Compliance to determine whether government contractors were observing policies of nondiscrimination. Truman's orders accomplished little, and they expired when he left office in January 1953.[36]

Shortly after Dwight Eisenhower succeeded Truman, Clarence Mitchell of the NAACP met with Attorney General Herbert Brownell to discuss the need for a contract compliance committee and a civil rights bill. Although the latter was not enacted until 1957—and then only in a highly eviscerated form—Eisenhower responded to the first request with Executive Order

10479 on August 13, 1953. This order created the President's Committee on Government Contracts (PCGC) to "receive complaints of alleged violations of the nondiscrimination provisions of government contracts."[37] Primary responsibility for enforcement of nondiscrimination resided within the particular government agency that actually transacted business with the contractor; for example, the Defense Department with defense contractors. The PCGC assumed a general supervisory role and managed those cases in which a specific agency could not achieve a satisfactory conciliation. To underscore the importance of PCGC within the administration, Eisenhower appointed Vice President Richard Nixon as chairman. Thus, the PCGC also was referred to as the "Nixon Committee"[38]

The PCGC was the first federal peacetime agency to bring about some improvement, albeit very modest, in black employment. The committee suffered an inauspicious beginning as few African Americans filed complaints the first year, generating skepticism on the part of some committee members as to the actual pervasiveness of job discrimination in the United States. Nixon himself conceded, however, that "even today there are many people who do not file complaints because they do not know whether it will accomplish anything."[39]

Eventually, due largely to NAACP activities, complaints began to pour in from all parts of the country. The NAACP directed charges of discrimination against the aircraft industry—Lockheed, Boeing, and Cessna—Du Pont, B.F. Goodrich, the tobacco, oil, and steel industries, and several building trades unions. In some cases, progress was achieved. The Lockheed plant in Marietta, Georgia, agreed to the merger of the black and white locals of the International Association of Machinists. Atlantic Steel eliminated separate lines of progression, and some tobacco companies modified their segregation policies. The government pressured Southern oil companies to discard their separate seniority lists. The PCGC published pamphlets and posters, conducted seminars and negotiations with business officers, and sometimes requested that companies receiving federal contracts develop minority training programs.[40]

As was true of state FEPCs, however, the accomplishments of the PCGC must be measured against the magnitude of the problems with which it had to contend. Although the committee achieved some modest successes, the nation's racial hiring patterns remained relatively unaffected. Black workers continued to be overrepresented in lower-paying occupations, and black unemployment remained twice that of whites.

One major reason for the ineffectiveness of Eisenhower's program was the failure of the president to delegate and of the committee to exercise the type of authority needed to challenge the monumental problem of employment discrimination. Like Roosevelt's FEPC, the PCGC lacked enforcement powers. From its inception, the committee adopted a policy of "education, conciliation, mediation and persuasion."[41] Although Nixon proposed in 1957 that the PCGC consider canceling the contracts of companies with a history of discrimination, no such actions were ever taken. Reliance on voluntary compliance and moral suasion appealed to the "moderate" temperament of the Eisenhower administration, but it severely restricted the committee's ability to compel businesses and unions to modify longstanding policies. Compounding this problem was the committee's approach to union discrimination, which consisted of channeling complaints against unions to the leadership of the AFL-CIO. Given the AFL-CIO's unimpressive record in confronting racism within its affiliates, it is not surprising that the PCGC made little impact in the area of union reform.

The inadequacy of the PCGC becomes evident in the reaction of businesses and unions to various committee initiatives. NAACP complaints against Du Pont and B.F. Goodrich produced "no tangible results." One major study characterized reforms within the tobacco industry as "a few small dents in the racial-occupational pattern," and the southern textile industry was ignored altogether. As one critic concluded, "Subsequent studies have shown that there was no appreciable increase in nonwhite employment in contractor firms over the life of the Nixon Committee."[42]The executive order that created the PCGC expired at the end of the Eisenhower administration. In 1961, the committee submitted its final report to the president. Of particular importance was the following observation: "Overt discrimination, in the sense that an employer actually refuses to hire solely because of race, religion, color or national origin, is not as prevalent as is generally believed. To a greater degree, *the indifference of employers to establishing a positive policy of nondiscrimination* hinders qualified applicants and employees from being hired and promoted on the basis of equality."[43] Although one might contest the committee's assertion regarding the extent of overt discrimination, it is significant that the PCGC, like the New York FEPC, affirmed the inadequacy of simple nondiscrimination. The reference to "a positive policy of nondiscrimination" implied that the responsibilities of employers regarding equal employment opportunity had to be redefined from a passive to an active (affirmative) role. Although the committee did not employ the phrase "affirmative action," it clearly suggested than an employer must do more than wait for "qualified" nonwhite job candidates to appear when openings were available. This new philosophy would be implemented and expanded by subsequent administrations.

An examination of government equal employment opportunity policies from Roosevelt through Eisenhower reveals a pattern in which African Americans received only a fraction of what they requested, and then only in a modest fashion. The civil rights laws passed by Congress in 1957 and 1960 contained mild provisions for protecting the voting rights of southern blacks and made no mention of school desegregation, public integration, open housing, or equal employment opportunity. The subordinate status of African Americans in the U.S. economy in 1960 provided eloquent testimony to the deficiencies of policies based solely on voluntary compliance. That the government embraced such policies is not surprising, given the lack of African-American voting strength and the absence of mass protest activities throughout these years. In his autobiography, Hubert Humphrey attributed congressional failure to enact meaningful civil rights legislation prior to 1964 to the absence of outside pressures.[44] In the 1960s, civil rights demonstrators lobbyists supplied the necessary pressures to force the government to expand and develop the concept of affirmative action that it gradually and reluctantly came to acknowledge during the 1940s and 1950s.

NOTES

1. David Burner, *Herbert Hoover: A Public Life* (New York: Alfred A. Knopf, 1979), p. 215-216; and David S. Day, "Herbert Hoover and Racial Politics, The DePriest Incident," *The Journal of Negro History* 65 (Winter, 1980), pp. 6-17.

2. Wilson quoted in Weiss, *National Urban League*, p. 6.

3. Roosevelt from Weiss, *National Urban League*, p. 5; Sitkoff, *New Deal*, p. 20; and Henry F. Pringle, *Theodore Roosevelt: A Biography* (New York: Harcourt, Brace and World, 1931, 1956), pp. 322-327. Wilson from Sitkoff, pp. 20-21; Weiss, p. 6; and Arthur S. Link, *Wilson: The New Freedom* (New Brunswick, NJ: Princeton University Press, 1956), pp. 241-252.

4. Robert K. Murray, *The Harding Era: Warren G. Harding and His Administration* (Minneapolis: University of Minnesota Press, 1969), pp. 401-402.

5. Burner, *Herbert Hoover*, p. 216.

6. William E. Leuchtenburg, *Franklin D. Roosevelt and the New Deal* (New York: Harper and Row, Harper Colophon Books, 1963), p. 185; Burner, *Herbert Hoover*, pp. 215-216 & 235; Murray, *Harding Era*, pp. 397-402; Sitkoff, *New Deal*, pp. 27 & 85; and Day, "Herbert Hoover," pp. 7-8.

7. Spear, *Black Chicago*, pp. 187ff. Quote p. 192.

8. Weaver, *Negro Labor*, p. 9.

9. *Ibid.*, pp. 8-10; Myrdal, American Dilemma, p. 297; Weiss, *National Urban League*, p. 282; Osofsky, *Harlem*, pp. 161-169; Sitkoff, *New Deal*, pp. 35-38; and Day, "Herbert Hoover," p. 8.

10. For a discussion of tenant farmers and STFU see David E. Contrad, *The Forgotten Farmers* (Urbana: University of Illinois Press, 1965). Other information from Leuchtenburg, *New Deal*, pp. 50-74; and Naison, *Communist Party in Harlem*, p. 217.

11. Ickes quoted in Robert C. Weaver, "An Experiment in Negro Labor," *Opportunity* XIV (October, 1936): 295. Other information from Kirby, *Black Americans in the Roosevelt Era*, pp. 20-21; Mark W. Kruman, "Quotas for Blacks: The Public Works Administration and the Black Construction Worker," *Labor History* 16 (Winter, 1975): pp. 38-40; and Leuchtenburg, *New Deal*, pp. 133-134.

12. Quote from Weaver, *Negro Labor*, p. 11. Also, Weaver "Experiment," p. 295; and Kruman, "Quotas," p. 39.

13. Weaver, "Experiment," p. 296.

14. Interview with Robert Weaver, April 25, 1984; Weaver, *Negro Labor*, pp. 11-13; Weaver, "Experiment," pp. 295-296; and Kruman, "Quotas," pp. 40-46.

15. Weaver, *Negro Labor*, p. 13.

16. Mark I. Gelfand, *A Nation of Cities: The Federal Government and Urban America, 1933-1965* (New York: Oxford University Press, 1975), p. 64; Kruman, "Quotas," pp. 47-48; Myrdal, *American Dilemma*, pp. 1104-1105; Weaver, *Negro Labor*, pp. 11-14; Weaver, "Experiment," pp. 295-298; and Weaver interview.

17. Louis Ruchames, *Race, Jobs and Politics: The Story of FEPC* (New York: Columbia University Press, 1952, 1953), p. 12.

18. Executive order quoted in Gary W. Hubbard, "Affirmative Action: The Law and Politics of Equality," (Ph.D. dissertation, University of Nebraska, Lincoln, 1978), p. 106. Also, U.S. Equal Employment Opportunity Commission, *Legislative History of Titles VII and XI of Civil Rights Act* (Washington, DC: U.S. Government Printing Office), p. 1; Civil Rights Commission, *Twenty Years After Brown*, p. 3; Harris, *The Harder We Run*, pp. 116-117; Ruchames, *FEPC*, pp. vii, 9-21; and Newmann, *Protest, Politics and Prosperity*, pp. 12-13.

19. Gelber, *Black Men and Businessmen*, p. 27.

20. Hubbard, "Affirmative Action," p. 106.

21. Quote from Merl E. Reed, "FEPC and the Federal Agencies in the South," *The Journal of Negro History* 65 (Winter, 1980): 44. Also, Hubbard, "Affirmative Action," p. 106; Bureau of National Affairs, *The Civil Rights Act of 1964* (Washington, DC: Bureau of National Affairs, 1964), p. 10; U.S. Fair Employment Practice Committee, *Final Report* (Washington, DC: U.S. Government Printing Office, 1947), p. 21; and Ruchames, *FEPC*, pp. 35.

22. NAACP Memorandum of February 18, 1943, NAACP Files, U.S. Library of Congress, Group II, Series A, #208; U.S. EEOC, *Legislative History*, p. 2; FEPC *Final Report*, p. 2; Hubbard, "Affirmative Action," pp. 106-107; and Ruchames, *FEPC*, pp. 50-57.

23. Philadelphia transit strike from Hill, *Black Labor*, Chapter 11; and Ruchames, *FEPC*, Chapter 7. Other information from Earl Dickenson to Walter White, February 18, 1943, NAACP Files, Group II, Series A, #208; FEPC, *Final Report*, pp. viii, 4, 9, 11 & 31; Newmann, *Protest, Politics and Prosperity*, p. 12; Ruchames, *FEPC*, p. 159; Marshall, *The Negro and Organized Labor*, p. 215; Michael I. Sovern, *Legal Restraints on Racial*

Discrimination in Employment (New York: The Twentieth Century Fund, 1966), pp. 15-16; and Reed, "FEPC in the South."

24. Dies quoted in Ruchames, *FEPC*, p. 50.

25. Quote from Hubbard, "Affirmative Action," p. 108. Also, Hubbard, pp. 122-132; Newmann, *Protest, Politics and Prosperity*, p. 12; and Hill, *Black Labor*, p. 211.

26. U.S. FEPC, *Final Report*, p. xv.

27. *Ibid*, various entries.

28. Walter White to Mary Morton, August 31, 1944, NAACP Files, Group II, Series A, #264; Norton to White, September 1, 1944, *ibid*.; Memorandum, September 16, 1944, *ibid*.; William Hastie to Walter White, September 21, 1944, *ibid*.; U.S. EEOC, *Legislative History*, p. 7; Golden, *Meany*, p. 306; and Ruchames, *FEPC*, pp. 194-206.

29. Rebecca Chalmer Barton to Roy Wilkins, January 12, 1950, NAACP Files, Group II, Series A, #264; Alfred Bernheim to Wilkins, January 20, 1950, *ibid*.; Leslie Perry to Wilkins, February 28, 1950, *ibid*.; *Civil Liberties*, #82, *ibid*.; CIO Memorandum, May 19, 1950, *ibid*.; Jewish Labor Committee Memorandum, December 18, 1953, *ibid*.; Hubert H. Humphrey, The *Education of a Public Man* (Garden City, NY: Doubleday and Co., Inc., 1976), p. 268; U.S. EEOC, *Legislative History*, p. 8; Ruchames, *FEPC*, pp. 207-208; and Martin, *Democratic Party, 1945-1976*, p. 71.

30. New York State Law, Section 297(c), from Sovern, *Legal Restraints*, p. 248.

31. *National Labor Relations Act,* U.S. Code, Title 29, Section 160(c).

32. Herbert Hill, "State Laws and the Negro: Social Change and the Impact of Law," *African Forum* 1 (Fall, 1965): 97-100; Brooks, *Toil and Trouble*, p. 208; Gelber, *Black Men and Businessmen*, pp. 30 & 41; Sovern, *Legal Restraints*, pp. 20-46; and Vines, "Title VII," pp. 8-9.

33. Quotes from Gelber, *Black Men and Businessmen*, pp. 33 & 32.

34. Quote from Gelber, *Black Men and Businessmen*, p. 93. Also, Gelber, pp. 36-37; and Sovern, *Legal Restraints*, pp. 45-46.

35. "Civil Rights and 'FEPC'," *Congressional Digest* 43 (March, 1964): 68.

36. *Ibid*.; NAACP Memorandum, January 10, 1952, NAACP Files, Group II, Series A, #2 08; Civil Rights Commission, *Twenty Years After Brown*, pp. 4-5; Hubbard, "Affirmative Action," pp. 108-109.

37. Hubbard, "Affirmative Action," p. 109.

38. Clarence Mitchell to Walter White, June 28, 1953, NAACP Files, Group II, Series A, #208; NAACP Memorandum, April 22, 1984, *ibid*.;

Gelber, *Black Men and Businessmen*, p. 122; and Hubbard, "Affirmative Action," pp. 109-110.

39. Nixon quoted in Gelber, *Black Men and Businessmen*, p. 114.

40. Memorandum from Walter White, November 13, 1953, NAACP Files, Group II, Series A, #208; William Brown to PCGC, NAACP Files, Group II, Series A, #349; Report of Labor Secretary, March, 1957, NAACP Files, Group III, Series B, #139; Report of the Labor Secretary, January/February, 1958, *ibid.*; Report of the Labor Secretary, October, 1958, *ibid.*, *Quarles v. Philip Morris*, 279 F.Supp. 508; *Pattern for Progress*, Final Report to President Eisenhower from the Committee on Government Contracts (Washington, DC: U.S. Government Printing Office, 1961) , pp. 4-8; and Northrup, *Negro in Tobacco Industry*, p. 40.

41. Nixon quoted in Marshall, *Negro Worker*, p. 123.

42. Quotes from William Brown to PCGC, October 21, 1953, NAACP Files, Group II, Series A, #349; Northrup, *Negro in Tobacco Industry*, p. 40; and Gelber, *Black Men and Businessmen*, p. 116.

43. *PCGC*, Pattern for Progress, p. 14.

44. Humphrey, *Education*, p. 267.

III

From the Streets to the Courts: Kennedy and Civil Rights

The black protest movement that grew steadily but gradually throughout the 1950s exploded in the 1960s, dramatically transforming racial politics in the United States. Mass demonstrations, civil rights legislation, assassinations and political violence, voter registration drives, and lawsuits became a recurrent feature of the U.S. political scene. The founding of the Student Nonviolent Coordinating Committee (SNCC)—a militant, direct-action organization—early in 1960 provided a symbolic beginning to a period of unprecedented racial activity.

The 1960s witnessed a transformation of the *goals* as well as the strategies of the civil rights movement. Just as mass protest became as critical to the movement as legal actions, demands for specific remedial procedures—often involving the use of numbers—supplanted acceptance of vaguely defined pledges of nondiscrimination within the movement. The intensified African-American militancy of the 1960s helped to make civil rights a national priority and to generate the Civil Rights Act of 1964, which subsequently served as the cornerstone of a sustained legal battle against job discrimination.

The emphasis on civil rights throughout the 1960 presidential election reflected the growing public acknowledgment of the gravity of the racial issue in the United States. Although African Americans consistently had supported Democratic presidential candidates since 1936, the Republicans had made inroads on this voting bloc during the 1950s. Eisenhower had captured 40 percent of the black vote in 1956—the highest of any Republican candidate since Hoover—and the Republicans envisioned further progress in 1960. Eisenhower, after all, had ordered federal troops into Little Rock, had appointed Earl Warren as chief justice of the Supreme Court that issued the *Brown v. Board of Education* decision, and had signed civil rights bills into law in 1957 and 1960. Republican candidate Richard

Nixon had been exposed to civil rights issues, especially job discrimination, as chairman of the President's Committee on Government Contracts. In an attempt to attract black votes, Nixon, following a meeting with liberal Republican Nelson Rockefeller of New York, demanded that the Republican platform include strong civil rights language. Evoking the image of an earlier Republican administration, Nixon, in his acceptance speech, promised, "There shall be the greatest progress in human rights since the days of Lincoln."[1]

The Democrats, especially northern liberals, were equally determined to reverse the erosion of black Democratic support. Civil rights leaders and Democratic liberals were most comfortable with Hubert Humphrey or Adlai Stevenson and were skeptical of the liberal credentials of the Democratic candidate, John F. Kennedy. Although Kennedy had voted for civil rights bills in the Senate, African-American spokespersons like Roy Wilkins and Clarence Mitchell of the NAACP were unimpressed with Kennedy's knowledge of, or fervor toward, their cause. Early in 1960, Wilkins and Robert Weaver met with Kennedy to argue the need for civil rights legislation, but they found the senator noncommittal. Later in the campaign, however, Kennedy directed Senator Joseph Clark of Pennsylvania and Representative Emmanuel Celler of New York to draft a civil rights bill to be enacted early in 1961. Equally significant, Democratic National Chairman Paul M. Butler, a civil rights sympathizer, was determined to incorporate this pledge within the party platform. Under the leadership of liberals Chester Bowles and Harris Wofford, assisted by Clarence Mitchell, the Democrats drafted and approved a platform with a strong civil rights plank, including the abolition of poll taxes and literacy tests for voting, accelerated school desegregation, the prohibition of discrimination in federally funded housing, and passage of a civil rights law, including a fair employment (FEPC) provision, in 1961. This progressive civil rights posture, coupled with Kennedy's intervention on behalf of an incarcerated Martin Luther King, Jr., in Atlanta, helped to secure 70 percent of the African-American vote for the Democratic candidate. Given Kennedy's slight plurality over Nixon—his margin of victory was barely 113,000 votes —African-American votes were crucial to Kennedy's victory.[2]

Whatever enthusiasm Kennedy aroused on the part of African-American spokespersons during the campaign, however, quickly dissipated in response to his cautious approach toward civil rights. Having survived the closest presidential election of the century, Kennedy chose to pursue a moderate domestic policy, designed to appeal to diverse constituencies while alienating as few people as possible. Never a civil rights crusader, Kennedy became even more reluctant to embrace the cause of African Americans when confronted with the congressional results of the 1960 election—the Democrats lost twenty seats in the House and two in the Senate—and with the deeply entrenched power of the southern Democratic bloc in the Senate. Kennedy needed southern support for other "New Frontier" measures, especially aid to education and a tax cut, and did not wish to alienate southern Democrats by pursuing civil rights legislation. Kennedy also was warned of the futility of sponsoring a civil rights bill by personal advisors and congressional leaders, including Senate Majority Leader Mike Mansfield.

Despite his campaign promises and the Democratic platform plank, Kennedy announced at a March 1961 press conference that his administration would not pursue a civil rights bill that year. "When I feel that there is a necessity for a congressional action," he explained, "with a chance of getting that action, then I will recommend it to the Congress."[3] Kennedy further catered to the southern bloc, and frustrated African-American and liberal supporters, by refusing to sever federal funds from institutions that practiced discrimination and by appointing federal judges like Harold Cox of Mississippi, who referred to African-American litigants as "niggers" and to African-American voting registrants as "a bunch of chimpanzees."[4]

Kennedy's approach to job discrimination and to the race issue in general was similar to that of the previous administrations: executive orders; conferences and private negotiations with businesses and labor unions; job training and education; and the substitution of moral suasion and cooperation for coercion. Burke Marshall, assistant to Attorney General Robert Kennedy, described the administration's strategy as "to work quietly with people behind the scenes and head off situations."[5]

To pursue these goals, the administration conducted seminars on minority hiring through the Labor Department, made greater efforts to bring African Americans into the federal government, and opened "apprenticeship information centers" in industrial cities. The Manpower Development and Training Act of 1962 provided job training for unskilled youths; by November 1963 about 20 percent of those enrolled in the program were nonwhite. Kennedy's proposals for government aid to education were prompted in part as a vehicle for equal employment opportunity. Kennedy pursued an economic policy described by economist James Tobin as "steady economic growth at full employment, avoiding cycles of employment and recession," designed to ensure employment for all workers, black and white. As Walter Heller, chairman of the Council of Economic Advisors, later argued: "Full employment is clearly the most powerful engine of black economic and social progress."[6]

Inherent in the administration's civil rights strategy was a rejection of the confrontational tactics that SNCC, CORE, the SCLC, and the NAACP were increasingly adopting. Long suspicious of "knee-jerk liberals" who were "more intent on virtuous display than on practical results," the "pragmatists" of the Kennedy White House were skeptical of many of the major civil rights and liberal organizations.[7] Assistant Attorney General Nicholas de B. Katzenbach, for example, criticized the recommendations of the Civil Rights Commission as "not calculated to induce cooperation."[8]

An example of the administration's preference for "cooperative" solutions in the economic sphere occurred in 1963 and involved union apprenticeship programs. Following numerous complaints by civil rights groups against these programs, the Labor Department announced in the fall of 1963 that all certified apprenticeship programs must admit future candidates strictly on a merit basis or must make a special effort to include a "significant" number of minorities. Contractors and building trades unions objected to this language, arguing that the minority requirements would lead to the imposition of a quota system. Rather than defend its proposal, the Labor Department agreed to modify its new requirements, removing all references to numbers and approving "any plan" that ensured "equality of opportunity." To assuage union fears, the regulations specified that: "Nothing contained in this part shall be construed to require any program sponsor or employer to select or employ apprentices in the proportion which their race, color, religion, or national origin bears to the population." Thus, the administration attempted to placate both civil rights proponents and construction unions, and most likely satisfied neither.[9]

Kennedy's most ambitious endeavor in the field of economic discrimination, and the clearest illustration of the administration's "pragmatic" philosophy, was Executive Order 10925, issued March 6, 1961. Like his predecessors, Kennedy chose to rely on executive orders rather than risk a confrontation with congressional conservatives. In January 1961, the President met with a group of civil rights leaders, who proposed an executive order to prohibit discrimination in federal employment, by government contractors, and in all programs receiving federal funds. Kennedy made no commitments and suggested that they submit a memorandum to presidential advisor Theodore Sorenson incorporating these suggestions.

As usual, the civil rights leaders received only a part of what they requested. Executive Order 10925, like Eisenhower's order, outlawed discrimination by employers holding federal contracts. The enforcement mechanism resembled that of Eisenhower's PCGC. Each federal agency assumed authority for enforcing nondiscrimination by its contractors, with overall supervision provided by the President's Commission on Equal Employment Opportunity (PCEEO), chaired by Vice President Lyndon Johnson. Two major differences, however, distinguished the PCEEO from previous committees. Unlike the previous orders, Order 10925 empowered government agencies to cancel contracts with unions and businesses that violated equal opportunity provisions (something that the NAACP had been demanding since the 1940s). In addition, the order contained the following statement: "The contractor will take affirmative action to ensure that applicants are employed, and that employees are treated during employment, without regard to their race, creed, color, or national origin."[10]

Executive Order 10925 thus became the first federal civil rights initiative to employ the phrase *affirmative action*. Two important observations concerning this terminology must be made. First, unlike the New York State FEPC law, Executive Order 10925 defined affirmative action as the obligation of the employer, and not as a power delegated to the courts. In this respect, Kennedy's order reflected the conclusion of the PCGC that employers must go beyond passive nondiscrimination in their equal opportunity efforts. Second, the order failed to define *affirmative action* or to state specific affirmative action requirements of employers. This vague wording constituted a major obstacle to effective enforcement throughout the life of the Commission.

If the administration failed to state what affirmative action *was*, however, it was more definite as to what affirmative action was *not*. Affirmative action in 1961 did not refer to hiring goals or targets. Secretary of Labor W. Willard Wirtz stated the administration's position: "It is clear that quotas are wrong. No one in government has proposed them." The president himself rejected the idea of quotas, declaring that "I don't think we can undo the past."[11]

The history of the PCEEO resembled that of previous commissions: some individual successes, but overall ineffectiveness. The prototypical PCEEO agreement was signed on May 25, 1961, with the Lockheed plant in Marietta, Georgia. Previously the target of FEPC and PCGC actions, Lockheed practiced the standard forms of discrimination, from segregated cafeterias to the concentration of black workers in semiskilled and custodial positions. In response to employee affidavits filed with the assistance of the NAACP, Lockheed agreed to integrate its facilities and to review the records of its African-American employees to determine those with the best chance of passing promotion examinations. Some of Lockheeds "reforms" seem unusual by today's standards, for example, providing paper cups to avoid conflicts over integrated drinking fountains. Nevertheless, Lockheed's efforts were successful. Two years after the program was implemented, the *Chicago Defender* and the Southern Regional Council—an organization concerned with job integration in the South—reported that the integration process was progressing "smoothly." Indeed, representatives from other companies visited Lockheed for ideas and suggestions.[12]

The Lockheed agreement, unfortunately, represented one of the few effective exercises of power by the PCEEO. Although delegated substantial enforcement authority, Vice President Johnson chose to imitate his predecessors' reliance on voluntary compliance. By the time the commission was abolished in 1965, it had failed to rescind a single federal contract. Its chief enforcement mechanism was Plans for Progress (PFP), an arrangement designed by Atlanta lawyer Robert Troutman in which employers and unions signed general pledges of nondiscrimination. The act of joining PFP satisfied the antidiscrimination obligations of Executive Order 10925. As an alternative to government coercion, PFP proved enormously popular with corporations and labor unions. By the end of 1962, dozens of major contractors including Chrysler, Ford, General Motors, IBM, and IT&T had joined PFP, along with more than one hundred AFL-CIO unions.[13]

As business leaders and politicians congratulated one another for their participation in this "progressive" program, civil rights groups attacked PFP as a vehicle for contractors to substitute vague promises of nondiscrimination for concrete affirmative actions. In April 1962, for example, Herbert Hill of the NAACP denounced PFP as "more publicity than progress."[14] The following year, a study conducted by the Southern Regional Council concluded that the program was "largely meaningless."[15] Throughout the course of its existence, PFP never clarified what definite steps were to be taken or what criteria for "progress" were to be employed by contractors and unions. Basic decisions regarding the implementation of nondiscrimination clauses remained in the hands of business officials. The steel industry official who claimed that "our obligations under the Plans for Progress program is to employ . . . on the basis of merit only" without reference to hiring goals or to the recruitment and training of minority workers illustrated the narrow interpretation of nondiscrimination espoused by PFP members.[16]

The lax attitude of PFP participants occasionally degenerated into public scandal. In 1962, for example, a PFP official resigned following the disclosure that he had sponsored a dinner for a southern congressional representative in a segregated hotel. The ultimate vindication of the civil rights leaders' antipathy towards PFP occurred in 1968 when a government agency investigating white-collar employment in New York City discovered that non-PFP employers exhibited a higher rate of minority utilization than PFP employers. In fact, non-PFP companies employed African-American managers at a rate four times that of PFP members. Plans for Progress, like so many federal civil rights programs, represented more show than substance.[17]

The PCEEO likewise was more of a paper program than a concerted attack on employment discrimination. It is true that in its scope and authority the PCEEO surpassed its predecessors in the Eisenhower and Truman administrations, especially after a second executive order of 1963 extended the commission's authority to federally assisted construction projects. By the end of 1963, the commission had received over 2,000 complaints, primarily from the NAACP, CORE, and other civil rights groups, and had resolved over 900 of them, a success rate well in excess of the Nixon Committee's record over a seven-year period. Responding to complaints, the PCEEO helped initiate the merger of separate union locals within the paper industry, the abolition of separate seniority lists within the tobacco industry, and the elimination of separate lines of progression within the steel industry .

Unfortunately, such "reforms" often produced, not real progress, but the development of more sophisticated forms of racism by employers. Within the tobacco industry, for example, the "merger" of black and white seniority lists consisted of adding the names of black employees to the bottom of the white list. The U.S. Steel plant in Fairfield, Alabama, agreed to merge its separate lines of progression, but it penalized workers who transferred from less-skilled to better-paying departments through salary reductions and loss of seniority.[18] Despite its reference to affirmative action, the PCEEO never developed a coherent strategy to address the circumvention of antidiscrimination regulations. The PCEEO also offered little assistance to African-American workers in dealing with the more intangible obstacles to job integration, such as the hostility directed against African-American "pioneers" in formerly all-white departments.

Unwilling to cancel contracts and unable to achieve more than token integration in most instances, the PCEEO also suffered from a number of debilitating political problems. Because enforcement responsibility was divided among the various government agencies, the government never adopted uniform standards and criteria. Thus, different contractors could be subject to different regulations, a situation that generated extensive confusion among contractors and unions and hindered effective enforcement of the order. Because the commission was based on an executive order rather than an act of Congress, it experienced severe funding restrictions, and many critics questioned its legality. Indeed, one federal official later stated that: "The failure of PCEEO to ameliorate discrimination . . . was one of the reasons for the passage" of the Civil Rights Act of 1964. Criticized by groups and individuals ranging from the Civil Rights Commission to Attorney General Robert Kennedy, the PCEEO was terminated as part of a reorganization effort of 1965.[19]

Significantly, although Kennedy's civil rights program clearly surpassed those of previous administrations, civil rights leaders emphasized, not its minor accomplishments, but, rather, its inadequacy in light of the monumental problems confronting African Americans. By the 1960s the civil rights movement had entered a more militant phase and had rejected as obsolete and unacceptable the traditional federal civil rights approach of moderate and piecemeal reform. Throughout the North and South, blacks and their white sympathizers challenged the inertia of the federal government by demonstrating and protesting in unprecedented numbers. The escalation of black activism in the 1960s was due to a number of interrelated factors: the proliferation and political maturation of civil rights organizations; the emergence of African-American leaders like Martin Luther King, Jr., and Malcolm X, who were capable of mobilizing grass-roots activism; an accelerated African-American migration from isolated southern rural communities to northern and southern urban centers; higher standards of education for whites and blacks, produced in part by federal monies made available through the GI Bill of Rights and the National Defense Education Act; a more tolerant intellectual environment resulting in part from attacks on racism by social scientists like Gunnar Myrdal, E. Franklin Frazier, Franz Boas, Ashley Montagu, and C. Vann Woodward; and a legal attack on Jim Crow culminating in, but not limited to, *Brown v. Board of Education.*

A distinct African-American leadership cadre had emerged by this time, including James Farmer of CORE; Whitney M. Young, Jr., of the National Urban League; Roy Wilkins of the NAACP; James Forman of SNCC; Adam Clayton Powell, Jr.; and Malcolm X. Despite their individual differences regarding strategies and philosophy, all these individuals contributed to the politicization of African Americans. Inspired by these prominent figures, as well as by numerous local leaders and organizations, black and white civil rights proponents, frustrated but undaunted by the constrained attitude of the White House, launched a massive attack on racial discrimination throughout the nation. [20]

Civil rights leaders not only mobilized greater numbers of people during the 1960s, but, frustrated by the token concessions of the 1950s, they adopted a more militant strategy as well. While continuing to eschew violence, the leadership of the organized civil rights movement, especially SNCC, CORE, and the SCLC, redefined nonviolence away from "nonviolent persuasion" and toward "nonviolent intervention" or "nonviolent coercion." The former, widely practiced during the 1950s, emphasized "converting" the movement's opponents by appealing to their consciences and sense of justice. The latter, although not refuting the moral superiority of nonviolence over violence, utilized nonviolence primarily as a *tactic* to attack discrimination directly and to force the power structure to respond. As Martin Luther King, Jr., stated in 1963: "The Negro in the South can now be nonviolent as a stratagem, but he can't include loving the white man. . . . Nonviolence has become a military tactical approach." In explaining the strategic role of nonviolence, King wrote: "Nonviolent direct action seeks to create such a crisis and foster such a tension that a community is forced to confront the issue. It seeks so to dramatize the issue that it can no longer be ignored."[21] Civil rights activists no longer argued that whites must accept racial justice "in their hearts" in order to practice it publicly.

Significantly, King and other leaders acknowledged that nonviolent intervention often elicited a violent response from racist whites. While decrying this development, they accepted it as the price for racial progress in the United States.[22]

Accompanying the emergence of this mass direct-action movement was the merging of diverse civil rights objectives into a well-integrated and thorough program. Rather than accept a piecemeal approach to voting rights, school integration, job discrimination, public accommodations, and general denial of constitutional rights, African Americans demanded the elimination of the Jim Crow system in all its aspects, North and South. As Bayard Rustin declared in 1963: "The package deal is the new demand."[23] Recognizing the limitations of executive orders, African-American leaders insisted that the enactment of a comprehensive civil rights law was crucial to the elimination of race discrimination in the United States. Although sensitive to the difficulties Kennedy faced in securing the passage of such a bill, civil rights leaders expected the president to exert the full powers of his office toward that objective. Martin Luther King, Jr., epitomized their sentiments: "Nevertheless, to understand difficulties should not be a preparation for surrendering to them."[24]

This new black activism manifested itself in a number of now-famous activities: "Freedom Summer" of 1964 and the voter registration drives of the Deep South; the Freedom Rides of 1961; lunch counter sit-ins; boycotting of stores in the North and South; the integration of state universities in Alabama and Mississippi; and mass demonstrations in Atlanta and Albany, Georgia. Protestors not unexpectedly suffered mass arrests, crowd violence and intimidation, beatings, and police brutality, while FBI agents passively stood on the sidelines taking notes. On those occasions when Kennedy acted decisively—for example, employing federal marshals during the Freedom Rides and during James Meredith's entry into the University of Mississippi—his actions were primarily a response to a situation created by the protesters. As James Farmer observed regarding the Freedom Rides: "We planned the Freedom Ride with the specific intention of creating a crisis. . . . We figured that the government would have to respond if we created a situation that was headline news all over the world and affected the nation's image abroad."[25]

Although many people identify civil rights protests with the South, a series of less publicized but equally significant protests were staged in northern towns and cities during the early 1960s. Because northern blacks had already secured basic voting rights and access to public accommodations, northern protests generally revolved around housing, schools, and jobs. Protestors, with CORE playing a prominent role, picketed and demonstrated outside banks, stores, and factories that failed to hire African Americans. In late 1962, for example, St. Louis CORE picketed Kroger Supermarkets, demanding preferential hiring of African Americans until they constituted 15 percent of the work force in all departments. The following year, on Long Island, New York, CORE secured an agreement with Meadow Brook National Bank to reserve 50 percent of all future openings for African Americans and Puerto Ricans. In December 1962, following a two-month boycott, Sealtest Dairy Company of New York agreed to give hiring priority to African Americans and Puerto Ricans. Several months later, A&P of New York City reached an agreement with CORE and the NAACP to hire 400 African Americans and Puerto Ricans over the subsequent two years, a number that represented almost the entire anticipated turnover for that period.

These agreements illustrated another characteristic of the heightened militancy of the 1960s—an increasing reliance on numerical formulas and preferential hiring to ensure equal opportunity. Disillusioned following decades of vague promises of nondiscrimination and unaffected by the *A.S. Beck* and *Hughes* decisions of an earlier period, a new generation of civil rights activists had become convinced that concrete, quantifiable solutions offered the only remedy to job discrimination. Rejecting the philosophy of gradualism, African Americans, especially in the North, demanded immediate, verifiable improvement in their economic status. African-American job demands from this time on regularly linked nondiscrimination with affirmative action. By 1962, CORE had established guidelines for preferential hiring, insisting that employers assume the responsibility for locating and training minority workers.[26]

Perhaps the most dramatic and significant protests were the construction demonstrations that erupted in northern cities in 1963. Frustration at being excluded from an industry so intimately connected with African-American neighborhoods exploded first in Philadelphia. The initial target was a school construction site at which African Americans were employed solely as unskilled laborers. Picketing began on May 24 as protestors demanded that African Americans be hired as skilled workers and apprentices. Peaceful at first, the demonstrations soon turned violent. Work at the project was halted, and the city's Commission on Human Relations began an investigation. On May 31, the various sides reached a "pact" in which contractors agreed to hire six black artisans. Meanwhile, a second demonstration began outside a construction project at the Philadelphia Municipal Services Building. Violence erupted when the police escorted construction workers through the picket lines. Mayor James Tate halted work on the project for two weeks until the sides came to terms. Although CORE initially had demanded that 15 percent of all skilled jobs be reserved for African Americans, they finally settled for an assurance of nondiscrimination and the hiring of additional African-American workers after the NAACP refused to endorse their hiring goals.

"Construction fever" spread rapidly to other cities, including Elizabeth, New Jersey, where 77 protestors were arrested in August following a violent clash with police. In the same month, Cleveland experienced a similar crisis when a community group titled the United Freedom Movement, which included representatives of the NAACP and CORE, staged demonstrations at the Municipal Mall construction site. When contractors finally consented to hire a small number of blacks, white workers walked off the job. The various sides eventually achieved an agreement to permit the hiring of minority workers, but few actually found jobs.[27]

The construction demonstrations in New York City in 1963 serve as a valuable case study of northern urban protests. The disruptions began in June and involved an annex to Harlem Hospital. Representatives of the Joint Committee on Equal Employment Opportunity (JCEEO), a community umbrella group consisting of CORE, the NAACP, the Urban League, the Negro American Labor Council, the Workers' Defense League, and the

Association of Catholic Trade Unionists, met with the construction contractors to extract a promise for increased minority hiring. When the negotiations proved unsuccessful, the JCEEO inaugurated a large-scale demonstration campaign at the Hospital, forcing acting Mayor Paul R. Screvane to halt work on the $25 million project. Protests soon spread to other construction sites, including the Downstate Medical Center in Brooklyn, as well as City Hall and the city headquarters of Governor Nelson Rockefeller. Demonstrators' tactics included "sitting down in front of trucks and bulldozers, chaining themselves to doorways, and even climbing cranes and girders."[28] As the protests dragged on through July and into August, tensions mounted and tempers flared. Violent confrontations erupted between demonstrators and the police, whom some pickets referred to as "storm troopers." Hundreds of protesters were arrested. One African-American minister summed up the situation in these words: "This proves there's no difference between New York and Alabama, between the United States and South Africa."[29]

Attempts to reconcile the opposing parties revealed the tremendous disparity between the perceptions of government officials and the building trades unions on the one hand and the demands of the JCEEO on the other. Mayor Robert Wagner, Jr., established an "action panel" to help locate "qualified" minorities to take the journeyman's exam for union membership. This proposal, as reported by *The New York Times*, "would depend on voluntary compliance."[30] In contrast, the protestors' demands included reserving 25 percent of all publicly assisted jobs for African Americans and Puerto Ricans and "the admission of Blacks and Puerto Ricans as apprentices in twice their proportion to the city's population."[31] Rockefeller immediately attacked these proposals as "un-American in concept and principle," and Peter Brennan, president of the city's Building Trades and Construction Council, denounced them as "unfair and un-American."[32] Proponents of hiring goals and targets defended the proposals as the only concrete alternative to vague promises of nondiscrimination, which historically had been ineffective. Responding to charges of "reverse discrimination," the *Amsterdam News* remarked sarcastically that: "The sudden concern about the ideal of equal opportunity now seems to be lavished solely on the white workers who are already unionized and working on these jobs that are being picketed around the city."[33]

After months of conflict, the JCEEO eventually agreed to the establishment of a special recruitment and referral program for minority workers, and the disruptions subsided. In mid-November, work resumed on the Harlem Hospital site. Unfortunately, the results of the referral programs were typical of most voluntary "solutions." Although thousands of African Americans applied for journeyman and apprenticeship positions, only a token number were accepted. The failure of voluntary compliance led to further construction demonstrations throughout the remainder of the decade. Equally important, it confirmed the protestors' distrust of general promises and their convictions regarding the necessity of numerical solutions.[34]

The northern protests demonstrated the emphasis attached to job discrimination by civil rights leaders in the 1960s. In 1963, Martin Luther King, Jr., observed that "Housing and employment opportunities seem most critical," and Roy Wilkins characterized job discrimination as "the most pressing problem confronting Negro Americans."[35] Almost every major civil rights proponent expressed similar views.

Although not abandoning the crusade for voting rights and social integration in the South, African-American leaders increasingly focused on the more subtle forms of discrimination encountered by northern urban blacks. In July 1963, at the National Urban League's annual convention, Whitney Young issued a call for a "domestic Marshall Plan" through which government, business, and voluntary associations would infuse millions of dollars into the nation's cities. In 1962, the SCLC formally "adopted" Operation Breadbasket, an organization created by the Reverend Leon Sullivan in Philadelphia in 1959 to pressure companies to hire African-American workers and to utilize the services of African-American businesses. The August 1963 March on Washington selected as its theme, not "Freedom," but "Freedom and Jobs."

Significantly, a consensus emerged among the most prominent African-American leaders as to the need for some type of affirmative action. James Farmer succinctly articulated these views: "Offering him (black individual) equal rights, even equal opportunity, at this late date, without giving him a special boost, is the kind of cruel joke American individualism has played on the poor throughout American history." Most major spokespersons agreed that the Jim Crow system could not be abolished without the enactment of a comprehensive civil rights bill.[36]

By early 1963 the pressure for civil rights legislation had become irresistible. In addition to nationwide protests, racial violence erupted in northern and southern cities—Harlem, Philadelphia, Kansas City, and Cambridge, Maryland—demonstrating that numbers of young African Americans were rejecting the philosophy of nonviolence. Aggressive, militant African-American spokespersons, epitomized by Malcolm X, electrified black audiences and frightened white Americans. The rhetoric of the Black Muslims and other groups designated by whites as "extremists" and "radicals" increased white liberal demands for civil rights legislation to offset what they perceived as a growing tendency toward violence. Disputes within CORE and the NAACP regarding armed self-defense and the presence of whites within black organizations alarmed and threatened to alienate white liberals.

Pressure from the streets inevitably reached the halls of government, as Democratic and Republican legislators flooded Congress with civil rights bills. Nelson Rockefeller, a potential Republican presidential candidate in 1964, accused President Kennedy of having "abdicated virtually all leadership towards achieving civil rights legislation."[37] Disconcerted by the ever-increasing African-American militancy, apprehensive of being upstaged by Republican opponents, determined to retain African-American support in the 1964 election, and emboldened by an unusually strong Democratic performance in the 1962 congressional elections, Kennedy finally submitted a civil rights bill on February 28, 1963. The Kennedy bill, which basically was an extension of the Civil Rights Acts of 1957 and 1960, authorized a four-year extension of the Civil Rights Commission and contained mild proposals regarding voting rights and school desegregation. Missing were any provisions for integration of public facilities, protection of Fourteenth Amendment rights, or equal employment opportunity. The proposal was far less comprehensive than many congressional bills already under consideration, and it made little headway. Even at this late date, Kennedy refused to champion even the minimal demands of civil rights leaders.[38]

Then came Birmingham. The "Johannesburg of the South," Birmingham enforced a rigid color line in all aspects of its economic, political, and social life. Birmingham was also a steel town, where the local U.S. Steel plant manifested all the city's Jim Crow traditions, and members of the steelworkers union participated in Ku Klux Klan activities. Late in 1962, the SCLC selected this bastion of segregation as the target of Project "C" (Confrontation), the most ambitious direct-action protest undertaken by the civil rights movement to that time. Initiated in the spring of 1963 after extensive planning and careful execution by King, the Reverend Fred Shuttlesworth, and other leaders, Project "C" was to consist of sit-ins, mass demonstrations, and boycotts. The project's concrete goals included the "adoption of fair hiring practices" by the city's downtown department stores, "equal employment opportunities for blacks" within city government agencies, and the desegregation of the stores' facilities, including lunch counters.[39] Among the project's more intangible objectives was the spiritual and psychological uplift that would accompany a successful challenge of this deep-seated racist system. As King observed: "If Birmingham could be cracked, the entire nonviolent movement in the South could take a significant turn." Another SCLC official expressed similar hopes: "And we felt that if we could crack that city, then we could crack any city."[40]

Finally, Birmingham offered the SCLC an opportunity to publicize the plight of southern blacks. Anticipating a violent reaction by Safety Commissioner Eugene "Bull" Connor and his men, the SCLC leadership counted on large-scale media attention, especially television coverage, to convey to the world the oppression and brutality of the Jim Crow system. Whereas the local southern press often ignored civil rights protests, television represented a national medium that could and did bring the black revolution into the homes of millions of white Americans.[41]

Launched April 2, 1963, Project "C" initially was characterized by restraint on both sides. Then on Thursday, May 3, Connor and his men lost their self-control. Throughout the following four days, police attacked unarmed demonstrators with clubs, fire hoses, and police dogs, while the news media disseminated graphic pictures and stories of police savagery to a worldwide audience. In Birmingham, however, unlike many previous demonstrations, African Americans no longer were willing to submit meekly to police violence. Instead, African-American youths pelted police with bricks and bottles, and a riot erupted in the city's business district. Peace was restored temporarily by the signing of a "pact" on May 10, calling for, among other things, the hiring and upgrading of African-American workers throughout the city. That same evening, however, the uneasy truce was shattered by bomb explosions at the home of King's brother, a local minister, and at the motel where King was staying. A riot ensued, and Kennedy eventually federalized the Alabama National Guard and moved U.S. Army troops close to the city.[42]

The events in Birmingham provided unequivocal evidence that the nation no longer could afford to downplay its racial problems. One writer summed up the significance of Birmingham: "America learned that the patience of 100 years is not inexhaustible. It is exhausted."[43] Inspired by the activities in Birmingham, African Americans throughout the nation staged 750 demonstrations in the month of May alone. The political ramifications of Birmingham were direct and dramatic. Between May 13 and June 20, 127 civil rights bills were introduced into Congress. Birmingham shattered White House complacency as Kennedy and his advisors began discussions regarding the contents of a new, more comprehensive civil rights bill. In a May 22 press conference, Kennedy announced that he would submit civil rights legislation, warning that African Americans must be provided with a "legal remedy" or else "they take to the streets, and we have the kinds of incidents we have in Birmingham." In a June 10 address to the National Conference of Mayors, Kennedy reaffirmed his objective of transferring the black revolution "from the streets to the courts."[44]

On June 19 the White House submitted to Congress the most comprehensive civil rights measure ever sponsored by a U.S. president. As with the previous bill, however, the White House failed to include an FEPC section. Fearing that such a provision would impede passage of the bill, Kennedy preferred that Congress consider a separate FEPC bill. Given the political developments of 1963, however, such expectations no longer were realistic.[45]

Kennedy's bill—H.R. 7152—was submitted to Subcommittee #5 of the House Judiciary Committee. Chaired by Emmanual Celler, the subcommittee included such civil rights sympathizers as Peter Rodino of New Jersey, William McCulloch of Ohio, and John Lindsay of New York. Hearings scheduled by the subcommittee provided an opportunity for representatives of the religious, labor, and civil rights groups that comprised the Leadership Conference on Civil Rights (LCCR) to express their views on the impending legislation. Such diverse individuals as George Meany, Roy Wilkins, Senator Jacob Javits of New York, and Will Maslow of the American Jewish Congress were unanimous in their support of an FEPC provision. From this point on, the question was no longer *whether* an equal employment opportunity section would be incorporated but, rather, what *type* of FEPC mechanism would be established and how nondiscrimination in employment was to be defined.[46]

The dispute regarding the nature and authority of the proposed fair employment board extended throughout the duration of the congressional debates on the civil rights bill. In July 1963, the House Committee on Education and Labor approved H.R. 405, a fair-employment bill that provided for a five member Equal Opportunity Commission modeled after the National Labor Relations Board, with the power to investigate charges of discrimination and issue cease-and-desist orders. (A similar bill, S. 1937, was introduced into the Senate by Hubert Humphrey, Paul Douglas, Harrison Williams, Abraham Ribicoff, and Clifford Case.) The Judiciary Subcommittee voted to incorporate H.R. 405 into the administration bill. After adding or strengthening several other provisions, the subcommittee on October 2 formally reported the modified proposal to the entire Judiciary Committee.[47]

While civil rights leaders expressed satisfaction with the modified language of the new bill, the administration maintained that the new bill could never pass Congress. The White House drafted its new bill carefully, devising a language that it felt would be amenable to liberal and moderate Republicans, whose support was considered critical for passage. The chief objection to the FEPC provision of the subcommittee bill was that it delegated to an appointed committee the power to modify hiring and promotion procedures. This arrangement reinforced the charges of southern opponents that the bill undermined the rights of white people. The negative reactions of many Republicans to the new language confirmed the Kennedys' convictions that the subcommittee bill had to be rejected by the Judiciary Committee. Thus, the battle lines were drawn: the LCCR and congressional liberals versus congressional moderates and the White House.[48]

The White House inaugurated its assault on the subcommittee bill in mid-October when Robert Kennedy retestified before the Judiciary Committee and arranged a series of private meetings with committee members. After nearly two weeks of deliberations, the administration finally achieved a consensus on the rewording of the FEPC and other provisions. Despite charges of "selling out" leveled by indignant liberals, administration representatives persuaded most committee members to diminish the power of the fair employment board in order to improve the bill's chances of passage. With the assistance of two legislative aides, Justice Department officials Burke Marshall and Nicholas de B. Katzenbach drafted a compromise bill. On October 29, the Judiciary Committee, in a carefully orchestrated vote, agreed to replace the subcommittee bill with the compromise bill, which it then approved by a 23-11 margin.

The modified bill retained the Equal Employment Opportunity Commission (EEOC), but it eliminated the cease-and-desist powers, substituting instead the authority to initiate court cases in the event of a finding of discrimination. Although this provision fell far short of the demands of civil rights spokespersons, it still was substantially stronger than the original Kennedy proposal. The House of Representatives approved H.R. 7152 in its amended form on February 10, 1964.[49]

The next, and most formidable, hurdle for the bill to overcome was the traditional death trap for civil rights legislation, the Senate filibuster. On February 26, the Senate voted to place H.R. 7152 directly on the Senate calendar, thereby concluding consideration of the more comprehensive S. 1937. By this time, responsibility for passage of the bill had passed from Kennedy to Lyndon Johnson. A master legislator, Johnson assumed a crucial behind-the-scenes role as the White House pursued the sixty-seven votes necessary for cloture, that is, the termination of a filibuster. In a series of compromises directed primarily at securing the support of Everett Dirksen, the influential ranking Republican on the Senate Judiciary Committee, the Democratic leadership agreed to a further weakening of the FEPC section. Rather than initiate court actions, the EEOC was restricted to investigating charges of discrimination and seeking voluntary conciliation. Thus, by the time the Senate considered H.R. 7152, the commission had been divested of all enforcement powers.[50]

Occurring simultaneously with the debate over the composition of the FEPC was an equally virulent debate regarding the concept of nondiscrimination. Opponents of H.R. 7152 denounced the proposal as a smokescreen for introducing hiring quotas. Senator Lister Hill of Alabama warned that the FEPC provisions would require employers to "hire by race." Hill insisted that "preferential treatment" already had been introduced into the U.S. system. Referring to the construction demonstrations in northern cities, Hill maintained that "crash programs to upgrade specific groups are being resorted to with growing frequency." Senator George Huddleston of Alabama condemned the bill as "legislation by duress which finds its origins in unlawful disturbances and demonstrations of minority groups seeking to obtain special privileges infringing upon the rights of all other Americans."[51]

Sponsors of H.R. 7152 denied the validity of charges of "preferential treatment" and "quotas" and insisted that the bill required only that employers practice simple nondiscrimination. Senator Harrison Williams maintained that "to hire a Negro solely because he is a Negro is racial discrimination." A Justice Department memorandum affirmed: "There is no provision . . . that requires or authorizes any federal agency or federal court to require preferential treatment for any individual or any group for the purpose of achieving racial balance." Senator Joseph Clark bluntly stated: "Quotas are themselves discriminatory."[52]

Southern critics, hoping to arouse the hostility of the working-class whites, also condemned the bill as infringing on the collective bargaining rights of labor unions, especially in the field of seniority. Union-management contracts, they predicted, would be abrogated to dispense special privileges to black workers. Supporters of the bill responded to these accusations with the assurance that previously established collective-bargaining accords were exempt from the bill's jurisdiction unless they were discriminatory in nature. The bill, they maintained, did not threaten the tenet of "last hired, first fired." In addition, Walter Reuther of the United Automobile Workers assured the Congress and union members that the bill's creators did not intend to provide jobs for blacks by dismissing white workers.[53]

When challenged regarding the compatibility of black economic progress with the retention of jobs and benefits by white workers, sponsors of H.R. 7152 responded with a fundamental liberal tenet of the 1960s: economic growth. Labor leaders and liberal politicians maintained that increasing the size of the economic "pie" would enable previously excluded groups to partake of U.S. affluence without injuring those who already benefited from the system. David McDonald, president of the United Steelworkers of America, argued that the nation must "speed up our rate of economic growth to the point that there are sufficient jobs for all Americans of all races and creeds." Secretary of Labor Wirtz professed: "I believe in fair employment, and in full employment." The AFL-CIO officially endorsed the contention that "full employment is indispensable to equal employment opportunity."[54] The administration's economic program, including tax cuts and the Manpower Development and Training Act, was designed to stimulate economic growth with the ultimate goal of achieving "full employment" (defined then as 4 percent unemployment). Such policies, administration officials contended, simultaneously could assure blacks of economic advancement and protect the interests of white workers.[55]

The only public challenge to this liberal dogma came from the African-American spokespersons themselves. A. Phillip Randolph, James Farmer, Whitney Young, and Bayard Rustin, among others, declared that civil rights progress could not wait for the establishment of a full-employment utopia and that, even in the event of economic growth, African Americans required—and deserved—special assistance in overcoming the effects of three centuries of discrimination. James Farmer testified that employers should make a concerted effort to locate qualified minority workers and to train less-than-qualified minority applicants. Roy Wilkins and Whitney Young argued that, when a black and white applicant exhibited *equal* qualifications, the black candidate should be hired. Adam Clayton Powell defended preferential treatment as a temporary expedient until blacks achieved an economic position that enabled them to compete effectively with whites. Whitney Young, while assuring critics that no "responsible organization or Negro leader advocates the establishment of a permanent quota system," asserted that "we are forced during the transitional and negotiation stages to discuss numbers and categories as the only way to assure more than token compliance." Commenting on administration attempts to placate white and black workers, Young warned: "You can't keep all elements in society completely happy."[56]

These arguments, although proposed by individuals deeply involved with the problem of job discrimination, never found a receptive audience within the political arena. In the optimistic environment of 1963-64, liberal politicians insisted that a combination of simple nondiscrimination and "pure" affirmative action—that is, enhancing the educational and job skills of African-American workers—would solve the employment problem. To exceed these limits would be to challenge liberal economic theories and to impede passage of the civil rights bill. Not until several years later did political liberals concede that they had underestimated the scope and complexity of job discrimination in the United States.[57]

The modification of the FEPC and other provisions and the assurances by the bill's advocates that the measure would require only pure nondiscrimination assuaged the fears of anxious legislators and paved the way for passage of the bill. In an unprecedented move, the Senate voted 71-29 on Wednesday, June 10, 1964, to invoke cloture on the civil rights debate. The Senate approved the final version of the bill on June 19, and the House followed suit on Wednesday, July 2, Following the House vote, the bill was rushed to the White House, which scheduled a special ceremony for 7:00 P.M. in the East Room. Among the several hundred invited guests were Martin Luther King, Whitney Young, Roy Wilkins, and Clarence Mitchell. Calling on the nation to "close the springs of racial poison," Lyndon Johnson signed into law the Civil Rights Act of 1964.[58]

The passage of the Civil Rights Act represented a watershed in the struggle for economic justice in the United States. The act served as the basis for a sustained legal and bureaucratic assault on employer and union discrimination. At the same time, however, the final version of the act reflected the debilitating consequences of the extensive compromises and modifications that political leaders had deemed the price of enactment.

The Civil Rights Act consisted of eleven sections or "titles." Title VII, which contained the FEPC provisions, prohibited discrimination against any individual "because of such individual's race, color, religion, sex, or national origin."[59] This stipulation applied to employers with more than 100 employees (to be reduced to 50 by 1967), labor unions, apprenticeship programs, and employment agencies. To monitor compliance, the act created the Equal Employment Opportunity Commission (EEOC), which consisted of five members, three from one party and two from the other, to be appointed by the president and approved by the Senate.

Originally intended as an enforcement body patterned after the NLRB, the EEOC emerged as a relatively powerless entity, authorized to investigate charges of discrimination and "to eliminate any such unlawful employment practice by informal methods of conference, conciliation and persuasion."[60] All EEOC efforts were to be conducted in private, and, when the alleged infraction occurred within a state which had its own antidiscrimination law, the EEOC was required to defer to the state agency for sixty days. In cases where the EEOC was unable to achieve conciliation, the aggrieved party then was required to initiate a civil action. The one concrete enforcement mechanism was the provision in Section 707 empowering the attorney general to initiate court actions in response to "a pattern or practice" of widespread discrimination. [61] (Such suits, known as 707 suits, have not been numerous.) In addition to conciliation efforts, Title VII authorized the EEOC to conduct hearings and technical studies, to cooperate with public and private state and local antidiscrimination agencies, and to recommend cases to the attorney general for 707 suits.

In the volatile area of affirmative action, Title VII remained ambiguous. The phrasing of certain sections clearly was intended to allay fears of preferential treatment. The most widely quoted language in this regard was that of Section 703(j): "Nothing contained in this title shall be interpreted to require any employer, employment agency, labor organization, or joint labor-management committee subject to this title to grant preferential treatment to any individual or to any group . . . on account of an imbalance which may exist with respect to the total number and percentage of persons of any race, color, religion, sex, or national origin" within a business or union.[62] Many individuals read this paragraph as an explicit prohibition of proportional hiring. Section 703(h) reaffirmed the legality of "a bona fide seniority or merit system"—provided it was not discriminatory—much to the relief of businesspeople and unions.[63] These sections appeared to reassert the liberal commitment of the early 1960s to pure nondiscrimination.

A closer reading of Title VII, however, reveals that the law's sponsors were unwilling to close the door entirely on the concept of affirmative action. Section 706(g), in language clearly reminiscent of the National Labor Relations Act and the Ives-Quinn Act, recognized the authority of the federal courts to "order such affirmative action as may be appropriate, which may include reinstatement or hiring of employees, with or without back pay."[64] Thus, although the EEOC could not dictate remedial procedures, such power was perceived as inherent in the judicial process.[65]

Title VII was far less comprehensive than civil rights advocates would have preferred. It did, however, represent the first national FEPC law, and civil rights groups immediately planned to test its application to all sectors of the economy. Title VII was scheduled to become effective in July 1965, providing employers and the government with an opportunity to prepare themselves for its implementation. Anticipating the maelstrom that the act would generate, W.P. Gullander, president of the National Association of Manufacturers, prophesized: "No piece of legislation since the Wagner Act of three decades ago will have a more significant bearing on industrial-relations procedures than Title VII of the new act."[66] The year 1965 marked the emergence of a new era in the struggle for racial economic justice in the United States. Although grass-roots racial protests continued throughout the decade, enactment of a civil rights law helped redirect the energies of the black revolution toward the courts and federal antidiscrimination agencies, as its authors had intended.

NOTES

1. Nixon quoted in James C. Harvey, *Civil Rights During the Kennedy Administration* (Hattiesburg: University and College Press of Mississippi, 1971), p. 12. Also: James L. Sundquist, *Politics and Policy: The Eisenhower, Kennedy, and Johnson Years* (Washington, DC: The Brookings Institution, 1968), pp. 252-253; Congressional Quarterly Service, *Politics in America 1945-1966* (Washington, DC: Congressional Quarterly Service, 1967), p. 37; Taylor Branch, *Parting the Waters: America in the King Years 1954-63* (New York: Simon and Schuster, 1988), pp. 321-23; Lewis, *King*, p. 129; and Martin, *Democratic Party 1945-1976*, p. 169.

2. Oral History Interview, John F. Kennedy Library: Clarence Mitchell, Jr., February 9, 1967, by John Stewart, pp. 1-5; Oral History Interview, Kennedy Library: Roy Wilkins, August 13, 1964, by Paul Bernhard, pp. 2-3 & 15; Carl M. Brauer, *John F. Kennedy and the Second Reconstruction* (New York: Columbia University Press, 1977), p. 23; Jim F. Heath, *Decade of Disillusionment* (Bloomington: Indiana University Press, 1975), p. 69; Lawrence Wittner, *Cold War America* (New York: Praeger Publishers, 1974), pp. 190-192; Harvey, *Civil Rights*, pp. 13-14; Chuck Stone, *Black Political Power in America* (New York: The Bobbs-Merrill Company, 1968), p. 48; David Burner and Thomas R. West, *The Torch Is Passed: The Kennedy Brothers and American Liberalism* (St. James, NY: Brandywine Press, 1984), Chapter 3; Gloster D. Current, "Why Nixon Lost the Negro Vote," *The Crisis* 68 (January, 1961), pp. 5-12; and Branch, *Parting the Waters*, Chapter 8.

3. Kennedy quoted in Harold Chase and Allen Lerman, eds., *Kennedy and the Press: The News Conferences* (New York: Thomas Y. Crowell, Company, 1965), p. 43.

4. Cox quoted in Victor S. Navasky, *Kennedy Justice* (New York: Athenium, 1971), p. 245. Also: Navasky, *ibid.*, pp. 133 & 244; Oral History Interview, John F. Kennedy Library: Burke Marshall, May 29, 1964, by Louis Oberdorfer, pp. 61 & 65; Wilkins Interview, p. 22; Arthur M. Schlesinger, Jr., *A Thousand Days* (Boston: Houghton Mifflin Company, 1965), p. 930; Theodore Sorenson, *Kennedy* (New York, 1965), p. 342; Barbara Carter, "The Role of the Civil Rights Commission," *The Reporter* 29 (July 4, 1963), pp. 10 & 13; Heath, *Decade of Disillusionment*, pp. 69-73; Sundquist, *Politics and Policy*, p. 256; Congressional Quarterly Service, *Politics in America*, p. 40; and Burner and West, *The Torch Is Passed*, pp. 159-160.

5. Marshall quoted in Carter, "Civil Rights Commission," p. 12.

6. Quotes from James Tobin, "The Political Economy of the 1960s," in *Toward New Human Rights: The Social Policies of the Kennedy and Johnson Administrations*, ed. David C. Warner (University of Texas, 1977), p. 33; and Walter W. Heller, "Economics of the Race Problem," *Social Research* 37 (Winter, 1970), p. 506. Also, U.S. Department of Labor, *Weekly News Digest* September 23, 1963, p. 3; October 21, 1963, p. 2; November 4, 1963, p. 5; November 9, 1963, pp. 2 & 5; Clarence Mitchell Interview, p. 8; Navasky, *Kennedy Justice*, p. 97; Sundquist, *Politics and Policy*, pp. 131-132.

7. Quotes from Navasky, *Kennedy Justice*, pp. 192-93; and Schlesinger, *Thousand Days*, p. 742.

8. Katzenbach quoted in Carter, "Civil Rights Commission," p. 12.

9. Quote from *Weekly News Digest*, December 17, 1963, p. 2. Also: *Weekly News Digest*, October 28, 1963, pp. 1-2; December 17, 1963, pp. 1-2; December 23, 1963, p. *5; The New York Times*, August 20, 1963, pp. 1 & 18.

10. Quote from Hubbard, "Affirmative Action," pp. 110-111.

11. Wirtz quoted in *Weekly News Digest*, November 18, 1963, p. 2. Kennedy quoted in Chase and Lerman, eds., *News Conferences*, p. 478. Also: *Public Papers of the Presidents*, John F. Kennedy, 1961 (Washington, DC: Government Printing Office, 1962), p. 150; Hubbard, "Affirmative Action," pp. 111-112; and *The New York Times*, March 7, 1961, pp. 1 & 27.

12. Quote from *Chicago Defender*, May 4, 1963, p. 6. Also: *The New York Times*, June 18, 1961, pp. 1 & 50; and Sobel, *Civil Rights*, pp. 98-99.

13. Lyndon B. Johnson, *A Time for Action: A Selection from the Writings and Speeches of Lyndon B. Johnson, 1953-1964* (New York: Atheneum Publishers, 1964), p. 95; Arthur Fletcher, *The Silent Sell-Out: Government Betrayal of Blacks to the Craft Unions* (New York: The Third Press, 1974), pp. 36-37; Alfred W. Blumrosen, *Black Employment and the Law* (New Brunswick, NJ: Rutgers University Press, 1971), p. 76; Sobel, *Civil Rights*, pp. 144-145; and *Weekly News Digest*, October 18, 1965, p. 2.

14. Hill quoted in Sobel, *Civil Rights*, p. 144.

15. *The New York Times*, March 1, 1963, pp. 1 & 4.

16. Quote from Rowan, *Negro in Steel Industry*, p. 95.

17. U.S. Equal Employment Opportunity Commission, *Hearings on Discrimination in White Collar Employment* (Washington, DC: EEOC, 1968), pp. 169-171, Fletcher, *Sell-Out*, pp. 36-37; and Brauer, *Second Reconstruction*, p. 149.

18. *Quarles v. Philip Morris, Inc.* 279 F. Supp. at 509; *U.S. v. U.S. Steel Corporation* 371 F. Supp. at 1055; NAACP *Annual Report* 1963, p. 70; Sovern, *Legal Restraints*, pp. 106 & 137; Northrup, *Negro in Tobacco Industry*, pp. 40-41; and Northrup, *Negro in Paper Industry*, pp. 54-58.

19. Quote from Blumrosen, *Black Employment and the Law* p. 68. Also: Robert Kennedy in Allen J. Matsunow, *The Unraveling of America: A History of Liberalism in the l960s* (New York: Harper and Row, 1984), pp. 65-66; Foster Rhea Dulles, *The Civil Rights Commission 1957-1965* (Michigan State University Press), pp. 141-143; Reginald Alleyne, "Current Developments under Title VII of the Civil Rights Act of 1964 and Executive Order 11246," in *Current Developments in Labor Law*, eds. Alleyne and Jan Vetter (Berkeley, CA: School of Law, 1970), pp. 23-24; Blumrosen, p. 68; and Fletcher, *Sell-Out*, pp. 37-39.

20. Francis Fox Piven and Richard A. Cloward, *Poor Peoples' Movements* (New York: Vintage Books, 1979), pp. 182-217; Sitkoff, *New Deal*, Chapters 8-9; and Peter Camejo, "The Civil Rights Movement: How It Began, What It Won," *The Militant* 38 (December 20, 1974), pp. 5-6.

21. Martin Luther King, Jr., quoted in David J. Garrow, *Bearing the Cross: Martin Luther King, Jr. and the Southern Christian Leadership Conference* (New York: Vintage Books, 1986, 1988), p. 273; and "Letter from Birmingham Jail," in *Why We Can't Wait* (New York: Harper and Row Publishers, 1963, 1964), p. 81.

22. *Ibid.*, Chapter 5; David J. Garrow, *Protest at Selma* (New Haven, CT: Yale University Press, 1978), especially pp. 2 & 222-23; Garrow, *Bearing the Cross*, pp. 273-274; and Bo Wimark, "Nonviolent Methods and the American Civil Rights Movement 1955-1965," *Journal of Peace Research* 10 (1974), pp. 115-132.

23. Bayard Rustin, *The Meaning of Birmingham* (Glen Gardner, NJ), p. 1; and Mitchell Oral Interview, p. 20.

24. Quote from Martin Luther King, Jr., "The Hammer of Civil Rights," *The Nation* 198 (March 9, 1964), p. 233. Also: Mitchell Oral Interview, pp. 19-21; and Wilkins Oral Interview, pp. 10-11.

25. Farmer quoted in Garrow, *Bearing the Cross*, p. 156. Also: Testimony of Timothy Jenkins, U.S. House of Representatives, Subcommittee #5 of Committee on the Judiciary, 88th Congress, 1st Session, on *Miscellaneous Proposals Regarding the Civil Rights of Persons within the Jurisdiction of the United States* (Washington, DC: Government Printing Office, 1963), p. 1247; and Testimony of James Farmer, *ibid.*, p. 2215. For accounts of civil rights activities during the years 1961-63, see

Branch, *Parting the Waters*, chapters 11-17; and Garrow, *Bearing the Cross*, chapters 3-4.

26. *Newsday* editorial, February 7, 1963, in NAACP Files, U.S. Library of Congress, Group III Series H, Box 67; August Meier and Elliot Rudwick, *CORE* (New York: Oxford University Press, 1973), pp. 187-192 & 235; and Harold Weiner, "Negro Picketing for Employment Equality," *Harvard Law Review* 13 (Spring, 1967), pp. 290-292.

27. Philadelphia disruptions from F. Ray Marshall and Vernon M. Briggs, Jr., *The Negro and Apprenticeship* (Baltimore: Johns Hopkins University Press, 1967), pp. 87-95; Meier and Rudwick, *CORE*, pp. 192 & 236; Sobel, *Civil Rights*, pp. 212ff; and *The New York Times*, June 1, 1963, p. 1.

Elizabeth demonstrations in *The New York Times*, August 17, 1963, p. 1. Cleveland protests in U.S. Commission on Civil Rights, *Hearings before the U.S. Commission on Civil Rights in Cleveland, Ohio* (Washington, DC: Government Printing Office, 1966), pp. 445-48; Hill in Jacobsen, *American Labor*, p. 296; Marshall and Briggs, *ibid.*, pp. 103-104; and Marshall, *Organized Labor*, pp. 124ff.

28. Meier and Rudwick, *CORE*, p. 228.

29. *The New York Times*, August 1, 1963, p. 1.

30. *The New York Times*, July 12, 1963, p. 1.

31. *The New York Times*, July 12, 1963, p. 51.

32. Rockefeller quoted in *The New York Times*, August 3, 1963, p. 1. Brennan quoted in *The New York Times*, August 17, 1963, p. 1.

33. *New York Amsterdam News*, July 27, 1963, p. 10.

34. James Haughton Interview; U.S. Department of Labor, Manpower Administration, *Negros in Apprenticeship,* Manpower/Automation Research Monograph No. 6 (Washington, DC: Government Printing Office, 1967), pp. 17-18; Marshall and Briggs, *Negro and Apprenticeship*, pp. 51-60; Meier and Rudwick, *CORE*, pp. 228 & 237; *The New York Times*, June 19-August 17, 1963; November 13, 1963; January 7, 1964; and *New York Amsterdam News*, June-December, 1963.

35. King quoted in "What the Marchers Really Want," *The New York Times Magazine*, August 25, 1963, p. 8. Wilkins quoted in *The New York Times*, June 12, 1963, p. 22.

36. Quote from James Farmer, *Freedom - When?* (New York: Random House, 1965), p. 170. For views of civil rights leaders, see: "What the Marchers Really Want," p. 7; "Five Angry Men Speak Their Minds," Gertrude Samuels, Chair, *The New York Times Magazine*, May 17, 1964,

p. 14; "Negro Leaders Tell Their Plans for '64," *U.S. News and World Report* 56 (February 24, 1964), p. 56ff.

Information on Breadbasket from "Negro Ministers Unfold 'Operation Breadbasket' in Atlanta," SCLC *Newsletter*, 1 (December, 1962), pp. 3-4; Bloom and Fletcher, "Supermarkets," p. 119; and Matusow, *Unraveling of America*, p. 209.

37. Rockefeller quoted in Congressional Quarterly *Almanac*, Vol. 19, 1963 (Washington, DC: Congressional Quarterly Service, 1964), p. 339.

38. Testimony of Robert Kennedy, Hearings before House Judiciary Subcommittee #5, p. 1395; Congressional Quarterly *Almanac* 1963, p. 339; Congressional Quarterly Service, *Politics in America*, pp. 46-47; and *The New York Times*, February 1, 1963, p. 1; March 1, 1963, pp. 1 & 5; June 15, 1963, p. 1. For fear of "radicals," see *The New York Times*, May-June, 1963.

39. Garrow, *Bearing the Cross,* p. 237.

40. Martin Luther King, Jr., "Birmingham, U.S.A.," *New York Amsterdam News*, June 8, 1963, p. 10; Wyatt Walker quoted in Garrow, *Bearing the Cross*, p. 228.

41. For civil rights movement and the media, see: Garrow, *Selma*, pp. 135-45; Hamby, *Liberalism*, pp. 158-59 & 181; Burner and West, *The Torch Is Passed*, pp. 155-57; and William B. Monroe, Jr., "Television: The Chosen Instrument of the Revolution," *Race and the News Media*, eds. Paul E. Fisher and Ralph L. Lowenstein (New York: Frederick A. Praeger, Publishers, 1967), pp. 83-97.

42. For a comprehensive account of Birmingham, see Lewis, *King*, chapter 7; Garrow, *Bearing the Cross*, chapter 5; and Branch, *Parting the Waters*, chapters 18-20. Also: Burke Marshall Oral Interview, pp. 95-102; King, "Birmingham, U.S.A.," p. 10; "Boycott Aids in Birmingham," SCLC *Newsletter* 1 (July, 1963), p. 7; Marshall, *Negro Worker*, pp. 47-49; Piven and Cloward, *Poor Peoples' Movements*, p. 241; Rowan, *Negro in the Steel Industry*, p. 102; and Garrow, *Selma*, pp. 135-136.

43. Len Holt, "Birmingham Demonstration, 1963," in *Black Protest*, Joanne Grant, ed. (New York: St. Martin's Press, 1968), p. 344.

44. Kennedy quoted in Chase and Lerman, eds., *News Conferences*, p. 450; and *The New York Times*, June 10, 1963, p. 20.

45. Contents of JFK bill in House Judiciary Subcommittee #5 *Hearings*, pp. 649-660. Also: Marshall Oral Interview, pp. 104-l06; King, "Hammer"; Humphrey, *Education*, pp. 272-273; Sundquist, *Politics and Policy*, p. 261; U.S. Equal Employment Opportunity Commission, *The First Decade* (Washington, DC: EEOC, 1974), p. 10; and *The New York Times*, June 4, 1963, p. 1; June 14, 1963, p. 1.

46. House Judiciary Subcommittee #5 *Hearings*, especially testimony of Meany, Wilkins, Maslow, and Javits; Archie Robinson, *George Meany and His Times* (New York: Simon and Shuster, 1981), pp. 234-36; *The New York Times*, June 4, 1963, p. 1; June 14, 1963, p. 1; and Congressional Quarterly, *Almanac 1963*, p. 342.

47. Bureau of National Affairs, *The Civil Rights Act of 1964* (Washington, DC: BNA, 1964), p. 41; Congressional Quarterly *Weekly* 21 (July 19, 1963): p. 1159; (August 9, 1963), p. 1419; 22 (January 24, 1964), p. 157; and *The New York Times*, July 31, 1963, p. 1; October 14, 1963, p. 1.

48. *The New York Times*, October 17, 1963, p. 1; October 18, 1963, p. 19, and testimony of Herman Talmadge, "Civil Rights and 'FEPC'," *Congressional Digest* 43 (March, 1964), p. 83.

49. Testimony of Richard Cramer, *Congressional Record*, Vol. 110, Part II (Washington, DC: Government Printing Office, 1964), pp. 1595-96; Bureau of National Affairs, *Civil Rights Act*, pp. 41 & 195; "Caught in the Crossfire: Halleck on Civil Rights," *U.S. News and World Report*, 55 (November 11, 1963), p. 24; Murray Kempton, "Heroes on the Right," *The New Republic* 149 (November 9, 1963), p. 4; "Halleck and McCulloch," *Newsweek* 62 (November 11, 1963), pp. 34-37; and *The New York Times*, October 18, 1963, pp. 1 & 19; October 24, 1963, pp. 1 & 24; October 29, 1963, pp. 1 & 20; October 30, 1963, pp. 1 & 22; February 11, 1964, p. 1.

50. Testimony of Everitt Dirksen, *Congressional Record*, Vol. 110, p. 13319; Neil MacNeil, *Dirksen: Portrait of a Public Man* (New York: The World Publishing Company, 1970), pp. 223 & 234; *The New York Times*, February 18, 1964, pp. 1 & 20; May 14, 1964, pp. 1 & 28; Congressional Quarterly *Almanac* 1964, pp. 354 & 364; and Bureau of National Affairs, *Civil Rights Act*, p. 41.

51. Hill quoted in *Congressional Record*, Vol. 110, p.487; and "FEPC," *Congressional Digest*, p. 81. Huddleston quoted in *Congressional Record*, Vol. 110, p.1605.

52. Williams quoted in *Congressional Record*, Vol. 110, Part 7, p. 8921. JD memo in Part 6, p. 7207. Clark quoted in Part 6, p. 7218.

53. Testimony of Lister Hill, *Congressional Record*, Vol. 110, pp. 487-88; and *Congressional Digest*, "FEPC," p. 77. JD Memo, *Congressional Record*, Vol. 110, Part 6, p. 7207. Reuther letter in Part 6, p. 7206. Testimony of Thomas Kuchel, p. 6563.

54. MacDonald quoted in U.S. Senate, Committee on Labor and Public Welfare, *Hearings before the Subcommittee on Employment and Manpower, 88th Congress, 1st Session* (Washington, DC: Government

Printing Office, 1963), p. 292. Wirtz quoted in *Weekly News Digest,* September 16, 1963, p. 1. AFL-CIO from "Equal Rights for All . . . The AFL-CIO Position," *The American Federationist* 71 (March, 1964), p. 2.

55. Tobin in Warner, *Towards New Human Rights,* pp. 33 & 41; Testimony of George Meany, Senate Committee on Labor and Public Welfare *Hearings,* p. 151; and W. Willard Wirtz, "Toward Equal Opportunity," *American Child* 45 (November, 1963), pp. 2-4.

56. Quotes from Whitney M. Young, Jr., "The Negro Revolt," *American Child* 45 (November, 1963), p. 8; and "Negro Leaders Tell Their Plans for '64," pp. 56-57. See also: Young, *To Be Equal* (New York: McGraw-Hill Book Company, 1964), pp. 25-29; Testimony of James Farmer, Senate Committee on Labor and Public Welfare *Hearings,* pp. 224-26; Testimony of Roy Wilkins, *ibid.,* pp. 204-205; Adam Clayton Powell, Jr., in "Five Angry Men Speak Their Minds," p. 110.

For a thorough discussion of the debates concerning preferential treatment during the consideration of the civil rights bill, see Hugh Davis Graham, *The Civil Rights Era: Origins and Development of National Policy* (New York: Oxford University Press, 1990), Chapter 4.

57. For later observations regarding affirmative action and job discrimination, see: Testimony of Edward Brooke, *Congressional Record,* Vol. 115, Part 29, December 18, 1969, pp. 39966-67; and House Labor Committee Report, in Bureau of National Affairs, *The Equal Employment Opportunity Act of 1972* (Washington, DC: BNA, 1973), p. 162.

58. Johnson quoted in *The New York Times,* July 3, 1964, p. 9. For passage of the act, see: Congressional Quarterly *Almanac* 1964, pp. 366-78; and *The New York Times,* June 11, 1964, p. 1; June 20, 1964, p. 1; June 18, 1964, p. 1; July 1, 1964, p. 1; July 3, 1964, p. 1.

59. *Civil Rights Act of 1964,* Public Law 88-352, 78 Stat. 253, Section 703(a).

60. *Ibid.,* Section 706(a).

61. *Ibid.,* Section 707(a).

62. *Ibid.,* Section 703(j).

63. *Ibid.,* Section 703(h).

64. *Ibid.,* Section 706(g).

65. *Civil Rights Act,* Title VII; and Bureau of National Affairs, *Civil Rights Act,* p. 41, provide basis for discussion of Title VII.

66. Gullander quoted in "Managing Your Manpower: How Employers Are Preparing for the Civil Rights Act," *Dun's Review* 84 (November, 1964), p. 57.

IV

Implementation: the Johnson Years

In June 1965, President Lyndon Johnson delivered the commencement address at Howard University in Washington, D.C. Referring to the long and arduous struggle for equality, Johnson declared: "You do not take a person who, for years, has been hobbled by chains and liberate him, bring him to the starting line of a race, and then say you are free to compete with all the others, and still just believe that you have been completely fair." "We seek not just freedom," the president added, "but opportunity."

In light of developments since 1965, Johnson's words may sound like a bold call for affirmative action programs. In fact, the speech contained no references to the types of hiring programs that became so widespread in later years. Rather, Johnson focused on overcoming poverty through such "safe" strategies as education and strengthening the black family. (The latter strategy reflected the philosophy of Daniel Patrick Moynihan, who authored the initial draft of the speech.)[1]

Nevertheless, Johnson's rhetoric demonstrated that many liberals were beginning to reconsider their traditional faith in simple nondiscrimination. In fact, the Johnson years marked a transitional period in the civil rights movement, during which certain trends from earlier periods reached their fruition and began to recede in the face of new, more complex issues. The mass protest activities that began during the 1950s and proliferated during the Kennedy years reached a dramatic climax at Selma, Alabama, in 1965, and in the northern urban riots that began that same year. Similarly, the decades-long crusade for black suffrage and public integration finally realized most of its goals with the enactment and implementation of the Civil Rights Act of 1964 and the Voting Rights Act of 1965.

The successful resolution of these issues, however, generated neither racial peace nor equality. Rather, another, more difficult set of issues replaced them, including housing, school integration, and affirmative action. Regarding the last of these three, the Johnson years witnessed both continued grass-roots protest against employment discrimination and the emergence of a legal and bureaucratic strategy to implement affirmative action. Many of the same civil rights groups that took the initiative in securing passage of the Civil Rights Act played a major role in ensuring its implementation. As the complexity of the jobs issue became evident during these years, liberal thought increasingly accommodated itself to the affirmative action demands of civil rights activists. By the end of 1968, the courts and federal bureaucracy, and not direct action protests, had emerged as the dominant vehicles for antidiscrimination/affirmative action efforts.

The establishment of a federal antidiscrimination apparatus was a painful, ad hoc process characterized by confusion and ineptitude. The critical year in this process was 1965, when the preeminent equal opportunity agencies—the Equal Employment Opportunity Commission (EEOC) and the Office of Federal Contract Compliance (OFCC)—came into being. The EEOC was a product of Title VII of the Civil Rights Act, which became operative in July 1965. Its inauspicious beginning foreshadowed the grave difficulties that were to obstruct this agency in the ensuing years. Although the act provided the administration with a one-year hiatus to facilitate a smooth inauguration, Johnson did not appoint an EEOC chairman until May 1965, when Franklin D. Roosevelt, Jr., was sworn in. A former congressman and sponsor of FEPC legislation, Roosevelt's tenure lasted only one year, terminating with his resignation in May 1966. Preparations for the commission were ad hoc and disorganized. Delays in assembling an experienced staff ultimately forced the commission to recruit members from other agencies. The commission's investigative staff received only one week of training before being sent into the field. The EEOC initially lacked its own headquarters and operated out of a series of offices "borrowed" from the Department of Commerce. Much early communication was addressed simply to, "FDR, Jr., Washington, D.C."[2]

In addition to their lack of training, EEOC members launched their agency in the absence of sufficient funding, support, and enforcement precedents. The commission's finances and staff for its first fiscal year—1966—were based on an anticipated caseload of 2,000 cases; in fact, the commission received 9,000. Despite the strenuous efforts of its overworked staff, the EEOC from its inception accumulated a backlog that would achieve monumental proportions in the ensuing decade. In addition, because no fair employment effort of this magnitude had ever been attempted previous to 1965, agency members often operated without guidance or precedents, devising strategies and "solutions" as situations unfolded. One attorney described the early commission as "a do-it yourself operation for the staff."[3] Finally, the low priority accorded to equal employment activities by the Johnson administration hindered Title VII enforcement efforts. The White House and Justice Department concentrated on other issues, especially voting rights. Not until Ramsey Clark became attorney general in 1967 did the Justice Department become a real factor in securing Title VII compliance.[4]

The general strategy adopted by the EEOC was to respond to the receipt of a complaint by conducting an investigation. If the commission found no "reasonable cause," it dismissed the complaint. If it determined the charge to be legitimate, it arranged a conference with the accused employer to work out a voluntary agreement between the parties. Although the commission could not impose remedial procedures, it could and did offer suggestions and issue general guidelines regarding employment practices, such as testing. In the event of a charge of discrimination against an AFL-CIO affiliate, the EEOC agreed to inform representatives of the international union, the local union, and the AFL-CIO Civil Rights Department, as well as the relevant employer. Only in extreme cases of discrimination did the Commission recommend a case to the Justice Department for a "707 suit," and only in rare cases did the department acquiesce. Commission members acknowledged the inadequacy of this system, and as early as 1965 they pressed Congress to authorize the cease-and-desist powers that had been deleted during the congressional debates. Congress refused, however, and the EEOC remained strictly a conciliatory body until 1972.[5]

As the Johnson administration established the EEOC, it also reorganized the federal antidiscrimination apparatus for government contractors. Responding to a set of recommendations submitted by Vice President Hubert Humphrey, Johnson, on September 24, 1965, issued Executive Order 11246. This order preserved the nondiscrimination/ affirmative action requirements of Kennedy's Executive Order 10925, but it added the stipulation that all federal contractors periodically submit written "Compliance Reports" indicating the level of minority participation on their projects. Responsibility for overseeing compliance remained in the hands of the "predominant interest agency" (PIA).[6] The order abolished the President's Commission on Equal Employment Opportunity (PCEEO) and replaced it with the Office of Federal Contract Compliance (OFCC), located within the Department of Labor. Thus, the order invested authority for enforcing nondiscrimination by government contractors in the secretary of labor (as opposed to the vice president in the Eisenhower and Kennedy orders), and it empowered him to cancel contracts, to debar businesses from future contracts, and to recommend cases to the Justice Department for prosecution in the event of noncompliance. To promote fair employment within the government itself, the order further required all federal agency heads to establish an equal employment opportunity effort within their agencies, to be supervised by the Civil Service Commission. Finally, the Plans for Progress program was continued as a separate entity.[7]

Executive Order 11246 was more specific regarding the requirements for contractors and the penalties for noncompliance than was Kennedy's order. Unfortunately, the new order, like the previous one, failed to define "affirmative action" or to provide precise criteria with which to evaluate compliance. The order did specify that affirmative action be extended to "employment, upgrading, demotion, or transfer; recruitment or recruitment advertising; layoff or termination; rates of pay or other forms of compensation; and selection for training, including apprenticeship."[8] It neglected to indicate, however, *how* affirmative action was to be applied in these areas.

The failure to define "affirmative action" createdsevere enforcement difficulties for the OFCC as well as for the affected contractors and unions. Other obstacles confronting the newly created OFCC were insufficient funding and an inadequate work force. In addition, many agency officials were former PCEEO employees who introduced to the OFCC their "cautious, non-enforcement oriented attitudes."[9] Johnson himself expressed the same attitude toward enforcement as president that he had as chairman of the PCEEO: "I strongly share the view that efforts to obtain voluntary compliance should receive priority."[10] Vice President Humphrey and Attorney General Nicholas Katzenbach expressed similar views. From its inception, then, the OFCC rejected the vigorous application of its authority in favor of cooperative efforts with contractors.

Enforcement of Executive Order 11246 was further weakened by the transfer of enforcement authority from the vice president to the secretary of labor. This move diminished the role of Hubert Humphrey within Johnson's civil rights program, an unfortunate circumstance in light of Humphrey's long-standing support for civil rights measures. Finally, in prohibiting discrimination due to "race, creed, color, or national origin," the order omitted any reference to "sex"—unlike Title VII—a deficiency that was not rectified until a subsequent executive order was issued in 1967.[11]

The relative weakness of both the EEOC and OFCC did not discourage civil rights proponents from pursuing the vigorous enforcement of Title VII and Executive Order 11246. As early as January 1965, the NAACP publicly declared: "It is now up to all of us as citizens to ensure implementation" of the act.[12] Even before Title VII became operative, the NAACP and NAACP Legal Defense Fund had begun to prepare job discrimination cases. These two organizations filed more than 2,500 charges during the first eighteen months of the EEOC, targeting such institutions as U.S. Steel, Philip Morris, and Sears Roebuck.

As previously mentioned, the EEOC received approximately 9,000 complaints during its first year. Of this total, 60 percent charged racial discrimination, and 37 percent were sex discrimination cases. The latter number demonstrated that womens' groups were actively pursuing the Title VII prohibitions against sex discrimination. The overwhelming majority of all charges—87 percent—were directed against employers, and 21 percent involved labor unions. (The overlap reflects those charges directed against unions *and* employers.) Nearly half the charges were directed against eleven southern states, a statistic that reflected, in part, the absence of state FEPCs in the South. The three most common sources of grievances were hiring, promotion, and seniority practices.[13]

Beginning in 1965, civil rights organizations expanded the struggle against job discrimination to every sector of the U.S. economy. Not surprisingly, much of this activity focused on improving the position of African-American workers in those industries in which they already were represented: steel; pulp and paper; tobacco; textiles; automobiles; and construction. Many of the issues were familiar ones, such as separate lines of progression, segregated union locals, plant versus departmental seniority, and hiring and promotion practices. With the enactment of Title VII, civil rights proponents initiated legal suits against alleged offenders and submitted complaints to federal agencies, while at the same time sustaining more traditional forms of protest, such as pickets, demonstrations, and boycotts.[14]

The first major EEOC and OFCC conciliation agreement involved the Newport News Shipbuilding Company of Virginia. A sizable Navy contractor and the largest private employer in the state, Newport News epitomized the Jim Crow system of the South. African Americans held only 32 of 2,000 supervisory positions and only 6 of more than 500 apprenticeship positions. African-American employees generally could attain no position above that of "mechanic." Promotions occurred largely at the discretion of the company, with African Americans having little input. Compounding this discriminatory system were such demeaning Jim Crow practices as segregated locker and shower facilities and inferior wages for equal work.

After Title VII took effect in July 1965, forty African-American employees, including the Reverend J.C. Fauntleroy, head of the local NAACP chapter, filed complaints with the EEOC. Because Newport News was a defense contractor, the OFCC also became involved. On March 25,

1966, Secretary of Labor W. Willard Wirtz ordered that all federal contracts to the company be suspended until the company was judged to be in compliance with federal antidiscrimination laws. Extensive negotiations involving the EEOC, the OFCC, the Justice Department, and Newport News finally produced an agreement on March 30 that modified departmental-transfer and apprenticeship-selection procedures and commissioned an outside expert to determine which employees had suffered discrimination in wages and promotions. Within months after the development of this accord, almost 3,000 African Americans had been promoted, and 60 percent of African-American workers hired after March 30 were employed in previously all-white departments.[15]

The Newport News agreement unfortunately was exceptional in both the rapidity of its settlement and the degree of cooperation among the diverse government agencies. A case illustrating the circuitous and exasperating process that was more typical of affirmative action cases was that of the Allen-Bradley company in Milwaukee. A producer of sophisticated electronic equipment, Allen-Bradley in 1964 employed over 6,000 workers, of whom *4* were black. The company conducted most of its recruitment via word-of-mouth among employees, thereby reserving most job openings for employees' friends and relatives. The company justified its hiring policies by arguing that African Americans lacked the necessary technical skills to produce sensitive equipment.

Local civil rights leaders refused to accept this rationalization. Beginning in 1964, Milwaukee CORE and other community groups lodged formal complaints against Allen-Bradley with the federal government. Because government contracts comprised 25 percent of the company's business, the complaints eventually were directed to the OFCC, which conducted an investigation. On May 24, 1968, the OFCC declared Allen-Bradley and four other large corporations to be in violation of federal affirmative action regulations and warned that they must request a hearing by June 4 or else face a possible severing of federal money. Allen-Bradley appealed the ruling, while civil rights groups in Milwaukee mobilized their forces for direct-action protests.

On August 13, demonstrations by African-American and Latino groups organized by the controversial civil rights figure Father James Groppi began outside the Allen-Bradley plant. Protestors' demands included the hiring of minority workers until the work force was 12 percent African-American and 5 percent Latino, figures roughly equivalent to the respective proportions of these groups within the city's population. Allen-Bradley, meanwhile, unconditionally rejected "any hiring quotas or training programs."[16]

In August 1968, a three-member Labor Department panel chaired by Professor Bernard Meltzer conducted a hearing into Allen-Bradley's employment situation. The panel's report, submitted to the secretary of labor in December, charged Allen-Bradley with violating the nondiscrimination and affirmative action requirements of Executive Order 11246. Since 1964, the panel discovered, African-American employment in the plant had increased only from 4 to 32, representing one-half of 1 percent of the company's labor force. Although the company did not discriminate *actively* by 1968, the panel maintained, it had failed to take such affirmative steps as recruiting in African-American schools and cooperating with local civil rights and employment agencies. The company thus maintained an anti-black image that discouraged minorities from seeking employment. The panel denied company charges that the Labor Department sought to impose hiring quotas. Despite these findings, however, the panel recommended further negotiations between Allen-Bradley and the OFCC.

By the end of 1968, the OFCC appeared to be in a commanding position regarding the Allen-Bradley case. Neither the company nor the federal government, however, seriously considered the threat of a funding cutoff; both sides realized that such a maneuver would result in the loss of more than 1,000 jobs. Consequently, before leaving office in 1969, Secretary of Labor Wirtz accepted the panel's recommendations and awarded Allen-Bradley additional time to develop a viable affirmative action program. Wirtz also assured the company: "Any 'quota' practice would be wrong."[17]

Thus, the problem passed to the Nixon administration, where in 1969 Secretary of Labor George P. Shultz accepted with "reservations"a plan in which Allen-Bradley agreed to advertise job openings publicly, to cooperate with minority schools and organizations, and to maintain a list of all job applicants by race. Thus, after five years of agitation, Milwaukee blacks received no concrete proposals for minority hiring. Although protests continued under the auspices of James Groppi, the Allen-Bradley case was officially "solved." Significantly, the protracted Allen-Bradley controversy illustrated the reliance of African-American activists on both traditional forms of protest—Groppi's demonstrations—*and* government intervention—the OFCC—a pattern characteristic of the mid- and late-1960s.[18]

As previously mentioned, campaigns for equal employment opportunity often comprised one segment of a larger crusade for civil rights. No case provided a more dramatic illustration of this process than the bitter and protracted racial conflict in Bogalusa, Louisiana. Founded as a sawmill camp in the early twentieth century, bordered by pine forests and the East Pearl River, Bogalusa was situated close to the Mississippi border and was described by one observer as "just an extension of Mississippi."[19] Bogalusa resembled Mississippi in its ruthless application of the Jim Crow system. The town served as a bastion of the Ku Klux Klan, which "periodically whipped blacks and burned crosses."[20]

Bogalusa was also a paper mill town. Situated at the heart of the town's political and social life was "the Mill," an imposing paper plant that, since 1955, had been the property of Crown-Zellerbach, the nation's second largest paper company. Although Crown-Zellerbach was a northern-based corporation, it "adopted a strict hands-off policy in community affairs" and acquiesced in the imposition of a rigid color line within the plant.[21] The mill was highly unionized, and Local 189 of the United Papermakers and Paperworkers constituted a potent—and racially reactionary—political force within the community. Many union members participated in Klan activities. Meanwhile, African Americans, who comprised one-third of the town's population, represented only one-seventh of the mill's work force, and these workers were generally relegated to the lowest-paying jobs. African Americans were confined to separate lines of progression and segregated facilities and were restricted to a separate union local (189-A).[22]

Even this citadel of reactionary politics was not immune, however, to the forces of change. Much of the initial impetus was economic, being generated by changes within the company itself. Responding to intense competition within the paper industry, Crown-Zellerbach began to mechanize the Bogalusa plant in the late 1950s, with the result that more than 500 employees lost their jobs between 1961 and 1965. Unemployed workers—black and white—were placed in a pool to serve as temporary workers. The heightened economic insecurity and competition for jobs produced by these layoffs in turn produced increased racial tensions in Bogalusa. By the mid-1960s, the town claimed "reportedly the highest concentration of Klan members" in the South.[23]

It was at this time that the civil rights movement reached Bogalusa. As a government contractor, Crown-Zellerbach fell within the jurisdiction of Executive Order 10925 and joined Plans for Progress, but it modified few of its practices. In 1964, CORE personnel entered the town to assist in voter registration and general integration drives. Their efforts were offset by the violent resistance of the racist power structure in the area. Undeterred, CORE launched a renewed assault in 1965, including a campaign by the

Civic and Voters League, a predominantly African-American middle-class organization, to secure increased minority employment at Crown-Zellerbach. Again, the town reacted violently, physically attacking and intimidating civil rights proponents. When two CORE activists were beaten early in 1965, Louisiana Governor John McKeithen claimed that the wounds were self-inflicted and denounced the victims as "professional trouble makers" attempting to "stir something up."[24] After civil rights leaders finally pressured the local police into hiring two African-American deputies, one, O'Neal Moore, was murdered, ostensibly by a Crown-Zellerbach employee.

In response to these activities, young Bogalusa African Americans organized the Deacons for Defense and Justice, a self-defense group that carried guns and conducted regular drills. Although the national CORE leadership attempted—unsuccessfully—to dissuade the Deacons from pursuing this path, James Farmer gratefully accepted their protection when he visited Bogalusa in April 1965. As the violence proliferated in Bogalusa, CORE began to apply greater pressure on Crown-Zellerbach. It picketed the corporation's national headquarters in San Francisco, demanding that company officials exert moral leadership concerning the situation in Louisiana, beginning with the firing of all Klan members in their plant. Company officials reluctantly agreed to confer with CORE leaders in Bogalusa on July 15, 1965, by which time Title VII had become operative. Following the meeting, Crown-Zellerbach announced that it would comply with Title VII requirements by desegregating all of the plant's facilities. At the same time, the Justice Department initiated suits against the Klan as well as against segregated restaurants and movie theaters in the town.

Despite these actions, however, racial violence continued unabated, highlighted by a police riot in the African-American ghetto in October 1965. In January 1966, a former radio-station operator who had been driven from his business testified before Congress that "the Klan has won its battle in Bogalusa."[25]

The "battle" for equal opportunity in the Crown-Zellerbach plant, however, was far from over. The history of this "battle" throughout the subsequent five years was one of bureaucratic entanglements that illustrated the hardships and frustrations that civil rights activists encountered in their struggle for economic justice. Although Crown-Zellerbach had promised in the summer of 1965 to integrate its facilities, many serious problems remained, including separate lines of progression and separate locals. In addition, beginning in 1964, the company required all employees seeking transfers to previously all-white departments to pass standardized tests, on which blacks historically achieved lower scores than whites.

Following complaints by African-American workers, the EEOC in December 1965 secured an agreement with Crown-Zellerbach in which the lines of progression were intermeshed. In fact, the company dovetailed the lines so that black workers were added to the bottom of the white list. Although black local 189-A opposed this arrangement, it was outvoted by the white local. Continued complaints led to the involvement of the OFCC in 1967, which nullified the EEOC agreement.

Unable to achieve a new accord with the company, both the government and African-American employees turned to the courts. In a series of major decisions culminating in *Hicks v. Crown-Zellerbach* in 1970, the courts ordered the merger of the union locals, the implementation of a new seniority list based on time in the mill rather than time in a particular department, and the abolition of tests for employees. Significantly, the courts ruled that testing procedures and seniority arrangements that on the surface seemed neutral still could violate Title VII if they perpetuated *past* discrimination. The African-American workers of Bogalusa, then, achieved a major victory in the field of affirmative action, but only after years of bloodshed and costly legal maneuvering. Although the contest began in the streets, it ultimately was settled in the courts, a course of events illustrative of the changes in civil rights strategies brought about by the Civil Rights Act.[26]

Most job discrimination cases lacked the dramatic elements of the Bogalusa affair. Although grassroots protests continued throughout the decade, jobs protests increasingly involved the less dramatic processes of initiating lawsuits and filing complaints with federal agencies. In addition to companies previously mentioned, targets of NAACP and NAACP Legal Defense Fund charges included the Ingalls Shipbuilding Corporation of Mississippi, the International Paper Company, Southern Bell Telephone Company, Timken Roller Bearing Company of Rockdale, Texas, and the U.S. Steel Corporation. Civil rights groups also filed more than seventy complaints against Ryder and other trucking companies. Many of these complaints resulted in EEOC and OFCC involvement and/or legal suits. The EEOC, for example, ruled against Planters Manufacturing Company of Clarksdale, Mississippi, following complaints by five African Americans and the Chemical Workers Union regarding segregated locker rooms and differential wage scales. Complaints filed by African Americans against Bethlehem Steel and U.S. Steel during the 1960s served as the basis for major judicial decisions in the 1970s. Some companies, such as International Paper and Timken Roller Bearing, agreed to develop affirmative action programs after threats of funding cutoffs by the OFCC.

The EEOC responded to complaints in certain areas by conducting hearings of entire industries. In the late 1960s, the commission investigated minority hiring patterns in the southern textile industry, in white-collar employment in New York City, and in several leading industries in the Los Angeles area, including aerospace, motion pictures, radio, and television. Besides publicizing hiring and promotion abuses, the commission occasionally developed industrywide agreements. Following the Los Angeles hearings, for example, the threat of a Justice Department suit convinced the movie industry to reserve 20-25 percent of all future skilled jobs for minority workers. The New York hearings enabled the EEOC to achieve a number of affirmative action agreements and to recommend other cases to the State Commission on Human Rights and to the federal government for further action. Conferences arranged in 1967 by the EEOC and the Federal Drug Administration contributed to an increase in minority employment in the drug manufacturing industry.[27]

At the same time that African Americans utilized the governmental antidiscrimination machinery, they continued to engage in independent activities to rectify economic injustices. Perhaps the most ambitious undertaking regarding employment during the 1960s was Operation Breadbasket. Instituted in 1959, "adopted" by the Southern Christian Leadership Conference in 1962, and transferred to Chicago in 1966, Operation Breadbasket, under the dynamic leadership of the Reverend Jesse Jackson, emerged as a national force. Following its establishment in Chicago, Breadbasket selected as its first target the Country Delight dairy company. Following an African-American boycott that cost the company more than $500,000 in sales, Country Delight conceded and signed an equal employment pact with the SCLC.

Breadbasket gradually became more ambitious, challenging such giants as Sealtest, DelMonte, and Kellogg, as well as such supermarket chains as Jewel and A&P. A typical agreement was that signed after a boycott of Sealtest in Cleveland in 1967, in which the company agreed to hire fifty African Americans, to conduct recruiting drives in African-American schools, to train African-American employees for personnel management positions, and to use the services of African-American businesses and suppliers. In a standard Breadbasket operation, the SCLC gathered data regarding a company's hiring and business practices, sought voluntary compliance with demands based on these data, and resorted to economic pressure if the company refused to negotiate. Although their chief weapon was the boycott, Breadbasket participants also engaged in sit-ins and demonstrations, and sometimes were arrested. Breadbasket also initiated boycotts in response to a company's failure to comply with its agreements.

In spite of these vigorous efforts, the programs's actual effectiveness was questionable. Although the SCLC claimed credit for the creation of thousands of jobs for African-American workers, critics charged that the program produced few tangible results due to a lack of follow-up and poor administration by its leadership. Historian Allan Matusow maintained that the operation benefitted primarily "middle-class black manufacturers." Whatever its accomplishments, however, Operation Breadbasket epitomized the types of initiatives that African-American activists had adopted by the mid-1960s to achieve their "share" of American wealth.[28]

These early antidiscrimination efforts primarily affected southern employers. Because southern firms historically practiced the most blatant forms of discrimination, they were the most susceptible to Title VII regulations. In addition, southern states generally lacked the state FEPCs to which the EEOC was required by law to defer for sixty days. A study of northern and southern businesses conducted in 1967 revealed that the changes generated by Title VII were confined largely to southern employers and included desegregation of facilities, the elimination of racial data from job applications, and the formalizing of the interview process. Significantly, some employers organized biracial groups within their plants "to keep CORE or any outside civil rights organization from getting credit for employment integration."[29]

Generally speaking, however, equal employment opportunity laws generated little substantive change within the business community during these years. In one study of more than 600 companies during the late 1960s, 60 percent of company executives claimed that FEPC laws had "no effect" or were of "limited importance" with respect to business practices. In fact, one-half of the respondents were not even aware of the existence of public antidiscrimination agencies.[30] Confronting job discrimination primarily on a complaint-by-complaint basis, federal equal opportunity agencies failed to influence a large number of employers.

One factor that limited the influence of federal antidiscrimination efforts was the unwillingness of employers who did not practice *overt* discrimination to acknowledge any necessity for affirmative action. In 1967, the EEOC reported that: "There is little quarrel about affirmative action when it involves merely broadening recruitment sources." It added, however, that "it has been found that purely affirmative actions may not produce affirmative results—and it is results that are needed."[31] Employers and unions sometimes accepted "pure" affirmative actions such as job training and recruitment in minority schools but opposed hiring targets or modification of seniority arrangements. One study of employers in the late 1960s discovered "very few companies anywhere with ongoing affirmative action programs."[32] With the gradual abolition of the Jim Crow system, the question of affirmative action, and not simple nondiscrimination, came to dominate the debate regarding economic justice in the United States.[33]

The reactions of business leaders to the civil rights movement in general were varied and often ambiguous. On the one hand, employers resented any incursions into their operations that they felt threatened their autonomy or the efficient conduct of business. A study of management attitudes toward equal employment opportunity during the 1960s claimed that business officials agreed that "special efforts must be made, but these should not compromise basic conventions in the company or the union."[34] The greatest fears, of course, involved the imposition of hiring quotas, which some employers claimed were necessary on a formal or informal basis to comply with affirmative action rules. In 1965, for example, Boeing, a NASA contractor, claimed to be importing African-American craftsmen from northern states to satisfy its contractual obligations. That same year, the *Wall Street Journal* warned that the EEOC would demand "preferential treatment" as a sign of compliance with Title VII. Ironically, according to one study, the idea of "quotas" was more acceptable in the South, which traditionally had adhered to a concept of "racial balance."[35]

At the same time, however, many business leaders recognized that the racial situation in the United States had changed irrevocably and that the business world would have to accommodate itself to this new environment. As Stephen Gelber explained, businesspeople found it easier to modify their policies than to "remake the world to fit the ideology of the profit ethic." A Birmingham businessman was more blunt: "I'm no integrationist, but I'm no goddamn fool, either."[36]

A major objective of the business community was to avoid any social and economic dislocation that impeded the normal functioning of business. Thus, pressured by a growing black activism, businesses often engaged in civil rights activities—sometimes substantial, sometimes token—designed to maintain social cohesion. One example of this process occurred in Rochester in 1966, when a local activist group called FIGHT demanded that the Kodak company hire 600 hard-core unemployed. When Kodak refused, FIGHT responded by inviting Stokely Carmichael to Rochester. Fearing an outbreak of racial hostilities, religious and business leaders in the city organized Rochester Jobs, Inc., with the goal of training and finding employment for 1,500 of Rochester's unemployed.

The most serious disruptions of the 1960s—the urban race riots—led to the creation of the National Alliance of Businessmen and the Urban Coalition to diffuse the nation's racial crisis by helping ghetto youngsters find employment. Many corporate leaders held sizable investments in the areas decimated by the riots. Henry Ford's reaction following the Detroit riot of 1967 was typical of many of these individuals: "That was pretty close to home."[37] Both the National Advisory Commission on Civil Disorders (Kerner Commission) and the president of the National Association of Manufacturers listed the absence of job opportunities as a major catalyst of the urban disturbances.

The foregoing does not imply that business leaders actively embraced the civil rights movement. On the contrary, employers and unions spent much time and energy circumventing equal opportunity laws. It can be argued, however, that many employers, accepting the inevitability of change and hoping to ameliorate racial conflict, offered at least token concessions to African Americans. By mid-1968, the *Wall Street Journal* observed: "Big business has been dragged kicking and screaming into the civil rights movement. But it is in."[38]

Following the implementation of Title VII and Executive Order 11246, civil rights groups initiated a major campaign against discrimination not only against employers, but against unions as well. Business and union discrimination often were intertwined and mutually reinforcing. For this reason, complaints and lawsuits directed against many companies also incorporated the local unions. The lawsuits against Crown-Zellerbach in Bogalusa named the pulp and paper unions as codefendants. Attacks on discriminatory practices in the steel industry included complaints against the United Steelworkers of America. Initial targets of NAACP complaints included locals of the International Chemical Workers Union, the International Brotherhood of Electrical Workers, and the International Association of Machinists.[39]

Not surprisingly, civil rights groups leveled charges against the building trades unions (BTUs), including Sheet Metal Workers, Electricians, and Plumbers. By the mid-1960s, the construction industry had become a primary target of African-American animosity, for several reasons. The volume of construction work expanded throughout this period, exceeding $100 billion by the end of the decade, while membership in the BTUs climbed steadily and approached 3 million persons. An increasing percentage of construction projects—nearly one-half—were financed with the assistance of government money. The use of public funds to finance projects that denied skilled positions to African Americans exacerbated the already tense situation between minority workers and the BTUs. In addition, African Americans coveted skilled construction jobs because wage rates were considerably higher than those in the manufacturing fields that historically employed nonwhite workers.

Construction projects were concentrated in metropolitan centers that, in the wake of "white flight," housed a steadily growing nonwhite population. Between 1950 and 1967, for example, the African-American population of Newark increased from 17 percent to 49 percent of the total; in Chicago, from 14 percent to 30 percent; and in Philadelphia, from 18 percent to 33 percent. Because construction projects were so visible in minority neighborhoods, they became obvious as well as accessible targets for job demonstrations. Compounding African-American frustration at the inability to secure skilled construction jobs was the presence of many African-American unskilled and semiskilled laborers within the industry who could not penetrate the skilled crafts. Finally, the entry age for apprenticeship programs, usually 18-25 years of age, made these programs attractive among African-American youths as a possible remedy for unemployment, which registered 25 percent during the prosperous 1960s.[40]

The first Justice Department Title VII action against a labor union evolved from complaints by African Americans against the Jefferson National Expansion Memorial project, better known as the Gateway Arch, in St. Louis. Responding to the absence of skilled African-American workers from a project funded primarily by state and federal money, the NAACP and other civil rights groups submitted complaints to the OFCC. Under OFCC pressure, one contractor, the Hoel-Steffen Construction Company, subcontracted with the E. Smith Plumbing Company, an African-American organization. E. Smith was associated with the independent Congress of Industrial Unions, rather than with the AFL-CIO (of 1,200 AFL-CIO plumbers in St. Louis, none was African-American.) When the African-American plumbers arrived at the site on Friday, January 7, 1966, white workers immediately walked off the job. Throughout the ensuing weeks, whites boycotted the project, maintaining that the critical issue was AFL-CIO membership, and not race. Following renewed NAACP complaints, OFCC Chairman Edward Sylvester, Jr., appealed to the Justice Department to take "appropriate action" against the unions.[41]

In February, the Justice Department responded by initiating a "707 suit" against several St. Louis BTUs, including the Plumbers, the Pipefitters, and the Electrical Workers. That same month, the Justice Department secured a temporary restraining order from the U.S. District Court, which declared the walk-out to be a secondary boycott and therefore in violation of Taft-

Hartley. The white workers reluctantly returned to their jobs, and the walk-out ended. Unfortunately, this proved to be a pyrrhic victory for black workers, as few ultimately gained membership in the BTUs.[42]

Similar scenes took place in other cities, including Philadelphia, Cleveland, and New York. In New York in 1964, for example, members of Plumbers Local #2—George Meany's home local—walked off their jobs to protest the introduction of four nonunion plumbers, three Puerto Ricans and one African American, to a construction site in the Bronx. Although the union—and Meany—insisted that union membership, and not race, was the pivotal issue, newspeople investigating the site reported "racial epithets and profanity" by some union members. The two sides eventually reached an agreement that permitted the four minority plumbers and other minority candidates recruited by the Civil Rights Commission to take the journeyman's exam, and work resumed.[43]

Beginning in 1967, the federal government, encouraged by civil rights organizations, abandoned this piecemeal approach to discrimination within the construction trades and instituted several "special area plans" that applied to publicly assisted construction projects throughout given metropolitan areas. The first such plan—the Cleveland Plan—evolved from a class action suit initiated by two African-American workers with the assistance of the Columbus NAACP against Governor James Rhodes and the State of Ohio. The city of Cleveland was in a state of turmoil by 1967. Demographically, the African-American proportion of the city's population had more than doubled from 16 percent to 34 percent in less than twenty years, raising racial tensions. Such activities as the 1963 Municipal Mall protests and the busing of African-American schoolchildren into the Italian Murray Hill neighborhoodexacerbated the city's already tense racial situation. In 1966, the Civil Rights Commission conducted hearings on civil rights violations in Cleveland, focusing, among other areas, on the construction industry. Later that year, tensions finally erupted, catapulting the city into "the year's most severe racial rioting," in which four people were killed and fifty wounded.[44] The following year, Cleveland elected its first African-American mayor, Carl Stokes, although he received only 20 percent of the white vote.

Racial discontent spread to other parts of the state, producing, among other results, a class action suit against the state involving the construction of the Medical Basic Sciences Building at Ohio State University. The plaintiffs, William Ethridge and Jerome Welch, charged the construction unions with systematically excluding African-American workers. Because the union hiring halls supplied *all* of the skilled labor to the site, African-

American workers could not participate in the Ohio State project. Judge Joseph Kinneary, in a decision known as *Ethridge v. Rhodes*, agreed with Ethridge and Welch and prohibited the state from awarding contracts to any construction firm or union guilty of discrimination.

Rather than accept a vague pledge of nondiscrimination, the court devised a compliance system reminiscent of the PWA housing projects of the 1930s, involving "manning tables." Construction contractors routinely calculated "manning tables," which projected employment needs at various stages of construction. NAACP representatives recommended that contractors expand these tables to include a "social specification" detailing the proportion of minority workers to be employed in each phase of the operation. Kinneary accepted this proposal and established minority hiring targets of approximately 20 percent for all skilled jobs.

Meanwhile, African-American protests and NAACP complaints and lawsuits against construction projects in Cleveland continued. Seeking to defuse these conflicts, Secretary of Labor Wirtz met with NAACP Labor Secretary Herbert Hill, who proposed the extension of the *Ethridge* ruling to Cleveland job sites. Wirtz concurred, and he ordered the Ohio State arrangement to be expanded to include all government-assisted construction in the Cleveland area. The Cleveland Plan required all bidders who were awarded contracts to assure minority representation in all occupational categories. The federal government actually suspended over $80 million in construction money later that year until recalcitrant contractors agreed to hire African-American workers.

The Cleveland Plan survived a legal challenge two years later growing out of a construction project at Cuyahoga Community College. Reliance Mechanical Contractors, Inc., submitted the lowest contractual bid but was rejected in favor of the second-lowest bidder because Reliance could not assure minority participation in every sector of the project. Reliance challenged this action in court, arguing that the affirmative action obligations under the Cleveland Plan amounted to hiring quotas. The Supreme Court of Ohio, in July 1969, rejected this contention, maintaining that a distinction existed between flexible hiring goals, which were legal, and inflexible quotas, which would violate Title VII. Legitimized by this decision, the Cleveland Plan emerged as one of the more successful government affirmative action programs of the 1960s and 1970s.[45]

The federal government subsequently introduced a similar plan in Philadelphia. Like Cleveland, Philadelphia had experienced construction demonstrations since 1963, but African Americans had made only token incursions into the skilled crafts. In October 1967, officials of the

Philadelphia OFCC and other federal agencies developed the Philadelphia Plan, which required employers, after receiving a government contract, to develop a viable affirmative action program, assuring minority participation on their projects. The OFCC originally did not require Cleveland-style manning tables, but it later mandated their use.

As in Cleveland, the BTUs were outraged. While construction workers organized public protests, the unions complained to Congress regarding this new "quota" system. Complaints reached U.S. Comptroller General Elmer Staats, whose authority included determining the legality of financial transactions of the federal government. In November 1968, Staats ruled the Philadelphia Plan to be in violation of federal law. According to Staats, the government's failure to provide prospective contractors with specific affirmative action standards *prior* to the awarding of contracts imposed unfair obligations on contractors after their bids were accepted. In Staats's own words: "Until provision is made for informing bidders of definite minimum requirements to be met by the bidder's program and any other standards or criteria by which the acceptability of any such program would be judged," all contracts were to be awarded to the lowest bidder, affirmative action notwithstanding. This ruling not only terminated the Philadelphia Plan, but it also prevented other cities from establishing similar programs.[46]

Similar integration efforts in San Francisco were also unsuccessful. The most critical construction project undertaken in that city during the 1960s was Bay Area Rapid Transit (BART). Complaints by African Americans of being excluded from skilled jobs on that project were supported by an investigation by the Civil Rights Commission, which revealed a black participation rate of less than 1 percent among several BTUs. The federal government subsequently suspended $13 million in payments to BART pending the institution of a citywide affirmative action agreement. Early in 1967 the OFCC developed a set of guidelines for BART contractors, which included job training for minority youths and greater dissemination of information regarding affirmative action requirements to unions and subcontractors. These stipulations were vague and were laxly enforced and therefore accomplished little.[47]

Despite their limited success, the special area plans constituted a significant phase in the evolution of antidiscrimination/affirmative action enforcement. By instituting citywide plans, the federal government acknowledged the need for concrete, large-scale remedies to the pervasive problem of discrimination within the construction industry. After a disappointing beginning during the 1960s, area wide plans became a staple of federal antidiscrimination efforts during the 1970s, as we shall see in the later chapters.

The Cleveland Plan also illustrated an increasing acceptance of numerical solutions to discrimination. African-American jobs protests since the 1960s, especially in construction, had incorporated demands for specific hiring targets, indicating that civil rights activists had rejected gradualism in favor of immediate gains. This transition reflected disillusionment with the slow rate of racial progress prior to the 1960s. Sociologists Leonard Broom and Norval Glenn, for example, estimated that, based on the trends of the 1950s, the "natural" equalizing of black-white median family income would occur in the year 2410! Blacks would also require several centuries to achieve proportional representation in such professions as law and sales. Within the construction industry, the number of black apprentices had increased from 2,190 in 1950 to 2,191 in 1960.[48] By the 1960s, African Americans exhibited little inclination to wait for their "fair share" of American wealth, and they argued that employers and unions would continue to evade affirmative action obligations in the absence of government pressure.

Significantly, by 1967 the federal government had begun to share these sentiments. A district court approved the "social specifications" of the *Ethridge* proposal, and the Department of Labor approved similar arrangements in the special area plans. By the late 1960s, then, liberals had begun to question their previous espousal of simple nondiscrimination. This process accelerated in the 1970s, straining the New Deal liberal coalition and transforming the nature of the civil rights debate.

Special area plans represented one strategy for integrating the BTUs. Another policy initiated primarily by nongovernment groups was to increase the participation of African-American youths in union apprenticeship programs. Pioneering this endeavor was the Workers' Defense League (WDL). Comprised primarily of young African-American males, including Ernest Green of the "Little Rock Nine," the WDL offered "cram courses" for apprenticeship entry exams and provided such services as medical exams and loans for tools and for apprenticeship application fees. Although inaugurated during 1963-64, this program received little publicity until 1965, when a confrontation with Sheet Metal Workers Local 28 of New York City propelled it into the public eye. In January of that year, Local 28 administered its apprenticeship test, on which African Americans performed poorly. The WDL then instituted an intensive program to prepare its pupils for a subsequent exam in November. On that second test, WDL tutees demonstrated a marked improvement, accumulating scores comparable to white testees. On another exam conducted on November 12, 1966, WDL applicants posted nine of the top ten scores and 75 percent of the top sixty-five scores. Local 28 refused to accept these results, accusing the WDL of preparing their pupils through "some nefarious means."[49] The State Commission on Human Rights responded to the union's actions by initiating a lawsuit on behalf of the WDL pupils, with the NAACP filing a brief of *amicus curiae*. Early in 1967 the New York State Supreme Court upheld the validity of the test results and ordered Local 28 to accept the African-American applicants.[50]

The WDL in fact had "doctored" its pupils by concentrating its sessions almost entirely on the types of questions asked on apprenticeship exams. As a general rule, the success of a WDL training program correlated directly with the league's ability to predict the contents of an apprenticeship exam. Despite the use of "test-busting" techniques and the antipathy of Local 28, however, union reaction to the WDL program was predominantly favorable. In 1967, the AFL-CIO Constitutional Convention officially endorsed the program, and in February 1968 the AFL-CIO Building and Construction Trades Department assured its cooperation. The rationale for this behavior is not difficult to determine. Rather than challenge union dominance of the apprenticeship system, the WDL confined its activities to enhancing its clients' attractiveness within the system. Confronted with the alternative of government-enforced affirmative action programs, organized labor opted for an arrangement that appeared to stimulate racial progress without threatening union control of entry into its ranks. The federal government added its approval when it initiated large-scale funding of these programs in 1967. By the following year, WDL-style programs had appeared in more than fifty cities.

The very features, however, that endeared this system to organized labor often operated to the detriment of the program. Although thousands of youngsters entered these programs, the drop-out rates of WDL pupils from apprenticeship programs was very high, and those who did complete their apprenticeship received no guarantees of job referrals or union membership. Moreover, union sponsorship evolved into union dominance as the AFL-CIO "took tacit control of the WDL program."[51] The result was the Apprenticeship Outreach Program, supervised by the AFL-CIO and funded largely by the Labor Department, which brought thousands of youths into apprenticeship programs but had a limited effect on the racial composition of the BTUs.[52]

The antidiscrimination activities of civil rights activists during the 1960s further strained the precarious alliance between African Americans and organized labor. Adhering to the traditional views of economic opportunity, white workers often considered blacks to be responsible for their own subordinate position. As one steelworker explained: "Everything you read now says the Negro is treated unfairly in jobs and housing. I don't think it's that bad. You can only get ahead by hard work, and if the Negro works hard, he'll do all right like anyone else." Their inability to discern the racist underpinnings of U.S. society left many white workers perplexed as to the motivations behind the growing black militancy in the United States. "I know a lot of older Negroes, and they don't cause trouble. It is the young ones that are in the riots that worry me. They want everything too fast, and they don't care who gets hurt. Some of them are Commies."[53] Whites generally considered blacks to be inferior workers, and resented what they regarded as the "special privileges" accorded minority workers.[54]

Not surprisingly, such sentiments were especially characteristic of the construction industry. The anxiety of job competition combined with racial animus to produce a volatile situation. Illustrative of these sentiments was the reaction of a white construction worker to a black official during the 1964 New York City plumbers' walkout: "I want a crack at his job right now just like they want to take mine."[55]

Underscoring this racial hostility was the threatened loss of control over the construction profession that the civil rights movement represented. A study by the New York City Commission on Human Rights concluded: "The unions consider control of membership admission and job control to be their own private domain. They resist any attempt to change the status quo."[56] Under duress, union leadership acquiesced to certain changes, but only within the established framework. Early in 1968, C.T. Haggerty, President of the AFL-CIO Building and Construction Trades Council, informed Secretary of Labor Wirtz of the affirmative action procedures that his unions considered acceptable. The list included greater dissemination of job and apprenticeship information, support for apprenticeship outreach programs, minority recruitment, and cooperation with "appropriate organizations directly representative of minority groups."[57] Conspicuously missing were any references to hiring targets or government-sponsored affirmative action programs. Yet many rank-and-file workers would not accept even these minimal concessions. As one construction worker explained: "Animals don't mix, why should people have to?"[58] White construction workers often complained that the allegedly inferior skills of black workers constituted a safety hazard to coworkers. These problems continued throughout the Johnson and Nixon presidencies.[59]

Often exasperated by the bureaucratic machinations of government fair employment agencies, African-American activists increasingly turned to the courts for enforcement of equal employment opportunity laws. John Kennedy had characterized the Civil Rights Act as a device for transferring the black revolution from the streets to the courts; by the mid-1960s, the legal revolution had begun to emerge. Reliance on the courts was not a novel strategy for African Americans. The NAACP had employed litigation as a weapon against segregation since the organization's inception and had achieved concrete results by the 1930s. During that decade, federal courts upheld the right of African Americans to picket stores that practiced discrimination, and, in the *Murray* and *Gaines* decisions, ordered the integration of state university law schools. The latter decisions served as precursors for *Brown v. Board of Education* in 1954. In a 1960 decision, *Boynton v. Commonwealth of Virginia*, the Supreme Court ordered the integration of all interstate transportation facilities; it was to test compliance with this decision that CORE inaugurated the Freedom Rides of 1961.[60]

The mass action movement of the late 1950s augmented, rather than replaced, the legal component of the civil rights struggle. Lawyers accompanied civil rights activists on protest marches and defended protestors threatened with fines and/or imprisonment. The refusal of southern lawyers to represent civil rights figures led to an influx of northern lawyers and law students into the South. The 1960s, moreover, witnessed the rise of public service law. Prompted by the enactment of Great Society legislation, lawyers, usually young and idealistic, adopted all the leading causes of the period, including the rights of welfare recipients and the poor, protection of the environment, defense of political radicals, and civil rights.[61]

In the midst of these legal developments, Congress passed the Civil Rights Act. The result was an avalanche of Title VII suits, often generated by the NAACP and the NAACP Legal Defense Fund. Significantly, many of these cases arose from unsuccessful EEOC conciliation attempts. Federal judges sometimes based their decisions on EEOC guidelines, thereby delegating to the commission a sort of quasilegislative authority. Among the crucial judicial decisions of the Johnson years were *Ethridge v. Rhodes* and the early Crown-Zellerbach cases. One of the most consequential decisions of the 1960s involved the question of class action suits. Rule 23(A) of the U.S. Federal Rules of Procedure provides that, when actions against a class of people are too numerous to file as individual grievances, "one or more, as will fairly insure the adequate representation of all," may file a class action suit on behalf of the entire group.[62] In *Hall v. Werthan Bag Company*—a suit that arose from an NAACP complaint and was filed with the assistance of the NAACP Legal Defense Fund—a U.S. district court ruled that Title VII authorized class actions, declaring: "Racial discrimination is by definition a class discrimination." Since 1966, most landmark job discrimination cases have been class action suits.[63]

The most critical affirmative action case to be resolved during the Johnson years was *Quarles v. Philip Morris* in 1968. Philip Morris in Virginia historically had adopted all of the Jim Crow practices characteristic of the tobacco industry, including segregated locals, "black" versus "white" departments, and unequal pay for equal work. Although the company, under government pressure, abolished these practices during the 1960s, it retained the policy of *departmental* seniority, whereby an individual transferring from one department to another sacrificed all accumulated seniority. When an African-American employee named Douglas Quarles transferred from the formerly all-black prefabrication department to the formerly all-white warehouse department, he was informed of the company's seniority arrangement. Quarles, however, refused to surrender his seniority status, and he appealed to the EEOC. When the commission was unable to achieve an agreement, Quarles filed a class action suit against Philip Morris and Local 203 of the Tobacco Workers International Union. Supporting Quarles was the NAACP Legal Defense Fund, which received the assistance of "a task force of legal scholars" from prominent universities, as well as the EEOC, which filed a brief of *amicus curiae*.[64]

In a landmark decision, a U.S. District Court ordered the company's seniority procedures modified so as not to penalize workers formerly restricted to segregated departments. Although departmental seniority was not in itself discriminatory, the court ruled, it had the effect of perpetuating *past* discrimination, and it therefore violated Title VII. In its most famous dictum, the court maintained: "It is apparent that Congress did not intend to freeze an entire generation of Negro employees into discriminatory patterns that existed before the Act."[65]

The significance of the *Quarles* decision lay in its broad interpretation of Title VII. The court's language rejected the argument that Title VII authorized nothing beyond simple nondiscrimination. The *Quarles* decision also indicated the degree to which judicial thought regarding job discrimination had changed in the course of the decade. In a 1959 case involving the Armco Steel Corporation and the United Steelworkers of America, the U.S. Court of Appeals conceded that the plant's departmental transfer provisions adversely affected African-American workers. Nevertheless, it ruled that: "This is a product of the past. We cannot turn back the clock."[66] In the *Quarles* decision, the Court, if not "turning back the clock," at least extended Title VII prohibitions to all actions that reinforced the subordinate status of African-American workers arising from past discrimination. By the late 1960s and into the 1970s, federal courts increasingly assumed the authority to modify or abolish such time-honored business traditions as seniority, hiring, and testing if they perpetuated previous injustices.[67]

While blacks turned to the courts for relief, the Johnson Administration took certain actions after 1965 to contribute to equal employment opportunity, including the expansion and clarification of Executive Order 11246. In October 1967, Johnson issued Executive Order 11375, which extended the affirmative action stipulations of Executive Order 11246 to include sex discrimination. The Labor Department attempted to reduce some of the confusion regarding affirmative action obligations of federal contractors by issuing a more concrete set of guidelines. The new regulations, effective July 1, 1968, required every employer with more than fifty employees and a contract in excess of $50,000 to submit a "written affirmative action compliance program" with goals and timetables for minority hiring, to be updated annually.[68] Although these regulations were more specific than the vague language of Executive Order 11246, according to one study, "the concept of 'affirmative action' remained fuzzy." Not surprisingly, some contractors equated the new regulations with imposed quotas.[69]

The proliferation of Great Society programs also provided the administration with an opportunity to expand equal employment procedures. The Federal-Aid Highway Act of August 1968 contained an equal opportunity clause; the Nixon administration later directed the Federal Highway Administration to establish a training program for minority workers. The Model Cities program, established in 1966, awarded preference to areas of "concentratedunemployment or underemployment," including minority neighborhoods such as Northern Philadelphia, the South Bronx, and Roxbury-Dorchester in Boston. Model Cities contracts required "maximum opportunities for employing residents of the area in all phases of the program."[70] The administration perceived Model Cities as a vehicle, not only to rebuild cities, but to increase the volume of construction work, thereby creating opportunities for minorities without displacing white workers. Model Cities was administered under the auspices of Secretary of Housing and Urban Development Robert Weaver, creator of the PWA minority hiring program of the 1930s. As with Executive Order 11246, however, the equal opportunity provisions of the Model Cities program remained vague, leaving each locality to interpret them according to its own circumstances. As a result, according to historian James Patterson, local government "rarely paid more than lip service to the ideal of maximum feasible participation." One exception to this rule was New York City, which required the introduction of minority apprentices to Model Cities programs.[71]

The nondiscrimination and affirmative action efforts of the Johnson administration clearly exceeded those of its predecessors. As with previous administrations, however, their actual effect was limited and inadequate. The predominant federal equal employment agency, the EEOC, remained understaffed, poorly financed, and overburdened. During the period 1965-68, combined funding for the EEOC, OFCC, and the Civil Rights Division of the Justice Department totaled only $38 million. Although created to oversee Title VII compliance on a nationwide basis, at no point during the Johnson years did the EEOC's total staff exceed 400.

The administration's neglect of the commission impeded effective settlement of job discrimination charges. A 1970 study by the Civil Rights Commission revealed that the commission's rate of successful conciliations was less than 50 percent. Moreover, those cases that the EEOC *did* resolve usually required between one and two years to complete. This inordinate amount of time, juxtaposed with the poor chances of successful resolution and fears of retaliation by employers and union officials, dissuaded many victims of discrimination from submitting complaints. One early study of the Title VII compliance process concluded that EEOC activities benefitted 8,500 workers (approximately 70 percent African-American) in Fiscal Year 1967 and 28,000 workers in Fiscal Year 1968. These numbers reflected those workers who benefitted *directly* from EEOC actions; many others undoubtedly profited from changes initiated by employers to avoid government intervention. Nevertheless, in light of the millions of African-American workers suffering from job discrimination, these numbers do not represent large-scale change within the nation's work force.

Another major obstacle hindering the EEOC was the commission's lack of enforcement powers. As previously noted, the final version of Title VII deprived the EEOC of the power to issue cease-and-desist orders. The administration was unable to persuade Congress to restore this power. In 1966, the House of Representatives approved the Roosevelt-Hawkins bill, which invested the commission with cease-and-desist powers, but the bill died in the Senate. Further attempts to fortify the EEOC were equally fruitless.

Compounding all these deficiencies was a debilitating lack of leadership. In the brief period from July 1965 until the end of Johnson's presidency, the EEOC had three chairmen. Franklin Roosevelt, Jr., the original chairman, lasted only until May 1966. The commission then struggled without a permanent chairman until September, when Johnson appointed Stephen Shulman. Shulman's brief tenure expired in July 1967; one month later, Clifford L. Alexander, Jr., former director of the Harlem Youth Project and Johnson's deputy special counsel for civil rights, assumed the position. This high turnover rate characterized EEOC offices at all levels and precluded any sense of continuity within the agency. The inadequacy of funding, staffing, and leadership within the EEOC provided evidence of the low priority accorded the commission by the administration.[72]

The OFCC likewise experienced funding and manpower problems. Like the EEOC, the OFCC lacked an adequate staff to review the volume of complaints it received. Unlike the EEOC, however, the OFCC possessed substantial enforcement powers, but it refused to exert them. Although authorized to sever funds from any contractor who engaged in discriminatory behavior, the OFCC, from the beginning, opted for a policy of voluntary compliance. Although it threatened several companies, it did not debar a single contractor until May 1968. OFCC reliance on voluntary compliance, according to the NAACP, "has meant the administrative nullification of the Executive Order." Finally, the lack of cooperation and coordination between the OFCC and EEOC often led to a duplication of efforts, thereby wasting valuable and scarce resources.[73]

The Justice Department also accumulated an unimpressive record in the field of job discrimination. Title VII empowered the department to file 707 suits in cases of pervasive discrimination; two years after Title VII became operative, five such suits had been initiated. Reflecting the administration's priorities, the Civil Rights Division of the Justice Department concentrated on other issues, especially voting rights, and relegated job discrimination to a lower status. Thus, the onus of initiating Title VII litigation lay primarily with the NAACP Legal Defense Fund. The situation improved, however, with the appointment of Ramsey Clark as attorney general in 1967. Clark refocused much of the Justice Department's energies toward economic discrimination, inaugurating twenty-three suits during Fiscal Year 1968.[74]

Other government programs designed to increase minority employment also met with limited success. The shortcomings of the pre-apprenticeship programs and Model Cities have already been explored. Likewise, programs established under the Manpower Development and Training Act of 1962, while assisting some minority youths, failed to achieve the lofty expectations that surrounded their creation. MDTA trainees generally did *not* represent the least-educated or hard-core unemployed among the African-American community, and they often received training for "dead-end" jobs.[75]

An analysis of employment data during the late 1960s offers some insight into the limited progress achieved by African Americans during this period. By 1969, more African Americans worked in "white-collar, craftsmen or operative occupations" than in "laborer or service jobs," a turnabout from 1960.[76] Nonwhite unemployment declined from 12.4 percent in 1961 to 6.7 percent in 1968. The percentage of nonwhite families with annual incomes exceeding $8,000 had doubled since the beginning of the decade. Much of this improvement resulted from the economic expansion of the decade—African Americans received nearly 10 percent of the 13 million jobs created during the 1960s—although antidiscrimination activities also contributed. The fact that younger African Americans benefitted the most from this progress provided some cause for optimism.

Observed from a different perspective, however, the picture remained bleak. In 1968, 35 percent of black families—as opposed to 10 percent of whites—resided below the poverty level. The black unemployment rate remained twice that of whites, and black median family income was only 60 percent of white income. Unemployment among black teenagers reached 25 percent. In 1969, 11 percent of black men and 12 percent of black women were employed in "professional, technical, and managerial" positions; for whites, the respective numbers were 29 percent and 19 percent.[77] Blacks were far more likely to be employed as nonfarm laborers and private household employees than whites. In the construction trades, despite years of protest, blacks continued to be excluded from the skilled crafts. A study of the New York State construction industry published in 1969, for example, found no increase in African-American and Puerto Rican participation during the course of the decade. In 1969, the Labor Department revealed that the African-American participation rate in seven Philadelphia BTUs was below 2 percent, although African Americans constituted one-third of the city's population. Blacks, then, exhibited little progress *relative to whites* during this period. Surveying the economy as a whole, *Business Week* reported in August 1967 that: "The profile of the Negro's job dilemma today is virtually unchanged from 1961."[78]

The limited affirmative action accomplishments of the Johnson administration were symptomatic in part of political undercurrents buffeting the nation at this time. The twin pressures of race relations and the Vietnam War steadily unraveled the overwhelming majority that Johnson had assembled in 1964. White liberals were distraught at the shift from integration and nondiscrimination to black nationalism and affirmative action. As historian William O'Neill asserted: "Northern liberals had staked a lot on integration, and many took its decline personally."[79] As previously noted, some liberals converted to the philosophy of affirmative action, precipitating a split in liberal ranks. Many working-class and middle-class whites who historically had sympathized little, if at all, with the black struggle for equality, reacted antagonistically to demands for open housing, school busing, and hiring goals. Perhaps more significantly, many whites who supported the initial goals of the civil rights movement became disillusioned with the movement's shifting objectives and strategies. Polls and studies indicated a steady liberalizing of racial attitudes, even among working-class whites, during the 1960s. Ironically, at the same time, the political schism between whites and blacks increased in many areas. By 1966, 52 percent of white respondents to a Gallup Poll criticized the administration for "moving too fast" in the field of civil rights. Two years later, 61 percent of those surveyed agreed that the black movement was "moving too fast."[80]

Significantly, the civil rights movement itself had been transformed from a southern crusade for voting rights and access to public accommodations to a "northern, proletarian" movement "concerned with 'gut' issues like who gets the money."[81] CORE demonstrations at the 1964 World's Fair, open housing marches in Milwaukee and Chicago, and the urban violence of 1965-68 elicited white responses ranging from "white flight" to the suburbs to violent counterdemonstrations. Felled by a rock during a protest march in Chicago in 1966, Martin Luther King declared: "I have seen many demonstrations in the South, but I have never seen anything so hostile and so hateful as I've seen here today."[82] Northern whites who had perceived the civil rights movement as an assault on the southern Jim Crow system responded very much like southern whites when their own schools, jobs, and neighborhoods became the targets of black protests. Studies indicated that whites exhibited greatest tolerance with regard to jobs (meaning pure nondiscrimination) and public accommodations and the greatest hostility toward job quotas and school busing, which directly affected economic security and family life.[83]

For their part, African Americans increasingly pursued an independent course by the late 1960s, disdaining what they considered the piecemeal and superficial reforms espoused by white liberals. By this time, African-American activists were far more concerned with achieving concrete progress than with placating their traditional liberal and labor allies. For example, CORE and SNCC dismissed their white volunteers, assuming an all-black identity. The Black Panthers armed themselves and engaged in violent confrontations with police. African-American steelworkers, organized into a caucus titled the Ad Hoc Committee, demanded an African-American vice presidency within the United Steelworkers of America. African-American teachers developed a black caucus with the American-Federation of Teachers in 1969. Militant young African Americans within the automobile industry, lacking seniority and fearing layoffs, organized independent unions such as DRUM (Dodge Revolutionary Union Movement) and FRUM (Ford) that conducted wildcat strikes, cooperated with the Black Panthers and radical white groups, and demanded the firing of UAW President Walter Reuther. One white auto worker vocalized the sentiments of many of his colleagues towards these developments: "They have taken over. You do your work, keep your mouth shut, and get the hell out when the whistle blows." Despite the civil rights progress of the 1960s, the dream of an integrated society appeared as remote in 1968 as it had a decade earlier.[84]

Another specter that haunted the civil rights movement and U.S. politics during the late 1960s was the Vietnam War. The administration's Vietnam policies alienated many liberals from the Democratic Party and consumed funds that African-American leaders considered vital for domestic reforms. Funding for the war in 1966 alone was three times the total allocation for the Office of Economic Opportunity, the nation's most prominent antipoverty agency, for the period 1965-1970. Although Johnson insisted that the nation could afford "guns and butter," Congress remained skeptical. By 1966, the Great Society legislative honeymoon was over, as Congress increasingly rejected or eviscerated White House proposals. The fear of federal deficits, which rose from $3.8 billion in 1966 to $25.2 billion in 1968, displaced social reform as the compelling force behind government activities. Among the major victims of the Vietnam War was the "Domestic Marshall Plan" envisioned by Whitney Young and other African-American leaders. The optimism of the early 1960s did not survive the grim realities of the ensuing years.[85]

The U.S. political system could no more ignore the nation's shifting political *zeitgeist* than it could Birmingham or the Freedom Rides earlier in the decade. Politicians began to campaign on "law and order" themes rather than on Great Society platforms. This posture benefited the Republican Party, which gained forty-seven seats in the House of Representatives, three in the Senate, and eight gubernatorial positions in the 1966 elections. Ronald Reagan capitalized on the Watts riot and the Berkeley demonstrations to depose Governor Pat Brown in California, and Lester Maddox was elected governor of Georgia. The myth of the "white backlash" has been greatly exaggerated, given that most of the new Republicans characterized themselves as "moderates." In the Maryland gubernatorial election, for example, Democratic candidate George P. Mahoney, who adopted the motto, "Your home is your castle - protect it!", was defeated by the more moderate Spiro Agnew, who captured the state's African-American vote.[86] Also, Massachusetts Republican Edward Brooke became the first African-American U.S. Senator of the twentieth century. Nevertheless, the elections illustrated a growing uneasiness among white voters concerning the nation's racial situation.[87]

Graphic evidence of these new attitudes was the failure of the president's civil rights initiatives in Congress after 1965. In 1966, the Senate refused to act on the Roosevelt-Hawkins bill to strengthen the EEOC after the bill had passed the House. That same year, Congress rejected an administration civil rights bill, primarily on account of its open housing provisions, which, unlike previous civil rights laws, affected the North more than the South. The only consequential civil rights bill to pass Congress after 1965 was the Civil Rights Act of 1968, enacted following the assassination of Martin Luther King in April of that year. This law incorporated open housing provisions, but it also expressly prohibited the transportation of firearms and ammunition and the use of any means of transportation or communication for the purpose of inciting violence. The Civil Rights Act of 1968 was as much a law-and-order statement as a civil rights bill, and it probably could not have passed Congress in any other form.[88]

Even the White House could not escape the nation's shifting political ethos. In August 1965, a White House Conference on Equal Employment Opportunity divided over the question of "colorblindness" versus "color-consciousness." Especially disruptive were the issues of seniority and the recall of laid-off workers. By 1966, the President had equated black rioters with the Ku Klux Klan, denounced "lawbreakers," and considered it necessary to remind the nation that "While there is a Negro minority of 10 percent in this country, there is a majority of 90 percent who are not Negroes."[89]

The issues of race, inflation, social disruption, and Vietnam converged in the election of 1968. The Republicans selected former vice president Richard Nixon as a "centrist" candidate over conservative Ronald Reagan and liberal Nelson Rockefeller. In the Democratic camp, Johnson's refusal to seek reelection and Robert Kennedy's assassination assured the nomination of Vice President Humphrey. Perhaps the most foreboding feature of the Democratic primary race was the impressive strength of George Wallace in northern urban blue-collar wards. The "Wallace factor" offered startling evidence of working-class hostility to the black and antiwar movements. In November, Nixon scored a narrow victory over Humphrey. Nixon benefited heavily from the white southern vote, capturing every southern state except Texas. Humphrey, meanwhile, received 85 percent of the African-American vote. Significantly, after his strong primary showings, Wallace received only 9 percent of the votes of "northern manual workers."[90] An intensive lobbying effort by the AFL-CIO leadership convinced many recalcitrant workers to return, at least temporarily, to the Democratic fold. Nixon's election in 1968, four years after Johnson's landslide victory, provided evidence that the labor-liberal-southern-civil rights coalition that had constituted the foundation of Democratic Party strength since the New Deal had begun to unravel.[91]

In conclusion, then, the Johnson years witnessed a major transformation in the civil rights movement in general and the struggle for economic opportunity in particular. Civil rights activists had won many of their immediate objectives, including the passage of major civil rights legislation, increased voting rights, and the abolition of the most blatant forms of social segregation. These developments, coupled with the assassinations of such grass-roots leaders as Martin Luther King, Jr., and Malcolm X, helped redirect the movement away from large-scale public protests and toward legal and governmental channels. At the same time, both civil rights groups and government agencies began to embrace a more expansive view of the types of measures needed to overcome the effects of centuries of discrimination. The next few chapters focus increasingly on the responses of the federal government to these various trends.

NOTES

1. Johnson quoted in *Public Papers of the Presidents:* Lyndon B. Johnson, Vol. 2, 1965 (Washington, DC: Government Printing Office, 1966), p. 636. For analysis of speech *see* Hugh Davis Graham, *The Civil Rights Era: Origins and Development of National Policy 1960-1972* (New York: Oxford University Press, 1990), pp. 174 & 511, note # 55; and Stephen Steinberg, *Turning Back: The Retreat from Racial Justice in American Thought and Policy* (Boston: Beacon Press, 1995), pp. 113-119.

2. U.S. Equal Employment Opportunity Commission, *The First Decade*, p. 13; Richard P. Nathan, *Jobs and Civil Rights* (Washington, DC: Government Printing Office, 1969), p. 18; Rowan, *Negro in Steel Industry*, p. 111; and Erbin Crowell, Jr., "EEOC's Image: Remedy for Job Discrimination?," *Civil Rights Digest* 1 (Spring, 1968): 29-30.

3. Quote from EEOC, *First Decade*, p. 13.

4. U.S. Commission on Civil Rights, *Federal Civil Rights Enforcement Efforts* (Washington, DC: Government Printing Office, 1970), pp. 317-18 & 376; U.S. EEOC, *First Annual Report FY 1966* (Washington, DC: EEOC, 1967), p. 17; Blumrosen, *Black Employment and the Law*, p. 85; EEOC, *First Decade*, p. 13; and Nathan, *Jobs and Civil Rights*, pp. 45-46 & 80-81.

5. *AFL-CIO News*, December 25, 1965, p. 8; Civil Rights Commission, *Federal Enforcement Efforts*, pp. 307ff.; EEOC, *First Annual Report*, p. 11; and Nathan, *Jobs and Civil Rights*, pp. 20 & 76-79.

6. Thompson Powers, ed., *Now Hear This! Equal Employment Opportunity: Compliance and Affirmative Action* (New York: National Association of Manufacturers, 1969), p. 24.

7. Executive Order 11246, 30 F.R. 12319; Hubbard, "Affirmative Action," pp. 113-118; Ruth P. Morgan, *The President and Black Civil Rights: Policy-Making by Executive Order* (New York: St. Martin's Press, 1970), pp. 49-50; Rowan, *Negro in Steel Industry*, p. 7; and *Washington Post*, September 25, 1965, pp. 1 & 7.

8. Executive Order 11246, Section 202(1).

9. Fletcher, *Silent Sell-Out*, p. 39.

10. Johnson quoted in *Presidential Papers*, Vol. 2, p. 787.

11. Quote from Executive Order 11246, Section 101. Also: Civil Rights Commission, *Federal Enforcement Efforts*, pp. 145-149 & 156ff.; Fletcher, *Sell-Out*, p. 46; Hubbard, "Affirmative Action," p. 118; *The New York*

Times, December 5, 1968, p. 79; and *Washington Post*, September 25, 1965, p. 7.

12. Statement of January 13, 1965, NAACP Files, U.S. Library of Congress, Group III, Series B, #362.

13. NAACP, *Annual Report for 1965* (Washington, DC: Government Printing Office, 1966), pp. 6 & 45-46; NAACP Legal Defense Fund, *Report '66* (Washington, DC: 1967), pp. 10-12; EEOC, *First Annual Report*, pp. 6-7; and *Weekly News Digest*, February 8, 1965, pp. 1-6.

14. NAACP *Annual Reports*, 1965-68; NAACP Legal Defense Fund, *Annual Reports*, 1966-68; and *Wall Street Journal*, October 13, 1965, p. 14.

15. EEOC, *First Annual Report*, pp. 8-10; *Weekly News Digest*, May 2, 1966, pp. 1-2; Blumrosen, *Black Employment and the Law*, pp. 329ff.; and Fletcher, *Sell-Out,* pp. 49-50.

16. "Not Discriminating Becomes Not Enough," *Business Week*, January 11, 1969, pp. 88-92.

17. Wirtz quoted from "Decision of the Secretary of Labor in the Matter of Allen-Bradley Company," OFCC Docket No. 101-68, in Powers, *Now Hear This*, p. 90.

18. Shultz quoted in *Wall Street Journal*, August 11, 1969, p. 6. Also: Powers, *Now Hear This*, pp. 89-92; Ruth G. Schaeffer, *Nondiscrimination in Employment: Changing Perspectives 1963-1972* (New York: The Conference Board, Inc., 1973), p. 11; *Milwaukee Journal*, September 25, 1968, p. 9; August 11, 1968, p. 1; August 14, 1968, p. 11; August 15, 1968, p. 1; August 16, 1968, p. 1; August 17, 1968, p. 11; August 20, 1968, p. 1; December 20, 1968, p. 1; December 21, 1968, p. 1; January 17, 1969, pp. 1 & 7; *Weekly News Digest,* June 3, 1968, p. 1; July 29, 1968, p. 1, August 18, 1969, p. 1; *Wall Street Journal*, August 11, 1969, p. 6; *The New York Times*, May 25, 1968, p. 70; August 11, 1968, p. 41; January 18, 1969, p. 16; "Cracking Down on Job Bias," *Business Week*, June 1, 1968, p. 34; "A 'Model Employer' Fights Back on Bias," *Business Week*, October 12, 1968, pp. 122-126; "Not Discriminating Becomes Not Enough," *Business Week*, January 11, 1969, pp. 88-92; and "Demonstrating Again at Allen-Bradley," *Business Week*, August 16, 1969, p. 44.

19. *The New York Times*, April 4, 1965, p. 55.

20. Quote from Meier and Rudwick, *CORE*, p, 347.

21. Northrup, *Negro in the Paper Industry*, p. 96.

22. *Crown-Zellerbach Corporation v. Wirtz* 281 F. Supp. 337; Vera Rony, "Bogalusa: The Economics of Tragedy," *Dissent* 13 (May-June, 1966): 235-239; *The New York Times*, January 6, 1965, p. 28; January 9,

1965, p. 13; Meier and Rudwick, *CORE*, pp. 346-347; and Northrup, *Negro in Paper Industry*, pp. 96-97.

23. Quote from Rony, "Bogalusa," p. 237.

24. McKeithen quoted in *The New York Times*, February 5, 1965, p. 17.

25. Quote from *The New York Times*, January 6, 1966, p. 11. Also: *The New York Times*, January 6, 1965, through January 6, 1966; *St. Louis Post Dispatch*, December 29, 1965, p. 4; Farmer, *Freedom - When?*, p. 20; Sobel, *Civil Rights*, pp. 352-353 & 407; Meier and Rudwick, *CORE*, pp. 346-350; Northrup, *Negro in Paper Industry*, pp. 96-98; Rony, "Bogalusa," pp. 234-241, and "Caught in the Civil Rights Crossfire," *Business Week*, August 7, 1965, pp. 102-106.

26. For court decisions, see *Hicks v. Crown Zellerbach Corporation* 319 F. Supp. 314 (1970); *Local 189, United Papermakers and Paperworkers, AFL-CIO v. U.S.* 416 F. 2d 980 (1969); *Oatis v. Crown Zellerbach Corporation* 398 F. 2d 496 (1968); and *Crown Zellerbach Corporation v. Wirtz* 281 F. Supp. 337 (1968). See also *Weekly News Digest*, April 4, 1968; Northrup, *Negro in Paper Industry*, pp. 98ff.; and Rony, "Bogalusa," pp. 241-242.

27. For drug industry, see F. Marion Fletcher, *The Negro in the Drug Manufacturing Industry*, The Racial Policies of American Industry Report #21 (Philadelphia: University of Pennsylvania Press, 1970), especially pp. 30-45. For Los Angeles, see U.S. Commission on Civil Rights, *Federal Enforcement Efforts*, pp. 365-366; and U.S. Equal Employment Opportunity Commission, *Hearings before the EEOC on Utilization of Minority and Women Workers in Certain Industries* (Washington, DC: EEOC, 1969). For New York City, see *Hearings before the U.S. EEOC on Discrimination in White-Collar Employment* (Washington, DC: EEOC, 1968); and Nathan, *Jobs*, pp. 28-29.

Other information from Press Releases, July 17, 1965; July 31, 1965; September 17, 1965; May 7, 1966; December 10, 1966; January 28, 1967; and May 29, 1967, NAACP Files, U.S. Library of Congress, Group III, Series B, #362; NAACP Legal Defense Fund, "The Quiet Revolution," *Report* for 1968, pp. 12-13; *AFL-CIO News*, September 3, 1966, p. 1; "Cracking Down on Job Bias," *Business Week*, June 1, 1968, pp. 34-38; U.S. EEOC, *Third Annual Report FY1968* (Washington, DC: EEOC, 1969), pp. 22ff.; *U.S. v. U.S. Steel Corporation* 371 F. Supp. 1045; and *U.S. v. Bethlehem Steel Corporation* 446 F. 2nd 652 (1971).

28. Quote from Matusow, *The Unraveling of America*, p. 209. Also: Matusow, *ibid.*, p. 210; *Cleveland Plain Dealer*, August 9, 1967, p. l; Bloom and Fletcher, *The Negro in Supermarket Industry*, pp. 118-129;

"Negros Go National with Demands for Jobs," *Business Week,* August 19, 1967, pp. 37-38; and "The Sit-In at A&P Was No Tea Party," *Business Week,* February 6, 1971, p. 21.

29. Quote from Vines, "The Impact of Title VII," p. 126.

30. Frances Reissman Cousens, *Public Civil Rights Agencies and Fair Employment: Promise v. Performance* (New York: Frederick A. Praeger, Publishers, 1969), pp. 43-44 & 58-61.

31. EEOC, *First Annual Report,* p. 8.

32. Cousens, *Public Civil Rights Agencies,* p. 55.

33. Vines, "The Impact of Title VII"; Nathan, *Jobs and Civil Rights,* p. 57; Cousens, *Public Civil Rights Agencies.*

34. Louis A. Ferman, *The Negro and Equal Employment Opportunities: A Review of Management Experiences in 20 Companies* (New York: Frederick A. Praeger, Publishers, 1968), p. 123.

35. Quote from *Wall Street Journal,* October 13, 1965, p. 1. Also: Gelber, *Black Men and Businessmen,* pp. 3-7; Ferman, *Equal Employment Opportunities,* p. 123; and *Weekly News Digest,* July 19, 1965, p. 5.

36. Quotes from Gelber, *Black Men and Businessmen,* p. 14; and Charles E. Silberman, "The Businessman and the Negro," *Fortune* 68 (September, 1963): 99.

37. Ford quoted from *Wall Street Journal,* June 14, 1968, p. 1.

38. Quote from *Wall Street Journal,* June 11, 1968, p. 1. Also: *Wall Street Journal,* June 11, 1968, p. 23; June 14, 1968, p. l; *Report of the National Advisory Committee on Civil Disorders* (New York, 1968), especially pp. 111 & 132ff.; Gelber, *Black Men and Businessmen,* especially p. 157; Silberman, "Businessman and Negro," especially pp. 97-99; and Ferman, *Equal Employment Opportunities.*

39. Press Release, September 17, 1965, NAACP Files, U.S. Library of Congress, Group III, Series B, #362; *Wall Street Journal,* October 13, 1965, p. 14; NAACP, *Annual Report 1966,* pp. 55-56; and *Hicks v. Crown Zellerbach* 319 F. Supp. 314.

40. *NAACP Annual Report 1966,* p. 55; U.S. Commission on Civil Rights, *The Challenge Ahead,* pp. 12-15; Dennis Derryck, *The Construction Industry: A Black Perspective* (Joint Center for Political Studies, 1972), pp. 2-5; Charles Edward Donegan, "The Philadelphia Plan: A Viable Means of Achieving Equal Opportunity in the Construction Industry or More Pie in the Sky?," *University of Kansas Law Review* 20 (Winter, 1972): 195; Daniel Quinn Mills, *Industrial Relations and Manpower in Construction* (Cambridge, MA: MIT Press, 1972), pp. 4-5; Strauss and Ingermann, "Public Policy and Discrimination in

Apprenticeship," pp. 300-301; U.S. Department of Labor, Bureau of Labor Statistics, *The Social and Economic Status of Negroes in the United States, 1969* (Washington, DC: Government Printing Office, 1969), pp. 5 & 30; and U.S. Department of Commerce, Bureau of the Census, *1972 Census of Construction Industries* (Washington, DC: Government Printing Office), Vol. 1, Part A, pp. 1-9. For cases against BTUs, see *The New York Times*, June 28, 1967, p. 21.

41. *St. Louis Post-Dispatch*, January 22, 1966, p. 1.

42. NAACP, *Annual Report 1966*, p. 55; *St. Louis Post Dispatch*, January-February, 1966; *Weekly News Digest*, January 31, 1966, pp. 1-2; February 28, 1966, p. 1; Civil Rights Commission, *Federal Enforcement Efforts*, p. 168.

43. Quote from *The New York Times*, May 2, 1964, p. 28. Also:*The New York Times*, May 1, 1964, pp. 1 & 22; May 2, 1964, p. 1; May 15, 1964, p. 1; May 19, 1964, p. 1; *AFL-CIO News*, May 23, 1964, p. 5; Testimony of Herbert Hill, NAACP Files, U.S. Library of Congress, Group III, Series B, #363; *Commonwealth of Pennsylvania et al. v. Local Union 542, International Union of Operating Engineers* 469 F. Supp. at 338-342; and *Hearings before the U.S. Commission on Civil Rights in Cleveland, Ohio* (Washington, DC: Government Printing Office, 1966), pp. 487-490.

For a thorough discussion of 1964 Plumbers walk-off, see Herbert Hill, "The New York City Terminal Market Controversy: A Case of Race, Labor, and Power," reprint from *Humanities in Society* 6 (Fall, 1983): 351-391.

44. Sobel, *Civil Rights*, p. 440.

45. For decision, see *Weiner v. Cuyahoga Community College District et al.* 249 N.E. 2d 907. Also: *Ethridge v. Rhodes* 268 F. Supp. 83 (1967); Herbert Hill interview and telephone conversation, December 9, 1984; Civil Rights Commission, Cleveland *Hearings*; Civil Rights Commission, *Federal Enforcement Efforts*, pp. 169-170; *The New York Times*, 1967: May 19, p. 25; June 2, p. 42; June 28, p. 21; July 3, p. 6; *Cleveland Plain Dealer*, 1967: February 23, p. 6; May 18, p. 6; June 12, p. 1; Lewis M. Steel, "A Second 17th of May Landmark Decision," *The Crisis* 74 (June, 1967): 259-263; "NAACP Launches Drive for Construction Jobs," *The Crisis* 74 (July, 1967): 303; James E. Jones, Jr., "The Bugaboo of Employment Quotas," *Wisconsin Law Review*, 1970, p. 346; Robert Kuttner, "Red and Green in Civil Rights," *Commonweal* 90 (September 5, 1969): 535; Earl M. Leiken, "Preferential Treatment in the Skilled Building Trades," *Cornell Law Review* 56 (November, 1970): 90-91; Jeffrey Hadden, et al., "The Making of the Negro Mayors, 1967," in *The Transformation of*

Activism, ed. August Meier (Trans-Action Books, 1970), pp. 93-110; Fletcher, *Sell-Out*, p. 64; and Derryck, *Construction Industry*, p. 18.

46. Staats quoted from James E. Remmert, "Executive Order 11246: Executive Encroachment," *American Bar Association Journal* 55 (November, 1969): 1037. Also: *Commonwealth of Pennsylvania* 469 F. Supp. at 342ff.; Herbert Hill, *Labor Union Control of Job Training*, Howard University Institute for Urban Affairs and Research, Vol. 2, No. 1 (Washington, DC: 1974), pp. 16-17; Fletcher, *Sell-Out*, pp. 64-66; Hubbard, "Affirmative Action," pp. 122-129; Donegan, "Philadelphia Plan," pp. 196-197, and testimony of Sam Ervin in *Congressional Record*, Vol. 115, Part 29 (Washington, DC: Government Printing Office, 1969), p. 39949.

47. *Hearings before the United States Commission on Civil Rights, San Francisco, California* (Washington, DC: Government Printing Office, 1967), especially p. 323; Civil Rights Commission, *Federal Enforcement Efforts*, p. 169; Jones, "Bugaboo," p. 345; and Thomas O'Hanlon, "The Case against the Unions," *Fortune* 77 (January, 1968): 190.

48. Statistics from Leonard Broom and Norval D. Glenn, "When Will America's Negroes Catch Up?," *New Society* 130 (March 25, 1965): 6; and U.S. Department of Labor, *Negroes in Apprenticeship*, p. 7. Also: Herbert Hill, "The New Judicial Perception of Employment Discrimination—Litigation of Title VII of the Civil Rights Act of 1964," *University of Colorado Law Review* 43 (March, 1972): 244.

49. Edward C. Pinkus, "The Workers' Defense League," in *Programs to Employ the Disadvantaged*, ed. Peter B. Doeringer (Upper Saddle River, NJ: Prentice Hall, Inc., 1969), pp. 183-184.

50. *Ibid.*, pp. 171-184; Civil Rights Commission, *Challenge Ahead*, p. 114; Brooks, *Toil and Trouble*, p. 260; Goulden, *Meany*, p. 408; and "Apprenticeship Test is Upheld," *The Crisis* 74 (March, 1967): 104.

51. Goulden, *Meany*, p. 409.

52. Civil Rights Commission, *Challenge Ahead*, p. 114; Hill, *Union Control of Job Training*, pp. 6-9, *AFL-CIO News*, February 17, 1968, p. 1; Goulden, *Meany*, p. 409; Pinkus, "Workers' Defense League," pp. 169 & 185ff. The Apprenticeship Outreach Program is discussed in more detail in Chapter 7.

53. Quotes from Ferman, *Equal Employment Opportunities*, pp. 97-98.

54. See Ferman, *Equal Opportunities*, especially pp. vi & 97ff.; and *Wall Street Journal*, December 3, 1970, p. 25.

55. *The New York Times* May 2, 1964, p. 1.

56. Quote from James Haughton, "The Role of the Board of Education in Perpetuating Racism in the Building Trades and Vice-Versa," in *Schools Against Children*, ed. Annette T. Rubenstein (New York: Monthly Review Press, 1970), p. 167.

57. *Weekly News Digest*, February 26, 1968, p. 1

58. *The New York Times*, May 2, 1964, p. 1.

59. *Ibid.*, pp. 1 & 28; *Wall Street Journal*, August 3, 1964, p. 1; Hill, *Union Control of Job Training*, pp. 33-35; Strauss and Ingermann, "Discrimination in Apprenticeship," pp. 302-303; and Donegan, "Philadelphia Plan," p. 199.

60. Sitkoff, *New Deal*, pp. 237-240; *Boynton v. Commonwealth of Virginia* 81 S Ct 182; Simba, "Neo-Concept of Equal Employment," p. 20; and Aryeh Neier, *Only Judgment: The Limits of Litigation in Social Change* (Middletown, CT: Wesleyan University Press, 1982), pp. 49-50.

61. Neier, *Only Judgement*, p. 5; Jerold S. Auerbach, *Unequal Justice* (New York: Oxford University Press, 1976, 1980), pp. 265 & 278ff.; and Robert Borosage, et al., "The New Public Interest Lawyers," *The Yale Law Journal* 79 (May, 1970): 1069-1152.

62. *Hall v. Werthan Bag Corporation* 251 F. Supp. 185.

63. Quote from *ibid.*, p. 186. Also: *Ibid.*, pp. 184ff.; Press Release, July 31, 1965, NAACP Files, U.S. Library of Congress, Group III, Series B, #362; William B. Gould, *Black Workers in White Unions* (Ithaca, NY: Columbia University Press, 1977), p. 40; Blunrosen, *Black Employment and the Law*, p. 85.

64. NAACP Legal Defense Fund, *Report 1967*, p. 10.

65. *Quarles v. Philip Morris, Inc.* 279 F. Supp. 516.

66. *Whitfield v. United Steelworkers of America* 263 F. 2d 551.

67. *Ibid.*, pp. 505ff. Also: NAACP Legal Defense Fund, *Report 1967*, p. 10; Alleyne, "Current Developments under Title VII," pp. 14-15; and Simba, "Equal Employment," pp. 273-276.

68. Hubbard, "Affirmative Action," p. 118.

69. Quotes from Remmert, "Executive Order 11246," p. 1037; and Schaeffer, *Nondiscrimination in Employment*, p. 11. Also: *Weekly News Digest*, June 3, 1968, p. 1; *U.S. Code of Federal Regulations*, Vol. 41, Chapter 60, Section 1.4 .

70. Quotes from *Weekly News Digest*, December 25, 1967.

71. Quote from James T. Patterson, *America's Struggle Against Poverty 1900-1980* (Cambridge, MA: Harvard University Press, 1981), p. 149. Also: Patterson, *ibid.*, pp. 148-149; James MacNamara Interview, April 12, 1984; *Wall Street Journal*, March 9, 1968, p. 4; *Weekly News*

Digest, December 25, 1967, pp. 1-5; "Crafts Ease Their Stand on Bias," *Business Week*, December 9, 1967, pp. 133-34; "Building for Peace in Construction," *Business Week*, March 16, 1968, p. 100.

Federal Highway information from U.S. Commission on Civil Rights, *From the Highways to the Skyways: A Study of Contract Compliance Programs of the Department of Transportation* (Washington, DC: Government Printing Office, 1973), pp. 12 & 20.

72. EEOC analysis from Civil Rights Commission, *Federal Enforcement Efforts*, pp. 269-366; National Advisory Committee on Civil Disorders, p. 419; Bureau of National Affairs, *The Equal Employment Opportunity Act of 1972* (Washington, DC: Bureau of National Affairs, 1973), p. 28; Oliver Lee E. Mbatia, "The Economic Impact of the 1964 Fair Employment Practices Act and Subsequent Executive Orders on Black Americans" (Ph.D. dissertation, Oregon State University, 1972), especially pp. 102ff,; James E. Jones, Jr., "Equal Employment Opportunities: The Promises of the '60s—The Reality of the '70s," *The Black Law Journal* 2 (Spring, 1972): 8; "Job-Rights Unit Asks New Power," *U.S. News and World Report* 59 (August 2, 1965): 63; Nathan, *Jobs and Civil Rights*, pp. 18 & 45-46, and Cousens, *Fair Employment*, p. 14.

73. Quote from NAACP, *Annual Report 1967*, p. 98. Also: Civil Rights Commission, *Federal Enforcement Efforts*, pp. 156ff.; Advisory Committee on Civil Disorders, p. 419; and Powers, *Now Hear This*, pp. 3-27,

74. *The New York Times*, August 13, 1968, p, 21; Civil Rights Commission, *Federal Enforcement Efforts*, pp. 370ff.; NAACP Legal Defense Fund, *Report 1966*, p. 12; Nathan, *Jobs and Civil Rights*, pp. 79-81; and Allan Wolk, *The Presidency and Black Civil Rights* (Philadelphia: Fairleigh Dickinson University Press, 1971), p. 77.

75. Quote from Advisory Committee on Civil Disorders, p. 416. Also: James L. Sundquist, *Politics and Policy* (Washington, DC: 1968), pp. 131-132; and Patterson, *Poverty*, p. 127. MDTA discussed in Chapter 3.

76. Bureau of Labor Statistics, *Profile*, p. 40.

77. *Ibid.*, p. 42.

78. Quote from "For Negroes, The Pie Cuts Too Thin," *Business Week*, August 5, 1967, p. 26. Also: Bureau of Labor Statistics, *Profile*; Adam Walinsky et al, *Official Lawlessness in New York State Construction Employment, Government Inaction, and the $275 Million Annual Cost*, Published 1969, p. 1; Kuttner, "Red and Green," p. 535; Civil Rights Commission, *Last Hired*, p. 81; U.S. Department of Labor, Bureau of Labor Statistics, *Handbook of Labor Statistics* (Washington, DC: Government Printing Office, 1983), p. 63; Bernard E. Anderson and Phyllis A. Wallace,

"Public Policy and Black Economic Progress: A Review of the Evidence," *American Economic Review* 65 (May, 1975): 47-48; Claire C. Hodge, "The Negro Job Situation: Has It Improved?" *Monthly Labor Review* 92 (January, 1969): 20-28; Lloyd Hogan and Harry Harris, "The Occupational-Industrial Structure of Black Employment in the United States," *The Review of Black Political Economy* 6 (Fall, 1975): 8-28; and Albert W. Niemi, Jr., "The Impact of Recent Civil Rights Laws: Relational Improvement in Occupational Structure, Earnings and Income by Nonwhites, 1960-1970," *The American Journal of Economics and Sociology* 33 (April, 1974): 138-39.

79. William O'Neill, *Coming Apart* (New York: Quadrangle Books, 1971), p. 194.

80. Sar A. Levitan, ed., *Blue-Collar Workers: A Symposium on Middle America* (New York: McGraw-Hill Book Company, 1971), p. 52.

81. O'Neill, *Coming Apart*, p. 166.

82. King quoted in *Chicago Tribune*, August 6, 1966, p. 1.

83. For "reverse discrimination" and "white backlash" see: "Labor Drive for LBJ Hits Own 'Backlash'," *Business Week*, September 12, 1964, pp. 49-54; "Now It's Whites Who Are Claiming Their Job Rights," *U.S. News and World Report* 60 (May 16, 1966): 86ff.; O'Neill, *Coming Apart*, pp. 165-194; and Matusow, *Unraveling of America*, p. 214.

World's Fair demonstrations from *The New York Times*, 1964: April 13, p. 19; April 23, p. 1; April 24, p. 19. King in Chicago from Lewis, *King*, Chapter 11; *Chicago Tribune*, 1966: January 25, p. 3; January 26, p. 8; February 24, p. 3; July 11, p. 1; August 6, p. 1; September 5, p. 1; and Matusow, p. 204. Studies cited were Levitan, *Blue-Collar Workers*, especially pp. 139-140; and Judith Caditz, *White Liberals in Transition* (New York: Spectrum Publications, Inc., 1976), especially pp. 61-85.

84. For changes in CORE, see later chapters of Meier and Rudwick, *CORE*. Quote from B.J. Widdick, "Black City, Black Unions?" in *The World of the Blue-Collar Worker*, ed. Irving Howe (New York: Quadrangle Books, 1972), p. 127.

Labor issues from Brooks, *Toil and Trouble*, pp. 327-341; Brooks, "Black Upsurge in the Unions," *Dissent* (March-April, 1970): 124-134; Brooks, "DRUM Beats in Detroit," *Dissent* (January-February 1970): 16-25; and Fujita, *Black Workers' Struggles*, pp. 79ff.

85. James Tobin, "The Political Economy of the 1960s," in Warner, ed., *New Human Rights*, pp. 36, 41, & 50; Congressional Quarterly Service, *Politics in America*, pp. 64-65; Gerard R. Gill, *Meanness Mania*

(Washington, DC: Howard University Press, 1980), p. xii; Heath, *Decade of Disillusionment*, p. 261; and O'Neill, *Coming Apart*, p, 187.

86. Mahoney quoted in Sundquist, *Politics and Policy*, p. 281.

87. James Sundquist, *Dynamics of the Party System*, rev. ed. (Washington, DC: Brookings Institution, 1983), p. 385; Sundquist, *Politics and Policy*, pp. 281-86; Congressional Quarterly Service, *Politics in America*, pp. 64-67; Heath, *Decade of Disillusionment*, p. 261; and Levitan, *Blue-Collar Workers*, p. 126.

88. *Civil Rights Act of 1968*, Public Law 90-284; *New York Amsterdam News*, February 18, 1967, p. 1; Heath, *Decade of Disillusionment*, p. 224.

89. Johnson quoted in *Presidential Papers*, Vol 2, 1965, p. 898; and Doris K. Goodwin, ed., *Press Conferences*, p. 506. White House Conference from *Weekly News Digest*, March 14, 1966; and Georgena Potts, "Conference on Equal Employment Opportunity," *Monthly Labor Review* 89 (May, 1966): 503-509.

90. Quote from Matusow, *Unraveling of America*, p. 438.

91. *Ibid.*, pp. 422-26 & 438; Heath, *Decade of Disillusionment*, p. 287; Robinson, *George Meany,* pp. 275-279; and Steinberg, *Turning Back*, pp. 97-99.

V

Evolution: Nixon and Affirmative Action

Richard Nixon assumed office in 1969 without any carefully formulated agenda for dealing with civil rights issues. Nixon's major concern was foreign policy, particularly achieving "peace with honor" in Vietnam. During the Nixon presidency, the White House served as a battleground between Republican liberals and conservatives. Moderate-liberal Republicans achieved certain civil rights victories during Nixon's first term, especially in the field of job discrimination and affirmative action. By the 1972 election, however, Nixon increasingly aligned himself with his conservative supporters and advisers at the expense of liberals and civil rights proponents in general. This election was a catalyst in the development of independent, organized opposition among whites to welfare, busing, and affirmative action. At the same time, uncertain White House support for affirmative action led proponents to rely increasingly on the courts.

Richard Nixon's victory in November 1968 terminated eight years of Democratic control of the White House. Many liberals and civil rights proponents feared that his election would seriously diminish the federal government's commitment to equal opportunity. Early in 1969, Senator Jacob Javits expressed the sentiments of many liberals: "There is much concern in the country over how conservative this administration might be."[1] Unlike John Kennedy in 1960 and Lyndon Johnson in 1964, Nixon did not stress civil rights issues during his campaign. Elected despite overwhelming African-American support for Hubert Humphrey, Nixon was not indebted to African-American voters and was under far less pressure to placate this constituency than were his Democratic predecessors.

Nor were liberals reassured by Nixon's rhetoric during the election. Seeking to capitalize on the fearful and hostile reactions of millions of white voters to the urban violence of the late 1960s, Nixon claimed that the cities needed a greater police presence, and he promised to "meet force with force, if necessary, in the cities." He also criticized the Kerner Commission for relying "too much on federal programs" to promote jobs and housing.

At the same time, he opposed severing federal funds for segregated school systems.[2] It is not surprising, then, that many civil rights advocates interpreted Nixon's election as a threat to their hard-won gains.

Equally disconcerting to civil rights leaders was Nixon's unabashed pursuit of white southern votes in 1968. Especially valuable to Nixon was the "pledge of support" he received from Senator Strom Thurmond of South Carolina in May 1968.[3] A former Democrat, standard-bearer of the Dixiecrats in 1948, and long-time opponent of civil rights laws, Thurmond played a pivotal role in diverting white southern votes from conservative Ronald Reagan during the Republican primary campaigns and from Humphrey during the election. This "Southern Strategy" was remarkably successful as Nixon captured every southern state except Texas, leading many liberals to wonder what steps the president would pursue to ensure the continued loyalty of the South.[4]

Counteracting these forces, however, were several political factors that worked against an overall civil rights retreat by the new administration. To begin with, the closeness of the election discouraged any radical shift in presidential policies. Like Kennedy in 1961, Nixon initially pursued a moderate domestic program, avoiding sweeping attacks on the Great Society programs of the Johnson years. Moreover, having been nominated as a centrist over the conservative Ronald Reagan, Nixon owed his election in part to the support of the moderate-liberal wing of the Republican Party. The president could not afford to alienate this constituency and actually appointed several progressive Republicans to key governmental positions.

The most important factor mitigating against "turning back the clock" in racial matters was the momentum of the civil rights movement itself. The New Frontier-Great Society reforms had expanded, rather than satisfied, African-American demands in several areas, including employment. Civil rights groups intended to pursue affirmative action and busing as aggressively under a Republican administration as they had under its Democratic predecessors. By 1969, Republicans as well as Democrats no longer questioned the willingness or ability of African Americans to engage in disruptive and sometimes violent behavior. Having been elected on a "law-and-order" platform, the new administration avoided confrontational tactics that might recreate the mass demonstrations of the 1960s. In addition, since the passage of the Civil Rights Act of 1964, civil rights proponents had established a legal and administrative apparatus for combating discrimination that was firmly embedded in the federal bureaucracy and could not be ignored by the Nixon White House. As political scientist Allan Wolk explained, Nixon "has sworn to faithfully execute six civil rights laws, a host of Supreme Court holdings, several executive orders, and numerous administrative actions." The dynamism of racial change in the United States could not be arrested merely by the displacement of a Democratic president.[5]

This ambivalence surrounding the administration's civil rights strategy was reflected in the 1968 campaign. As previously stated, many civil rights advocates reacted apprehensively to Nixon's "law and order" rhetoric, which seemed designed to capitalize on the widely publicized "white backlash." On other occasions when he addressed the race question, Nixon, like many people, adopted the general position that much progress had been achieved but that more remained to be done. "Never have we been so close," he asserted during a 1968 radio broadcast, "to the achievement of a just and abundant society."[6] Particularly successful, in his eyes, was the crusade against such Jim Crow practices as public segregation and denial of voting rights, a movement that he felt had run its course by 1968. During his campaign he announced: "The old vocabulary of the civil rights movement has become the rhetoric of the rearview mirror."[7]

By 1969, Nixon had come to perceive the race issue largely in economic terms. With the legal barriers to integration eliminated, the major impediment to the equal participation of blacks in U.S. society was the absence of jobs, purchasing power, and economic opportunity. As early as 1967, Nixon had asserted: "Jobs is the gut issue. If you don't have jobs, you don't have housing, and you don't get off welfare."[8] Nixon, however, broke ranks with Great Society Democrats, accusing them of attempting "to buy off the Negro" with welfare and housing programs that he believed only perpetuated poverty and dependence on government.[9] Nixon's proposed solutions to black economic problems included creating jobs through business incentives, particularly within inner-city neighborhoods; promoting black capitalism; reforming the welfare system; and combating job discrimination. The president's emphasis on the economic aspects of discrimination reflected in part his experience as chairman of Eisenhower's President's Committee on Government Contracts.[9]

By 1969, having made substantial progress in the areas of social integration and voting rights, African Americans also increasingly perceived their struggle in economic terms. The demand for equal employment opportunity, always a basic component of civil rights demands, had become paramount by the late 1960s. While stressing the need for more jobs, African-American spokespersons were especially sensitive to the continued effects of job discrimination on nonwhite workers. Having abandoned both gradualism and simple nondiscrimination earlier in the decade, civil rights organizations during the Nixon years demanded carefully defined affirmative action in all sectors of the economy, public and private. The use of numerical targets, introduced tentatively during the Johnson years, became a staple of the demands of the 1970s.

Always a controversial issue, affirmative action would prove even more divisive during the Nixon years. Not only was a Republican administration in office, but the economy, after a sustained period of economic growth, experienced a downturn during the 1970s. Unemployment, which had declined steadily after 1961, begin to rise after 1969. After reaching a low of nearly 3 percent in 1969, unemployment rose to 6 percent by the end of Nixon's first term and continued to increase after 1972.[10] Affirmative action had been introduced as a full-employment concept: As more jobs were created, blacks could advanced without displacing whites. The economic downturn, however, created a situation in which black progress increasingly would occur at the *expense* of whites. This development made white acceptance of affirmative action even less likely.

Nixon, then, tried to maneuver a difficult path in affirmative action while attempting to placate opposing forces. On the one hand, he supported measures to improve the economic status of African Americans during uncertain economic times. At the same time, he sought to incorporate many disillusioned white Democratic voters—particularly in the South—into the Republican Party. The result of these contradictory goals was a lack of consensus and clear direction within the Nixon administration concerning civil rights issues.

The administration's ambivalent approach to civil rights was reflected in many of its actions. Many administration actions bore the imprint of Nixon's "Southern Strategy" and suggested a declining civil rights effort within the White House. For example, Nixon appointed many southern conservatives to federal positions, including former Strom Thurmond aide Harry Dent, who became deputy counsel to the president. Nixon also was determined to appoint a southern Supreme Court justice. His first candidate was Clement Haynsworth, Jr., of South Carolina, a conservative judge who had been accused of presiding over cases in which he had a financial interest. The Senate rejected the nomination after extensive lobbying by civil rights and labor groups. Following Haynsworth's defeat, Nixon proposed G. Harrold Carswell of Florida, whom the Senate also rejected. Nixon characterized Carswell's defeat as an "act of regional discrimination" against the South by the Senate.[11]

Other White House actions suggested an indifference, if not hostility, toward the concerns of African Americans. In contrast to Johnson, Nixon failed to deliver a specific civil rights message to Congress during his first year. His attorney general—John Mitchell—opposed automatic extension of the Voting Rights Act of 1965, proposing a weaker substitute. In 1970 Nixon accepted a report from Presidential Counsel Daniel P. Moynihan suggesting that "The time may have come when the issue of race could benefit from a period of 'benign neglect'." In the eyes of many civil rights leaders, White House commitment to the cause of African Americans had dissipated under the Nixon administration. Commenting on Nixon's performance in 1969, *Congressional Quarterly* concluded: "In the first year of the Nixon administration, White House support for the civil rights movement declined sharply." In a similar vein, the NAACP decried the "slow-down policy and philosophy of the Nixon administration."[12]

As previously suggested, however, Nixon also made several moves to maintain the support of moderate and liberal Republicans. Significantly, he appointed several progressive Republicans to federal positions, including former Michigan governor George Romney as Secretary of Housing and Urban Development (HUD). Health, Education and Welfare (HEW) provided a haven—albeit temporarily—for moderates and liberals such as Secretary Robert Finch; Leon Panetta, head of the Office of Civil Rights; Assistant Secretary for Education James Allen; and Assistant Secretary James Farmer, former national director of CORE. These individuals often came under fire from within and outside the administration for their advocacy of school desegregation.[13]

The pivotal appointments affecting job discrimination were those within the Department of Labor which, since the issuing of Executive Order 11246 in 1965, enforced affirmative action compliance by federal contractors. For secretary of labor, Nixon chose George P. Shultz, former dean of the Graduate School of Business of the University of Chicago. Characterized by *Business Week* as "moderate-conservative," Shultz proved acceptable to business and organized labor as well as to liberal senators Jacob Javits, Harrison Williams, and Walter Mondale. At his Senate confirmation hearing, Shultz indicated his support for equal employment opportunity, but he reiterated the now-familiar endorsement of voluntary compliance. In his own words: "The more we can accomplish by the mediation approach of persuasion and acceptance, the better off we are going to be in the long run because it is only when people accept these things that they really do work well."[14]

Even more significant for civil rights activists was the appointment of Arthur Fletcher as Assistant Secretary of Labor for Employment Standards. A former professional football player and a veteran of numerous manpower and urban affairs projects, Fletcher quickly established himself as the preeminent African-American official within the administration. Fletcher's position was especially important because the Office of Federal Contract Compliance (OFCC) fell within his jurisdiction. A strong advocate of affirmative action, Fletcher maintained that, "goals and timetables are essential to the extent that they fall short of establishing quotas." He also conceded that "the black community doesn't have a very high opinion of" OFCC due to the agency's unwillingness to invoke its enforcement powers. For director of OFCC, the administration selected black former longshoreman John Wilks.[15]

The Nixon administration perceived its civil rights role as ensuring the efficient implementation of already existing civil rights laws and executive orders rather than pursuing new legislation. Nixon criticized the "performance gap" of the previous administrations, whose "fancy speeches" were never converted into reality. His administration, by way of contrast, would stress "deeds" over rhetoric. Arthur Fletcher concurred, referring to "the shambles I inherited called OFCC."[16]

The most dramatic challenge to the administration's capacity for efficient management and problem solving occurred within the construction industry. Although the last of the major urban riots occurred in 1968 following the assassination of Martin Luther King, many violent confrontations took place throughout the nation's cities in 1969—including Pittsburgh, Seattle, Chicago, New York, and Boston—usually between construction workers, blacks, and the police. In Pittsburgh, for example, 50 blacks and 12 police officers were injured in a fracas, while construction workers in Chicago carried pistols to their job sites. Other cities, such as Buffalo and East St. Louis, declared a moratorium on publicly financed construction projects to avoid similar outbreaks.[17]

The 1969 construction demonstrations reflected the frustration of African-American workers at their continued inability to penetrate the most prestigious construction crafts, despite years of protest. In Pittsburgh, a city nearly 25 percent African-American, African Americans constituted less than 2 percent of the membership of 21 of the city's 25 building trades unions. Philadelphia, where African Americans comprised one-third of the population, had seven building trades unions with a black representation of less than 2 percent. An EEOC study revealed that African-American membership in the building trades unions actually declined from 1968 to 1969. The construction unions responded to these charges with assurances that various apprenticeship outreach programs would, *over time*, ensure a more equitable participation in the skilled crafts. Such arguments, however, could not assuage the fears and anger of black workers, who had rejected the philosophy of gradualism. Herbert Hill of the NAACP issued a challenge on the part of civil rights activists: "The time has come to take a completely new approach and bypass the entire obsolete structure of union control over hiring and training in the construction industry."[18]

As with Birmingham and Selma earlier in the decade, the protest activities of 1969 prompted government actions to defuse these incendiary situations. Following the example of the Johnson administration, the Department of Labor assumed a dominant role, rejecting case-by-case intervention in favor of citywide solutions. Assistant Labor Secretary Arthur Fletcher selected Philadelphia, with its especially deplorable record of minority hiring, as its initial laboratory. Wracked by construction demonstrations since 1963, Philadelphia was the site of the unsuccessful Philadelphia Plan of 1967 to establish minority hiring targets. In his decision of 1968, Comptroller General Elmer Staats declared the plan illegal because contractors were not made aware of their affirmative action obligations until *after* their bids were accepted.

In a Department of Labor order of June 27, 1969, Fletcher unveiled a revamped Philadelphia Plan, in which all federal contractors on projects in excess of $500,000 were required to submit with their bids a written affirmative action plan "which includes specific goals of minority manpower utilization."[19] Because the goals and timetables were included in the original bids, Fletcher reasoned, employers would be fully aware of their affirmative action requirements *prior* to being awarded a contract. These regulations were extended to six building trades unions with a black participatory rate below 2 percent.[20] A second Department of Labor order of September 23 established general ranges of minority hiring on which contractors were to base their goals and timetables. The department envisioned an increase in black participation in construction projects from a minimum of 5 percent in 1969 to a general range of 19-26 percent by 1973.[21]

Significantly, the department distinguished goals and timetables from inflexible quotas in that contractors who made a "good faith effort" to achieve their goals were exempt from sanctions and penalties if their efforts proved unsuccessful. Under this system, however, the contractor assumed the burden of proof to demonstrate that such a "good faith effort" in fact had been made. The department would determine compliance through periodic reviews of employment data. By demanding that specific hiring goals be submitted with construction bids rather than *after* these bids were accepted, the department intended the plan to conform with Staats's 1968 ruling.[22]

Intended as the prototype of the Nixon administration's assault on job discrimination within the construction industry, the Philadelphia Plan was launched with a great deal of publicity. Fletcher formally announced creation of the plan in June during a public ceremony. He introduced the order with some dramatic rhetoric: "Segregation didn't occur naturally—it was imposed. In that process, quotas, limits, boundaries were set. Sometimes written—sometimes unpublished." Because extraordinary efforts had been exerted to enforce discrimination, he argued, equally vigorous measures were required to eliminate discrimination. "Visible, measurable goals to correct obvious imbalances are essential." Fletcher's statements represented one of the most unequivocal endorsements of affirmative action ever pronounced by a federal official, and they illustrated the extent to which liberal theories had evolved since the espousal of pure nondiscrimination in the early 1960s.[23]

The Philadelphia Plan represented the most ambitious and dramatic civil rights undertaking of the Nixon administration in the area of job discrimination. It also precipitated bitter infighting within the already fragmented liberal-labor-civil rights coalition. Civil rights spokespersons generally applauded the plan as vociferously as labor leaders condemned it. Whitney Young of the National Urban League sent a letter to the president endorsing the plan and commending the efforts of Shultz and Fletcher. Herbert Hill and Clarence Mitchell of the NAACP lobbied for support of the plan on Capitol Hill. Construction contractors and unions, meanwhile, opposed the plan from its inception. Donald Slaiman, head of the AFL-CIO Civil Rights Department, accused the administration of "a calculated attempt to confuse the public . . . about doing something on the job front to cover up a retreat in civil rights." George Meany concurred, condemning the plan as administration chicanery to "offset their shortcomings in the civil rights area as a whole."[24]

The AFL-CIO projected their dispute into the political arena, appealing to both the legislative and judicial branches. The result was an unusual alliance pitting the Nixon administration and civil rights leaders against organized labor. As they did in response to the previous Philadelphia Plan, contractors and labor unions protested to Comptroller General Staats, who again ruled in their favor. Staats dismissed the distinction between goals and quotas as "largely a matter of semantics," because both committed contractors "to making race or national origin a factor for consideration in obtaining their employees," which, he argued, violated Title VII of the Civil Rights Act. Staats further argued that imposing hiring goals constituted discrimination against white workers, which also violated the Civil Rights

Act as well as Executive Order 11246. Allusions to "affirmative action" in Title VII and the executive order, Staats maintained, did *not* refer to hiring goals or quotas. Attacking the very ideological premise of affirmative action, Staats stated: "Even if the present composition of an employer's work force or the membership of a union is the result of past discrimination, there is no requirement imposed by the Constitution, by mandate of the Supreme Court, or by the Civil Rights Act for an employer or a union to affirmatively desegregate its personnel or membership." Staats concluded by ruling the revised plan to be in violation of federal law.[25]

Unlike the Johnson administration, however, the Nixon administration fought for its program. On September 22, 1969, Attorney General John Mitchell officially rebutted Staats's decision and declared the plan to be consistent with the Civil Rights Act and Executive Order 11246. Like Arthur Fletcher and many liberal senators, Mitchell espoused a broader interpretation of national antidiscrimination ordinances. Directly contradicting Staats, Mitchell argued that affirmative action as stipulated by the Kennedy and Johnson executive orders "imparts something more than the merely negative obligation not to discriminate." "The legal definition of discrimination is an evolving one," he continued, "But it is now well recognized in judicial opinions that the obligation of nondiscrimination, whether imposed by statute or by the Constitution, does not require and, in some circumstances, may not permit obliviousness or indifference to the racial consequences of alternate courses of action which involve the application of outwardly neutral criteria." "There is no inherent inconsistency," he added, "between a requirement that each qualified employee and applicant be individually treated without regard to race, and a requirement that an employer make every good faith effort to achieve a certain range of minority employment." Mitchell proposed that although Philadelphia-style plans were not specifically *authorized* by the Civil Rights Act, they were not *prohibited*, either. Buttressed by this ruling, the administration proceeded to implement the plan. In late October, the government awarded the first contract under the plan to Bristol Steel and Iron Works of Richmond, Virginia.[26]

Although overruled by Mitchell's ruling, Staats's decision fueled a congressional debate regarding funding of the Philadelphia Plan. Significantly, these debates provided a forum for various individuals and groups to define acceptable civil rights policies. Conservatives like Sam Ervin of North Carolina and Paul Fannin of Arizona, who had filibustered against the Civil Rights Act in 1964, now condemned the Philadelphia Plan as a quota system that contradicted that law. Liberal defenders like Jacob

Javits and Edward Brooke replied that the plan was established, not under the Civil Rights Act, but under Executive Order 11246, which not only authorized but required "affirmative action" by federal contractors. Commenting on the transition in liberal ideology from simple nondiscrimination to affirmative action, Brooke explained: "Since 1965, however, we have learned that simple prohibition of discrimination is not enough." Only "positive action," he maintained, could eradicate the "systemic discrimination" inherent in the U.S. economy.[27] Brooke's statement represented a concession on the part of many congressional liberals that they had underestimated the scope and magnitude of economic discrimination in the United States during previous civil rights debates.

In late December, the Senate threatened to negate the plan by approving an amendment to the Supplemental Appropriations Act withholding federal funds from any program that the comptroller general deemed illegal. In the wake of administration pressure, however, the House rejected the Senate amendment, and the Senate quickly reversed itself and followed suit, clearing the way for implementation of the plan. In the final Senate vote, liberal Democrats such as Walter Mondale, Edward Kennedy, Birch Bayh, Thomas Eagleton, George McGovern, and Alan Cranston joined moderate-liberal Republicans George Aiken, Hugh Scott, Jacob Javits, and Charles Percy in supporting the plan. Casting opposition votes were such traditional conservatives as Roman Hruska, John Stennis, and Strom Thurmond.

Significantly, the final tally revealed that opposition to the Philadelphia Plan was not limited to the traditional conservative bloc. Instead, several liberals and moderates, including Howard Baker, Robert Dole, William Fulbright, and William Proxmire, also voted against the plan. This voting pattern marked the early stage of an ongoing process in which many moderates and liberals who equated equal employment opportunity with nondiscrimination (and perhaps "simple" affirmative actions) withheld their support from the expanding definition of affirmative action. For liberal politicians, the Philadelphia Plan represented both an ideological dilemma—choosing between nondiscrimination and affirmative action—and a political dilemma—choosing between black and labor constituents. Representative William Moorhead of Pittsburgh, a city with sizable black and blue-collar populations, typified this quandary. Moorhead voted in favor of the plan but confessed, "This could cost me my job."[28]

Rebuffed by the White House and Congress, the contractors and unions sought their final refuge in the courts. The Contractors Association of Eastern Pennsylvania, an organization of large contractors that "collectively perform more than $150,000,000 of federal and federally assisted construction in that area annually," initiated a suit against Shultz, Fletcher, and Wilks, charging that the Philadelphia Plan violated federal antidiscrimination laws.[29]

In 1971, the U.S. Court of Appeals rejected this contention, approving the plan as "a refined approach" to the affirmative action requirements of the Kennedy and Johnson executive orders. The court cited previous rulings, including the *Quarles* and *Crown-Zellerbach* decisions, that defended the legality of affirmative action and asserted that Congress had not intended the Civil Rights Act as a defense of the racial status quo. Like John Mitchell, the court ruled that the failure of the act to authorize Philadelphia-style plans did not make such plans illegal as long as the act did not explicitly *prohibit* them. Conceding that "the Philadelphia Plan is color-conscious," the Court maintained "the only meaning which can be attributed to the 'affirmative action' language which since March of 1961 has been included in successive Executive Orders is that Government contractors must be color-conscious."[30] Finally, the court ruled that the Department of Labor, and not the comptroller general, was empowered to interpret the affirmative action clause of the executive orders.

This decision constituted a critical victory for civil rights forces and a crushing defeat for the contractors and unions. The court forcefully established the power of the executive branch to demand affirmative actions by federal contractors that transcended the nondiscrimination requirements of the Civil Rights Act.[31]

The alliance of civil rights leaders and the Nixon administration throughout the battle over enactment of the Philadelphia Plan merits further analysis. To begin with, the administration itself was divided over the issue. Fletcher reportedly put his job on the line after Staats ruled against the plan. In addition, congressional conservatives expressed their misgivings to the White House. Influential Senator Everett Dirksen, for example, warned the president that "this thing is about as popular as a crab in a whorehouse."[32]

Nixon's decision to override conservative opposition in favor of the Shultz-Fletcher-Wilks contingent reflected a number of converging factors regarding race, labor, and the construction industry. Throughout the 1960s, the steady increase in construction projects had produced a tight labor market that substantially increased all construction costs, including labor. By 1970, according to economist Daniel Quinn Mills, "average hourly earnings in contract construction exceeded those in all manufacturing by 55 percent."[33] The increased demand for construction labor dramatically reduced unemployment among construction workers and actually created labor shortages during "boom" periods.

Meanwhile, having inherited the full-employment economy of the 1960s when he assumed office, Nixon had targeted inflation as the nation's overriding economic concern. Determined to reverse the inflationary spiral within the construction industry, Nixon blamed rising construction costs on the ability of contractors and unions to control entry into the labor market. The unions abused this power, he charged, by maintaining an artificially low labor supply. "Skilled construction labor," he declared, "has been in disturbingly short supply."[34] His contentions were reinforced by a 1969 study financed by the Department of Labor Manpower Administration that forecasted manpower shortages in the construction industry throughout the coming decade.

Nixon's proposed solution (mirrored in the Department of Labor study) was to increase entry into the skilled labor force through manpower training and vocational education programs, through enforcement of equal employment opportunity laws, and through "special arrangements for returning Vietnam veterans."[35] Minority workers constituted one abundant source of potential construction labor. In addition to increasing the supply of labor, Nixon also sought to decrease demand by ordering a 75 percent cutback in federally financed (but *not* federally assisted) construction contracts in the fall of 1969. The Philadelphia Plan, then, enabled Nixon to increase the construction labor force while appeasing African-American protesters and moderate-liberal Republicans.[36]

The hostile reaction of the building trades unions to the plan evolved from a different set of circumstances. By the end of 1969, the economic growth of the 1960s had ceased, and the nation moved into a period of "stagflation" and recession. Unemployment rose throughout the economy, but it was especially severe in the construction industry, where it nearly doubled between 1969 and 1970, due in part to a decreased demand resulting from rising costs. In addition, labor leaders dismissed the declining unemployment rates of the 1960s as misleading because, due to the seasonal nature of construction work, the dominant concern was not *un*employment, but, rather, *under*employment. The AFL-CIO estimated that the average construction worker actually worked 500 fewer hours annually than his or her counterpart in the manufacturing sector.

In the economy in general, and in the construction industry in particular, the economic decline following 1968 increased the stakes and transformed the context of the struggle over affirmative action. By 1969, black demonstrators and white construction workers were engaged in a bitter struggle for increasingly scarce resources. Elected without substantial blue-collar support in 1968, Nixon was not beholden to this constituency as his Democratic predecessors had been and consequently was less reluctant to risk alienating them through imposing affirmative action plans.[37]

Probably no official within the Nixon administration reacted more enthusiastically to the Philadelphia Plan than Arthur Fletcher, who intended the plan as a model for similar arrangements in other cities. Within two years, the federal government had established affirmative action programs in Washington, D.C., Seattle, St. Louis, Atlanta, and San Francisco. The San Francisco and Atlanta plans were imposed after Department of Labor hearings revealed that blacks were substantially underrepresented in the construction unions. In San Francisco, for example, despite a minority population of 30 percent, nonwhites constituted only 15 percent of building trades members and a much smaller percentage of skilled workers.[38] Seattle attempted to avoid federal imposition of a plan by initiating a voluntary arrangement in February 1970. By June, 1971, however, the Department of Labor determined the Seattle plan to be so ineffective that a federally imposed solution was deemed necessary.

The Washington Plan originated in protests by African-American workers against their exclusion from the METRO project, financed in part by Department of Transportation funds. Following complaints by the Urban League, the NAACP, the Council of Churches, and other groups, the Department of Labor initiated hearings into the project in April 1970, while Transportation Secretary John A. Volpe temporarily suspended federal METRO funds. Fletcher sent notices to the various contractors, unions, and federal agencies establishing a June 1 deadline for finalizing a voluntary agreement. When the disparate factions failed to achieve a consensus by that date, the government imposed the Washington Plan in June 1970. That plan established general minority hiring ranges for 11 trades with African-American membership below 10 percent (Washington was approximately 70 percent African-American), with individual employers to select specific targets within those ranges. As with the Philadelphia Plan, compliance was evaluated according to the "good faith effort" of the employer.[39]

Despite Fletcher's fervor, however, the "imposed plan" did not become the primary strategy for implementing equal employment opportunity during the Nixon years. As with previous administrations, most officials within the Nixon government preferred voluntary compliance to federal coercion. In 1969, even as it was battling for implementation of the Philadelphia Plan, the Department of Labor issued an official policy statement declaring "It is recognized in these disputes that the best solution is a hometown solution."

George Shultz's affinity for voluntarism already has been noted. When Shultz departed Labor for the newly created Office of Management and Budget in 1970, his successor, former Lockheed vice president James Hodgson, expressed similar views: "Voluntarism is the hallmark of successful labor relations." John Wilks echoed these sentiments: "A hometown solution is the best solution."[40]

In addition to the collective persuasions of government officials, several important political undercurrents mitigated against the continued imposition of affirmative action plans. Chief among these was Nixon's pursuit of blue-collar votes in 1972. Detecting a steady erosion of Democratic identification among blue-collar workers, Nixon hoped to capitalize on what were perceived as working-class racial antipathies and prowar sentiments to shatter the New Deal Democratic coalition. Although later studies revealed the portrayal of blue-collar workers as hawkish and antiblack to be exaggerated, belief in a racial "backlash" was widespread. Not only did polls indicate a national preoccupation with the "social issue" of race, crime, and counterculture, but certain visible elements within the working class, including construction workers, did manifest those characteristics commonly attributed to blue-collar America.[41]

The Pittsburgh construction workers who chanted "Wallace, Wallace, Wallace" during 1969 demonstrations and their New York City counterparts who attacked antiwar protestors the following year apparently evidenced a "hard-hat" mentality attractive to Nixon. Following the latter episode, Peter Brennan, president of the New York City Building and Construction Trades Council, was invited to the White House, where he presented the president with a hard hat engraved "Commander in Chief." This episode symbolized a rapprochement between the White House and construction workers. To cultivate this relationship, the administration rejected the proliferation of government-mandated affirmative action plans in favor of "hometown solutions" in which unions and contractors retained substantial power. Reliance on local, voluntary plans was also consistent with Nixon's "New Federalism," in which state and local governments would play an increased role in addressing most domestic problems.[42]

The term *hometown solutions* refers to local arrangements among community officials, contractors, and unions to increase nonwhite employment on construction projects. Representatives of these three parties generally formed supervisory boards to oversee compliance and to resolve conflicts. Eschewing the carefully defined goals and timetables of imposed plans, most hometown solutions established general minority participation targets for the entire industry, thus alleviating the burden on individual contractors and unions. As with imposed plans, compliance was usually contingent on a "good faith effort" to achieve the established goals. Participation in these programs was voluntary, but, beginning in 1972, nonsigners were subject to more stringent requirements by the Department of Labor. Hometown solutions proved to be far more acceptable to the construction industry than were imposed plans. By 1975, more than 60 voluntary plans were in operation throughout the country.[43]

If Philadelphia served as the standard for imposed plans, Chicago performed the same function for voluntary plans. Perhaps more than any other federal affirmative action program, the Chicago Plan was the direct product of black protest. The site of racial violence and open housing marches in 1966, Chicago witnessed an outbreak of construction protests beginning July 22, 1969. The driving force behind these demonstrations was the Coalition for United Community Action (CUCA), a powerful and well-organized umbrella association whose membership ranged from the SCLC to "Southside street groups" including the Vice Lords and Black P. Stone Nation.[44] Led by the Reverend C.T. Vivian, CUCA threatened to halt construction projects in African-American neighborhoods by "any means" unless contractors and unions agreed to certain demands, including elimination of the union hiring hall and the establishment of an on-the-job training program for 10,000 minority workers to be supervised by CUCA.[45] The coalition argued that African Americans constituted only 3 percent of the city's construction labor force. The contractors and unions rejected these demands, deemed "extortion" by one official, and insisted that African-American participation in the construction industry was several times greater than the coalition claimed.[46]

The resulting impass led to a violent and protracted struggle between the two sides. CUCA demonstrators halted $80,000,000 of construction work at 20 projects. One picket sign epitomized their sentiments: "This job is closed by the community."[47] Demonstrators "backed by force provided by black youths" broke into the offices of the Chicago Building Trades Council.[48] Community people attended protests accompanied by German shepherds and Doberman pinschers, while white workers carried pistols to their job sites. Intervention by police led to violence—including gunfire—on both sides, especially between police and youth gang members. Many people were arrested, including the Reverend Jesse Jackson, director of Operation Breadbasket.

In early September, the Building and Construction Trades Council proposed a training program for 4,000 minority workers to be supervised by an administrative board consisting of two representatives each of the contractors, unions, and CUCA. Vivian rejected the offer as "unjust and unresponsive to the needs of black people."[49] He argued that the contractors and unions would outvote the coalition on strategic issues and thereby retain control of the training program. Jesse Jackson insisted that 4,000 position were insufficient to alleviate the economic plight of black Chicagoans. This new deadlock prompted Alderman William Cousins to warn: "We're sitting on a powder keg. Unless something is done about this in a few days, this city is going to go up in flames."[50]

At this point, the federal government became involved. Fletcher scheduled Labor Department hearings into the Chicago situation for September 24-25. On the appointed date, Fletcher, Wilks, and other Labor Department personnel arrived in the city to begin their investigations. Unfortunately, the hearings, intended to disarm a volatile situation, in fact exacerbated tensions. Embittered white workers, apprehensive that the government would institute a Philadelphia-style plan, initiated a series of counterdemonstrations. Construction workers forced a postponement of the hearings by entering the hearing room and shouting down Department of Labor representatives. It was now the construction workers who protested in the streets, battling blacks and the police and singing "God Bless America." White demonstrators rushed Jesse Jackson and his wife on their way to a meeting, while Fletcher, subjected to threats of violence, slept in a secret room surrounded by armed guards.[51]

Fortunately, within a few days the violence peaked and slowly abated. Acquiescing to requests by union and construction officials, white workers returned to their jobs on Monday, September 29. The DOL hearings belatedly got underway, and Mayor Richard Daley offered to assist the quest for a solution. After months of negotiations, the various parties agreed to the Chicago Plan on Monday, January 12, 1970. Similar to the Building and Construction Trades Council proposal of the previous September, the plan consisted of "an offer of immediate job opportunities for 1,000 qualified black workers in the building trades, apprenticeship ratings for upwards of 1,000 youths with previous experience, and pre-apprenticeship on-the-job training for 2,000 additional minority youths."[52] The plan created a supervisory board comprised of seven members: two each from the contractors, the unions, and the coalition, plus a representative of the mayor's office. Policy decisions required five votes; the mayor's representative therefore served as a "wild card" to prevent total domination by the contractors and unions. All sides appeared satisfied with the agreement. George Shultz announced: "I am delighted with the Chicago agreement"; C.T. Vivian declared: "We're on our way."[53]

The administration presented the Chicago Plan as evidence that most construction controversies were best approached through cooperative local efforts. Having secured an agreement in Chicago, the Labor Department applied the same formula to numerous other cities, including Pittsburgh. In April 1968, Pittsburgh attempted to address the construction problem—and to avoid racial conflict—by instituting Operation Dig, a program designed to incorporate minority workers into the construction crafts. The project failed, however, due to a series of problems ranging from "negative work attitudes" and drug abuse by trainees to economic recession.[54]

The project's failure helped spark large-scale demonstrations in August 1969, which were organized by the Black Construction Coalition, whose membership included the NAACP and Operation Dig participants. Dissident blacks blocked traffic, grappled with police, and ultimately suspended over $200,000,000 of construction work. According to one writer, "more than once downtown Pittsburgh was close to a bloodbath."[55] Black demonstrations led to white counterdemonstrations, which further inflamed racial tensions. A march on City Hall by white construction workers became a "victory parade" as onlookers cheered and threw confetti from windows. Chanting "We want work" and "We want jobs," the workers bore placards reading "White is dependable" and "Wallace in '72."[56] As occurred in Chicago, tempers eventually cooled, and the conflicting parties agreed to discussions, with the assistance of the city government and the Labor Department. Key points of contention included the number of African Americans to be incorporated into the industry and control of job-training programs. Negotiations continued into May 1970, when the Pittsburgh Plan officially was unveiled. The foundation of the Pittsburgh Plan was a program, supervised by African-American organizations, to train and employ 1200 African Americans on local construction projects.[57]

Buoyed by the success—as the administration perceived it—of voluntarism in Chicago and Pittsburgh, Secretary of Labor Hodgson compiled a list of 73 cities to receive DOL assistance on initiating local plans. Hometown solutions soon appeared in dozens of cities, including New York, Boston, Denver, and Indianapolis. Most of these programs were designed to appease minority demands for construction employment while minimizing outside incursion into traditional union prerogatives. As such, the plans often succeeded in disappointing both sides while satisfying neither. White workers combined racial antipathy with complaints of "favoritism" for nonwhites and disparaging observations regarding the ability and dedication of black workers. In the words of one Pittsburgh ironworker: "I don't mind working with a nigger, But when we're up there, he better know the ropes. And these guys don't know nothing."[58] Many minority trainees undoubtedly had less job experience and formal education than their white counterparts; such differences often reinforced racial stereotypes and perpetuated racial animosities. Unions and contractors continued to justify racial membership disparities by claiming the absence of properly educated and skilled minority workers. White workers sometimes cited "inferior" black skills as a safety hazard for coworkers.[59]

For their part, civil rights activists often denounced hometown solutions as carefully designed mechanisms for evading affirmative action obligations. Critics cited such practices as "motorcycling"—in which contractors transported minority workers from site to site so as to be counted in several projects simultaneously—and "checker boarding"—in which a contractor transferred his minority workers from his *private* projects to inflate their representation on *public* projects—as evidence of the industry's "paper" commitment to affirmative action. (To negate the latter practice, the Philadelphia Plan was modified and later programs were designed so as to include *all* of a contractor's jobs, public and private.) Hometown plans, as previously mentioned, offered no guarantees of long-term employment or union membership. Moreover, the phrase "good faith effort," fundamental to every construction affirmative action program, provided an "out" for employers who failed to reach their hiring goals.

Although appearing impressive on paper, the hometown programs generally failed to achieve impressive results. Herbert Hill of the NAACP vocalized the feelings of many civil rights activists when he categorized hometown plans as "a hodgepodge of quackery and deception." Even Arthur Fletcher later conceded that, by 1971, "around the country, hometown plans were failing."[60] Even as organized labor signed voluntary affirmative action agreements, African-American organizations and federal agencies initiated legal actions against recalcitrant building trades unions. Integrating the construction crafts proved a frustrating and arduous endeavor as African Americans increasingly battled, not only racism, but a receding economy that victimized white as well as nonwhite workers.[61]

The Nixon administration reserved its most impressive affirmative action efforts for the construction industry in part because of the pressure exerted by the grass-roots protests, which did not materialize in other fields of employment. By 1969, the struggle against economic discrimination increasingly was a bureaucratic and legal one. This struggle continued throughout the Nixon years. The administration risked an early confrontation with civil rights forces through its relationship with the EEOC. Under Chairman Clifford Alexander, the commission launched a series of investigations whose targets included the southern textile industry, white-collar employment in New York City, and, in March 1969, the aerospace, motion picture, and television industries in Los Angeles. The latter hearings especially produced hostile reactions that reverberated to Capitol Hill. Following these hearings, Alexander requested a Justice Department suit against the motion picture industry, which Attorney General Mitchell opposed.

This situation climaxed during hearings into job discrimination by the Senate Judiciary Committee in April 1969, when Everett Dirksen, referring to "your carnival hearing out in Los Angeles," warned Alexander: "Either this punitive harassment is going to stop, or somebody is going to lose his authority, or I am going to the highest authority in this government and get somebody fired." Edward Kennedy attempted to reassure Alexander: "I think those who threaten you because you are doing the job do a great disservice to you and the American people."[62] Within the new administration, however, Dirksen's voice overruled that of Kennedy, and, within a few days, Alexander submitted a "bluntly worded letter of resignation" to the White House. "Vigorous efforts to enforce the laws on employment discrimination," he charged, "aren't among the goals of this administration." Alexander cited "a crippling lack of administration support" as a major cause of his resignation. [63]

Blacks and liberals who mistrusted Nixon followed this drama closely. Clarence Mitchell of the NAACP, for example, expressed consternation that "a change in the White House would automatically result in the ousting of Mr. Alexander for political reasons."[64] Nixon acted quickly to neutralize a potential conflict, nominating African-American Republican William Brown III, a former deputy district attorney of Philadelphia, to replace Alexander. Originally recommended by the Johnson administration, Brown secured the support of liberal senators through his advocacy of contract severance for discriminatory employers and of cease-and-desist powers for the EEOC. "The only way to ever get any effective use out of a power," he insisted, "is the use of that power in appropriate cases."[65] The Senate approved Brown's nomination and, one year later, accepted the nomination of EEOC member Cotton Lewis, an African-American lawyer from Virginia who was active in desegregation cases and who believed in contract severance and Justice Department suits in cases of noncompliance.[66]

The administration also attempted to expand the commission's enforcement powers. Unwilling to support cease-and-desist powers, the administration instead submitted a bill in 1969 to empower the EEOC to initiate lawsuits in cases in which it failed to achieve voluntary compliance.

William Brown, who formerly supported cease-and-desist authority, reversed himself and adopted the White House position, infuriating in the process many Senate liberals, including Eagleton, Javits, and Mondale. The dispute proved academic, however, as the measure died in Congress. A similar bill met the same fate in 1971.[67]

Despite these setbacks, African Americans and liberals continued to exploit the EEOC and OFCC in the struggle against job discrimination. The first consequential affirmative action controversy under the new administration materialized in April 1969 and involved the Defense Department and the textile industry. The largest single department within the federal government, the Defense Department accounted for more than three-quarters of all federal contracts, affecting 20,000,000 workers. Compliance by defense contractors was a controversial issue. Conservatives like J. Mendel Rivers of South Carolina, chairman of the House Armed Services Committee, argued that investigations and debarments hindered the production of military equipment deemed essential to national security. Moreover, some contractors were the sole manufacturers of certain items, making debarment an unfeasible option. Despite these obstacles, the Defense Department initially maintained an active compliance program following the promulgation of Executive Order 11246, issuing show-cause orders to 40 companies. Complaints by contractors, however, found a sympathetic audience within the department. Consequently, in 1967, the compliance program was decentralized and deemphasized within the Defense Department. By Fiscal Year 1969, DOD reviewed less than 10 percent of its contractors for affirmative action.[68]

The Defense Department awarded numerous contracts to southern textile firms. As discussed in Chapter 1, this industry excluded African Americans until the mid-twentieth century and then relegated them to the lowest-paying positions. By 1969, African Americans constituted 12 percent of the overall labor force of the nation's three largest textile companies—Burlington Mills, J.P. Stevens, and Dan River Mills—but less than 1 percent of officials and managers, professionals, and salesworkers. An "unwritten rule" at one plant mandated that blacks, but not whites, use paper cups at a desegregated drinking fountain. A Defense Department investigation of the three textile giants, begun in January 1968, uncovered pervasive discrimination and underutilization of minorities. The Defense Supply Agency (DSA) rejected affirmative action proposals submitted by the companies as inadequate and recommended sanctions against them.

In February 1969, in the midst of this controversy, Assistant Secretary of Defense David Packard approved nearly $10,000,000 in contracts for field uniform cloth to Burlington, J.P. Stevens, and Dan River. Despite the DSA's recommendations, and despite Executive Order 11246 and the July 1968 Labor Department regulations that explicitly required written affirmative action programs for large contracts, Packard settled for a verbal "gentleman's agreement" in which "the firms would cease racial discrimination in their hiring practices." Packard received assurances that the companies would submit "quarterly reports on their progress" to Defense.[69]

Packard's flexible enforcement policy received the support of Labor Secretary Shultz. The Senate, however, was less sympathetic. News of this arrangement reached Edward Kennedy, who was chairing a Senate subcommittee hearing into job discrimination. The issue became a public scandal and a potential partisan conflict. Despite a defense of the textile industry by Strom Thurmond, the government ruled the firms to be in noncompliance of federal affirmative action laws. All three companies subsequently developed written affirmative action plans.[70]

A second Defense Department controversy arose a year later and involved the McDonnell-Douglas plant in St. Louis. Although the 1970 census reported the population of the St. Louis SMSA to be 40 percent black, blacks constituted only 7.5 percent of the McDonnell-Douglas work force. More significantly, blacks represented only 2 percent of supervisors and less than 1 percent of officers, and they accused the company of discriminatory hiring and promotion policies. In December 1969, the Defense Department awarded McDonnell-Douglas a multibillion-dollar contract for the F-15 fighter plane without reviewing the company's affirmative action policy. The Civil Rights Commission conducted its own investigation in January 1970 and, determining the firm's plan to be "inadequate," directed correspondence to this effect to the Defense Department. In his response to the commission, Defense Secretary Melvin Laird conceded a "serious error" in compliance procedures had been made, but he denied any "conscious disregard of regulations" by the Air Force.[71]

The White House faced a potential embarrassment as Edward Kennedy threatened to raise the issue in Congress as he had the textile controversy of the previous year. A major confrontation was avoided, however, when the Defense Department, the OFCC, and McDonnell-Douglas agreed on an affirmative action plan on February 10. This arrangement included "expanded, inplant educational and training opportunities" for African-American workers; regular meetings of supervisors to discuss affirmative action regulations; employment and promotion "targets"; and efforts to secure housing for African-American employees. With the acceptance of this plan, the McDonnell-Douglas controversy abated.[72]

The textile and McDonnell-Douglas cases represented two of the more dramatic episodes of antidiscrimination activities during Nixon's first term. By the 1970s, complaints to government agencies had become as common as pickets and demonstrations had been during the previous decade. In its first year, the EEOC received 2,000 complaints; in Fiscal Year 1972 it received 39,000. The majority of these charges continued to be directed against employers, although complaints against unions also were numerous. The South continued to generate the most complaints of any geographical area, followed by the industrial states. To deal with this rapidly increasing caseload, the White House significantly increased EEOC funding and personnel. In 1968, the EEOC staff numbered about 360, with a total budget of just over $13 million. By 1972, the numbers were 1,640 and nearly $30 million, respectively.

Despite increased funding and personnel and streamlined compliance procedures, the EEOC remained a paragon of bureaucratic inefficiency. By June 1972, the commission's backlog exceeded 50,000 cases and continued to grow. The OFCC, while threatening several employers with contract severance, remained hesitant to exert this power, clinging tenaciously to its commitment to voluntary compliance. Cooperative efforts between these two agencies remained the exception rather than the rule. Federal enforcement of equal employment opportunity laws remained inadequate throughout the Nixon years. In a study published in 1973, the Civil Rights Commission charged: "There is no government-wide plan for civil rights."[73]

In addition to expanding the EEOC, the Nixon administration took certain steps to broaden and clarify federal affirmative action regulations. Central to this effort was the Department of Labor, which issued a series of orders regarding the obligations of federal contractors. Order #1, issued October 1969, attempted to streamline the enforcement process by reducing the number of federal compliance agencies from 26 to 15. Order #14 of January 1972 augmented this process by requiring uniform equal opportunity enforcement procedures from all federal agencies.[74]

The most consequential Labor Department efforts were those designed to clarify the vague affirmative action requirements of Executive Order 11246. In February 1969, the Civil Rights Commission informed Shultz that "The failure of OFCC to provide guidance on the substance of affirmative action requirements has given rise to the use of vague or otherwise ineffectual standards by the contracting agencies."[75] Conceding the need for more concrete affirmative action regulations, John Wilks prepared a memorandum late in 1969 proposing proportional hiring as evidence of contract compliance. Senator Sam Ervin angrily exposed a draft of this proposal to his colleagues and the press in January 1970. An apprehensive Wilks quickly retreated, assuring the public that the document did not represent administration policy and had been released "prematurely."[76]

In February, the Labor Department officially released its new regulations in a policy directive titled "Order #4." Expanded and re-released December 4, 1971, as Revised Order #4, the published version deleted all references to proportional hiring. Instead, it required that "within 120 days from the commencement of a contract each prime contractor or subcontractor with 50 or more employees and a contract of $50,000 or more develop a written affirmative action compliance program for each of its establishments," even if only one of its establishments received federal money.[77] Appropriate compliance programs included analyzing all phases of production and operation to determine if female and minority workers were underutilized. Acceptable levels of minority and female employment were contingent on several factors, including their representation in the local labor force and the severity of unemployment among minority and female workers. When such analysis determined underutilization, employers were to rectify the deficiencies through the development of "significant, measurable, and attainable" goals and timetables.

Order #4 carefully distinguished between goals, defined as "targets reasonably attainable by means of applying every good faith effort," and "rigid and inflexible quotas." Employers were required to compile "support data," including seniority rosters and lines of progression, and submit them to the OFCC or to the appropriate federal agency upon request. Failure to comply with these requirements could result in contract cancellation and future debarment.[78]

Revised Order #4 exceeded all previous government orders in its detailed outlining of federal affirmative action stipulations. Its strictures, however, were entirely nonquantitative and therefore imprecise. Even if a contractor compiled all the requisite data, which numerical criteria would determine "underutilization?" To what extent were these definitions left to the discretion of the employer and/or contracting agency? What constituted a "good faith effort," and to what extent did it relieve a firm of its failure to achieve hiring targets? Despite the improved wording of Revised Order #4, the question of affirmative action remained ambiguous and continued to hinder effective compliance efforts.[79]

The executive branch also focused some attention on "cleaning up its own house" by promoting affirmative action within the federal bureaucracy.

Women and minorities traditionally found employment within the federal government but were concentrated in the lower job-classification levels. Kennedy and Johnson restricted their affirmative action efforts to seeking more "qualified" minorities for federal positions. In 1965, Executive Order 11246 vested responsibility for affirmative action within the federal government in the Civil Service Commission. These actions increased the overall *number* of minorities and women but failed to improve their *status* perceptibly. By the time Nixon assumed office, a survey by the Civil Rights Commission of federal employment revealed that, of all federal workers with a status of GS 13 or above (on a scale of 1-18), 2 percent were black and 0.7 percent were Spanish-surnamed. At the same time, a study ordered by Nixon claimed that 20 percent of all federal employees were minorities, a proportion that exceeded that of private business. Thus, the Nixon administration emphasized "upward mobility" of those already employed rather than recruitment of additional minority workers.[80]

Executive Order 11478 of August 1969 listed affirmative action steps for federal agencies. Three months later, the administration created the Office of Federal Equal Employment Opportunity (OFEEO) within the Civil Service Commission to monitor antidiscrimination efforts. The investment of enforcement authority within the Civil Service Commission created a dilemma for that agency. Instituted in the nineteenth century to replace the corrupt "spoils system" with a policy of merit employment, the commission was adverse to abandoning or modifying its merit principles, especially as embodied in its Civil Service exam. In the words of Robert Hambleton, head of the Civil Service Commission, "Merit systems were born of the need . . . to divorce the civil service from politics."[81] Although the commission accepted the adoption of goals and timetables by federal agencies in 1971, it did so reluctantly, and it limited their use.

The Civil Service Commission's perception of its role as guardian of merit employment led to a protracted struggle with the Civil Rights Commission, which decried the overrepresentation of minority workers in the lowest job echelons. By the mid-1970s the occupational status of female and minority federal employees had improved, but it remained inferior to that of white males. In 1974, for example, females represented 35 percent of all federal employees but only 10 percent of those in categories GS 9 and above.[82]

Among the most comprehensive and far-reaching federal affirmative action efforts during the Nixon years were those undertaken by the federal courts. Intended by John Kennedy to redirect the black revolution "from the streets to the courts," the Civil Rights Act had in fact engendered a legal revolution by the beginning of the 1970s.[83] Mass demonstrations for voting rights and desegregation of public facilities had all but disappeared, and disputes involving job discrimination increasingly were settled in the legal arena. Unlike the legislative process, judicial actions did not require activists to assemble political coalitions with their inevitable compromises and infighting. This was of particular importance to a minority group like blacks, whose affirmative action demands often lacked widespread white support. More insulated from shifts in public opinion than the legislative branch and less encumbered by bureaucracy than the executive branch, the judicial system emerged as the most consistent promoter of equal employment opportunity within the government.

As previously discussed, an incipient legal revolution emerged during the Johnson years, illustrated by the *Hall, Ethridge*, and *Quarles* decisions. By 1969, the federal courts had affirmed the legitimacy of class action suits under Title VII and had assumed the authority to modify ostensibly "neutral" business practices that perpetuated past discrimination. This legal momentum accelerated during the Nixon years. Ironically, one critical component of Nixon's "Southern Strategy" was an assault on the "judicial activism" of the 1960s, which had embittered many conservatives. Nixon's 1969 nomination of Supreme Court Justice Warren Burger, a conservative critic of the Warren Court with a strong "law-and-order" reputation, was directed towards this end and was applauded by southern conservatives such as Strom Thurmond, James Eastland, and Sam Ervin. Similar considerations prompted Nixon's unsuccessful nominations of Haynsworth and Carswell. To the chagrin of conservatives, however, these actions did not arrest the momentum inherited from the Warren Court. Regarding school integration, the Supreme Court, in the *Alexander* decision of 1969, ordered school desegregation efforts accelerated; two years later, in *Swann v. Charlotte-Mecklenburg*, the Supreme Court affirmed the right of district courts not only to order school integration, but to devise their own busing plans when municipalities failed or refused to do so.[84]

The Burger Court also authored several landmark affirmative action decisions. Perhaps the most consequential was the *Griggs v. Duke Power Company* decision of March 1971. Duke Power Company's Dan River Steam Station in Draper, North Carolina, historically had segregated its labor force into "black" and "white" departments, with blacks confined to "laborer" positions, until Title VII became effective in July 1965. By that time, the *lowest* white wage at the plant exceeded the *highest* black wage. Although the company abolished formal discrimination in 1965, it required all prospective transferees to take standard aptitude tests and to possess a high school diploma. Significantly, the requisite test scores for transfers exceeded the national average and thereby automatically eliminated from consideration one-half the nation's high school graduates. Given the inferior quality of black education in the South, these requirements effectively served as *de facto* barriers against integration. As late as 1970, the lowest occupational stratum—"labor"—remained entirely black.

In 1966, Duke Power Company refused promotions to janitor Willie Griggs and 12 African-American coworkers on the basis of inadequate qualifications. The 13 men subsequently filed a complaint with the EEOC charging that the requirements were discriminatory in nature. When the commission failed to convince the company to modify its transfer procedures, Griggs and his companions initiated a Title VII suit against their employer with the assistance of the NAACP Legal Defense Fund. The EEOC filed an *amicus curiae* brief and, in August 1966, issued formal testing guidelines that linked the validity of testing procedures to their ability to measure skills necessary for job performance. In the absence of enforcement powers, however, the EEOC was unable to impose these guidelines on Duke Power Company.

The litigants suffered setbacks in both the district court and the U.S. court of appeals. The district court ruled that EEOC guidelines lacked statutory basis and therefore were not obligatory. The appeals court argued that the company's equal application of transfer requirements to blacks and whites proved the absence of any *intent* to discriminate, even if these requirements adversely affected blacks.

Griggs and the Legal Defense Fund carried their battle to the Supreme Court, which unanimously voted to overturn the lower court decisions. In a carefully worded ruling, Chief Justice Burger held that business practices that unequivocally produced discriminatory *results* violated Title VII even if they were not *intended* as discriminatory devices. In Burger's own words, "Under the Act, practices, procedures, or tests neutral on their face, and even neutral in terms of intent, cannot be maintained if they operate to 'freeze' the status quo of prior discriminatory employment practices."[85] Because the racist system of the South prevented blacks from attaining the same academic status as whites, Burger reasoned, requirements such as a high school diploma and "acceptable" test scores were inherently discriminatory.

In addressing the question of whether tests or requirements that disproportionately eliminated particular groups were *ever* permissible, Burger accepted the EEOC criterion of "business necessity."[86] A test's validity was contingent on its predictive value and/or its ability to measure skills required to perform a job. In the case of the Dan River Station, the court found no justification for requiring a high school diploma to perform most jobs. Likewise, standard aptitude tests measured something called "general intelligence" rather than specific skills and therefore were not job-related.[87] The court, for example, could not discern how a test that included spelling questions and a definition of "vernal equinox" determined an individual's qualifications for a coal-handler position. Based on these criteria, the court determined the company's transfer procedures to be in violation of Title VII. In rendering this verdict, the Supreme Court essentially affirmed the district court ruling in *Hicks v. Crown-Zellerbach*.

Griggs proved to be a landmark decision for several reasons. First, its endorsement of EEOC testing guidelines served notice to employers that commission decrees could not be ignored with impunity. Although the EEOC lacked direct enforcement powers, the possibility that its guidelines could be adopted as legal strictures convinced many employers to comply with the commission's doctrines rather than risk a legal defeat. More significantly, the court's determination that aggrieved individuals need not prove an *intent* to discriminate subjected numerous business practices—testing, interviews, academic requirements, and even prior criminal records—to a more stringent scrutiny. This was particularly critical in a modern society in which educational requirements often reflected a general preference for a "well-educated" individual and sometimes were only tangentially relevant to the specific demands of an occupation. Business reactions to such rulings often were negative, as will be discussed later in the chapter.[88]

The federal courts also increasingly applied numerical formulas, long advocated by civil rights activists, in job discrimination cases. One such case involved Local 53 of the International Association of Heat and Frost Insulators and Asbestos Workers in New Orleans. Like so many businesses and unions, especially those within the construction industry, Local 53 refused membership to African Americans and Mexican Americans until passage of the Civil Rights Act. Although the union abolished formal exclusion at that time, it maintained a number of stringent employment requirements, including written recommendations from three current members, four years of work experience, and a majority vote by the rank and file, all of which benefited friends and relatives of union members to the detriment of nonwhites. Although all 1,200 insulation workers in the New Orleans area were "required by contract to recognize Local 53 as the exclusive bargaining agent for such employees," fewer than 300 of these workers actually were admitted into the local.[89]

In 1966, African-American workers with NAACP assistance filed a complaint with the EEOC charging that the entrance stipulations constituted discrimination against nonwhites. In November of that year, the EEOC found "reasonable cause," but it failed in its conciliation efforts with Local 53. The black workers, including Paul Vogler, Jr., subsequently instituted a legal action against Local 53 on November 25. The following month the Justice Department instituted a Title VII suit; the two legal actions were combined shortly thereafter.

In the ensuing legal battle, a succession of federal courts found Local 53 to be in violation of Title VII. The courts cited, among other decision, *Quarles v. Philip Morris* to the effect that practices that appear neutral on the surface—in this case, nepotism—can be discriminatory in *effect* when applied under a particular set of circumstances—in this case, by an all-white union. Having ruled against Local 53, the courts devised their own remedial procedures. Specifically, they ordered Local 53 to award membership status to several African-American and Mexican-American applicants, to develop more objective membership criteria, and to refer white and black workers alternately until some semblance of racial equity was achieved. These rulings, in what became known as the *Vogler* case, served as a precedent for the adoption of numerical solutions by other courts.[90]

One case that accepted the authority of the *Vogler* decision was *Carter v. Gallagher*, which involved the Minneapolis Fire Department. Local police and fire departments historically had excluded African Americans from their ranks. The Minneapolis Fire Department provided a case study of this practice. The department required all applicants to possess a high school diploma and to pass a written exam and an agility test, and it automatically rejected any individual with a prior arrest record. It ranked applicants according to test performances, with special preference for armed service veterans, and selected them from the top of the list down. The total absence of African-American firefighters as late as 1970 offered irrefutable evidence of the exclusionary effects of this system.

In October 1970, five African Americans introduced a class-action suit against the department charging, among other things, that the written exam was discriminatory in that it was biased towards a white, middle-class vocabulary. The following March, a district court upheld these accusations and ordered the fire department to create separate seniority lists for whites and nonwhites and to select 20 candidates from the nonwhite list before admitting any additional whites. The department appealed to the appeals court, which, in September, overruled the district court, characterizing its hiring dictates as reverse discrimination against whites. Having made this ruling, however, the court agreed to rehear the case, and in January 1972 it modified its own decision. Citing *Vogler* as a precedent, the court ordered the alternate hiring of 1 nonwhite for every 2 white firefighters until 20 minority workers were employed. The court carefully distinguished between *temporary* preference for *qualified* minority workers, which conformed to Title VII stipulations, and fixed quotas, which did not.[91]

In numerous other cases, the courts ordered the use of numerical formulas to offset past discrimination. In 1972, for example, a district court cited the disproportionately high rate of African-American and Latino failures as evidence of the discriminatory nature of the Cleveland Police Department entry examination. It ruled that 18 percent of future openings be reserved for minority-group applicants. Significantly, the courts generally justified numerical formulas as temporary expedients designed to enable blacks to compete with whites on a more equal basis. Court-ordered affirmative action procedures represented less a rejection of equal opportunity than a redefinition of that precept. Acknowledging that "neutral" practices often perpetuated the disadvantages of past discrimination, and cognizant of the historical failure of nonquantitative remedies, the courts espoused "preferential treatment" as a mechanism for negating past discrimination and thereby creating equal opportunity in *fact* rather than just in *theory*. The ultimate goal remained fair competition, and not permanent reliance on quotas. Underlying this approach was the conviction that, in the absence of discrimination, black achievement would have approximated or equaled that of whites.[92]

The cumulative impact of judicial decisions, administrative enforcement activities, and federal regulations on the business community was significant. Federal requirements of EEO-1 forms and affirmative action plans created additional paperwork and consumed valuable time. Employers began to scrutinize their employment, testing, and promotion procedures for practices and requirements that might generate complaints and job discrimination suits. Shortly after the *Griggs* decision, for example, the EEOC reported that "a large petroleum factory" had abandoned its requirements of tests and a high school diploma for promotions.[93] Business officials complained of the burdens—financial and otherwise—of validating tests and other selection criteria. The multiplicity of possible validation standards and lack of consensus among social scientists as to the legitimacy of testing procedures compounded business resentment. In *Commentary*, Elliot Abrams, arguing the side of the employers, accused the EEOC of "making it impossible for an employer to insist on any but the most simplistically conceived job qualifications." Moreover, the lack of coordination and cooperation among the numerous federal compliance agencies confused and frustrated employers and impeded effective enforcement of antidiscrimination laws.[94]

In addition to these complaints, employers sometimes found themselves confronted with problems not traditionally associated with business enterprises. Some employers were forced to deal with such issues as employees' court appearances, parole officers, and inferior medical care. One study conducted in 1970 revealed that trainees from the "hard-core unemployed" were late and absent more often and were less familiar with work rules than other employees. Segregated housing patterns often created transportation difficulties for minority workers. "Business as usual" seemed increasingly remote to many employers by the 1970s.[95]

These complaints must be viewed in perspective. Affirmative action regulations constituted a form of government intervention in business operations and thus were perceived by many employers as an infringement on their autonomy. The responsibility of recruiting and training minority workers conflicted with the traditional personnel policy—regularly violated throughout history—of hiring the most "qualified" worker. Unquestionably, many minority candidates possessed inferior job skills and educational backgrounds. The concept of affirmative action, however, required employers to redefine their social responsibilities, a process against which many would have rebelled under any circumstances.

A related problem was increased reliance on racial statistics. The numerical issue, which was simultaneously a moral and a pragmatic one, plagued both business people and liberals. No precise criteria existed to govern the application of quantitative formulas. Should a firm's minority employment record, for example, be evaluated against the overall minority population, the percentage of minority-group members within the labor force, the number of minority workers possessing particular skills, or some other yardstick? What geographical parameters realistically demarcated an "available" supply of labor? What precise level of discrepancy between available minority workers and actual minority employees constituted "underutilization?" These questions illustrate the difficulties involved in implementing and enforcing affirmative action.

The numerical issue also posed a moral dilemma to proponents of nondiscrimination. One of the goals of the early civil rights movement was the removal of racial considerations from employment. By the late 1960s, however, affirmative action regulations required employers to use racial data, albeit for inclusionary, and not exclusionary, purposes. W. Willard Wirtz, who, as secretary of labor under Kennedy and Johnson, monitored the early stages of this process, remarked with irony as early as 1965 that "a good many of us have spent a good part of our lives trying to get rid of race identification on employment cards."[96] With the advance of time, an increasing number of people rejected as naive any "solutions" that ignored the realities of race. Race-conscious policies had created economic disparities, and only race-conscious policies could eliminate them. Statistics, as ambiguous as they are, provided the only concrete criteria by which to gauge the efficacy of nondiscrimination efforts.

Affirmative action proponents also denied the validity of the term "preferential treatment," arguing that the goal of affirmative action was to negate the special privileges accrued by whites over the years as a result of consciously applied racial policies. An official statement by the New York City Commission on Human Rights explained: "What is lost, therefore, to the majority is not a right, but an expectation of benefits flowing from illegal practices and systems, to which the majority class was never entitled in the first place."[97] Affirmative action, then, was not "reverse discrimination," but, rather, a mechanism for instituting *real* equality of opportunity.

Especially disconcerting to some individuals were the negative connotations surrounding the concepts of racial identification and quotas. The perpetuation of racial identification violated the ostensibly American ideal of "treating all persons as individuals." Jewish groups cited the historical use of quotas to limit Jewish participation in various institutions. American history provided too many examples of the misuse of the concept of race. Prior to the 1960s, for example, the most recent Supreme Court affirmation of the validity of racial categorization was *Korematsu v. United States* in 1944, which sanctioned the internment of Japanese Americans during World War II. Although affirmative action proponents justified reliance on statistics as a means to an end, the continued use of racial information, even on a temporary basis, suggested that the traditional liberal dream of a colorblind society was being deferred, if not abandoned. Finally, viewed from a different perspective, hiring goals also could function as a "double-edged swords by serving *maximum* as well as *minimum* targets."[98]

Despite all these objections, the federal courts and bureaucracy increasingly accepted the validity of numerical solutions during the late 1960s and early 1970s. In contrast to the 1930s and 1940s, when the courts, in the *A.S. Beck* and *Hughes* decisions, prohibited proportional hiring, the courts of the 1970s approved and implemented the quantitative plans espoused by civil rights groups. For this reason, the NAACP and other organizations were able to expand affirmative action.

If any single event served to crystallize the growing opposition to affirmative action, it probably was the 1972 presidential election. Nixon's strategy during that campaign reflected the arguments contained in Kevin Phillips's *The Emerging Republican Majority* and Richard Scammon and Ben Wattenberg's *The Real Majority*. Although differing in details, both monographs asserted that a majority of Americans had grown disillusioned with the developments of the liberal welfare state of the 1960s. By appealing to white middle-class voters by adopting a firm "law-and-order" posture and criticizing the "excesses" of busing, welfare, and affirmative action, they argued, the Republican Party consistently could win the presidency and become the nation's majority party.[99]

Nixon implemented many of these ideas during his first term. His "Southern Strategy" appealed to Sun Belt voters, many of whom had deserted the Democratic Party in 1968. His antipathy toward busing and the welfare state struck a responsive chord with many whites, North and South. By 1970, Nixon was clearly in pursuit of white, working-class votes. That year, Nixon hosted a massive Labor Day dinner for labor leaders, including George Meany, an outspoken critic of the administration. In December 1971, the president commuted the sentence of former Teamsters president James Hoffa, who served less than five years of a thirteen-year term for pension-fund fraud and jury tampering. In the construction industry, the administration adopted the "hometown solution" instead of imposed plans. In 1972, Nixon approved a bill allocating $1,000,000,000 in construction funds over a two-year period. The 1972 Republican convention removed planks that had appeared in the 1968 platform supporting "right-to-work" laws and "vigorous enforcement" of the Taft-Hartley Act.[100]

Significantly, Nixon's blue-collar strategy exploited the racial animus of the time. Nixon's characterization of Italian immigrants as "not asking for something, asking only for the opportunity to work," appealed to white ethnics through a thinly veiled reference to the widely held stereotype of black affinity for welfare. The president's 1972 Labor Day speech attacked busing and "the rise of the fixed quota system"; condemned "master planners who want more power in a central government"; and contrasted America's traditional "work ethic" with the emerging "welfare ethic."[101] This racial typecasting provided official sanction for the portrayal of blacks as seeking special privileges and helped unite the opposition to affirmative action. That same year the president asked Congress to establish a "moratorium" that would prevent federal courts from issuing future busing orders. He later publicly raised the possibility of a constitutional amendment prohibiting busing.[102]

Perhaps more consequential was Nixon's exploitation of the black-Jewish rift over affirmative action. Recounting that Jews historically had been victimized by quotas, many Jewish intellectuals and professionals interpreted their personal success as a triumph of the merit system over a pernicious quota system, and they resisted what they charged were efforts to reverse this process. As Ben Halpern stated in *Midstream*: "The fact is that the merit criterion is a matter of interest to the Jews as a group." To many Jews, black affirmative action proposals represented "a principle of ascribed equality." In 1972, Elliot Abrams of *Commentary* referred to the EEOC as the "quota commission," and Carl Schiffman, senior investigator for the commission, resigned his position, claiming discrimination because he was white and Jewish rather than black or Spanish-surnamed. Jewish hostility toward the goals of civil rights activists was especially significant because Jews historically had been in the forefront of the civil rights struggle.[103]

Jewish organizations helped to make affirmative action an election-year issue. In May and June of 1972, representatives of the American Jewish Congress, B'nai B'rith, and other Jewish groups conferred with HEW Secretary Elliot Richardson to request that the agency repudiate "preferential treatment" for minorities, especially within the academic world. Distressed over rumors that Democratic presidential nominee George McGovern had promised to reserve 10 percent of all federal patronage jobs for blacks, Phillip E. Hoffman, president of the American Jewish Committee, drafted a letter to both candidates requesting that they clarify their respective positions on quotas. Chairman Louis Stokes of the Congressional Black Caucus condemned this action as "high-handed at best and racist at worst."[104]

The letters had their desired effect, however. McGovern promptly responded: "I share the concerns you have expressed and reject the quota system as detrimental to American society."[105] Despite this statement, many white voters continued to perceive McGovern as the "quota" candidate. This image arose in part from a policy change implemented by the Democratic Reform Committee following the debacle of Chicago in 1968. The committee adopted new regulations requiring state Democratic parties to take "affirmative steps to encourage . . . representation of minority groups on the national convention delegation in reasonable relationship to the group's presence in the population of the states."[106] The adoption by the Democratic Party of a platform plank in 1972 supporting the right of the Supreme Court to mandate school busing, while consistent with the law, reinforced the image of McGovern as a "pro-black" candidate.[107]

Nixon, by way of contrast, handled the quota issue as a masterful politician. In response to the Hoffman letter, Nixon declared his opposition to quotas and ordered all federal agencies to analyze their affirmative action procedures to ensure that they did not promote quotas. These orders confused federal officials, who maintained from the beginning that their regulations required goals and timetables but prohibited quotas. Nixon, however, intended his statement for rhetorical, and not administrative, effect. The president's actions reinforced his image as the defender of traditional American values against the assault of busing and welfare.[108]

To maintain this image, Nixon increasingly distanced himself from the causes of African Americans. By 1970, despite the proliferation of construction affirmative action plans, Nixon clearly was strengthening ties with conservative supporters at the expense of blacks and liberals. The administration's civil rights record for 1970, for example, generated little enthusiasm among black leaders: submission of the Moynihan "benign neglect" report; nomination of Carswell for the Supreme Court; the March 24 antibusing address; implementation of the Chicago Plan, substituting hometown solutions for imposed plans; and belated White House endorsement of the extension of the Voting Rights Act.

Accompanying this process was the removal of black and liberal spokespersons from administration positions. The first victim was EEOC Chairman Clifford Alexander, who resigned his position in 1969 following a confrontation with Everett Dirksen. The following year witnessed a large-scale "housecleaning" of HEW liberals who advocated strong school desegregation measures, including busing. Among this group were Leon Panetta, James Allen, James Farmer, and Secretary Robert Finch. Finch's resignation in June induced one official to remark: "I see this as the reactionaries coming out of the woodwork."[109] In September 1971 the White House "promoted" Arthur Fletcher to the position of alternate delegate to the United Nations. This move may have been generated by complaints that Fletcher had attained too much power within the Labor Department. Following Nixon's reelection in 1972, Theodore Hesburgh, chairman of the Civil Rights Commission and a leading critic of federal civil rights enforcement efforts in general and the Nixon administration in particular, resigned his position.[110]

By 1972, White House support for civil rights activities had reached its lowest point in years. Observers from *Business Week* to the Civil Rights Commission to *The New York Times* were unanimous in their negative appraisals of Nixon's civil rights policies. In November 1972, a federal district judge charged that Nixon's antibusing posture had permitted recalcitrant school districts to continue to receive HEW funds, a practice that severely curtailed enforcement of school integration laws. In the field of job discrimination, in October 1972 HEW issued revised guidelines for university hiring that placed greater emphasis on "good faith efforts" and ordered that affirmative action results be evaluated against a pool of "qualified" black candidates, as opposed to the black percentage of the overall population. Meanwhile, the Office of Civil Rights within HEW investigated 15 charges of race discrimination filed by white faculty members. A December 1972 *New York Times* survey of OFCC officials found them united in their accusations that the administration had abandoned all pretense of enforcing contract compliance. Agency officials who pressed federal contractors to meet their affirmative action obligations were overruled or reprimanded. The NAACP Annual Report for 1972 issued a similar charge: "Contract compliance enforcement has become moribund." The *Wall Street Journal* reported in September 1972: "The Nixon administration appears to be moving toward a softening of its (affirmative action) regulations." *Business Week* decried the "steady erosion" of contract compliance efforts. The abominable state of federal antidiscrimination efforts was illustrated by the abbreviated tenure of George Holland, who was appointed director of OFCC in February 1972 and resigned in June, dismissing the agency's activities as illusionary and cosmetic.[111]

So drastic was the deterioration of federal antidiscrimination efforts that Labor Department officials publicly had to deny rumors that the administration intended to abandon the Philadelphia Plan, a move that *Business Week* predicted "probably will put an end to all serious government contract hiring requirements for race, sex, and religion."[112] The Philadelphia Plan ultimately survived, although its achievements were limited. The NAACP succinctly characterized the overall situation as a "tragic retreat of the Federal Government on every civil rights issue during 1972."[113]

Richard Nixon scored a monumental victory over George McGovern in 1972, capturing the electoral votes of every state except Massachusetts. Nixon's popularity extended to almost every constituency. The "Southern Strategy" proved successful as Nixon completed the sweep of the South he nearly had attained in 1968, receiving 70 percent of the popular vote in some states. A Gallup Poll of December 1972 revealed that "54 percent of labor union members and persons in their families voted for Mr. Nixon."[114] Thirty-five percent of Jewish voters—double the percentage of 1968—cast their ballots for Nixon, the highest percentage of Jewish Republican votes since the 1950s.[115]

Numerous issues contributed to Republican electoral success. Labor union votes reflected approval of many administration policies, including Vietnam. Significantly, the AFL-CIO refused to endorse McGovern, citing their opposition to his Vietnam policies, while the Teamsters leadership officially endorsed Nixon following the release of Jimmy Hoffa. Jews who voted for Nixon sometimes were more appreciative of his support for Israel than his opposition to busing and quotas. Other issues, including an economic upswing and *detente* with China and the Soviet Union, also attracted many voters. Moreover, references to a political "realignment" in 1972 must be qualified, given that the Democrats retained control of the House and gained two seats in the Senate. The Congress that assembled in 1973 included more African Americans, including newcomers Barbara Jordan and Andrew Young, and females than its predecessors, although these groups remained severely underrepresented.[116]

To these factors must be added the racial issue. The Nixon campaign would not have focused on busing, quotas, and welfare had they been empty issues. Roy Wilkins referred to race as the "secret issue" of the campaign, and *Newsweek* labeled quotas the "sleeper issue" of the election. In addition, the *American Jewish Year Book* stated: "The heaviest volume of Jewish votes for the Nixon-Agnew ticket was in areas of racial tension."[117] The disparity between the popular vote for Nixon—61 percent—and the African-American vote for Nixon—approximately 13 percent—illustrated the huge chasm between black and white political perceptions.[118] Richard Nixon forged a powerful coalition in 1972 in which African Americans were conspicuous by their absence.

The period 1969-72 marked a crucial transitional phase in the equal employment campaign. During this period, the federal bureaucracy and the courts expanded affirmative action beyond what could have been anticipated in 1964. At the same time, lax and inefficient enforcement of affirmative action laws produced increased expectations but disappointing results. As affirmative action expanded throughout the economy, opposition to affirmative action likewise increased. Various members of the New Deal Democratic coalition, especially organized labor and Jewish Americans, who had supported the movement's earlier goals increasingly found themselves in opposition to affirmative action demands. Opposition to a complex and volatile issue like affirmative action, unlike voting rights and simple nondiscrimination, did not automatically constitute racism. Indeed, many former "allies" who challenged affirmative action continued to perceive themselves as pro-civil rights. In their eyes, the movement, and not themselves, had become misdirected.[119]

By 1972, especially in presidential politics, the "pro-black" label had become a liability. This development, coupled with the growing public opposition to affirmative action, would force African Americans—and other underrepresented groups—to rely increasingly on the courts in the ensuing years.

NOTES

1. Javits quoted from U.S. Congress, Senate Committee on Labor and Public Welfare, *Hearing of George P. Shultz to be Secretary of Labor* (Washington, DC: Government Printing Office, 1969), p. 9.

2. Nixon quoted in Stephen E. Ambrose, *Nixon: Volume Two: The Triumph of a Politician, 1962-1972* (New York: Simon & Schuster, 1989), p. 144. See also Tom Wicker, *One of Us: Richard Nixon and the American Dream* (New York: Random House, 1991), p. 489.

3. Richard Nixon, *RN* (New York: Grosset and Dunlap, 1978), pp. 304-5.

4. Nixon, *RN*, pp. 304-5; Leon Panetta and Peter Gall, *Bring Us Together: The Nixon Team and the Civil Rights Retreat* (New York: J. B. Lippincott Company, 1971), p. 5; Reg Murphy and Hall Gulliver, *The Southern Strategy* (New York: Charles Scribner's Sons, 1971), pp. 204ff.; and Heath, *Decade of Disillusionment*, p. 287.

5. Quote from Allan Wolk, *The Presidency and Black Civil Rights* (Pennsylvania: Fairleigh Dickinson University Press, 1971), p. 219. See also, Richard Nathan, *The Plot that Failed: Nixon and the Administrative Presidency* (New York: John Wiley and Sons, Inc., 1975), pp. 5 & 16; and Panetta, *Bring Us Together*, pp. 1-3.

6. Nixon quoted from *Nixon Speaks Out* (Nixon-Agnew Campaign Committee, 1968), p. 35.

7. *Ibid.*, p. 59.

8. Nixon quoted in Ambrose, *Nixon: Volume Two*, p. 125.

9. *Ibid.*, pp. 124-26 & 186-88; *Nixon Speaks Out,* p. 60.; Interview with Leon Panetta, May 22, 1984; *The Nixon Presidential Press Conferences*, Helen Thomas, ed. (New York: Earl L. Coleman Enterprises, Inc., 1978), p. 289; *Public Papers of the Presidents: Richard M. Nixon, 1970* (Washington, DC: Government Printing Office, 1971), pp. 305ff.; *The New York Times*, September 24, 1969, p. 1; and Nixon, *RN*, p. 437. For Eisenhower and PCGC, see Chapter II.

10. U.S. Department of Labor, Bureau of Labor Statistics, *Handbook of Labor Statistics* Bulletin #2715 (Washington, DC: Government Printing Office, 1983), pp. 63 & 155.

11. Quote from Ambrose, *Nixon: Volume Two,* p. 338. See also Ambrose, pp. 296, 301, 315-17, 330, 337-38; Wicker, *One of Us*, pp. 496-99; *The New York Times*, May 22, 1969, pp. 1 & 36-37; and Archie

Robinson, *George Meany and His Times* (New York: Simon & Schuster, 1981), p. 21.

12. Quotes from Congressional Quarterly, *Nixon: The First Year of His Presidency* (Washington, DC, 1970), p. 49, and NAACP, *Annual Report for 1969* (Washington, DC, 1970), p. 5. Moynihan quoted in Ambrose, *Nixon: Volume Two,* p. 332. See also: Congressional Quarterly, *First Year,* pp. 50-51; *Second Year,* p. 70; NAACP *Annual Report, 1969,* p. 6; *The New York Times,* March 1, 1969, pp. 1 & 69; June 23, 1970, p. 1; October 30, 1969, pp. 1 & 34; Murphy, *Southern Strategy,* pp. 132-36 & 199-200; Nixon, *RN,* p. 442; Wicker, *One of Us,* p. 492; and Panetta, *Bring Us Together,* Chapter 13.

13. Wicker, *One of Us,* Chapter 12; Nathan, *Plot,* p. 5; Ambrose, *Nixon: Volume Two,* pp. 364-65 & 460-61; and Panetta, *Bring Us Together,* and interview.

14. Shultz quote from Senate *Hearings,* p. 26. See also: "New Secretary Leans to a Middle Course," *Business Week,* December 21, 1968, pp. 74-75.

15. Fletcher quote from *Hearing before the Committee on Labor and Public Welfare, U.S. Senate, 95th Congress, 1st Session, on Arthur Fletcher to be an Assistant Secretary of Labor,* April 15, 1969 (Washington, DC: Government Printing Office, 1969), pp. 10 & 12. See also Fletcher, *Silent Sell-Out,* p. 17.

16. Quotes from Nixon, *Public Papers, 1970,* pp. 39-40; and Fletcher, *Silent Sell-Out,* p. 77.

17. NAACP, *Report 1969,* p. 113; *The New York Times,* August 28, 1969, p. 27; *Wall Street Journal,* September 26, 1969, p. 1; and Fletcher, *Sell-Out,* pp. 69ff..

18. Hill quote from *Wall Street Journal,* September 26, 1969, p. 1. See also; NAACP, *Report 1970,* p. 85; Robert Kuttner, "Red and Green in Civil Rights," *Commonweal* 90 (September 5, 1969): 535; Peter Nash, "Affirmative Action under Executive Order 11246," *NYU Law Review* 46 (April, 1971): 238; and *Congressional Record,* Volume 115, Part 29 (Washington, DC: Government Printing Office, 1969), p. 39951.

19. Quote from Hubbard, "Affirmative Action," p. 123.

20. The six trades were Ironworkers; Plumbers and Pipefitters; Steamfitters; Sheetmetal Workers; Electrical Workers; and Elevator Construction Workers. A seventh trade, Roofers and Water-proofers, originally was included but later was exempted. *Congressional Record,* Volume 115, Part 29, p. 39951.

21. *Ibid.*

22. Labor Department orders from *Congressional Record*, Vol. 115, pp. 39951-39957. See also: *Memorandum in the United States District Court of Pennsylvania for Taylor v. United States Department of Labor*, December 7, 1982, pp. 5-8; U.S. Department of Labor, *Weekly News Digest*, July 7, 1969; *Wall Street Journal*, June 30, 1969; Hubbard, "Affirmative Action," pp. 123-127; and Nash, "Affirmative Action," pp. 236-238.

23. Fletcher quote from *Weekly News Digest*, July 7, 1969. Other information from *Taylor Memorandum*, pp. 5-7; *The New York Times*, June 28, 1969, p. 61; September 24, 1969, p. 1; *Wall Street Journal*, June 30, 1969; and Hubbard, "Affirmative Action," pp. 123-124.

24. Slaiman quote from *AFL-CIO News*, January 10, 1970, p. 5; Meany quote from January 17, 1970, p. 9. For views of African Americans, see *Weekly News Digest*, July 21, 1969; and NAACP, *Report 1969*, p. 116.

25. Staats decision in *Congressional Record*, Vol. 115, Part 29, pp. 40019-40022. See also Sam Ervin in *Congressional Record*, p. 39949; and Hubbard, "Affirmative Action," pp. 127-129.

26. Mitchell ruling in *Congressional Record*, Vol. 115, pp. 40019-40022. See also: *Weekly News Digest*, November 3, 1969; Fletcher, *Sell-Out*, p. 67; Hubbard, "Affirmative Action," pp. 130-33; and Kuttner in *Commonweal*, p. 535.

27. Brooke quote from *Congressional Record*, Vol. 115, pp. 39966-39967.

28. Moorhead quote from Joseph Alsop, "The Philadelphia Plan: A Dilemma with Sharp Horns," *Los Angeles Times*, January 6, 1970, p. 7. See also: *Congressional Record*, Vol. 115, Part 17, pp. 22332-22333; pp. 23268-23269; Part 24, pp. 32667ff.; Part 29, pp. 39949ff.; Stephen Steinberg, *Turning Back: The Retreat from Racial Justice in American Thought and Policy* (Boston: Beacon Press, 1995), pp. 107ff.; Fletcher, *Sell-Out*, p. 68; and *The New York Times*, December 19, 1969, p. 27, and December 23, 1969, p. 1. For final vote see *Congressional Record*, Part 30, p. 40749.

29. *The Contractors Association of Eastern Pennsylvania v. the Secretary of Labor* 442 F. 2d 165.

30. 442 F. 2d 170 & 173.

31. 442 F. 2d 159ff.; and NAACP *Report 1971*, pp. 46-47.

32. Dirksen quote from Nixon, *RN*, p. 438.

33. Mills, *Construction*, p. 56.

34. Nixon quote from *Public Papers 1970*, p. 270.

35. *Ibid.*, p. 269.

36. *Hearing before the Committee on Labor and Public Welfare, U.S. Senate, 91st Congress, 2nd Session, on James D. Hodgson to be Secretary of Labor, June 16, 1970* (Washington, DC: Government Printing Office, 1970), p. 8; Leonard Lecht, *Manpower Needs for National Goals in the 1970's* (New York: Frederick A. Praeger, 1969), especially pp. 81ff.; Goulden, *Meany,* p. 412; U.S. Department of Labor, *Black News Digest,* September 6, 1971; *The New York Times,* September 5, 1969, p. 23; *Wall Street Journal,* September 26, 1969, p. 22; Nixon, *Public Papers, 1970,* pp. 268ff.; and Mills, *Construction,* pp. vii-92.

37. *Washington Post,* November 7, 1970, p. Al; W. Elliot Brownlee, *Dynamics of Ascent* (New York: Alfred A. Knopf, 1979), p. 463; Robinson, *George Meany,* pp. 275ff.; NAACP, *Report 1969,* p. 112; Mills, *Construction,* pp. 26 & 91-92; and John T. Joyce, "Construction Unions in the 70s," *The American Federationist* 80 (October, 1973): 10.

38. Murray Friedman, "Intergroup Relations and Tensions in the United States," *American Jewish Year Book,* Vol 73, 1972, p. 139; *Black News Digest,* June 14, 1971.

39. San Francisco, St. Louis and Atlanta plans from *Black News Digest,* 1971: March 29, June 14, June 18, and July 7. Seattle from *Black News Digest,* June 18, 1971; and Charles Edward Donegan, "The Philadelphia Plan: A Viable Means of Achieving Equal Opportunity in the Construction Industry or More Pie in the Sky?", *University of Kansas Law Review* 20 (Winter, 1972): 204. Washington Plan from *Weekly News Digest,* April 20, 1970; June 8, 1970; *AFL-CIO News,* June 6, 1970, p. 11; Richard Rowan and Lester Rubin, *Opening the Skilled Construction Trades to Blacks* (Philadelphia: University of Pennsylvania Press, 1972), pp. 32ff.; and Courtland Milloy, Jr., "Plan to Get More Blacks into Washington Construction Jobs Fails," *Washington Post,* March 10, 1981. For Fletcher's views, see *Weekly News Digest,* June 23, 1969; and Irwin Dubinsky, *Reform in Trade Union Discrimination in the Construction Industry* (New York: Praeger Publishers, 1973), p. 175.

40. Department of Labor statement from *Weekly News Digest,* October 20, 1969. Hodgson from Senate *Hearings,* p. 3. Wilks from *Weekly News Digest,* December 15, 1969. For Shultz transfer, see Robinson, *Meany,* p. 298; and Ambrose, *Nixon: Volume Two,* p. 328.

41. "Social Issue" in Richard M. Scannon and Ben J. Wattenberg, *The Real Majority* (New York: Coward-McCann, Inc., 1970), pp. 37-43. See also Steinberg, *Turning Back,* p. 98.

42. Fletcher, *Sell-Out,* pp. 11-13; Herbert Hill, "Nixon and the 'Hard Hats': 'Law and Order' vs. 'Hometown' Solutions," *Social Policy* 1

(November-December, 1970): 41; Dubinsky, *Reform*, pp. 142 & 175; Ambrose, *Nixon: Volume Two*, pp. 473-74; Wicker, *One of Us*, pp. 524-29 & 638-39; and *The New York Times*, April 24, 1969, p. 1; May 27, 1970, pp. 1 & 18. Analysis of blue-collar attitudes from Sar E. Levitan, ed., *Blue-Collar Workers: A Symposium on Middle America* (New York: McGraw-Hill Book Company, 1971).

43. U.S. Commission on Civil Rights, *The Challenge Ahead* (Washington, DC: Government Printing Office, 1976), pp. 154-160; *Black News Digest*, March 6, 1972; Derryck, *The Construction Industry*, p. 20; Dennis Yeager, "Litigation under Title VII of the Civil Rights Act of 1964, the Construction Industry and the Problem of the 'Unqualified' Minority Worker," *Georgetown Law Journal* 59 (June, 1971): 1267, 1271-72.

44. *Chicago Defender*, August 18, 1969, p. 20.

45. *Chicago Defender*, July 23, 1969, p. 3.

46. *Chicago Tribune*, September 4, 1969, p. 2.

47. *Chicago Defender*, July 24, 1969, p. 36.

48. *Chicago Tribune*, September 11, 1969, p. 4

49. *Chicago Defender*, September 6, 1969, p. 1.

50. Quote from *Chicago Tribune*, September 10, 1969, p. 3. See also: *Tribune*, 1969: September 4, p. 1; September 5, pp. 1 & 9; September 8, p. 5; September 9, pp. 1 & 2; September 10, p. 3; September 11, pp. 1 & 4; September 12, p. 14; September 13, p. 2; September 19, p. 5; September 23, p. 9. *Chicago Defender*, 1969: July 23, p. 1; July 24, p. 2; July 29, p. 3; July 30, pp. 3 & 24; August 7, p. 3; August 13, p. 3; August 18, pp. 3 & 20; August 25, p. 20; August 26, p. 3; September 6, p. 12. See also: Fletcher, *Sell-Out*, pp. 69ff.; *Wall Street Journal* September 22, 1969, p. 22.

51. Fletcher, *Sell-Out*, p. 72; *Weekly News Digest*, September 22, 1969; *Chicago Tribune*, September 25, 1969, p. 3; September 26, pp. 1 & 2; September 30; *The New York Times*, September 27, 1969, p. 18.

52. *Chicago Tribune*, January 13, 1970, p. 1.

53. Shultz quote from *Weekly News Digest*, January 26, 1970; Vivian from *Chicago Tribune*, January 13, 1970, p. 1. See also: *Chicago Tribune*, January 13, 1970, p. 18.

54. Dubinsky, *Reform*, p. 5.

55. Stanley Plastrik, "Confrontation in Pittsburgh," *Dissent* (January-February, 1970): 28.

56. Dubinsky, *Reform*, pp. 140-142.

57. *Ibid.*, especially pp. 6 & 140-146; *AFL-CIO News*, February 7, 1970, p. 2; *The New York Times*, September 24, 1969, p. 18; "Pittsburgh Blacks Try Negotiating," *Business Week*, September 6, 1969, pp. 32-33;

"Integration Drive Fails to Overcome," *Business Week*, June 6, 1970, p. 52; and Plastrik, "Confrontation," pp. 25-31.

58. "Pittsburgh Blacks," *Business Week*, September 6, 1969, p. 32.

59. *Weekly News Digest*, June 29, 1970, and August 31, 1970; *The New York Times*, September 5, 1969, p. 23; *Wall Street Journal*, December 3, 1970, p. 25; "Integration Drive," *Business Week*, June 6, 1970, p. 48; Dubinsky, *Reform*, pp. 5 & 101; and Donegan, "Philadelphia Plan," p. 199.

60. Hill quoted in *Social Policy*, p. 41; Fletcher quoted in *Sell-Out*, p. 79.

61. Civil Rights Commission, *Challen*ge, pp. 199-200; Caditz, *White Liberals*, p. 25; Derryck, *Construction Industry*, pp. 21-22; Nash, "Affirmative Action," pp. 238-240; Kevin McGuiness, *Government Memoranda on Affirmative Action Programs* (Washington, DC: Equal Employment Advisory Council, 1976), p. 62; "New York Job Plan Opposed," *The Crisis* 77 (June-July, 1970): 209; Hill in *Social Policy*; and Fletcher, *Sell-Out*, p. 79. For an example of lawsuits involving the construction industry, see Appendix IV in U.S. General Accounting Office, *Federal Efforts to Increase Minority Opportunities in Skilled Construction Craft Unions Have Had Little Success* (Washington, DC: Government Printing Office, 1979). Note: Particular programs, including the Chicago, New York, and Philadelphia Plans, will be discussed in more detail in later chapters.

62. Quotes from *Hearings before the Subcommittee on Administrative Practice and Procedure of the Committee on the Judiciary* U.S. Senate, 91st Congress, 1st Session, March 27-28, 1969 (Washington DC: Government Printing Office, 1969), pp. 22 & 24.

63. Quotes from *Wall Street Journal*, April 10, 1969, p. 3; and Wicker, *One of Us*, p. 492. Other material from U.S. Commission on Civil Rights, *Federal Civil Rights Enforcement Efforts* (Washington, DC: Government Printing Office, 1970), pp. 365-66; U.S. EEOC, *Hearings before the EEOC on Utilization of Minority and Women Workers in Certain Major Industries* (Washington, DC: EEOC, 1969); *AFL-CIO News*, April 5, 1969, p. 8; *The New York Times*, April 10, 1969, p. 1; and *Wall Street Journal*, April 10, 1969, p. 3.

64. Mitchell quote from *Hearing before the Committee on Labor and Public Welfare, U.S. Senate, 91st Congress, 1st Session, on William Hill Brown III to be a Member of the Equal Employment Opportunity Commission* (Washington, DC: Government Printing Office, 1969), p. 8.

65. *Ibid.*, pp. 16-17.

66. *Ibid.*; *Hearing before the Committee on Labor and Public Welfare, U.S. Senate, 91st Congress, 2nd Session, on Colston A. Lewis to be a Member of the EEOC* (Washington, DC: Government Printing Office, 1970); *Wall Street Journal*, May 7, 1969, p. 16.

67. 1969 bill from *Wall Street Journal*, August 11, 1969, p. 6; and *Chicago Defender*, August 18, 1969, p. 20. 1971 bill from *Hearings before the Subcommittee on Labor of the Committee on Labor and Public Welfare, U.S. Senate, 92nd Congress, 1st Sessions on S. 2515, S. 2617, H.R. 1746* (Washington, DC: Government Printing Office, 1971); and Charles Culhane, "Battle Over Enforcement Powers for EEOC Pits Business Against Labor, Civil Rights Groups," *National Journal Reports* 3 (November 13, 1971): 2249-59. A more detailed analysis of the attempts to strengthen the EEOC, culminating in the passage of the Equal Employment Opportunity Act, appears in Chapter VI.

68. Testimony of Barbara McIntosh in *Oversight Hearings before the Subcommittee on Equal Opportunities of the Committee on Education and Labor, U.S. House of Representatives, 94th Congress, 1st Session* (Washington, DC: Government Printing Office, 1975); Civil Rights Commission, *Federal Efforts*, pp. 235-239 & 252; Testimony of William Ryan in Blumrosen, *Black Employment and the Law*, pp. 405-407; William Ryan, "Uncle Sam's Betrayal," *The Progressive* 32 (May, 1968): 25-29; and "Minority Hiring Under New Attack," *Business Week*, June 13, 1970, p. 110.

69. Quotes from Rowan, *The Negro in the Textile Industry*, pp. 119-120; and testimony of Leonard Biermann in March 1969, Senate Judiciary *Hearing*, p. 46.

70. Rowan, *Textile Industry*, pp. 119-20; *Weekly News Digest*, May 5, 1969; *AFL-CIO News*, April 5, 1969, p. 1; and Congressional Quarterly, *Nixon: First Year*, p. 52. For general background on the textile industry, see Rowan.

71. U.S. Commission on Civil Rights, "The System Can Work: A Case Study in Contract Compliance" Clearinghouse Publication #29 (Washington, DC: Government Printing Office, 1970). Laird quote from *St. Louis Post Dispatch*, January 16, 1970, from Civil Rights Commission, Publication #29.

72. Quote from Department of Defense, *News Release* No. 11370, February 10, 1970, from Civil Rights Commission, Publication #29. See also general references in Publication #29; and Civil Rights Commission, *Federal Enforcement Efforts*, pp. 139-40 & 232-34. Population statistics from U.S. Department of Commerce, Bureau of the Census, *County and*

City Data Book 1977 (Washington, DC: Government Printing Office, 1978), p. 696.

73. Quote from U S. Commission on Civil Rights, *The Federal Civil Rights Enforcement Effort—A Reassessment* (Washington, DC: Government Printing Office, 1973), p. 5. See also pp. 7 & 69-89; *Federal Enforcement Efforts*, pp. 156-58 & 269-352; Senate Committee on Labor and Public Welfare, *Hearings*, 1971, especially, pp. 55, 80, & 196; U.S. EEOC, *Fifth Annual Report, FY1970* and *Sixth Annual Report, FY1971* (Washington, DC: EEOC); U.S. Commission on Civil Rights, "Statement on Affirmative Action for Equal Employment Opportunities," Clearinghouse Publication #41 (Washington, DC: Government Printing Office, 1973), p. 3. Data on staff and funding from Steinberg, *Turning Back*, p. 101.

74. Order #1 from Civil Rights Commission, *Federal Enforcement Efforts*, p. 195. Order #14 from *Black News Digest*, January 31, 1972.

75. *Weekly News Digest*, February 9, 1970.

76. *The New York Times*, January 16, 1970, p. 15.

77. Revised Order #4, U.S. *Code of Federal Regulations*, 60-2.1.

78. Quotes from *CFR* 60-2.12

79. *CFR* 60-2; Civil Rights Commission, *Federal Enforcement Efforts*, pp. 190-92; *Weekly News Digest*, February 9, 1970; and *The New York Times*, February 4, 1970, p. 26. For examples of criticism, see Civil Rights Commission, *Federal Efforts—Reassessment*, p. 66.

80. Robert E. Hampton, "The Response of Government and the Civil Service to Antidiscrimination Efforts," in *Equal Rights and Industrial Relations*, Industrial Relations Research Association Series (Madison: University of Wisconsin Press, 1977), pp. 144-45.

81. *Ibid.*, p. 141

82. For a comprehensive discussion of affirmative action within the federal government, see David H. Rosenbloom, *Federal Equal Employment Opportunity: Politics and Public Personnel Administration* (New York: Praeger Publishers, 1977). See also Clifford Alexander, "Equality under the Law: A Review of the Programs," in *Towards New Human Rights*, ed. Warner, pp. 386-89; Michael Malbin, "Agency Differences Persist over Goals and Timetables in Nondiscrimination Plans," Part II, *National Journal Reports* 5 (September 29, 1973): 1430; Civil Rights Commission, *Federal Enforcement Efforts*, pp. 35-102; *Reassessment*, pp. 41-63; and Hampton, "Civil Service," pp. 141-65.

83. Kennedy quote from *The New York Times*, June 10, 1963, p. 20.

84. *Swann et al. v. Charlotte-Mecklenburg Board of Education et al.* 402 U.S. 1; Simba, "Equal Employment," p. 296; Paul Brest, "Race

Discrimination," in *The Burger Court*, Vincent Blasi, ed. (New Haven, CT: Yale University Press, 1983), pp. 114-117; *The New York Times*, May 22, 1969, pp. 1, 36 & 37; October 30, 1969, pp. 1 & 34; and Wittner, *Cold War America*, pp. 336-37. For description of a "typical" affirmative action program, see Gregory D. Squires, *Affirmative Action* (East Lansing: Michigan State University, 1977), pp. 35-44.

85. *Griggs et al v. Duke Power Company* 401 U.S. 430.

86. 401 U.S. 431.

87. 401 U.S. 427-428.

88. 401 U.S. 424; Ruth G. Schaeffer, *Nondiscrimination in Employment: Changing Perspectives 1963-1972* (New York: The Conference Board, Inc., 1973), p. 20; Alfred Blumrosen, "The Crossroads for Equal Employment Opportunity: Incisive Administration or Indecisive Bureaucracy?," *Notre Dame Lawyer* 49 (October, 1973): 55; Blumrosen, "Strangers in Paradise: *Griggs v. Duke Power Company* and the Concept of Employment Discrimination," *Michigan Law Review* 71 (November, 1972): 59-110; NAACP Legal Defense Fund, *Annual Report, 1970-1971*, p. 12; U.S. EEOC, *Sixth Annual Report*, p. 11; EEOC, *The First Decade* (Washington, DC: EEOC, 1974), pp. 17-18; and *The New York Times*, March 9, 1971, pp. 1 & 21. For Crown-Zellerbach cases, see Chapter IV.

89. *Local 53 of the International Association of Heat and Frost Insulators and Asbestos Workers v. Vogler* 407 F. 2d 1050.

90. 407 F. 2d 1047; U.S. EEOC, *Fourth Annual Report*, p. 15; Blumrosen, *Black Employment and the Law*, p. 245; and "Court Bans Asbestos Union Bias," *The Crisis* 77 (March, 1970): 112-113. *Quarles* decision in Chapter IV.

91. *Carter v. Gallagher* 452 F. 2d 315 (1971); Beverly Grazza, "*Carter v. Gallagher*: From Benign Classification to Reverse Discrimination," *University of Pittsburgh Law Review* 34 (1972): 130-144.

92. Cleveland Police Department in U.S. Commission on Civil Rights, Ohio Advisory Committee, *Affirmative Action or Inaction?* (Washington, DC: Government Printing Office, 1978), p. 14. Other information from Blumrosen, *Black Employment*, pp. 245 & 311; and *Carter* 452 F. 2d 330.

93. U.S. EEOC, *Sixth Annual Report*, p. 37.

94. Quote from Elliot Abrams, "The Quota Commission," *Commentary* 54 (October, 1972): 56. See also: Malbin, "Agency Differences," *National Journal Reports*, Part I, pp. 1400-1411; Part II, September 29, pp. 1429-1434; Rowan, *Negro in the Steel Industry*, p. 110; and *The New York Times*, December 3, 1984, p. B10.

95. Jonathan Bramwell, *Courage in Crisis* (New York: The Dobbs-Merrill Company, 1972), p. 10; Hjalmar Rosen and Melvin Blonsky, "Dual Standards in Employing the Hard-Core," *Personnel Administration* 33 (March-April, 1970): 4ff..

96. Wirtz quoted in *Weekly News Digest*, November 8, 1965, pp. 1 & 2.

97. Commission quoted in Walter Goodman, "The Return of the Quota System," *The New York Times Magazine*, September 10, 1972, p. 106.

98. For "practical" problems of statistics, see Malbin in *National Journal Reports*, Part II; U.S. Commission on Civil Rights, *To Know or Not to Know* (Washington, DC: Government Printing Office, 1973); Frank C. Morris, Jr., *Current Trends in the Use (and Misuse) of Statistics in Employment Discrimination Litigation* (Washington, DC: Equal Employment Advisory Council, 1977); and *The New York Times*, December 3, 1984, B10. For analysis of actual implementation, see: Morris; Kevin McGuiness, *Government Memoranda*, especially pp. 42ff.; and *Timken v. Vaughan* 413 F. Supp. 1183 (1976). For philosophical discussion *see*: *Weekly News Digest*, November 8, 1965, pp. 1-2; Ben Halpen, "The 'Quota' Issue," *Midstream* 10 (March, 1973): 3-12; John Harold Kettlekamp, "Reverse Discrimination," *Mississippi Law Journal* 45 (1974): 467-488; and Bramwell, *Courage*, p. 25. For views of civil rights leaders, see debates over Civil Rights Act in Chapter III. Statistics from U.S. Department of Labor, Bureau of Labor Statistics, *The Social and Economic Status of Negroes in the United States, 1970* (Washington, DC: Government Printing Office, 1970), p. 49; and Lester Sobel, ed., *Affirmative Action* (New York: Facts on File, 1980), p. 13.

99. Godfrey Hodgson, *America in Our Time* (Garden City, NY: Doubleday and Company, Inc., 1976), pp. 414-415; Scannon and Wattenberg, *Real Majority*; and Wittner, *Cold War America*, p. 335.

100. Republican platform in *The New York Times*, August 19, 1972, pp. 1 & 26. Other information in Goulden, *Meany*, pp. 414-419; White, *Making of the President 1972*, p. 229; *Wall Street Journal*, October 10, 1969, p. 14 and June 19, 1972, p. 4; *The New York Times*, December 24, 1971, pp. 1, 12 & 24; and Friedman in *American Jewish Year Book 1973*.

101. Nixon quoted in Friedman, *American Jewish Year Book* 1973, p. 143; and *Public Papers*, 1972, pp. 851-52.

102. Ambrose, *Nixon: Volume Two*, pp. 520-24, 556, 623.

103. Ben Halpern, "The 'Quota' Issue," *Midstream* 19 (March, 1973): 12; Earl Raab, "Quotas by Any Other Name," *Commentary* 53 (January, 1972): 42; Abrams quoted in "The Quota Commission," *Commentary* 54

(October, 1972): 54. Schiffman episode in *The New York Times*, June 6, 1972, p. 28.

104. Stokes quoted in Friedman, *American Jewish Year Book 1973*, p. 176. See also Friedman, pp. 175-76; *Washington Post*, August 25, 1972, p. Al; *The New York Times,* September 4, 1972, p. 16; May 14, 1972, p. 20; June 30, 1972, p. 11.

105. McGovern quoted in Friedman, *American Jewish Year Book 1973*, p. 176.

106. White, *President 1972*, p. 32.

107. *Ibid.*, pp. 22-33; Friedman, *American Jewish Year Book 1973*, p. 179.

108. Friedman in *American Jewish Year Book 1973*, pp. 175-76; "Quotas: The Sleeper Issue of '72," *Newsweek* 80 (September 18, 1972): 36; and *Washington Post*, August 25, 1972, p. Al.

109. *The New York Times*, June 13, 1970, p. 14.

110. Congressional Quarterly, *Nixon: Second Year*, p. 70; *The New York Times*, June 13, 1970, p. 14; December 5, 1971, p. 53ff.; Panetta, *Bring Us Together*; Fletcher, *Sell-Out*, p. 81; and Friedman, *Year Book*, pp. 186-87. Hesburgh resignation from *The New York Times*, December 17, 1972, pp. 1 & 22.

111. Quotes from NAACP, *Annual Report 1972*, p. 60; *Wall Street Journal*, September 5, 1972; "Politics May Kill Quotas for Hiring," *Business Week*, September 9, 1972, p. 36. Holland quote from *Business Week*, September 9, 1972, p. 36.

112. *Business Week*, September 9, 1972, p. 36.

113. Quote from NAACP, *Annual Report 1972*, p. 60. Also: *Business Week*, September 9, 1972, pp. 36-37; *Wall Street Journal*, September 5, 1972; *The New York Times*, December 19, 1972, pp. 1 & 24; and Friedman in *Year Book*, p. 177.

114. Gallup Poll in *The New York Times*, December 14, 1972, p, 27.

115. Information on the South from Friedman in *Year Book*, p. 140; and White, *President 1972*, p. 342. Working class from White, pp. 237 & 343-344; and *The New York Times*, December 14, 1972, p. 27. Jewish votes from Friedman, p. 139. See generally: Fletcher, *Sell-Out*, pp. 1112; and Wittner, *Cold War America*, pp. 370-71.

116. Friedman in *Year Book*, pp. 140 & 164-65; Wittner, *Cold War America*, p. 371; Nixon, *RN*, p. 658; and *The New York Times*, July 19, 1972, p. 36. For analysis of changes in Congress, see Thomas P. Murphy, *The New Politics Congress* (Lexington, MA: D. C. Heath and Company, 1974).

117. Wilkins quoted in Friedman, *Year Book*, p. 163; *Year Book* quote, p. 158; and *Newsweek* quote September 18, 1972, p. 36.

118. Statistics from Wittner, *Cold War America*, p. 370; Friedman, *Year Book*, p. 140; and *The New York Times*, December 14, 1972, p. 27.

119. For an illustration, see Goodman, "Return of the Quota System."

VI

Moving Ahead: Nixon, Ford, and Affirmative Action

Richard Nixon's landslide reelection in 1972 could not have been encouraging to civil rights activists. Having campaigned against busing, job quotas, and welfare, Nixon interpreted his victory as a mandate against the liberal "excesses" of the 1960s. Nixon's agenda for his second term—dubbed the "New American Revolution"—involved reducing the size of the federal bureaucracy, cutting back or eliminating funding for Great Society programs, and restricting the executive branch of government. His budget for FY1973 called for "the elimination of the Job Corps and the Model Cities program, a virtual dismantling of the Office of Economic Opportunity, and drastic cuts in the funding of health, housing, education, and other social programs."[1] Nixon also supported increased defense spending, and he claimed the right to impound funds appropriated by Congress for federal programs. Accompanying the president to Washington in January 1973 was the new secretary of labor, Peter Brennan, former president of the New York City Building and Construction Trades Council and longtime opponent of affirmative action programs within the construction industry. Brennan's appointment was Nixon's reward to blue-collar workers, especially construction workers, for their electoral support.

One of the few White House concessions to African Americans during 1973 was approval of the Comprehensive Employment and Training Act (CETA), which incorporated, among other things, the Apprenticeship Outreach Program to increase minority participation in construction apprenticeship programs. Clearly, support of federal antidiscrimination activities did not seem to be a high administration priority in 1973.[2]

Nevertheless, the mid-1970s did *not* witness a major retreat in the area of affirmative action, for several reasons. First, the Congress, with its increased African-American, female, and liberal representation, sought to strengthen equal opportunity measures. A series of federal court decisions had created a legal foundation for affirmative action that the administration could have challenged only with great difficulty, if it had wanted to. In fact, the White House, despite its attacks—rhetorical and real—against Great Society programs, was not necessarily hostile to the concept of affirmative action. Enforcement of equal opportunity statutes was consistent with Nixon's espousal of the "work ethic." Elimination of racial barriers to employment, it was felt, would facilitate black economic advancement through private employment, thereby decreasing reliance on public services and assistance. Viewed in this perspective, the invigoration of federal antidiscrimination agencies not only complemented but helped justify the abolition of social welfare programs.[3]

Critically important to the perpetuation of affirmative action were the activities of civil rights groups, especially the NAACP and the NAACP Legal Defense Fund, as well as women's groups such as the National Organization for Women (NOW). Acting almost exclusively through the courts and federal bureaucracy, these groups continued to submit complaints and to initiate lawsuits, demanding increasingly broad and controversial modes of relief. The acceleration of affirmative action demands was, in part, a product of the momentum that had accumulated during previous decades.

By the 1970s, however, civil rights leaders also advocated affirmative action as a buffer against the economic downturn that disproportionately hurt African Americans. African-American workers were particularly vulnerable because they were concentrated in the construction and heavy manufacturing industries that were especially hard hit by the downswing. Thus, by 1975, black unemployment was nearly 15 percent. Herbert Hill estimated black male unemployment in Detroit at that time to be 40 percent. To prevent a recurrence of "last hired, first fired," civil rights activists pursued affirmative action even more vigorously, despite the widespread antiquota sentiments exhibited during the 1972 election.[4]

The foregoing does not imply that the period 1973-76 was one of uninterrupted affirmative action victories. As was true during previous years, much of the enforcement effort existed primarily on paper, hindered by a backlogged and inefficient bureaucracy. Also, many settlements, although more comprehensive than those of previous years, failed to satisfy the growing expectations of African-American and female groups. The issue of affirmative action remained complex and controversial, and it refused to go away.

Crucial to equal opportunity efforts after 1972 was the passage in March of that year of the Equal Employment Opportunity Act, which increased the power of the EEOC. In the initial drafts of the 1964 Civil

Rights Act, civil rights activists and congressional liberals had modeled the EEOC after the National Labor Relations Board, with the power to restrain employers and unions from engaging in discriminatory behavior. In the course of the debates over passage of the act, however, the agency's powers were steadily weakened, to the point where it was forced to rely almost exclusively on conciliation and voluntary compliance. From the inception of the EEOC in July 1965, advocates of equal employment opportunity had lamented the agency's relative impotence. Various groups, including the NAACP and the Kerner Commission, argued that cease-and-desist authority was vital to the effective functioning of the EEOC. The Johnson administration attempted to secure such authority, but its efforts failed.[5]

The Nixon administration also recognized the need for EEOC enforcement authority. The agency's steadily increasing caseload and backlog, coupled with criticism by civil rights and liberal groups, left little doubt of the commission's inadequacy in confronting the mammoth problem of economic discrimination. No consensus existed, however, on the nature and extent of the powers to be conferred. On one side, liberal activists expressed dissatisfaction with any arrangement short of cease-and-desist authority. Diametrically opposed to these views were business groups, which argued for continued reliance on voluntary compliance. The Nixon administration selected a middle ground, espousing legislation to empower the EEOC to initiate legal suits in the event of noncompliance, but still opposing any direct commission authority over business practices. The administration's approach instigated an early controversy when EEOC Chairman William Brown III, in his 1969 Senate confirmation hearings, championed cease-and-desist powers, only to reverse himself later and adopt the White House position, to the chagrin of congressional liberals.[6]

The struggle over EEOC enforcement authority continued throughout Nixon's first term. In 1969, the administration submitted a bill empowering the EEOC to initiate suits in federal courts and extending Title VII coverage to employees of state and local governments. The bill made little headway in Congress. The following year, the Senate approved a bill awarding cease-and-desist authority to the commission, but the House killed a similar measure.[7]

By 1971, the EEOC question had emerged as a major civil rights controversy within Congress. Consideration of a new bill generated "one of the most intensive offstage lobbying campaigns of 1971."[8] The battle began in January 1971 when Representative Augustus Hawkins of California, vice chairman of the Congressional Black Caucus, introduced a bill to the House conferring on the EEOC both cease-and-desist powers and the authority to initiate legal suits. The proposal, known as the Hawkins-Reid bill, became a focus of liberal support and a lightning-rod for conservative opposition.

Cognizant of the growing consensus in Congress of the pressing need for *some* reform of the EEOC, business groups, including the National Association of Manufacturers (NAM), the U.S. Chamber of Commerce, and the Associated General Contractors of America, lobbied in support of an alternative bill sponsored by Representative John Erlenborn of Illinois that limited the EEOC to initiating lawsuits. A Chamber of Commerce spokesperson warned that were the Hawkins-Reid bill to pass, the commission "might harass the hell out of business".[9] Meanwhile, the AFL-CIO joined liberal and civil rights groups in support of Hawkins-Reid. Final victory belonged to the business lobbyists as the House, on September 16, narrowly approved the Erlenborn bill over the Hawkins-Reid measure. Significantly, many northern Democrats, who favored a more stringent bill, joined southern Democrats, who opposed any modification of the *status quo*, in voting against the Erlenhorn bill.[10]

The spotlight then shifted to the Senate, where liberal senators Jacob Javits of New York and Harrison Williams of New Jersey assumed the leadership in the movement to secure cease-and-desist powers for the EEOC. Subcommittee hearings chaired by Williams in October 1971 provided a forum for the Leadership Conference on Civil Rights (LCCR), a confederation of labor, liberal, and civil rights organizations, to recapture the dynamic spirit it had exhibited a decade earlier. Representatives of the AFL-CIO, NOW, Americans for Democratic Action, and the Civil Rights Commission expressed their support for recasting the EEOC in the mold originally intended by liberal activists. Administration spokespersons, meanwhile, remained committed to judicial recourses only.

By this time, the EEOC backlog exceeded 30,000 cases, and the agency was nearly two years behind in its processing of complaints, underscoring the urgent need for reform. The fact that the commission achieved successful conciliation in less than half the cases in which it found "reasonable cause" convinced many people of the limitations of voluntary compliance. Following the subcommittee hearings, Javits and Williams cosponsored a "cease-and-desist" bill in the Senate, igniting a conflagration reminiscent of the civil rights battles of the 1960s. In January 1972 the Senate twice rejected an amendment introduced by Peter Dominick of Colorado to substitute judicial intervention for direct authority. Finally, on February 15, unable to overcome a southern filibuster, the Senate reversed itself and approved the Dominick (and administration) version.[11]

Just as the congressional struggles regarding civil rights legislation in the early 1960s had served as a forum for conflicting views regarding racial discrimination in the United States, the debates over strengthening the EEOC gave rise to more fundamental clashes regarding the evolution of affirmative action since that time. The Javits-Williams bill was intended as an amendment to Title VII of the Civil Rights Act; Senate conservatives seized this opportunity to challenge developments in the interpretation and enforcement of this law since 1965. As with the debates over the Philadelphia Plan in 1969, conservatives, led by Sam Ervin, charged that affirmative action violated the same civil rights law they had so bitterly opposed a decade earlier. On January 28, Ervin introduced an amendment to the bill prohibiting "reverse discrimination" in hiring: "No department, agency or officer of the United States shall require an employer to practice discrimination in reverse by employing persons of a particular race, or a particular religion, or a particular national origin, or a particular sex in either fixed or variable numbers, proportions, percentages, quotas, goals, or ranges."[12] The Ervin amendment was directed against proportional hiring in general and the Philadelphia Plan in particular. It provided compelling evidence of conservative reluctance, as late as 1972, to accept the legitimacy of Philadelphia-style construction plans or the use of goals and timetables in other fields of employment.

Congressional liberals challenged Ervin's reading of Title VII. An illuminating report issued by the House Labor Committee illustrated the evolution of liberal thought over the course of the preceding decade. "During the preparation and presentation of Title VII of the Civil Rights Act of 1964," the report read, "employment discrimination tended to be viewed as a series of isolated and distinguishable events, due, for the most part, to ill-will on the part of some identifiable individual or organization." Under these circumstances, voluntary conciliation and simple nondiscrimination were the preferred solutions. "Experience, however," the report continued, "has shown this to be an oversimplified expectation, incorrect in its conclusions." Job discrimination was more "complex and pervasive" than had been imagined in 1964.[13] Liberals increasingly employed the phrase *systemic* to describe economic discrimination.[14] Rather than being the product of malevolent individuals, discrimination was an inherent feature of the U.S. economic system and was reinforced and perpetuated by a vast array of institutions, practices, and beliefs.

As a remedy for systemic discrimination, voluntarism had been tried and found wanting. Only strict enforcement of nondiscrimination and affirmative action laws could prevail against a problem of the magnitude of job discrimination. Moreover, as Javits pointed out, Ervin's definition of nondiscrimination was inconsistent with a series of federal court decisions that had significantly broadened the reading of Title VII. Rather than adhere to static interpretations of economic discrimination predicated on the perceptions of the early 1960s, many liberals adopted a more evolutionary—and controversial—attitude toward equal employment opportunity as the complexity of the issues increasingly belied these earlier precepts. The paucity of support for the Ervin amendment—it attracted only 22 votes—demonstrated that most senators had rejected the strict differentiation between nondiscrimination and affirmative action.[15]

Although unsuccessful in their struggle to prohibit proportional hiring, southern conservatives did force the substitution of the Dominick bill for the more liberal Javits-Williams proposal. Following this maneuver, the Senate approved the modified bill in February, and the House followed suit in March. *The New York Times* reported: "The legislation is very close to what President Nixon had asked for."[16] As in 1964, civil rights leaders received an eviscerated version of what they had requested.

The new law, known as the Equal Employment Opportunity Act of 1972, modified several dimensions of the original Title VII. Most significantly, the EEOC was empowered to initiate suits in federal courts, rather than to rely on the Justice Department to do so. The act directed that the EEOC and the Justice Department exercise this power concurrently for two years, at which time the commission would assume exclusive authority. The law created the Office of General Counsel within the EEOC to conduct the commission's legal activities. This office was separated from the investigative branches to prevent any one individual or office from acting as prosecutor and judge. Employees of state and local governments, who had been exempt from the 1964 act, received Title VII coverage. Included in this stipulation were northern police and fire departments and southern county sheriff's offices, which historically had excluded African Americans. The act also expanded Title VII jurisdiction from employers with 25 or more employees to those with 15 or more workers.

In addition, the Equal Employment Opportunity Act made educational institutions subject to Title VII requirements for the first time. Prior to 1972, educational issues were handled primarily by the Department of Health, Education and Welfare (HEW), which was empowered by the 1964 act to withhold monies from any institution that practiced discrimination. With the passage of the 1972 law, the EEOC also could involve itself in cases of discrimination within the educational system, so far as they applied to employment. By expanding the scope of Title VII to encompass state and local employees and educational institutions, Congress extended Title VII coverage to an additional 15,000,000 workers.[17]

Passage of the 1972 act signaled the beginning of a more activist phase in the history of the EEOC. To reinforce the agency's new powers, Congress and the White House allocated increased financial and human resources to the commission. In November 1972, for example, the commission's staff included only 40 lawyers; six months later, the number was 222.[18]

Within a year after receiving its new powers, the EEOC concluded perhaps its most celebrated conciliation agreement when it signed a pact with the world's largest private employer, AT&T. The history of the AT&T agreement was a long and convoluted one, involving substantial amounts of time, money, and frustration. The company's hiring patterns reflected traditional racial and sexual typecasting. Women traditionally were confined to operator and clerical positions, while African Americans, hindered by what they denounced as discriminatory tests, were underrepresented among white-collar employees and overrepresented among service workers. As late as 1973, for example, women constituted 94 percent of all clerical workers and 95 percent of all operators. Black males comprised 25 percent of all service workers, but less than 2 percent of officials and managers. White males, conversely, held nearly 75 percent of all official and managerial jobs and dominated the skilled crafts, including lineman positions.

Following the passage of the Civil Rights Act, dissatisfied female and minority workers submitted hundreds of complaints to the EEOC regarding the company's employment policies. From 1967 to 1969, the commission negotiated with the company without achieving an agreement. The situation remained at an impasse until November 1970, when AT&T formally requested authorization for a rate increase from the Federal Communications Commission (FCC). EEOC attorney David Copus petitioned the FCC to deny this request, charging AT&T with race and sex discrimination. Cosponsoring this petition were the NAACP and NAACP Legal Defense Fund, NOW, the ACLU, and the Mexican-American Legal Defense Fund. The following April, the EEOC created a special AT&T task force under Copus's supervision.

Pressured by federal agencies and private complaints, AT&T eventually devised an affirmative action plan that was approved by the General Services Administration but not the EEOC. The latter agency complained to the Labor Department, which "ruled that the GSA had not acted in the best interests of all parties and decided to enter the case itself."[19] Thus, a new series of negotiations began late in 1972 involving the Justice Department, the Labor Department, the EEOC, and AT&T. Discussions continued into January 1973, when the parties achieved a landmark agreement.

The AT&T agreement provided for the restructuring of the company's hiring and promotion policies and the restitution of back pay to minority and female employees. The company agreed to open all job classifications to all workers, with annual goals and timetables for female and minority workers based on projections of job openings. The company also established transfer and promotion goals and, in some circumstances, agreed to a seniority "override"; that is, promoting minority workers with less seniority than their white coworkers. AT&T also promised a special review of all female employees with a college degree hired since the establishment of Title VII to identify cases of underutilization. The cost of these modifications was estimated at $23,000,000. The most widely publicized feature of this agreement was the awarding of $15,000,000 in back pay to 2,000 minority and 13,000 female employees as compensation for past discrimination. (In 1975, the company agreed to additional payments of $2,500,000 after it failed to achieve some of its goals.)[20]

As was frequently true in job discrimination settlements, various parties expressed discontent with the final agreement. Representatives of NOW charged that the employment provisions and monetary compensation were inadequate. Labor unions (the chief AT&T unions were the Communications Workers of America and the International Brotherhood of Electrical Workers) challenged (unsuccessfully) the seniority override provisions, claiming they constituted reverse discrimination. Significantly, the company, even after signing the pact, continued to deny any wrongdoing. When asked why an "innocent" employer would agree to such terms, one official replied: "It's just that the rules of the game have changed."[21]

Despite these criticisms, the AT&T agreement was a crucial one, for several reasons. Most obvious, of course, was the size of the corporation. The government's willingness to challenge the nation's largest private employer served as a warning to other companies that at least token compliance with affirmative action regulations must be observed. As one business official observed: "There's a lot of teeth-chattering going on around here."[22]

The AT&T case was also significant in that it illustrated the growing urgency of the issues of seniority and back pay to African-American workers. The question of seniority was not a novel one; rather, it had preoccupied African Americans throughout the century, especially during periods of economic downturn. The special hiring arrangements implemented by Henry Ford after World War I and the "superseniority" controversy following World War II demonstrated the concern of civil rights advocates with the tradition of "last hired, first fired." The issue was raised throughout the 1960s and 1970s when economic recessions—especially those of 1970-71 and 1974-75—threatened the newly won gains of African-American workers. The growing disparity between white and black unemployment rates prompted blacks to focus on the discriminatory effects of seniority provisions of collective bargaining agreements.

The willingness of civil rights organizations to challenge this basic tenet of labor relations illustrated the evolution of liberal/civil rights thought since World War II. In the 1940s, the NAACP denounced "superseniority" as a communist-inspired, antilabor tactic; by the 1970s, the NAACP Legal Defense Fund advocated the policy of "retroactive seniority" to combat the effects of economic recession. By the 1970s, frustration with the limited achievements of decades of civil rights activities superseded the fear of alienating labor unions. Buttressing the position of civil rights groups were federal court decisions that modified seniority arrangements that perpetuated past discrimination. Labor unions, not surprisingly, condemned interference with seniority as a violation of both collective bargaining procedures and Title VII, which protected "a bona fide seniority or merit system." The controversy regarding seniority and affirmative action was never effectively resolved and continued into the 1980s and 1990s.[23]

The question of back pay, which affected employers rather than unions, similarly moved to the forefront during the 1970s. The concept of back pay as a remedial affirmative action dates at least to the passage of the National Labor Relations Act of 1935, which empowered the NLRB to order compensatory payments to workers penalized for engaging in union activities. Its application to the field of civil rights became a major issue in the 1970s and reflected a growing consensus that certain groups were entitled to compensation for past discrimination. The issue was a complex one, because the pertinent administrative or legal body not only had to determine the propriety of back pay, but it had to identify the legitimate recipients as well. Given the preponderance of Title VII class action suits, the courts frequently had to decide whether back pay should be awarded to entire classes of workers—as in the AT&T case—or whether it should be restricted to individuals who could demonstrate that they had suffered specific acts of discrimination.

Significantly, the courts ruled during the mid-1970s that an *intent* to discriminate was not necessary for back pay to be awarded. Reflecting *Griggs v. Duke Power Company* of 1971, the courts ruled that employment practices that confined blacks to lower-paying jobs, when not justified by "business necessity," constituted grounds for monetary compensation, whether or not an intent to discriminate existed. Complicating this issue even further was the fact that many employers—like AT&T—never accepted the changing definitions of employer affirmative action obligations and considered themselves equal opportunity employers. An employer who denied any wrongdoing would especially oppose the granting of back pay. Like seniority, the back pay issue remained a staple of affirmative action disputes in the ensuing years.[24]

The AT&T case also illustrated the growing convergence of race and sex discrimination cases. Inspired by the black movement, women's groups initiated a series of lawsuits and administrative actions following passage of the Equal Pay Act of 1963 and the Civil Rights Act of 1964. A 1972 law extended the protections of the Equal Pay Act to "executive, administrative, and professional employees" as well as to salespersons and preschool workers.[25] Just as they did with laws against race discrimination, the courts expended the stipulations of laws against sex discrimination throughout the 1960s and early 1970s. Meanwhile, women entered the labor force in unprecedented numbers, challenging traditional sexual typecasting within the job market. By 1973, most major affirmative actions cases and settlements involved both women and minorities.[26]

Finally, the AT&T decision was significant because it signaled a transition in the operational methodology of the EEOC. In its formative years, the commission addressed complaints on a case-by-case basis, treating each individual complaint as a separate entity. To pursue this same policy against AT&T, against which the commission received more than 2,000 complaints, would have constituted a lifelong endeavor. By securing a companywide pact, the EEOC successfully consolidated thousands of complaints into one comprehensive conciliation agreement. Buoyed by this achievement, Chairman William Brown introduced a "track" system that established a four-tier hierarchy of categories based on the size of the accused company or unions. Track One referred to national corporations or unions; Track Two to regional institutions; and Tracks Three and Four to smaller businesses.

The EEOC accorded highest priority to "Track One" cases. Brown created a National Programs Division within the agency to deal exclusively with these cases. By September 1973 the EEOC had filed charges against such giants as General Motors, Ford, General Electric, Sears Roebuck, and the United Automobile Workers of America (UAW), challenging a host of practices and procedures, including "wages, benefits, union representation, layoffs, apprenticeship and training, promotion, and seniority."[27] As with

AT&T, each case incorporated numerous commission charges. Also as with AT&T, the accused parties generally denied engaging in discriminatory behavior. One UAW official complained "We still don't know what they're after."[28] This sudden burst of activity seemed to indicate a new forcefulness by the commission. A year later, however, all the cases were still in process, and little had been resolved.[29]

The EEOC also pursued another giant—the steel industry. The history of racial policies in the steel industry was one of pervasive discrimination. African-American steelworkers were concentrated in the lowest-paying positions and often were victimized by separate seniority lists and segregated facilities. White workers received preferential treatment, including, on some occasions, an upgrading of test scores. One federal judge characterized a Bethlehem Steel plant in Lackawanna, Pennsylvania, as "a microcosm of classic job discrimination in the North."[30]

Early attempts to rectify these conditions were fruitless. In 1957, NAACP Labor Secretary Herbert Hill submitted a compilation of charges and complaints by black steelworkers to the United Steelworkers of America and the NLRB, but he achieved little satisfaction. Following the implementation of Title VII, the industry and unions gradually eliminated their most blatantly racist practices. Discrimination was perpetuated, however, by such practices as departmental versus plant seniority.

As the volume of complaints increased during the 1960s, the federal government became involved. Chief among the government's targets were U.S. Steel and Bethlehem Steel. In December 1967, in response to NAACP charges registered with the EEOC, the Justice Department initiated a Title VII suit against the Bethlehem Steel plant at Lackawanna. In June 1971, the U.S. Court of Appeals ordered a series of modifications in hiring and promotion procedures, including the development of objective hiring, promotion and apprenticeship criteria, "priority transfer rights" for workers in eleven predominantly African-American departments, and the adoption of plant rather than departmental seniority. In addition, the company implemented "rate retention," a system in which transferees were entitled to retain their previous salary if it exceeded that of entry-level positions in their new department.

A similar scenario unfolded in the Bethlehem Steel plant in Sparrows Point, Maryland. Throughout the 1960s, the OFCC pressured the plant—a federal contractor—to adopt plant seniority and rate retention. Bethlehem refused, citing "business necessity." The Labor Department assigned a three-man panel headed by Fr. Dexter Hanley to investigate the situation. The panel determined in a 2-1 decision that, although current practices perpetuated past discrimination, any alteration of the seniority system would be "unduly disruptive" to business operations. However, the secretary of labor rejected this contention and ordered the plant's procedures modified along the same general lines as the Lackawanna plant.[31]

Black steelworkers and the Justice Department also launched a suit against the U.S. Steel plant in Fairfield, Alabama. The charges were analogous to those against Bethlehem Steel, with the exception that the claimants added back pay to their list of demands. The Justice Department presented the corporation with a number of affirmative action stipulations, threatening a lawsuit if they were rejected. U.S. Steel Chairman Edwin Gott replied that implementing the Justice Department terms would require that 50 percent of all workers hired for office and clerical jobs and 40 percent of those promoted to management positions over a five-year period be black, an arrangement he denounced as a violation of Title VII. Denying any "pattern or practice" of discrimination, Gott decided to risk a lawsuit rather than accede to the Justice Department's "grossly outrageous demands."[32]

Gott's strategy backfired, however. In January 1973, a district court sustained the accusations against the company and ordered plant seniority and back pay for victimized workers. The court ruled that "Back pay is an integral part pf the whole of relief," an important statement in light of increased demands for compensatory payments by female and minority-group workers.[33]

These actions, however, failed to mollify African-American and female hostility toward the steel industry. African-American workers lodged over 1,000 complaints against steel companies, and private class action suits against U.S. Steel sought back pay for more than 450 African-American steelworkers. In 1974, NOW and two female employees filed a class action suit against the Bethlehem Steel Sparrows Point plant.

To avoid becoming overwhelmed by the volume of complaints, the EEOC sought to apply the "AT&T formula" to the steel industry. By the end of 1973, intense negotiations were underway between the commission and steel officials to effect an industrywide agreement and to halt the proliferation of litigation against steel employers. As one steel company attorney observed: "As the legal situation came to be clarified, we decided an affirmative action approach would be a better way to do things."[34] Discussions continued into 1974, with the two parties divided primarily over the question of back pay, which the industry opposed but the EEOC insisted on. The commission hinted that it might file suit against ten major steel producers if a voluntary agreement could not be worked out.

Finally, in April 1974, the EEOC, the United Steelworkers of America, and nine steel corporations reached an agreement that included the adoption of plant seniority and rate retention, the use of hiring goals for minorities and females for one year, and $30,000,000 in back pay to approximately 4,000 female and 40,000 male minority-group workers. The steel pact was applauded by Secretary of Labor Peter Brennan but was criticized by the NAACP and NOW. Especially pernicious in their eyes was the stipulation that workers accepting a back pay settlement forfeited the right to sue their employer. Were such a worker to file a suit, the Justice Department would enter the suit on the side of the employer. A worker who declined back pay was required to lodge a complaint with the EEOC, which could initiate a suit only if conciliation efforts failed. The NAACP also decried the absence of black workers from the negotiations. Finally, the NAACP contended that the actual sums involved—estimated to average $400 per worker—were far less than what a judge would award in a job discrimination suit. Herbert Hill charged: "Through this agreement, the major steel corporations and the steelworkers union are attempting to buy immunity from litigation under Title VII of the Civil Rights Act of 1964."[35]

The steel pact, like the AT&T agreement, illustrated how the passage of the Civil Rights Act had transformed civil rights activities. In the 1960s, pressure from the streets provided a major impetus for the enactment of civil rights laws. A decade later, the fear of legal actions based on these laws convinced many employers to accept affirmative action. As Kennedy and Johnson had anticipated, the arena of conflict had largely shifted "from the streets to the courts." In both the 1960s and 1970s, of course, the initial efforts were undertaken by female and minority-group members with the support of civil rights organizations. By the 1970s, however, the passage of antidiscrimination laws and the creation of enforcement agencies enabled the government to intervene decisively in, and often assume control of, this process. Significantly, those civil rights organizations unable to effect a successful transition from direct protest to legal/bureaucratic channels—CORE and SNCC, for example—ceased to be a major factor in the struggle for equal employment opportunity.[36]

By the time of the signing of the steel pact, the burst of activity that began with the AT&T case apparently had run its course. During this period, the EEOC enjoyed an unusual degree of latitude due to White House preoccupation with the emerging Watergate scandal. Brown's "track" system and his pursuit of large corporations endeared him to African-American and women's groups but disturbed businesses and unions. Complaints reached the White House, which, in August 1973, announced it intended to remove Brown. Senate consideration of his successor—John Powell, Jr.—was held up for months as a liberal coterie led by Jacob Javits of New York awaited (and received) White House assurances that Brown's removal did not mean that the EEOC enforcement process was to be abandoned. In December 1973 the Senate confirmed Powell, a former general counsel to the Civil Rights Commission and U.S. attorney in Brooklyn with law degrees from Harvard and New York University. Powell acknowledged that cease-and-desist powers would expedite the resolution of complaints, but he refused to demand such powers. He stated a preference for conciliation over litigation and expressed reservations regarding his predecessor's "tracking system." Although the steel pact was finalized under Powell's tenure, the removal of Brown diminished much of the commission's zeal.[37]

The overall performance of the EEOC during these years was uneven. By the end of the Ford years, the commission could boast many real accomplishments. Thousands of charges, ranging from individual complaints to the AT&T and steel pacts, had been addressed, and thousands of people had received some degree of assistance. Many people who dealt with the EEOC were impressed with the quality of its investigations. The implicit threat of administrative or legal action sometimes convinced employers to modify discriminatory practices even in the absence of formal charges. The EEOC participated in many antidiscrimination lawsuits, and EEOC guidelines provided a basis for several judicial decisions, including *Griggs*. Funds provided by the EEOC assisted state and local antidiscrimination agencies. In 1974, the first EEOC training academy opened in Washington, D.C. Finally, the Equal Employment Opportunity Act empowered the agency to initiate Title VII suits in federal courts.[38]

Unfortunately, the commission's shortcomings often overshadowed its accomplishments. Despite its increased resources, the EEOC remained ill-equipped to administer its rapidly multiplying caseload, which, in 1973 alone, numbered almost 50,000 complaints, compared to 9,000 in its first year. By June 1975 the agency's backlog exceeded 125,000 cases, including more that 2,000 cases remaining from 1968. The average case took two years to resolve, and many took substantially longer. Brown's "tracking system," although effective against such giants as AT&T, did little to ameliorate the backlog, as 90 percent of all cases fell within low-priority categories three and four. The commission also failed to screen charges, a serious procedural flaw given that up to 10 percent of charges were spurious, including the 150 complaints filed by one individual of discrimination based on national origin—Transylvanian vampire. Agency requirements of racial data from employers resulted in the receipt by the EEOC of 260,000 forms annually. Compounding all of these difficulties was the absence of interagency cooperation within the federal bureaucracy. Despite assurances of OFCC-EEOC cooperation by secretaries of labor Hodgson in 1970 and Brennan in 1974, the two agencies functioned separately and independently, with little constructive interaction.[39]

Moreover, EEOC conciliation agreements often were less impressive in their implementation than they were on paper. As one example, the AT&T settlement, although widely heralded in the press, was denounced by Dr. Ann Scott, NOW vice president for legislation, as "chickenfeed."[40] A reimbursement of $15,000,000 appeared less generous when actually divided among 15,000 employees. In fact, NOW calculated that female workers alone lost $500,000,000 in income between 1965 and 1972. Actual company payments to some individual employees totaled as little as $100. Moreover, although the percentage of African Americans in administrative and sales positions had increased significantly by the end of the 1970s, the benefits for women were less certain, because more male employees transferred into formerly female departments than females into male lines. Nor was AT&T an isolated case. One General Accounting Office (GAO) study found no differences in racial hiring patterns between firms that had implemented EEOC agreements and those that had not.[41]

Under these circumstances, the allocation of additional powers to the EEOC constituted a mixed blessing. On the one hand, the ability to initiate legal actions made the commission more formidable. On the other hand, enactment of the 1972 law conferred legal responsibilities on an already overburdened agency. Just as the EEOC was ill-prepared to assume its administrative role in 1965, it was poorly equipped to assume an expanded role in 1972. The commission created the office of general counsel to coordinate legal activities, but it lacked adequate resources for extensive litigation. Lack of intra-agency cooperation between the litigation and compliance divisions created additional obstacles. In its first year, the commission launched only 25 suits, many of which were resolved before they came to trial. Significantly, the American Bar Association criticized the performance of the EEOC's inexperienced legal staff. Consideration of these difficulties prompted former chairman Clifford Alexander to label the Equal Employment Opportunity Act a "sham."[42]

The personnel problems that debilitated the EEOC during the Johnson years continued throughout the Republican administrations. The White House removed two chairmen, Clifford Alexander and William Brown, for pursuing their jobs too aggressively. The White House replaced Brown with

John Powell, only to find itself embroiled in further controversies. An autocratic, determined leader, Powell alienated his fellow commissioners with what they perceived as his disregard of their proper role. In 1975, the commissioners censured Powell. Civil rights and womens' groups shared this disillusionment with Powell's destabilizing effect on the commission. Finally, in March 1975, President Gerald Ford removed Powell, replacing him with Lowell Perry, an African-American automobile industry official with no previous civil rights experience. Perry thus became the fourth EEOC chairman since Nixon assumed office in 1969. In the words of one observer: "Since the fall of 1969, the commission has been in a perpetual state of reorganization."[43]

As a result of infighting, inadequate resources, irregular leadership, and reliance on voluntary compliance, enforcement of equal opportunity laws was often ineffective. Responding to the economic downturn and the increased costs of job discrimination settlements, business institutions resisted EEOC pressures more vigorously. The EEOC achieved success in only half of the cases in which it found probable cause. A 1976 GAO study concluded that "the direct results of the commission's individual charge and systemic discrimination activities have been minimal." Employing a more informal vocabulary, one congressional representative declared: "I have yet to see a federal agency quite as goofed up as the EEOC," while *Business Week* labeled the commission "the government's most notorious administrative mess."[44]

While the EEOC addressed complaints of job discrimination, the OFCC continued to monitor compliance by 250,000 government contractors. In Fiscal Year 1973 the OFCC conducted 31,000 agency reviews, and it anticipated an increase the following year. In October 1975 the agency officially was renamed the Office of Federal Contract Compliance Programs (OFCCP), and it expanded its definition of "minorities" to include persons with disabilities and Vietnam veterans. As was true of earlier periods, the agency recorded some concrete achievements. In April 1973, for example, the OFCC and Delta Airlines concluded an agreement promising increased opportunities for female and minority-group employees. *Business Week* reported in 1975 that the absolute number of minority employees at Lockheed—a major federal contractor—had increased since 1970, although the company's overall work force had declined by 35,000 during that period. The agency also created a new category of "nonresponsible" through which an employer could be debarred from *future* contracts without being entitled to a hearing. (Cancellation of existing contracts required a hearing.)

Finally, the OFCCP, along with other federal agencies, adopted a quantitative formula to gauge employment discrimination. Known as the Opportunity Index (OPI), the formula dictated that the success rate of female and minority-group members with respect to employment, testing, and other procedures measure at least 80 percent of that of white males. Put simply, a company that accepted 50 percent of white male applicants should accept at least 40 percent of female and minority applicants. Failure to do so constituted *prima facie* evidence of "adverse impact." This formula for the first time provided employers and contractors with a concrete basis by which to evaluate business practices.[45]

These developments, however, must be balanced against the agency's deficiencies, including inadequate staff and resources and lax enforcement. The OFCCP continued to rely on voluntary compliance, prolonging negotiations with offending contractors well beyond official deadlines in lieu of severing contracts. Through the end of 1974, the OFCC had debarred only nine contractors, replying on the *threat* of debarment to ensure compliance. By 1976, Herbert Hill dismissed the agency as "functionally useless."[46]

The other federal agencies accumulated similar records regarding contract compliance. One GAO study revealed that most agencies responsible for nonconstruction contractors reviewed less than 20 percent of all federal contracts. Moreover, agencies that monitored compliance often approved inadequate affirmative action plans. Lack of adequate personnel contributed greatly to this problem. One study of the Detroit metropolitan area in 1970 revealed a major shortage of federal equal employment opportunity staff members. The Defense Department, Veterans Administration, Agriculture Department, and HEW had *no* full-time equal opportunity officers in that area, and the Small Business Administration assigned one individual to cover twelve states. Effective enforcement of equal opportunity laws was virtually impossible under these circumstances.[47]

The OFCCP channeled much of its enforcement energy into the construction industry, with disappointing results. Although minority-group participation in the skilled crafts exceeded that of previous years, African Americans, Hispanics, and women continued to experience difficulties in entering the highest-paying professions. A GAO study of 1979 concluded: "Ineffective enforcement and inadequate monitoring by federal agencies resulted in minorities making little progress from 1972 through 1976 in increasing their representation among journeymen in skilled construction craft unions."[48] Minority-group representation in the skilled crafts increased from 7.2 percent in 1972 to 8.4 percent four years later. These statistics, however, were suspect—and possibly inflated—because most construction unions failed to complete the required EEO-3 forms, which recorded racial data.

Overall, minority-group workers continued to be overrepresented in the lowest-paying occupations. A 1972 study, for example, revealed that, although only one-fourth of all construction workers were located in the "Laborers, roofers, and trowel trades group," one-half of all Spanish-surnamed and three-fourths of all African-American workers belonged to these categories.[49] Data from the Bureau of Labor Statistics, moreover, revealed an inverse relationship between black membership and wage rates. By 1974, blacks comprised 3 percent or less of six of the seven highest-paying crafts, in contrast to 25 percent of "laborers," the lowest-paying occupation. Minority and female construction workers were also concentrated in certain large locals. In 1969, 40 percent of all locals reported no black members; five years later, almost 20 percent of all locals reported no black members, and 40 percent were less than 2 percent black.

Moreover, reported numbers of minority workers often included apprentices and trainees, many of whom never attained full-time journeyman status. According to the GAO, OFCCP "compliance strategies get minorities temporary employment rather than union journeyman membership."[50] One hometown plan, for example, placed 1,100 minority workers in construction projects over a four-year period, but only 26 became union journeymen. Contractors often issued temporary work permits that enabled minority-group workers to participate on a particular job but did not lead to union membership. "Checkerboarding"—transferring minority workers from private to public sites—also served to inflate minority representation. Those nonwhite workers who achieved journeyman status received lower wages and more often were assigned to short-term jobs than white workers. After nearly a decade of agitation and affirmative action plans, African Americans, Hispanics, and females continued to be underrepresented—and often unwelcome—in the skilled construction crafts.[51]

One major obstacle to black progress during the 1970s was the sluggish performance of the construction industry during this period. Although the total dollar volume of construction work increased during the decade (reflecting, in part, the effects of inflation), the construction labor force, after increasing by approximately 700,000 during the years 1967-72, remained relatively constant (at approximately 4,300,000) thereafter. Significantly, white membership in the BTUs actually *declined* from 1970 to 1974, while nonwhite membership rose. During that time, 43 percent of new BTU members were members of minority groups.[52] This statistic indicates a certain amount of minority progress. Again, however, these figures must be treated carefully, because the majority of unions did not submit the EEO-3 forms from which membership data were accumulated. Furthermore, African Americans who entered construction unions did so disproportionately in the lower-paying job categories.[53]

The modest rate of black progress also reflected the shortcomings of the hometown programs that represented the cornerstone of the Labor Department's construction policy. By the end of the Nixon-Ford years, a few of the programs appeared to be effective. The Indianapolis Plan produced positive results, due largely to the strength of the minority coalition that helped implement the plan. A Carnegie-Mellon study claimed that the Pittsburgh Plan was successful, even though it recruited only half the targeted number of African-American workers.

In general, however, the hometown plans failed to realize the aspirations of their creators. The Detroit Plan, for example, was designed to place 2,000 black workers in training programs in its first year; it actually placed 200. The San Francisco Plan was denounced by one critic as a "paper compliance program," and Labor Department studies charged the Miami and Boston plans had failed to achieve their goals. So disappointing was the New York experience that, in January 1973, the city withdrew from the plan and established its own affirmative action arrangement. The overall paucity of results forced the Labor Department to assign mandatory goals to nineteen cities and two states (Delaware and Rhode Island) in 1974.[54]

The Chicago Plan serves to illustrate the difficulties inherent in affirmative action enforcement within the construction industry. Conceived as a response to violent confrontations and heralded by its authors as a landmark in voluntarism and cooperation, the Chicago Plan actually produced meager results. In June 1971 *The New York Times* announced that the plan had "collapsed," claiming: "Last year's construction ended with not a single minority at work under the plan." The *Times* further reported that the Labor Department intended to devise its own program, citing Arthur Fletcher: "It's not a question of whether we'll impose a plan in Chicago, but a question of how."[55]

By the end of the year, however, the White House had "promoted" Fletcher out of the Labor Department, and the imposed plan never materialized. Rather, the Labor Department initiated another series of negotiations with representatives of unions, employers, and civil rights groups, which in turn produced a second voluntary plan in October 1972. The revised Chicago Plan established general hiring "ranges" for the various crafts with the ultimate goal of employing 10,000 minority-group workers by 1976. Workers would attain union membership, and the Labor Department agreed to fund a training program supervised by the Urban League. The plan required unions and employers to submit monthly data reports to the Urban League.

Unfortunately, the second Chicago Plan was no more successful than its predecessor. According to Labor Department statistics, the participation rate of African Americans in eight important crafts remained below 2 percent. Disillusioned, the Urban League withdrew from the plan in 1973. After years of experimentation, the Labor Department finally conceded that its voluntary approach was inadequate. In January 1974 the DOL imposed a plan in Chicago, with goals and timetables for minority-group participation in every craft, effective through 1978. As with most affirmative action plans, compliance was contingent on an employer's "good faith efforts."[56]

A number of factors contributed to the failure of the hometown plans. The lack of growth in the construction labor force during the Nixon-Ford years increased union intransigence toward affirmative action plans. It is not surprising that construction unions balked at admitting minority-group workers when union members themselves experienced difficulty securing employment.

Further difficulties arose from the nature of the programs themselves. The experimental nature of hometown plans, the uncertainty of union membership and job referrals, and the seasonal nature of construction work dissuaded many potential workers from becoming involved. Disputes among conflicting interests—usually unions, employers, and civil rights groups—often hindered effective management of the programs. Contractors successfully violated affirmative action regulations by failing to forward requisite data and by "motorcycling" minority-group workers from one work site to another.

As previously mentioned, one reason for OFCCP negligence was inadequate resources. The GAO reported, for example, that "one OFCCP area office had two people monitoring 29,000 contracts."[57] Technically required to audit affirmative action plans annually, the agency actually audited only half of such programs from November 1973 through March 1975. In addition, affirmative action enforcement within the construction industry had become extremely complicated and time-consuming. To determine whether an employer had made "good faith efforts," for example, the OFCCP had to evaluate fifteen major factors ranging from actual minority-group employment to the effects of the weather on construction. These circumstances made effective enforcement exceedingly difficult and sometimes created illusions of progress where none in fact existed.[58]

Compounding all these difficulties was the perpetuation of racist policies and attitudes within the BTUs. Despite the civil rights progress of the preceding twenty years, racial animosity remained a fact of construction life. Unions, which often accepted affirmative action programs under duress, devised sophisticated schemes like "motorcycling" to sabotage them, and white workers sometimes walked off their jobs when minority trainees arrived.

To be sure, the difficulties encountered by unions and contractors in hometown programs were real and must not be understated. Black workers often came from impoverished backgrounds and sometimes possessed inferior educations and job skills. The argument that *no* qualified black workers were available, however, was a specious one. The Bureau of Labor Statistics, for example, confirmed the existence of many already skilled black workers who could qualify for union membership. In some areas, the bureau claimed, black participation in the BTUs would double without *any* job training if the unions simply would admit qualified workers. Given the self-contained environment of the construction world and the overall state of the economy, such a prospect seemed unlikely at best. Citywide affirmative action plans were hurriedly designed to defuse explosive controversies within an industry—and perhaps a society—that never accepted the legitimacy of affirmative action. Under these circumstances, the ineffectiveness of these programs is neither surprising nor unexpected.[59]

Besides hometown plans, the other major strategy for integrating the building trades in which the Labor Department participated was the Apprenticeship Outreach Program. Generally funded by the Labor Department and administered by the AFL-CIO, the Workers' Defense League, and the National Urban League, these programs endeavored to introduce blacks into the construction crafts through the time-honored vehicle of apprenticeship. As with hometown plans, the statistics reveal a degree of progress—some of it real, some of it illusory. The scope of the program could not be denied. From its inception in 1967 through the end of 1975, Outreach programs in more than 100 cities placed between 25,000 and 30,000 minority youths in apprenticeship programs at a cost of tens of millions of dollars. These numbers were especially impressive when compared to the paltry numbers of black apprentices—approximately 2,000—in the United States as late as 1960. Indeed, statistics appeared to indicate that minority apprentices had attained nearly proportional representation. By 1974, 18 percent of all apprentices in the building trades were from minority groups. That same year, Apprenticeship Outreach Programs began to accept female candidates.

Again, however, the statistics were misleading. As was true throughout the construction industry, black apprentices were overrepresented in the lower-paying, less-skilled trades. More than half of Outreach placements were in the less-skilled crafts. In addition, the official statistics were not adjusted for dropout rates, which were far higher among nonwhites than whites. In fact, on a national basis, Outreach dropout rates exceeded completion rates in apprenticeship programs. Reasons for dropping out ranged from nonpayment of union dues to commuting difficulties to the absence of consistent employment. Finally, completion of an apprenticeship program, like participation in a hometown plan, offered no guarantees of long-term employment. Not only were apprenticeship graduates dependent on the unions for job referrals—which might or might not be forthcoming— but apprentices sometimes received training for nonexistent jobs. One GAO report concluded that "AOP placements appear overstated and that there was a high unemployment rate among those placed."[60]

Outreach programs were designed to minimize loss of union control over entry into the skilled crafts. Although they facilitated the entry of minority youths into the construction industry, they did not substantially modify the racial composition of the industry. Indeed, by 1976, 60 percent of all Outreach placements were *outside* the construction industry. The GAO eventually recommended the abolition of the program, a suggestion rejected by the Labor Department.[61]

By the mid-1970s, the courts, and not the federal bureaucracy, were spearheading the drive for affirmative action. Previous judicial rulings had contributed to the attack on separate lines of progression, discriminatory testing and hiring requirements, and other obstacles to the advancement of African-American workers. As we saw in the previous chapter, with the onset of economic recession in the 1970s, antidiscrimination suits more frequently focused on the issues of seniority and back pay. In rulings against such companies as U.S. Steel, Bethlehem Steel, Albemarle Paper Company, and Timken Roller Bearing Company, the courts modified seniority arrangements, usually substituting departmental for plant seniority, and approved back pay as modes of affirmative relief, even in class action suits. The *Albemarle* decision was particularly significant in its determination that the awarding of back pay was *not* contingent on a demonstration of employers' "bad faith."[62]

The courts continued to expand and liberalize Title VII during the mid-1970s. In January 1973, for example, a U.S. court of appeals upheld a district court ruling requiring a Cincinnati local of the IBEW to participate in a minority hiring and training program. Arguing that Title VII permitted affirmative relief, the judge cited the opinion of a previous court: "Any other interpretation (of Title VII) would allow complete nullification of the Civil Rights Act of 1964."[63]

The *Rios* decision of June 1974 produced an even broader reading of Title VII. The case stemmed from lawsuits filed by private parties and the Justice Department against Steamfitters' Local 638 in New York City. In June 1973, Judge Dudley Bonsal ruled that, despite the local's participation in the New York Plan, it continued to discriminate against minorities in its apprenticeship program, job referrals, and awarding of journeyman status. Bonsal ordered the local to develop an affirmative action program to ensure a nonwhite membership of 30 percent within four years. The local turned to the appeals court, which agreed to reassess the 30 percent figure but affirmed Bonsal's ruling. Responding to the union's contention that hiring targets violated Title VII prohibitions against preferential treatment to redress racial imbalances, the court held that these stipulations applied only to situations "attributable to causes other than unlawful discriminatory conduct."[64] The absence of minority workers due to discrimination did not constitute an "imbalance" but, rather, a deliberate denial of opportunity. Therefore, the Title VII restrictions did not apply to this situation. According to this interpretation, the courts retained extensive latitude in prescribing remedies in cases of discrimination.

The *Rios* decision was not unanimous. Claiming the absence of "textual justification" for the majority ruling, Justice Paul Hays dissented, arguing that Title VII "is not concerned with the causes of imbalances, past, present, or future. It provides for no exception from its broad prohibition for imbalances caused by past discrimination."[65] The juxtaposition of the minority and majority opinions provides a striking illustration of the evolution of judicial—and liberal—thought over the course of a decade. Hays employed a strict interpretation of Title VII that, one could argue, seemed relatively consistent with the oratory of liberal senators during the debates over the Civil Rights Act. In the ensuing years, however, the acknowledgment of systemic discrimination by liberal politicians, the demands of civil rights groups, and the progressively broader judicial reading of Title VII had transformed liberal perceptions of acceptable antidiscrimination measures. Hence, by 1974 Hays's opinion sounded far removed from prevailing civil rights ideology.[66]

By 1976, the long history of antidiscrimination and affirmative action activities had produced almost contradictory results. From one perspective, mass protests, judicial rulings, administrative pressures, and civil rights legislation had transformed business and union practices in ways probably unimaginable in 1960. The widespread implementation of goals and timetables and hometown plans; the modification of testing procedures, seniority arrangements, and employment requirements; and the preponderance of antidiscrimination complaints and legal actions were all indications of a dramatically different business environment. Although businesses and unions continued to challenge and subvert this new order, affirmative action had left an indelible mark on the U.S. economic scene. General Electric, for example, required every one of its 26,000 company managers to complete forms tracing the progress of minority employees throughout the firm. The annual performance evaluation of IBM managers included an assessment of their affirmative action record. In January 1975, *Business Week* proclaimed affirmative action to be "well under way," insisting that "most executives have come to accept affirmative action as a cost of doing business."[67]

Nor was this process a futile one. Statistics indicated that African Americans had achieved real economic progress over a 25-year period. In 1950, for example, 3.4 percent of nonwhites were employed in professional and technical occupations; by 1973, that number had increased to 9.9 percent. For clerical and kindred work, the respective numbers were 3.5 percent and 14.9 percent. Meanwhile, the number of African Americans employed as private household workers declined from 14.6 percent to 5.7 percent, and those working as nonfarm laborers declined from 15.7 percent to 9.7 percent. Black median income as a percentage of white income increased throughout this period, whether measured for males, females, or families. Black females exhibited the most dramatic relative gains, attaining approximate income equality with white females by 1970. In the skilled construction crafts, according to EEOC data, minority membership from 1972-1976 increased from 9.3 percent to 12.8 percent. Black participation in most professional and technical occupations exceeded that of previous decades. The battle against economic injustice had achieved some successes.[68]

The figures, however, present a skewed picture of the economic progress of African Americans, for two reasons. First, although black workers demonstrated *absolute* gains, the position of blacks relative to whites tended to remain static, or even to deteriorate, in many areas. Also, although many African Americans benefited from the advancements of the preceding years, many others fell victim to economic recession and ineffective enforcement of civil rights laws. A Civil Rights Commission report published in 1977 warned: "The recession has reversed much of the limited progress that had been achieved by triggering massive layoffs of new minority and women employees."[69] By mid-1975 unemployment among nonwhites exceeded 14 percent. This number, of course, did not include those who dropped out of the labor force as well as part-time workers who were unable to secure full-time jobs. Incorporating these groups, the National Urban League calculated the actual unemployment rate among African Americans to be 26 percent. In January 1975 the *Christian Science Monitor* reported that "the overall rate of urban black unemployment now is higher than during the great depression of the 1930's."[70]

Meanwhile, black poverty increased, especially among female-headed families. Whereas blacks constituted one-fourth of the nation's poor in 1959, they were almost one-third by 1972. During those years, the percentage of black families headed by females rose from 22 percent to 33 percent, amplifying racial economic disparities. Surveying the overall situation, the National Urban League concluded that "many of the gains made over the past decade were either wiped out or badly eroded in 1975, and the portents for the future are not encouraging."[71]

A comparison of white and black economic status reinforces this negative picture. According to EEOC data, by 1975, 16.3 percent of white males, but only 3.8 percent of black males, were employed as "officers and managers." For professionals, the respective numbers were 10 percent and 2.1 percent; for sales jobs, 7.9 percent and 3.5 percent. Conversely, 19.2 percent of black men but only 7.3 percent of white men were categorized as "laborers"; a similar pattern emerged for service workers, 13.6 percent versus 4.7 percent. Viewed from a slightly different perspective, blacks, who constituted over 10 percent of the nation's work force, accounted for only 3.0 percent of managers and 3.2 percent of professionals, but 20 percent of laborers and 22.7 percent of service workers. In addition, the ratio of black-white unemployment increased during the 1970s.

Despite more than a decade of affirmative action, white males continued to dominate the upper echelons of the U.S. economy. An EEOC study of the employment structure of twenty-three metropolitan areas, for example, indicated the subordinate status of minorities and women as late as 1974. In Atlanta, white males held 85 percent of officer/manager positions and 80 percent of professional jobs. Black males, less than 12 percent of the city's labor force, comprised 35 percent of all operatives and 48 percent of laborers. In New York City, blacks represented 15 percent of the labor force, but only 5 percent of officer/manager personnel and 34 percent of service workers. In Philadelphia, blacks accounted for 4 percent of officers and managers but 33 percent of service workers and 30 percent of laborers. These numbers were especially incriminating to civil rights spokespersons who increasingly adopted proportional representation as the yardstick to measure economic progress. Although African Americans clearly had advanced since 1960, they appeared little closer to obtaining their "fair share" of American wealth than they were twenty years earlier.[72]

Concentrated in blue-collar manufacturing jobs, African-Americans suffered disproportionately from the recessions of the 1970s. In addition, the general transition within the economy from manufacturing to service occupations hurt African-American workers. Inferior education, lack of appropriate job skills in a shifting economy, and limited contact with the business and professional world continued to obstruct aspirations of African Americans. Collective bargaining seniority arrangements left black workers vulnerable to the nuances of a fluctuating economy. Moreover, African Americans increasingly found themselves in competition with white females, who were entering the job market in unprecedented numbers. Whereas the male labor force increased only 17 percent from 1966 to 1976, the female labor force increased by more than 40 percent.[73] Compounding all these developments, as the National Urban League observed, was the nation's irresolute posture toward economic discrimination, which was amplified by the economic suffering generated by a faltering economy.[74]

As African Americans struggled to deal with the effects of economic dislocation and recession, the opposition to affirmative action, which had manifested itself during the 1972 election, was becoming more vociferous and organized. As the nation celebrated its bicentennial and moved into the 1980s, it began to reconsider seriously the propriety of goals, timetables, quotas, and other remedial actions on which many African Americans—and women and other minority-group members—had come to rely to escape from poverty and unemployment.

NOTES

1. Stephen E. Ambrose, *Nixon: Volume Three: Ruin and Recovery, 1973-1990* (New York: Simon & Schuster, 1991), p. 62.

2. *Ibid.*, chapters 1-2; U.S. Department of Labor, *Black News Digest*, January 21, 1974; *AFL-CIO News*, March 17, 1973, p. 5; and Nathan, *The Plot that Failed*, pp. 63-74.

3. Karen E. DeWitt, "Strengthened EEOC Accelerates Actions against Business, Labor Employee Discrimination," *National Journal Reports* 5 (June 22, 1973): 913.

4. U.S. Bureau of Labor Statistics, *Handbook*, pp. 63 & 75; Harris, *The Harder We Run*, pp. 178-82, and "White America's Recession; Black America's Depression," *Christian Science Monitor*, January 21, 1975, p. 6.

5. NAACP, *Annual Report 1967*, p. 97; National Advisory Committee on Civil Disorders, *Report*, p. 419; and Congressional Quarterly, *Almanac*, Vol. 28, p. 247. For discussion of passage of the 1964 act, see Chapter III. Johnson administration attempts at cease-and-desist powers for EEOC from: Herbert Hill, "The Equal Employment Opportunity Commission: Twenty Years Later," reprint from *The Journal of Intergroup Relations* XI (Winter, 1983): 66-67, Footnote #12; and DeWitt, "Strengthened EEOC," pp. 914-15.

6. *Wall Street Journal*, August 11, 1969, p. 6. For elaboration of Brown incident, see Chapter V.

7. 1969 bill in *Wall Street Journal*, August 11, 1969, p. 6. 1970 bill from NAACP, *Annual Report 1970*, p. 13; and Congressional Quarterly, *Almanac 1972*, p. 247.

8. Quote from Charles Culhane, "Battle over Enforcement Powers for EEOC Pits Business Against Labor, Civil Rights Groups," *National Journal Reports*, 3 (November 13, 1971): 2249.

9. *Ibid.*, p. 2257.

10. Culhane, "Battle"; *Wall Street Journal*, September 17, 1971.

11. *Hearings before the Subcommittee on Labor of the Committee on Labor and Public Welfare, U.S. Senate, 92nd Congress, 1st Session, 1971, on S. 2515, S. 2617, H.R. 1746* (Washington, DC: Government Printing Office, 1971); Congressional Quarterly *Almanac 1972*, pp. 247-52; *The New York Times*, 1972: January 23, p. 3; January 27, pp. 1 & 17; February 9, p. 1; February 16, pp. 1 & 22; February 23, p. 1; and *Washington Post*, 1972: January 26, p. A2; January 27, p. A3; February 16, p. A1.

12. *Congressional Record*, Vol. 118, 1972, Part 2, p. 1662.

13. House Report from U.S. Bureau of National Affairs, *The Equal Employment Opportunity Act of 1972* (Washington, DC: Bureau of National Affairs, 1973), p. 162.

14. See, for example, Evelyn Idelson, *Affirmative Action and Equal Employment: A Guidebook for Employers*, Vol. 1 (Washington, DC: Government Printing office, 1974), p. 5.

15. Bureau of National Affairs, *Act of 1972*, especially House Report; *Congressional Record*, Vol. 118, Part 2, pp. 1662-76.

16. *The New York Times*, March 9, 1972, p. 25.

17. For analysis of 1972 act, see Bureau of National Affairs, *Act of 1972*, especially pp. 1-2 & 26ff. See also U.S. Commission on Civil Rights, *The Federal Civil Rights Enforcement Effort: A Reassessment*, pp. 84-88; "Interview with John Powell, Jr.," *Black Enterprise* 4 (July, 1974): 28; *The New York Times*, February 23, 1972, p. 25; March 9, 1972, p. 25; *Washington Post*, March 9, 1972, p. Al; and Commerce Clearing House, *New 1972 Equal Employment Opportunity Law* (Commerce Clearing House, Inc., 1972), pp. 13-14.

18. DeWitt, "Strengthened EEOC," pp. 914-16; and Powell in *Black Enterprise*, p. 29.

19. Herbert Northrup and John Larson, *The Impact of the AT&T-EEOC Consent Decree* (Philadelphia: University of Pennsylvania, Industrial Research Unit, 1979), p. 9.

20. History of AT&T case from Northrup and Larson, pp. 1-14, & *Washington Post*, January 19, 1973, p. A8. Analysis of settlement from: Northrup and Larson, pp. 10-14; *Black News Digest*, January 29, 1973; Schaefer, *Nondiscrimination in Employment: 1973- 1975*, pp. 5-6; Sally Hacker, "Sex Stratification, Technology, and Organizational Change: A Longitudinal Case Study of AT&T," *Social Problems* 26 (June, 1979): 540; "Ma Bell Agrees to Pay Reparations," *Newsweek* 81 (January 29, 1973): 53-54; and "Crossed Wires at Bell," *Time* 102 (October 22, 1973): 79. Statistics from Northrup and Larson, pp. 38-44; and Hacker, p. 540.

21. *Washington Post*, January 19, 1973, p. A8.

22. *Newsweek*, January 29, 1973, p. 53.

23. Quote from *Civil Rights Act of 1964*, Public Law #88-352, Section 703(h). Also: NAACP Legal Defense Fund, *Annual Report 1974-75*, p. 4; Civil Rights Commission, *Last Hired, First Fired* (Washington, DC: Government Printing Office, 1977). Discussion of economy from Brownlee, *The Dynamics of Ascent*, pp. 464-65; and Harris, *The Harder We Run*, pp. 180ff.

24. *National Labor Relations Act*, U.S. Code, Title 29, Section 160(c); *Albemarle Paper Company v. Moody* 95 SCt 2362 (1975); *Head v. Timken Roller Bearing Company* 486 F.2d 870 (1973); *U.S. v. U.S. Steel Corporation* 371 F. Supp. 1045 (1973); James Hyatt, "The Anti-Bias Bottleneck," *Wall Street Journal*, October 22, 1974, p. 20; James Singer, "Internal Problems Hamper EEOC Anti-Bias Efforts," *National Journal Reports* 6 (August 17, 1974): 1232-33; and Oscar Ornati and Edward Gilbin, "The High Cost of Discrimination," *Business Horizons* 18 (February, 1975): 39.

25. U.S. Department of Labor, Employment Standards Administration, Wage and Hour Division, "*Equal Pay for Equal Work*," in *Women's Legal Handbook*, Vol. 4, *Equal Pay*, ed. Lee Ellen Ford (Butler, IN: Ford Associates, 1974).

26. Ford, *Women's Legal Handbook*, especially pp. 1-12; and *Wall Street Journal*, September 20, 1976, p. 1.

27. *Washington Post*, September 19, 1973, p. A4.

28. Quote from "Tackling the Giants," *Newsweek* 82 (October 1, 1973): 84.

29. Delbert L. Spurlock, Jr., EEOC's Compliance Process: The Problem of Selective Enforcement," *Labor Law Journal* 26 (July, 1975): 400-403; "EEOC Wrestles with Backlog, Unemployment," *Industry Week* 183 (October 28, 1974): 25; "Government Shifts Strategy to End Job Discrimination," *U.S. News and World Report* 75 (October 8, 1973): 104-105; *Washington Post*, September 19, 1973, p. 84; *Newsweek*, October 1, 1973, p. 84; and Singer, "Internal Problems," pp. 1227-28.

30. *U.S. v. Bethlehem Steel Corporation* 446 F 2d 655. Background on steel industry in Chapter I.

31. Lackawanna: 446 F. 2d 652 (1971); *The New York Times*, June 22, 1971, pp. 1 & 14; "NAACP Hails Court Ban on Biased Job Practices," *The Crisis* 78 (September, 1971): 229. Sparrows-Point: 446 F. 2d at 664; *Black News Digest*, January 29, 1973; *The New York Times*, January 17, 1973, pp. 1 & 12. Quote, p. 12. Background from: Rowan, *Negro on the Steel Industry*; and Brooks, *Toil and Trouble*, pp. 328-31.

32. Gott quoted from *Wall Street Journal*, December 15, 1970, p. 12.

33. Quote from *U.S. v. U.S. Steel Corporation* 371 F. Supp. 1046. See also: 371 F. Supp. 1045ff.; *Wall Street Journal*, December 15, 1970, p. 12.

34. *Wall Street Journal*, April 15, 1974, p. 2.

35. Hill quote from *The New York Times*, April 14, 1974, p. 14.

36. Singer, "Internal Problems," pp. 1232-33; U.S. EEOC, *The First Decade*, p. 29; *U.S. v. U.S. Steel Corporation* 520 F. 2d 1047, *Wall Street*

Journal, April 15, 1974, p. 2; *The New York Times*, December 15, 1973, pp. 1 & 39; April 14, 1974, pp. 1 & 14; and "EEOC Appointee Faces Steel Bias Decision," *Industry Week* 180 (January 14, 1974): 10-21.

37. *Hearing before the Committee on Labor and Public Welfare, U.S. Senate, 93rd Congress, 1st Session, on John H. Powell, Jr., to Be a Member of the EEOC* (Washington, DC: Government Printing Office, 1974); NAACP, *Annual Report 1973*, p. 9; Paul Delaney, "U.S. is Spurring Efforts to Fight Job Prejudice," *The New York Times*, January 19, 1974, p. 43; Singer, "Internal Problems," pp. 1228-29; and *The New York Times*, December 13, 1973, p. 32; February 12, 1974, p. 36.

38. *Hearings before the Subcommittee on Equal Opportunities of the Committee on Education and Labor, House of Representatives, 93rd Congress, 2nd Session, on H.R. 15826, A Bill to Terminate Discrimination in Employment* (Washington, DC: Government Printing Office, 1974), for testimony of Augustus Hawkins, p. 2, and E.H. Norton, pp. 96-99; *Industry Week*, October 28, 1974, p. 25; U.S. GAO, *Report to the Congress by the Comptroller General of the United States. The Equal Employment Opportunity Commission Has Made Limited Progress in Eliminating Employment Discrimination* (Washington, DC: Government Printing Office, 1976), pp. 8 & 15; Benjamin Wolkinson, *Blacks, Unions and the EEOC* (Lexington, MA: Lexington Books, DC Heath & Company, 1973), p. 4.

39. GAO, *Equal Employment Opportunity Commission*, especially pp. 1-22 & 59; Daniel Seligman, "How 'Equal Opportunity' Turned into Employment Quotas," *Fortune* 87 (March, 1973): 162; Gregory J. Ahart, "Process Evaluation of the Contract Compliance Program in Nonconstruction Industry," *Industrial and Labor Relations Review* 29 (July, 1976): 570-71; Spurlock in *Labor Law Journal*, p. 403; and Singer, "Internal Problems," pp. 1226-27.

40. NOW quote from testimony of Ann Scott in Powell *Hearing*, p. 43.

41. Criticism of AT&T pact from *Ibid.*; Hacker in *Social Problems*; and *Time*, October 22, 1973, p. 79. Positive reviews from Northrup and Larson, *AT&T Decree*; and Theodore Purcell, S.J., "Management and Affirmative Action," in Industrial Relations Research Association, *Equal Rights and Industrial Relations*, pp. 81-83. See also *Washington Post*, January 19, 1973, pp. A1 & A8. GAO study from GAO, *Equal Employment Opportunity Commission*, pp. 41-42.

42. Quote from Clifford Alexander, "Equality Under the Law: A Review of the Programs," in *Towards New Human Rights*, David Warner, ed. (University of Texas, 1977), p. 381. See also: Seligman, "Equal

Opportunity," p, 161; Spurlock in *Labor Law Review*, pp. 400-401; and Singer, "Internal Problems," p. 1230.

43. Quote from Spurlock in *Labor Law Review*, p. 398. See also: *Hearings* on H R. 15826 for testimony of Powell; Powell *Hearings;* "An Industry Man Takes Over A Battered EEOC," *Business Week*, June 23, 1975, pp. 113-15; James Singer, "EEOC Censures Chairman, White House Probes Leadership," *National Journal Reports* 7 (March 1, 1975): 315-17; Singer, "Forced Resignations Allow Revamping of EEOC," *National Journal Reports* 7 (March 22, 1975): 447-48.

44. Quotes from *Business Week*, June 23, 1975, p. 113; Hyatt, "Bottleneck," p. 20; GAO, *Equal Opportunity Commission*, p. i. See also Arvil Adams, "Evaluating the Success of the EEOC Compliance Process," *Monthly Labor Review* 96 (May, 1973): 26-29; Mbatia, "The Economic Impact of the 1964 Fair Employment Practices Act," especially pp. 140ff.

45. Kevin S. McGuiness, *Government Memoranda on Affirmative Action Programs* (Washington, DC: Equal Employment Advisory Council, 1976), pp 5-11 & 77-79; "Acting Affirmatively to End Job Bias," *Business Week*, January 27, 1975, p. 94; and *Black News Digest*, April 30, 1973, & February 4, 1974. See also: Ahart, "Process Evaluation."

46. Quote from Herbert Hill, "Affirmative Action and the Quest for Job Equality," *The Review of Black Political Economy* 6 (Spring, 1976): 273.

47. Ahart, "Process Evaluation," pp. 565-71; and Derryck, *Construction Industry*, pp 16-17.

48. U.S. General Accounting Office, *Federal Efforts to Increase Minority Opportunities in the Skilled Construction Craft Unions Have Had Little Success* (Washington, DC: Government Printing Office, 1979), p. i.

49. Herbert Hammerman, "Minorities in Construction Referral Unions—Revisited," *Monthly Labor Review* 96 (May, 1973): 44.

50. GAO, *Federal Efforts*, p. 21.

51. Civil Rights Commission, *The Challenge Ahead*, especially pp. 1-63 & 176-203; Vera Libeau, *Minority and Female Membership in Referral Unions, 1974* (Washington, DC: Government Printing Office, 1977), especially p. 5; GAO, *Federal Efforts*, pp. 1-22; and Hammerman, "Minorities—Revisited."

52. Libeau, *Minority Membership*, p. 3; U.S. Department of Commerce, Bureau of the Census, *1972 Census of the Construction Industry* (Washington, DC: U.S. Department of Commerce), Part A, pp. 1-9; *1977 Census* (Department of Commerce, 1981), Section 1, pp. 2-5; and Mills, *Construction*, p. 26.

53. Libeau, *Minority Membership*, especially pp. ix-5.

54. Indianapolis Plan from Rowan and Rubin, *Opening the Skilled Construction Trades to Blacks*, pp. 123ff.; and Derryck, *The Construction Industry*, p. 22. Pittsburgh Plan from "Pittsburgh Blacks Gain in Construction Trades," *Industry Week* 182 (September 9, 1974): 21-22. Detroit Plan from Hill, *Labor Union Control of Job Training*, pp. 99ff. San Francisco Plan—and quote—from Donegan, "The Philadelphia Plan," p. 204. New York Plan from Hill, *Job Training*, p. 83. Boston and Miami from GAO, *Federal Efforts*, p. 23. Department of Labor actions from *Wall Street Journal*, July 3, 1974, p. 11.

55. *The New York Times*, June 5, 1971, pp. 1 & 24.

56. *Black News Digest*, October 30, 1972; October 29, 1973; *The New York Times*, June 5, 1971, pp. 1 & 24; and Hill, *Job Training*, pp. 73-77.

57. GAO, *Federal Efforts*, p. 27.

58. *Ibid.*, pp. 21-28; Civil Rights Commission, *Challenge*, pp. 176-203; Derryck, *Construction Industry*, pp. 21-22; and U.S. Office of Federal Contract Compliance Programs, *Construction Compliance Program Operations Manual* (Chicago: Commerce Clearing House, Inc., 1977), pp. 209-12.

59. Libeau, *Female Membership*, p. 34; Hill, *Job Trainings* pp. 33-35; and Civil Rights Commission, *Challenge*, p. 81.

60. GAO, *Federal Efforts*, p. 45.

61. "Outreach and OJT Programs Should Be Halted, GAO Says," *Engineering News Record*, May 11, 1978, p. 66; *Black News Digest*, December 11, 1972 & May 20, 1974; Civil Rights Commission, *Challenge*, pp. 113-34; Donegan, "Philadelphia Plan," p. 207; Hill, *Job Training*, pp. 27-32 & 45-46; and Libeau, *Female Membership*, p. 32.

62. *Albemarle Paper Company v. Moody* 95 S Ct 2362 (1975); *Head v. Timken Roller Bearing Company* 486 F.2d 870; *U.S. v. Bethlehem Steel Corporation* 446 F.2d 652 (1971); and *U.S. v. U.S. Steel Corporation* 371 F. Supp 1045 (1973).

63. *U.S. v. Local Union No. 212 International Brotherhood of Electrical Workers* 472 F. 2d 622 (1974) Quote p. 636.

64. *Rios v. Enterprise Association Steamfitters Local 638 of U.A.* 501 F. 2d 623.

65. *Ibid.*, p. 634.

66. *Ibid.*, pp. 622ff.

67. *Business Week*, January 27, 1975, pp. 94 & 98; Theodore V. Purcell, "How GE Measures Managers in Fair Employment," *Harvard Business Review* 52 (November-December 1974): 99-104; and William

Julius Wilson, *The Declining Significance of Race* (Chicago: University of Chicago Press, 1978), p. 100.

68. Civil Rights Commission, *Twenty Years After Brown* (Washington, DC: Government Printing Office, 1975), pp. 32-33; Civil Rights Commission, *Last Hired*, pp. 75 & 81; and GAO, *Federal Efforts*, p. 51.

69. Civil Rights Commission, *Last Hired*, p. 2.

70. "White America's Recession; Black America's Depression," *Christian Science Monitor*, January 21, 1975, p. 6.

71. Quote from National Urban League, *The State of Black America 1976*, p. 1. See also: Urban League, pp. 1-6; Gerard Gill, *Meanness Mania* (Washington, DC : Howard University Press, 1980), p. xii; U.S. Bureau of Labor Statistics, *The Social and Economic Status of Negroes in the United States, 1970*, p. 49; Civil Rights Commission, *Last Hired*, pp. 10-11; "Recession: Depression," *Christian Science Monitor*; Harris, *The Harder We Run*, Chapter 8; Sar A. Levitan, William B. Johnston, and Robert Taggart, *Still A Dream: The Changing Status of Blacks since 1960* (Cambridge, MA: Harvard University Press, 1975), especially pp. 32-34.

72. Kathleen McMillan, *Minorities and Women in Private Industry 1975* (Washington, DC: Government Printing Office, 1977), pp. 8 & 12; and U.S. EEOC, *Employment Profiles of Women and Minorities in 23 Metropolitan Areas 1974* (Washington, DC:Government Printing Office, 1976), pp. 9ff.

73. *Wall Street Journal*, September 20, 1976, p. 1.

74. National Urban League, *State of Black America*, pp. 16; Civil Rights Commission, *Last Hired*, pp. 14 & 23; Harris, *The Harder We Run*, pp. 178-82; "Recession: Depression," *Christian Science Monitor*, p. 6; and *The New York Times*, January 20, 1974, pp. 1 & 43.

VII

Reorganization, Reassessment, and Retreat: Carter, Reagan, and Affirmative Action

By the end of the Nixon/Ford years, affirmative action was firmly established within the U.S. economy. Mandated and legitimized by judicial rulings and enforced by a burgeoning federal (and state and local) bureaucracy, affirmative action programs had been implemented everywhere from construction unions to the U.S. Library of Congress.[1] Widespread implementation, however, did not translate into widespread acceptance. Large segments of society rejected the concept and practice of affirmative action for reasons ranging from concern for economic productivity to racism and sexism.

By the time Jimmy Carter assumed the presidency in 1977, this opposition was making itself felt. As the Carter administration struggled to streamline the federal antidiscrimination apparatus, the federal courts—the most consistent supporters of affirmative action within the government—began to reevaluate and qualify their previous positions. Ronald Reagan's electoral victories of 1980 and 1984 brought into power an administration openly hostile to affirmative action. By the 1980s, affirmative action was under attack by the White House and was receiving only qualified support from the courts. Supporters of affirmative action, primarily African-American and women's groups, found themselves increasingly isolated within the political arena as goals, timetables, and quotas became major targets of the rising conservative movement.

In 1976, James Earl Carter of Georgia narrowly defeated incumbent Gerald Ford to become the first Democratic president in eight years. Carter actually trailed Ford among white voters and owed his victory in part to a nearly monolithic black Democratic vote. On several occasions during the 1976 campaign, Carter addressed civil rights issues, praising the 1964 Civil Rights Act as "the best thing that ever happened to the South in my lifetime."[2] Carter especially focused on the question of sex discrimination. In a speech to the National Women's Agenda Conference, Carter criticized the EEOC both for its massive backlog and for the fact that it had only one female commissioner. He promised to rectify both situations.[3]

Once in office, Carter selected many individuals sympathetic to civil rights issues to serve in his government. Among them were F. Ray Marshall of the University of Texas, author of several prominent monographs on black workers, as secretary of labor, and long-time civil rights activist Andrew Young as ambassador to the United Nations.

For chairperson of the EEOC, Carter nominated Eleanor Holmes Norton, an African-American lawyer who had chaired the New York City Commission on Human Rights. A veteran of the sit-in movement and the Mississippi Freedom Democratic Party of the early 1960s, Norton became the agency's seventh chairperson in twelve years when she assumed office in June 1977. "When I came to the EEOC," she recounted in an interview, "I found an agency pretty much on its knees," saddled with a backlog of 130,000 complaints.[4] Norton introduced procedures to reduce the agency's backlog and to expedite the processing of complaints. She ordered all cases to be screened, a procedure that reduced by 30 percent the volume of complaints accepted by the commission. In addition, Norton retained the "Thirty Day Turn-Around Process" implemented by the EEOC in August 1976 and applied to all charges filed before 1974. Under this system, within 30 days of receiving a complaint, EEOC field personnel were to meet with the employer and employee in hopes of achieving a negotiated settlement. This policy was intended to reduce EEOC caseloads by accepting "reasonable" settlements, even if they fell short of the claimants' demands. The commission also substituted "fact-finding conferences" for the detailed interrogatory forms that it formerly required employers to complete.[5]

Norton also set out to redirect the agency' enforcement efforts away from individual complaints and toward broader "patterns and practices" suits, for reasons of both efficiency and effectiveness. According to Norton, focusing on the thousands of individual complaints received each year was very time-consuming and dissipated the commission's scarce resources. In addition, like most proponents of affirmative action, Norton did not believe that discrimination in the 1970s consisted of isolated, individual acts. Rather, the major obstacle to the advancement of female and minority workers was deeply entrenched systemic discrimination, defined by the EEOC as "institutional employment practices which, although often neutral in intent, operate to keep minorities and women from job opportunities available to others." As Holmes explained, "People are absorbed into the market place in stereotypical fashion. It's not because the market place is evil, but because it operates like a machine and does business the way it has always done."[6]

According to Norton, challenging basic business practices required a vigorous government effort. Toward this end, she introduced a number of internal changes to the EEOC to improve its performance. For example, she created an Office of Systemic Programs to focus exclusively on "patterns or practices" cases. She also announced an aggressive new policy in which the EEOC would file lawsuits against offending employers without waiting to receive complaints from employees. "There will be a sizable step-up," she warned, "in the number of class suits."[7] Among the "patterns or practices" that might lead to EEOC intervention were severe underutilization of women or minorities, concentration of female or minority-group workers in lower-paying positions, and any practices (such as hiring or promotion requirements) that adversely affected female or minority workers and that could not be justified by business necessity. To offset the anticipated increase in the volume of legal actions under this policy, the commission would simultaneously take steps to prevent individual complaints from evolving into class-action suits. Overall, then, Norton's policies were directed toward two goals: (1) rapid resolution of individual complaints, especially through the Thirty-Day program, and (2) more emphasis on systemic discrimination.[8]

To support Norton, the Carter admininistration submitted—and Congress approved—the Reorganization Act of 1978, which restructured the equal opportunity apparatus within the federal government. Among other things, this act transferred the authority to enforce antidiscrimination regulations within the federal government from the Civil Service Commission to the EEOC. In addition, it made the EEOC responsible for enforcing the Equal Pay Act and the Age Discrimination Act. That same year, the EEOC adopted the Uniform Guidelines for Employee Selection Procedures. These guidelines essentially extended the "80 percent rule" discussed in the previous chapter to private employers. The purpose behind establishing the guidelines was to assist employers in avoiding lawsuits by clarifying their responsibilities under federal antidiscrimination and equal opportunity laws, although critics charged they were too vague to be of much value.[9]

Apparently reinvigorated by these structural changes, the EEOC under Norton pursued an aggressive affirmative action campaign. In January 1978 Norton had expressed optimism that the commission would eliminate its backlog within two or three years. Although this goal proved unachievable, by June 1979 the backlog had been halved.[10]

To some civil rights advocates, however, the EEOC's newly found efficiency was a mixed blessing. To reduce their caseloads, commission personnel often had to conduct "minimally sufficient," rather than thorough investigations, and to encourage complainants to accept less than full relief. According to Herbert Hill, the EEOC "had become a backlog reduction mechanism rather than an enforcer of the law." In some cases, EEOC personnel themselves cautioned that insufficient time was being devoted to race and sex discrimination cases. Although the commission eventually abandoned the Thirty-Day program, it continued to stress the rapid resolution of complaints. Of course, given the voluminous backlog inherited by Norton, one might question what alternatives were available to the EEOC by that time.[11]

The Carter administration also reorganized and strengthened the OFCCP. In the waning days of the Ford administration, the OFCCP published a *Construction Compliance Program Operations Manual* detailing the responsibilities of contractors, federal contracting agencies, and the OFCCP regarding enforcement of nondiscrimination within the construction industry. The manual specified that contracting agencies monitor the day-to-day activities of all imposed plans under the supervision of OFCCP regional offices. The national office of the OFCCP would create general rules and guidelines "for implementing the construction compliance program" and would supervise and coordinate the activities of the various federal agencies.[12]

The Carter administration, rejecting this arrangement as too cumbersome, issued new regulations in April 1978 that abolished all imposed plans and special bid conditions. In their place, the Labor Department established national hiring targets for females and regional targets for minorities, applicable to all federally assisted construction projects in excess of $10,000. In October 1978, the White House followed with Executive Order 12086, which transferred enforcement authority from the various contracting agencies to the Department of Labor, and ultimately to the OFCCP. These modifications produced greater conformity and consistency within the enforcement process, but they placed additional responsibilities on an already overburdened OFCCP.[13]

Like the EEOC, the OFCCP pursued a fairly vigorous agenda during the Carter years. In May 1978 *The New York Times* reported that twenty federal contractors were facing debarment; this number exceeded the total number of debarments of all previous administrations combined. Moreover, whereas previous debarment efforts had been directed primarily against smaller employers, several of the current targets were large corporations. Among those contractors ultimately debarred by the OFCCP were Prudential Insurance, Firestone, and Uniroyal. Agency director Weldon J. Rougeau also announced that the OFCCP would investigate entire industries, including the banking and insurance industries. Moreover, the OFCCP, like the EEOC, was increasingly including back pay to members of aggrieved groups in its settlements. During Carter's first year, for example, the agency collected $9 million in back-pay settlements, three times the total of the previous year.

The actual effectiveness of OFCCP activities remains difficult to gauge. On the one hand, many contractors protested the agency's policies as too aggressive and heavy-handed; some even announced their intention to challenge the agency in court rather than be pressured into a settlement. On the other hand, some advocates of affirmative action charged that, as in previous years, the enforcement program appeared more imposing on paper than it actually was. They pointed out, for example, that, given the thousands of firms that received contracts from the federal government, threatening twenty such firms with debarment was not very consequential. In addition, the three large firms cited above were all reinstated within three months.[14]

The construction industry remained a problem area for federal antidiscrimination officials. The various imposed and hometown plans produced no greater successes under a Democratic administration that they had under its Republican predecessors. In the early 1980s the Philadelphia Plan became the focus of a legal suit by five African-American workers who charged the Labor Department with the failure to enforce the plan's affirmative action stipulations. The workers accused the union hiring hall of failing to refer black workers, often choosing white workers situated lower on the referral list. Blacks who challenged this system risked being stigmatized as "troublemakers."

By the time the case reached a district court in 1982, three of the plaintiffs either had moved from Philadelphia or had entered different occupations. Reviewing the history of the plan, the court maintained that, during the plan's first five years, the Labor Department took certain affirmative steps, including debarring some noncooperative contractors and collecting the names of potential construction workers from minority organizations. Following 1974, however, the Labor Department ceased to debar contractors and failed to collect adequate employment statistics. The department therefore lacked concrete data on which to evaluate contractor compliance. Significantly, the court found no improvement in enforcement activities following the reorganization efforts of 1978. A court memorandum asserted: "The evidence presented at trial shows that the Department of Labor has accomplished little by way of implementing the Philadelphia

Plan." "Thus," the court concluded, "in 13 years, equal opportunity in the building trades has remained an unfulfilled goal." (Despite this dictum, the court ruled against the plaintiffs on a technicality.)[15]

The Washington Plan failed for similar reasons. Established in 1970 in response to protests regarding the METRO project, the Washington Plan failed to upgrade blacks from the "trowel trades" to the skilled crafts. In a city that was 70 percent black, blacks accumulated less than 24 percent of total work hours on the project. Even this figure was misleading, because many of these hours were logged by "a small percentage of black union members."[16] When the Washington Plan was established, blacks comprised less than 10 percent of the membership of eleven skilled crafts; ten years later, they still failed to surpass the 10 percent level. Blacks remained concentrated in less-skilled occupations, and many who participated in the plan were trainees or held temporary work permits but never achieved journeyman status. Black workers often met with a hostile reception, enduring such epithets as "nigger," "coon," and "'bobcat."[17] Bureaucratic inefficiency impeded efforts by federal agencies to monitor the Washington Plan. "The enforcement procedures of the plan were so cumbersome," reported the *Washington Post*, "that most building projects were done by the time disciplinary steps against contractors were completed." The *Post* concluded that the plan "has failed by almost every measure."[18]

Perhaps no situation better illustrated the intricacies of the construction compliance process than the New York Plan. The New York Plan was the product of disparate forces that marked the political environment of the 1960s. Large-scale construction demonstrations dating to 1963, coupled with violent outbreaks in Harlem and Jamaica and the "long hot summers" throughout the nation's cities, generated tremendous pressure for New York City officials to avoid major violence. The election of John Lindsay, a leading congressional exponent of civil rights legislation, as mayor in 1965 brought into power an administration more sympathetic to racial issues than its predecessors. Finally, the expanding civil rights role of the federal government provided added incentive for the city to act decisively to avoid imposition of a federal plan.

The federal government provided the laboratory for the city's initial affirmative action construction experiment with the enactment of Model Cities legislation in 1966. Model Cities, which supplied funds for revitalization of depressed urban areas, stipulated that localities receiving federal monies provide "maximum opportunities for employing residents of the area in all phases of the program."[19] The federal government offered no specific guidelines for fulfilling this requirement, however. In a pilot Model

Cities project in Brooklyn, city officials instituted a training program requiring one minority trainee for every four journeymen on the project. Officials later extended the program to other sites, including East Harlem and the South Bronx. With a few exceptions—including locals of the electrical workers and sheet metal workers—most unions accepted the trainees but offered them no guarantees of future journeyman status.[20]

The unions were less cooperative, however, with plans to extend this program on a citywide basis. In April 1968, Mayor Lindsay issued Executive Order 71, which mandated that all contractors employed on city projects pursue affirmative action on private and public projects. Like Lyndon Johnson's Executive Order 11246, however, Lindsay's ruling failed to define "affirmative action." Moreover, the order purposely omitted goals and timetables in hopes of eliciting cooperation by the building trades unions.

The decisive element in securing the cooperation of the construction industry was not the Lindsay administration's goodwill, however, but the imposition of the Philadelphia Plan in 1969. Determined to avoid a similar scenario in New York, the New York Building and Construction Industry Board of Urban Affairs (BUA)—composed of union and contractor organizations—developed an alternative plan for New York in March 1970. The BUA's New York Plan proposed to train minority workers through a combination of formal instruction and counseling and on-the-job training at construction sites. The BUA's target for the first year was 800 trainees. Peter Brennan, president of the Building and Construction Trades Council (a member of BUA), announced that Governor Nelson Rockefeller had agreed to provide money for the project.

While the city and the BUA conducted extensive negotiations over the details of the plan, civil rights groups attacked the proposal as a charade to enable the construction unions to evade genuine affirmative actions. The NAACP denounced the plan as a "hoax" and threatened to prevent its implementation through legal challenges and mass demonstrations.[21] To resolve this controversy, James MacNamara, special assistant to the Commission of Manpower and Career Development Agency, recommended that a committee be created to elicit minority feedback.

The mayor's office responded by instituting a task force to discuss citywide implementation of affirmative action. Headed by Deputy Mayor Richard Aurelio, the task force included NAACP attorney Robert Carter, Harry Fleishman of the American Jewish Committee, Ernest Green of the Workers' Defense League (WDL) and the "Little Rock Nine," and James Haughton of Fight Back!, a Harlem-based organization dedicated to placing

African Americans within the construction industry.[22] At its recommendation, Lindsay issued Executive Order 20 on July 15, 1970, which extended the "one-to-four" ratio to all publicly financed city construction projects. By issuing this order, Lindsay prompted the building trades unions to pursue their negotiations with the city more vigorously. By December 1970, all remaining disputes were resolved, clearing the way for the implementation of the New York Plan.

City and state officials and the BUA formally signed the New York Plan on December 10 at a ceremony at the Commodore Hotel on 42nd Street. The plan was almost identical to that announced in March, providing for the training of 800 (later adjusted to 1,000) minority workers who would receive "consideration" for union membership upon completing the program.[23] Like most hometown solutions, the New York Plan omitted goals and timetables and preserved most of the power of the craft unions. The plan was to be administered by a supervisory board comprised of three union representatives, three management representatives, three representatives from minority groups (to be appointed by Rockefeller and Lindsay), and one BUA member.

On January 18, 1971, Lindsay issued Executive Order 31, which ruled that all city affirmative action programs must conform to the New York Plan. Although the "one-to-four" program was not abolished, a contractor's acceptance of the vague guidelines of the New York Plan generally satisfied his or her affirmative action obligations. As one city document later reported: "Participation by contractors in the New York Plan was taken as evidence of affirmative action meeting the requirements of both Executive Orders 71 and 20."[24]

The reaction of civil rights groups was predictably hostile. Demonstrators attending the ceremony at the Commodore, organized by Fight Back!, booed Lindsay and Rockefeller and punctuated the air with shouts of "Fraud" and "Phony."[25] Herbert Hill wrote to Assistant Secretary of Labor Arthur Fletcher urging the Labor Department to reject the plan, which he termed "the worst in the country."[26] Among Hill's complaints was the fear that the absence of goals and timetables for specific crafts would result in the continued concentration of blacks in the "trowel trades." An editorial in *The New York Times* criticized the plan as "vastly inferior" to the WDL apprenticeship program and questioned whether real progress would be achieved by introducing 800 minority trainees into an industry that employed more than 100,000 persons. Despite continued protests, however, the New York Plan remained the city's official affirmative action program for two years.[27]

Lindsay's determination to enforce the New York Plan was evidenced by his response to four union locals that refused to accept minority trainees. In 1971, Lindsay ordered a freeze on all public construction money until the recalcitrant locals agreed to conform to the plan's stipulations. Three of the four locals eventually devised acceptable arrangements. When the remaining holdout, Sheet Metal Workers Local 28, refused to capitulate, the city agreed to join an already pending federal lawsuit against the local. Lindsay then freed all contracts in September 1971, including those with Local 28.[28]

Despite Lindsay's optimism, the plan's disappointing results appeared to bear out the predictions of its liberal critics. Designed to create opportunities for 1,000 minority-group trainees, the plan actually placed approximately 600 through the end of 1972. Of far greater significance was the fact that less than 40 trainees actually received union books. These numbers forced city officials to concede that the plan actually hindered minority-group workers from attaining journeyman status. In January 1973, the city announced that it intended to withdraw from the plan and to devise its own program. On January 23, Lindsay "reactivated" Executive Order 20, the one-to-four order. Six months later, Lindsay expanded Executive Order 71 of April 1968 to include goals and timetables for specific crafts, contingent on an employer's "good faith efforts."

Lindsay's actions incurred the wrath of Peter Brennan, who had moved from president of the Building and Construction Trades Council to secretary of labor. On July 19, Brennan issued a memorandum declaring that "additional and/or supplementary state or local requirements may not be applied to federally assisted construction projects" when a federally approved affirmative action plan already was in operation.[29] Brennan threatened to withhold federal money from any locality that imposed stricter affirmative action guidelines than those required by the federal government.

The unions, meanwhile, challenged the executive order in the courts. They achieved a major victory in May 1976 when the U.S. Court of Appeals ruled in *Broidrick v. Lindsay* that "preferential hiring" violated the city's Administrative Code. In response, Lindsay's successor, Abraham Beame, modified the order by deleting the goals and timetables. In 1977, however, the courts negated this ruling as well, holding that the mayor needed legislative approval for a policy of this scope.[30]

The drama of the New York Plan unfolded against an uncertain economic backdrop. In 1962, construction employment in New York City achieved its pinnacle, employing 137,000 workers. By 1977, the industry had reached a twenty-year low, employing only 64,000 workers. Thus, many of the city's most vigorous affirmative action battles were waged during a period when the industry's work force was being halved. After 1977, the number of construction workers increased, although it never reached the 1962 level. These figures must be approached carefully, because they include both housing construction, which slumped during these years, and office construction, which did well. Throughout this period, economic tensions combined with racial animus to transform the New York City construction industry into a battleground between the unions and minority groups, who comprised a steadily increasing percentage of the city's population.[31]

The construction controversy continued into the next administration. Beame's successor, Edward Koch, issued Executive Order 50 in April 1980, which retained the one-to-four ratio for "economically disadvantaged" groups but rejected numerical formulas.[32] According to the Mayor's Office of Construction Industry Relations (OCIR), minorities (African Americans and Latinos) constituted 12.4 percent of all journeymen in the mechanical trades by 1980-81, an increase from 5.3 percent ten years earlier. These numbers indicated that minority participation in the construction industry had improved noticeably during the 1970s. At the same time, however, given that by 1980 the city's population was 24 percent African American and 20 percent Latino, these numbers also demonstrated that minority workers continued to be underrepresented among these crafts. In addition, many contractors claimed to have fulfilled their contractual obligations by hiring Jamaican immigrants. Moreover, the OCIR admitted that most construction unions refused to submit racial data, rendering these statistics "often impressionistic and not subject to audit."[33]

African Americans and other minorities denied that any substantial progress had taken place, and they continued to protest what they perceived as their exclusion from the construction crafts. In 1984, for example, African-American workers demonstrated at the Trump Towers construction site in mid-Manhattan, chanting "Jobs! Jobs! We want jobs!"[34] A struggle ensued in which one police officer was stabbed.

Complicating this issue even further was the existence of widespread corruption and the penetration of organized crime within the construction industry. The OCIR charged certain African-American groups with using the threat of disruptions to force contractors to hire "community coordinators" at $400-500 per week in addition to extorting "dues" or "referral fees" from African-American workers. The Teamsters, in turn, demanded the hiring of "security guards" to protect workers from disruptive protestors.[35] A 1982 *New York Times* exposé reported substantial underworld involvement in up to half the city's construction unions. After 20 years of activity, the situation remained volatile, and solutions remained elusive.[36]

Results in other cities were equally disappointing. According to EEOC data, African Americans constituted 8.4 percent of the nation's unionized construction labor force by 1979 but only half that proportion of the mechanical trades. Although these numbers represented an improvement over previous decades, they also indicated that African Americans continued to be underutilized in the skilled crafts. Moreover, despite increased numbers of African-American apprentices, prospects for continued progress were not good. While civil rights groups and federal agencies were pressuring the construction unions to admit minority workers, the unions themselves lost their preeminent position within the industry. The unions retained much of their power in northern, midwestern, and West Coast metropolitan areas, but nonunion labor came to dominate the industry in the Sun Belt and throughout the nation's suburbs. By 1984, nonunion labor comprised 60 percent of the nation's construction labor force, double the percentage of ten years earlier. Unfortunately for blacks, nonunion labor was even more exclusionist than union labor, and black-white wage differentials among nonunion construction workers exceeded those of union workers. These developments translated into limited prospects for African-American construction workers.[37]

Overall, then, the record of the executive branch in the arena of economic opportunity was one of real but limited progress. As was true during previous administrations, proponents of affirmative action relied heavily on the support of the federal judiciary. During the Carter years, the courts remained generally supportive of affirmative action. However, several judicial rulings from this period either rejected or restricted specific affirmative action programs.

The most highly publicized and controversial affirmative action ruling during the Carter years was *Regents of the University of California v. Bakke,* decided on June 28, 1978. The case involved an affirmative action plan initiated by the University of California-Davis medical school in 1969 that reserved sixteen admission slots for minority students. In 1973 and 1974, the school rejected Allan Bakke, a white man, even though his test scores significantly surpassed those of several minority admittees. Bakke initiated a suit, charging the university with violating his constitutional rights. The case eventually reached the Supreme Court, which ruled 5-4 that the special admissions program constituted an illegal quota system. In the court's own words: "Preferring members of any one group for no reason other than race or ethnic origin is discrimination for its own sake. This the Constitution forbids."[38]

The *Bakke* ruling has sometimes been misconstrued as a sweeping rejection of affirmative action. In fact, although the Supreme Court ruled against strict quotas, it affirmed the right of the university to use race as *one* factor (but not *the* factor) in determining admissions. In addition, the *Bakke* case involved entrance into a professional school and was not directly related to the question of job discrimination. Title VII played no part in the case. (Bakke originally claimed that the admissions program violated Title VI, which prohibited federal support for institutions that practiced discrimination. The court rejected this argument and based its decision on the Equal Protection Clause of the Fourteenth Amendment.)

Nevertheless, the *Bakke* ruling was highly significant. Although the Supreme Court did not outlaw affirmative action outright, it placed definite limits on its legality. Furthermore, the case helped bring together various "antiquota" groups. Among those arguing *amicus curiae* in support of Bakke were conservative groups such as the Young Americans for Freedom and the U.S. Chamber of Commerce; Jewish groups, including the American Jewish Committee and the AntiDefamation League of B'nai B'rith; professional groups like the American Federation of Teachers; and white ethnic groups, including the Italian-American Foundation, the Ukrainian Congress Committee of America, and the Polish-American Affairs Council. Although these groups differed on any number of political issues, they all opposed affirmative action (at least as implemented in the UC-Davis plan), and, when united, they constituted a formidable political bloc. The diverse nature of this opposition illustrated how widespread popular dissatisfaction with certain affirmative action programs had become by the late 1970s.

Among those supporting the special admissions program were, not surprisingly, the NAACP and NAACP Legal Defense and Education Fund, the American Civil Liberties Union, and the Puerto Rican Legal Defense and Education Fund. As time passed, these groups increasingly found themselves defending their policies and previous victories against an active opposition.[39]

Some decisions that more directly addressed the question of job discrimination reflected a dampening enthusiasm for affirmative relief. In the *McDonald v. Santa Fe* decision of 1976, the Supreme Court ruled that Title VII protections applied to white as well as to nonwhite workers. Although not a direct assault on affirmative action, this decision added credence to "reverse discrimination" suits filed by white workers. Significantly, the court relied heavily on the congressional debates surrounding the Civil Rights Act, which had stressed simple nondiscrimination and seldom referred to affirmative action.[40]

By the late 1970s, the courts had become increasingly uneasy with the pervasive use of numerical formulas. The courts modified the *Griggs* decision of 1971, which stated that employees need not prove an *intent* to discriminate to be entitled to remedies. Finding this decision too sweeping, other courts ruled that the question of intent was relevant to determining discrimination.

The courts also espoused a more narrow definition of "proportional representation." In two 1977 decisions, the Supreme Court ruled that parties charging underutilization must demonstrate the existence of a pool of *qualified* minority-group workers and could not rely on overall population or labor-force statistics.

The courts sometimes imposed geographical limitations on proportional representation as well. In 1976, for example, the Defense Department debarred a Timken Roller Bearing plant in Bucyrus, Ohio, charging the plant underutilized minority workers. Timken appealed to the district court, which ordered the debarment overturned. The court ruled that Defense Department statistics included a neighboring city with a substantial minority-group population that was not within normal commuting distance of the Timken plant. The court determined that when this city was eliminated from consideration, charges of discrimination against the plant became unfounded. Federal court decisions also nullified executive orders by mayors John Lindsay and Abraham Beame and Governor Hugh Carey ordering affirmative action within the New York construction industry.[41]

In other key cases, however, the courts reaffirmed the validity of affirmative action plans. The most important victory for affirmative action proponents during the Carter years was the *Weber* decision of June 1979. The case involved the Grammercy, Louisiana, plant of the Kaiser Aluminum and Chemical Corporation. As was true in so many southern businesses, African Americans in the Grammercy plant were concentrated in lower-paying, unskilled production jobs. Although African Americans constituted nearly 40 percent of the local labor force, they comprised less than 2 percent of skilled craft workers in the plant. The EEOC eventually investigated the plant and found both Kaiser and the United Steelworkers of America guilty of violating antidiscrimination laws. In addition, as a federal contractor, Kaiser was pressured by the Department of Labor to increase the proportion of skilled minority workers.

To remedy this situation, Kaiser agreed to train its own production workers for craft positions rather than to hire skilled craft workers from outside the plant. Half of all openings in these training programs were reserved for African-American candidates, until the proportion of African Americans among craft workers approximated their representation in the local labor force. Kaiser incorporated this arrangement into its 1974 collective bargaining agreement with the United Steelworkers of America. As often occurred in affirmative action programs, the company filled its minority slots even when doing so required it to bypass white candidates with greater seniority than black trainees.

One white worker thus bypassed, Brian Weber, initiated a class action suit against the company and the union. Citing *McDonald v. Santa Fe*, Weber challenged the training program as a violation of Title VII, that is, as discrimination in reverse. The district court and court of appeals supported his claim; the union, in turn, appealed to the Supreme Court. On June 27, 1979, the Supreme Court overturned the lower court decisions, ruling that "private, voluntary, race-conscious affirmative action plans" did not violate Title VII. The court further stated that any interpretation of Title VII "that forbids all race-conscious affirmative action would bring about an end completely at variance with the purpose of the statute and must be rejected."[42]

The *Weber* decision, although a clear victory for affirmative action supporters, epitomized the growing judicial uncertainty regarding this difficult subject. The Kaiser plan was acceptable because it was "voluntary" (despite the fact that Kaiser was under government scrutiny): What, then, was the status of *imposed* plans? The court also stressed the temporary and remedial nature of the plan: Did this imply restrictions on other plans? The court refused to address the question of what constituted an acceptable plan, maintaining instead: "It is not necessary in these cases to define the line of demarcation between permissible and impermissible affirmative action plans; it suffices to hold that the challenged Kaiser-USA plan falls on the permissible side of the line."[43] As important as the *Weber* decision was, it left unanswered many critical questions concerning affirmative action at a time when the concept was increasingly under attack in legal and intellectual circles.[44]

Other decisions indicated continued judicial support for affirmative action. In 1980, the Supreme Court in *Fullilove v. Klutznick* upheld a stipulation within the Public Works Employment Act of 1977 that required that "the Secretary of Commerce set aside 10 percent of all federal contracts for minority businesses." This decision was particularly important because such "set-aside" laws were widely used to provide opportunities for minority businesses. Two years later, the Supreme Court approved a Boston executive order that set aside 25 percent of all publicly financed construction jobs for minorities and 10 percent for females. [45]

The overall trend of judicial rulings during the Carter years revealed an attitude of cautious support for affirmative action. Affirmative action was acceptable under some circumstances and unacceptable in others, subject to guidelines that were never clearly articulated. The judicial rethinking of the propriety of affirmative action was especially significant because women and minority groups had come to rely so heavily on the courts. This reliance became even more obvious after 1981, when a conservative Republican administration occupied the White House.

The election of Ronald Reagan brought into power an administration that was less sympathetic to the concerns of African Americans than any of its recent predecessors. In denouncing "big government" and promising to reduce social welfare spending, the new administration clashed both politically and philosophically with the established civil rights leadership. Many of Reagan's actions seemed directly antithetical to the interests of African Americans and other minority groups. He attempted to award tax-exempt status to private schools that practiced racial discrimination; he opposed sanctions against South Africa; and he resisted efforts to establish Martin Luther King's birthday as a national holiday.[46]

Perhaps more important, Reagan staffed many government positions that deal with civil rights with individuals whose thinking diverged from that of congressional liberals and most civil rights leaders. At the Justice Department, for example, Reagan's selection for attorney general, William French Smith, was an opponent of affirmative action, as was his successor, Edwin Meese. Perhaps more important was the appointment of William Bradford Reynolds to the position of assistant attorney general for civil rights. Reynolds was to play a major role in the effort to divert antidiscrimination efforts from the course they had taken since the late 1960s. At the Civil Rights Commission, chairman Arthur S. Fleming, after repeatedly finding fault with the administration's civil rights record, was replaced in 1982 with Clarence M. Pendleton, Jr. A critic of the traditional civil rights leadership, Pendleton at one point charged that "a lot of black leaders are part of a race industry." Pendleton later criticized the concept of comparable worth—a policy espoused by many women's rights groups that is intended to equalize pay scales between traditionally male and female occupations —as "the looniest idea since Looney Tunes came on the screen." Linda Chavez, the commission's staff director, charged in 1984 that the EEOC Uniform Guidelines "eliminate valid tests in favor of quota selection." The appointment of individuals with these views disconcerted many civil rights leaders who had come to rely on these positions for at least qualified support.[47]

In contrast to the Carter administration, the Reagan White House generally rejected the broad definitions of systemic discrimination that underlay so many affirmative action programs. Rather, administration officials were more likely to interpret discrimination in terms of acts against individuals, with remedies being restricted to individuals who could demonstrate that they had been victimized by such acts. Such a philosophy, of course, questioned the legitimacy of class-action suits and of the use of numerical formulas to determine and alleviate past discrimination. In this sense, it conflicted head-on with the strategic approach of civil rights activists as it had evolved since the 1970s.[48]

Not all administration officials were opposed to affirmative action. By 1981, affirmative action, buttressed by scores of laws, court rulings, and oversight agencies, was more firmly entrenched than was the case in the 1970s. Many people within the federal bureaucracy—and within the business community—had come to accept affirmative action, to varying degrees. Within the administration, as we shall see, much of the impetus to modify existing affirmative action practices emanated from the Justice Department. At the same time, several other cabinet officials and agency members opposed fundamental or dramatic shifts in established policies. Thus, the Reagan government was characterized by "an inconsistency of purpose" among the OFCCP, EEOC, Justice Department, and other agencies. Nevertheless, the general tone of administration policies was more hostile to established affirmative action policies than had been true of any previous administration.[49]

Caught in the middle of these shifting currents was the EEOC. The administrations's initial choice to head the commission was William M. Bell. In 1982, however, the White House withdrew the Bell nomination in favor of Clarence Thomas. A graduate of Yale law school, Thomas originally had come to Washington as a legal assistant to Senator John Danforth. Thomas had long been skeptical of affirmative action, denouncing it as "a narcotic of dependency" on which African Americans had become addicted. Like many other administration officials, Thomas felt that antidiscrimination actions should be geared toward individuals rather than groups or classes. Thus, as chairman, he redirected agency efforts away from "patterns and practices" suits and back toward individual cases. During his tenure, the proportion of "patterns and practices" suits handled by the commission declined significantly. In contrast to Norton, Thomas "decided that the agency had to pursue every case of discrimination to the fullest, ending a practice of disposing of complaints as quickly as possible." To accomplish this objective, he computerized the agency and instituted a number of internal financial reforms.[50]

Despite Thomas's personal discomfort with affirmative action, he did not set out with any ambitious plan to reverse the cumulative policies of his predecessors. Rather, he argued that goals and timetables could be appropriate under extreme circumstances, and he resisted White House pressures to rewrite the Uniform Guidelines adopted under the Carter administration. Thus, Thomas found himself in conflict with both the established civil rights leaders and administration conservatives, especially Reynolds.[51]

As the years passed, however, Thomas moved steadily toward the right, becoming increasingly hostile toward affirmative action and liberalism in general. In this he mirrored the behavior of other administration officials. This trend became increasingly pronounced after 1984, when two defining events helped crystallize the administration's anti-affirmative action philosophy. The first was Reagan's landslide victory in the 1984 election. Many conservatives interpreted Reagan's triumph as a final repudiation of the liberal policies of the 1960s and 1970s, including affirmative action, and administration conservatives emerged from the election in a powerful position. Following the election, rumors spread that Thomas could be forced out of office if he did not modify his actions to conform to White House positions.

In that same year the Supreme Court issued a decision involving affirmative action and seniority that seemed to validate the administration's restrictive civil rights philosophy. The ruling, *Firefighters Local Union No. 1784 v. Stotts*, involved a case initiated by white firefighters in Memphis, Tennessee, challenging an affirmative action program that protected the jobs of black firefighters with less seniority than their white coworkers. In June 1984, the Supreme Court ruled in favor of the white men, maintaining that "Title VII protects bona fide seniority systems." In the majority opinion, Justice Byron White asserted that to be eligible for "retroactive seniority," an individual must prove that he or she personally experienced discrimination: "Mere membership in the disadvantaged class is insufficient." This ruling contrasted markedly from judicial sanctions for class-based remedies dating to the 1960s.[52]

The Justice Department, which had filed a brief of *amicus curiae*, celebrated the *Stotts* ruling as a landmark defeat for affirmative action and announced its intention to challenge similar programs around the country. As Reagan's second term began in January 1985, the department, now headed by Edwin Meese, requested that more than 50 state and local governments "modify affirmative action plans so as to end the use of numerical goals and quotas." The administration entered into litigation against affirmative action plans pending in several cities, including Detroit, New Orleans, and Washington, D.C., and initiated a suit against an affirmative action plan in Indianapolis. That same year Meese proposed amending Executive Order 11246 so as to eliminate all requirements for goals and timetables. Clarence Pendleton of the Civil Rights Commission publicly declared: "We believe that quotas are a dead issue."[53]

The EEOC began to adopt a similar hard-line approach. In November 1984, Clarence Thomas announced a new policy in which the EEOC would seek relief only for individuals who could demonstrate that they were victims of discrimination. In addition, the Office of Systemic Programs was abolished as a separate entity within the commission. The EEOC also took steps to terminate the use of goals and timetables, which Thomas denounced as "a fundamentally flawed approach." In 1985 Acting General Counsel Johnny Butler instructed commission attorneys not to include goals and timetables in future settlements. That same year Thomas supported Meese's efforts to eliminate numerical goals from Executive Order 11246.[54]

The administration's offensive against affirmative action met with only limited success, however. For example, Meese's proposals regarding Executive Order 11246 were ultimately rejected following opposition by other Cabinet members, including Secretary of Labor William Brock and Secretary of State George Shultz (who, as Nixon's labor secretary, had helped initiate the Philadelphia Plan; see Chapter V). This development revealed that, even this late into the Reagan presidency, administration officials remained divided in their views on the value of affirmative action.[55]

More significant was the position of the Supreme Court. The administration response to the *Stotts* decision reflected the hope that the court would apply the strict standards established in that decision to future cases. In two key 1986 decisions, however, the court instead demonstrated that the *Stotts* ruling was specific to the circumstances of the Memphis plan. In *International Association of Firefighters v. City of Cleveland*, the court upheld a local plan that reserved a specified number of officer positions in the city's fire department for Latinos and African Americans. In writing the majority opinion, Justice William Brennan, who had also authored the *Weber* decision, essentially extended the reasoning behind that decision to public as well as private employment. He further asserted that Title VII permits "employers and unions voluntarily to make use of reasonable race-conscious affirmative action."[56]

The second decision, *Local 28, Sheet Metal Workers International Association v. EEOC*, involved a case in which a federal court had found a New York construction union local guilty of discrimination and had imposed minority hiring goals on the local. (See the previous references to Local 28 in the discussion of the New York Plan.) The local protested that the hiring plan violated Title VII because it extended race-conscious preferences to individuals who could not demonstrate that they were victims of discrimination. The Supreme Court upheld the plan, reasserting the philosophy of many prior rulings that class-based remedies were appropriate measures for addressing widespread and pervasive discrimination. Significantly, in both cases the court asserted that, depending on the circumstances of the specific case, individuals need not necessarily provide evidence of personal victimization to be eligible for relief.

These two decisions severely curtailed the administration's anti-affirmative action initiatives. In August 1986, Reynolds announced that the Justice Department was abandoning its efforts to eliminate numerical formulas from state and local affirmative action plans. The following year the EEOC withdrew the 1975 Butler directive against goals and timetables.[57]

Thus, despite the philosophical opposition of many administration officials to affirmative action, by the time Reagan left office in January 1989 the federal equal employment opportunity apparatus was still largely intact. Of course, many civil rights leaders felt strongly that the administration's track record in promoting equal opportunity was especially inadequate. A 1984 article in *Black Enterprise*, for example, charged: "Since President Reagan was elected, enforcement of antidiscrimination statutes has hit an all-time low." Such feelings, of course, were only intensified by administration efforts to reverse affirmative action policies and programs that the civil rights leadership had fought so hard to establish.[58]

At the same time, however, conservative opponents of affirmative action were highly disappointed at the administration's failure to redefine and redirect in a fundamental way the antidiscrimination efforts of the federal government. By the end of Reagan's second term, goals and timetables remained widespread in both government and private equal opportunity plans, and the Supreme Court had upheld the validity of race-conscious, class-based remedies. Where the civil rights leadership saw retreat and opposition, many conservatives saw more consistency than change. Thus, Robert Detlefsen claimed that "no sweeping changes occurred during Reagan's two terms in office," and Herman Belz charged that "employment discrimination policy under the Reagan administration was characterized more by continuity than change."[59]

In truth, the final assessment of the Reagan administration and affirmative action remains to be written. Much of the criticism from both liberals and conservatives focuses on the policies and actions of administrative agencies such as the Justice Department and the EEOC. Ultimately, however, Reagan's most lasting and substantial influence in the affirmative action arena could well involve his judicial appointments, particularly to the Supreme Court.

As we have seen throughout this book, since the 1960s proponents of affirmative action have increasingly relied on the federal courts for legal affirmation of their policies. That such a development occurred under the generally liberal Warren Court of the 1960s is not surprising. In 1969, however, when Warren Burger replaced Earl Warren as chief justice, many people—liberal and conservative—expected the court to divert dramatically from many of its previous pathways. No such radical change occurred, however. In fact, in many decisions such as *Griggs,* the Burger court substantially expanded the definition and scope of acceptable affirmative remedies. This trend continued despite the fact that two Republican presidents—Nixon and Ford—had the opportunity to nominate several justices. In general, the individuals they appointed—such as Harry Blackmun, Lewis Powell, and John Paul Stevens—tended to be moderates who did not adopt a doctrinaire approach to civil rights issues. (The one obvious exception was Nixon's nomination of the highly conservative William Rehnquist.) The same could probably be said for Reagan's first appointment: Sandra Day O'Connor, in 1981.

In 1986, however, the court took a sharp turn to the right when Chief Justice Burger retired. Rather than look outside the court for Burger's successor, Reagan instead selected Rehnquist, probably the court's most conservative member. Moreover, to assume Rehnquist's seat, Reagan nominated another hard-line conservative, Antonin Scalia. The following year, when Lewis Powell retired, Reagan replaced him with yet another conservative—Anthony Kennedy—after the Senate rejected the president's original choice, Robert Bork. Thus, by promoting Rehnquist and adding a number of conservative justices, Reagan had dramatically transformed the nature of the Supreme Court.[60]

As the *Cleveland* and *Local 28* decisions of 1986 indicate, the effects of the new appointments were not immediately felt. Two major decisions handed down in 1989, however, dramatically illustrated the new leanings of the court. One case, *Wards Cove Packing Co. v. Antonio,* involved an Alaskan cannery in which minority workers—primarily Filipinos and Alaskan Natives—were concentrated in less-skilled positions. The minority workers claimed that the company's employment practices had produced a form of racial and ethnic segregation within the plant. They also charged that there were a sufficient number of minority workers from whom the plant could select candidates for the skilled office positions. The court, although conceding that disparities existed between the composition of the skilled and unskilled departments, ruled that these disparities were not themselves proof of discrimination. The court further held that to prove discrimination it was not sufficient for the plaintiffs to show that there was a pool of minority workers; they must prove there were a significant number of *qualified* minority workers. Finally, the plaintiffs must demonstrate that particular employment policies directly *caused* the disparity between the two groups. The *Wards Cove* decision, then, placed much more stringent requirements on workers who challenge their employer's policies.[61]

The second decision involved a minority set-aside program in Richmond, Virginia. In Richmond as in many other cities, minority-owned firms received a disproportionately low share of municipal construction funds. For example, although African Americans constituted 50 percent of the city's population, during the period 1978-1983 minority-owned firms were awarded less than 1 percent of municipal construction contracts. To remedy this situation, the city council in 1983 adopted a "Minority Business Utilization Plan" in which contractors were required to subcontract 30 percent of their business to "Minority Business Enterprises" (MBEs). A challenge to this plan reached the Supreme Court, which, in *City of Richmond v. J.A. Croson*, struck down the plan as constituting a strict racial quota. Writing for a 5-4 majority, Sandra Day O'Connor argued that all race-conscious policies must be subject to "strict scrutiny" to determine whether they are necessary and valid. The Richmond plan, she maintained, did not pass such scrutiny because the city failed to prove that the disparities in the awarding of contracts were the result of racial discrimination. According to O'Connor, the purpose of the plan was to achieve a racial balance rather than to alleviate well-defined acts of discrimination. Thus, the plan violated the rights of white contractors and was therefore unconstitutional.[62]

The *Croson* decision, like the *Stotts* decision, alarmed many civil rights proponents. Once again the burden seemed to have shifted to female and minority workers to prove specific acts of discrimination by employers. At a time when discrimination had become increasingly subtle and was often carried out unconsciously, this would prove extremely difficult, if not impossible.

As the United States entered the 1990s, then, the future of affirmative action as official government policy seemed to be in question. During the 1970s the definition and scope of affirmative relief programs expanded beyond what many people could have expected, despite often ineffective enforcement by various government agencies. During the 1980s, in contrast, the growing conservative movement had increasingly targeted affirmative action programs for retrenchment, if not abolition. Moreover, the government support that had contributed to the expansion of affirmative action was now clearly diminishing. This was especially true of the federal courts, in the wake of the *Wards Cove* and *Croson* decisions. The retirements of liberal Supreme Court justices William Brennan and Thurgood Marshall and the subsequent appointment of Clarence Thomas to the court during the Bush presidency made future judicial support for affirmative action even less likely. Not surprisingly, then, affirmative action remained one of the most unsettling political and social questions of the 1990s.

NOTES

1. Library of Congress program in U.S. Library of Congress, *Affirmative Action News*, Personnel Bulletin No. 3 (Washington, DC: U.S. Library of Congress).

2. Carter quoted in *The Presidential Campaign 1976*, Vol. I, Part I (Washington, DC: Government Printing Office, 1978), p. 261.

3. *Ibid.*, Vol. I, Part II, p. 879.

4. "A Conversation with Commissioner Eleanor Holmes Norton," June 29, 1979, American Enterprise Institute for Public Policy Research (Washington, DC, 1979), p. 7.

5. Herbert Hill, "The Equal Employment Opportunity Commission: Twenty Years Later." Reprint from *The Journal of Intergroup Relations* XI (Winter, 1983): 50-53; *The New York Times*, January 8, 1978, Sec. III, p. 5.

6. Quotes from *The New York Times*, March 21, 1978, p. 47; January 5, 1978, p. B7.

7. Norton quoted in *The New York Times*, January 5, 1978, p. 1.

8. Hill, "Equal Employment Opportunity Commission";   "A Conversation with Eleanor Holmes Norton"; *The New York Times*, January 5, 1978, pp. A1 & B7; January 8, 1978, Sec. III, p. 5; January 9, 1978, p. A18; March 21, 1978, p. 47.

9. Herman Belz, *Equality Transformed: A Quarter-Century of Affirmative Action* (New Brunswick, NJ: Social Philosophy and Policy Center & Transaction Publishers, 1991), pp. 129-33; and *The New York Times*, February 24, 1978, p. 1.

10. U.S. General Accounting Office, *Federal Efforts to Increase Minority Opportunities in Skilled Construction Craft Unions Have Had Little Effect* (Washington, DC: U.S. GAO, 1973), p. 13; and *The New York Times*, January 8, 1978, Sec. III, p. 5.

11. Quote from Hill, "Equal Employment Opportunity Commission," p. 53.

12. U.S. Department of Labor, Office of Federal Contract Compliance Programs, *Construction Compliance Program Operations Manual* (Chicago: Commerce Clearinghouse, Inc., 1977), pp. 4-6.

13. 1976 regulations from *ibid.*; 1978 regulations from *Memorandum in the United States District Court for the Eastern District of Pennsylvania, Taylor v. U.S. Department of Labor, Civil Action #75-1437*, December 7,

1982, pp. 2-4 & 8-9; U.S. GAO, *Federal Efforts*, p. 26; and *The New York Times*, February 24, 1978, pp. A1 & A14.

14. Barbara R. Bergmann, *In Defense of Affirmative Action* (New York: Basic Books, 1996), pp. 54ff; and *The New York Times*, May 26, 1978, pp. D1 & D5.

15. Quotes from *Taylor v. U.S. DOL*, pp. 22 & 21. Information from *ibid.* and Steve Askin and Edwin Newton, "Blood, Sweat and Steel," *Black Enterprise* 14 (May, 1984): 44.

16. Courtland Milloy, Jr., "Plan To Get More Blacks into Washington Construction Jobs Fails," *Washington Post*, March 10, 1981, p. A10.

17. *Ibid.*

18. *Ibid.*, p. Al. Other information from Richard Rowan and Lester Rubin, *Opening the Skilled Construction Trades to Blacks* (Philadelphia: University of Pennsylvania Press, 1972), pp. 32-90; U.S. Department of Labor, *Weekly News Digest*, June 8, 1970; and Sar Levitan, William Johnston, and Robert Taggart, *Still A Dream: The Changing Status of Blacks since 1960* (Cambridge, MA: Harvard University Press, 1975), p. 273.

19. "Building for Peace in Construction," *Business Week*, March 16, 1968, p. 100.

20. *Ibid.*, pp. 100-103; Interview with James MacNamara, April 12, 1984; Congressional Quarterly Services, *Politics in America*, p. 65; and James Patterson, *America's Struggle against Poverty, 1900-1980* (Cambridge, MA: Harvard University Press, 1981), pp. 148-49.

21. "New York Job Plan Opposed," *The Crisis* 77 (June-July, 1970): 234.

22. For a discussion of Ernest Green and the WDL apprenticeship training program, see Chapter IV.

23. "Memorandum from Harry J. Wexler to Stanley Ruttenberg re Minority Hiring in the New York City Construction Trades: The City's Contract Compliance System," April 17, 1979, p. 4.

24. Quote from Stanley Ruttenberg and Harry J. Wexler, "Recommendation for Achieving Equal Employment Opportunity Contract Compliance on City and City-Assisted Construction Projects," May 15, 1979, p. 3. See also Ruttenberg and Wexler, *ibid.*, pp. 2-3; Wexler "Memorandum," pp. 1-4; MacNamara interview; Interview with James Haughton, April 4, 1984; Telephone conversation with MacNamara, March 1, 1985; and *The New York Times*, 1970: March 22, pp. 1 & 72; April 2, p. 33; April 12, p. 28; December 11, pp. 1 & 42.

25. Haughton interview; MacNamara telephone conversation; and *The New York Times*, December 11, 1970, p. 42.

26. *The New York Times*, December 22, 1970, p. 26.

27. Quote from *The New York Times*, December 14, 1970, p. 42. Other information from Haughton interview; and *The New York Times*, December 11, 1970, p. 42; December 22, 1970, p. 26; January 22, 1971, p. 43; June 22, 1971.

28. MacNamara interview.

29. *The New York Times*, August 21, 1973, p. 37.

30. MacNamara interview; Ruttenberg and Wexler, "Recommendations," pp. 3-5; Wexler, "Memorandum," pp. 3-8; U.S. Commission on Civil Rights, *The Challenge Ahead* (Washington, DC: Government Printing Office), p. 159; Herbert Hill, *Labor Union Control of Job Training*, Howard University Institute for Urban Affairs Research Vol. 2, No. 1 (Washington, DC, 1974), pp. 83-99; *The New York Times*, December 16, 1972, p. 1; January 13, 1973, pp. 1 & 13; August 21, 1973, p. 37; and April 4, 1974, p. 41.

31. "Problems of Discrimination and Extortion in the Building Trades," Interim Report to Mayor Edward I. Koch prepared by the Mayor's Office of Construction Industry Relations, 2nd ed. (New York, 1982), p. 3; and Askin and Newton, "Blood, Sweat and Steel," p. 40.

32. MacNamara interview.

33. Mayor's OCIR, "Problems of Discrimination," pp. 4-5.

34. Askin and Newton, "Blood, Sweat and Steel," p. 40.

35. Mayor's OCIR, "Problems of Discrimination," pp. 15 & 18.

36. *Ibid.*, pp. 15-19; MacNamara interview; Askin and Newton, "Blood, Sweat and Steel," pp. 40-42; Michael Oreskes and Selwyn Raab, "Tainted Industry: Construction in New York," *The New York Times*, April 25-27, 1982; *The New York Times*, February 12, 1985, p. B4; and Diane Balmori, *Hispanic Immigrants in the Construction Industry: New York City, 1960-1982* (New York University Center for Latin American and Caribbean Studies Occasional Papers No. 38, May 1983), pp. 14-19 & 39.

37. Askin and Newton, "Blood, Sweat and Steel."

38. *Regents of the University of California v. Bakke* 438 U.S. 307.

39. Harris, *The Harder We Run*, p. 187; Terry Eastland and William Bennet, *Counting by Race: Equality from the Founding Fathers to Bakke and Weber* (New York: Basic Books, Inc., 1979), pp. 3-4; Clarence Stasz, *The American Nightmare: Why Inequality Exists* (New York: Schocken Books, 1981), pp. 29-31; *Bakke* 438 U.S. 265; and Hill, "Race and Ethnicity in Organized Labor," p. 40.

40. *McDonald et al. v. Santa Fe Transportation Co. et al.* 427 U.S. 273 (1976). For congressional debates, see Chapter III.

41. *Timken Co. v. Vaughan* 413 F. Supp. 1183 (1976); Theodore V. Purcell, Jr., "Management and Affirmative Action in the Late Seventies," in Equal Rights and Industrial Relations, ed. Industrial Relations Research Association Series, p. 72; Stephen Rose, "Reverse Discrimination Developments under Title VII," *Houston Law Review* 15 (October, 1977): 136-56; Ruttenberg and Wexler, "Recommendations," p. 3; and MacNamara interview.

42. *United Steelworkers of America, AFL-CIO, v. Weber et al.* 443 U.S. 194 (1979).

43. *Ibid.*, p. 195.

44. *Weber* 443 U.S. 193; Brest, "Race Discrimination," pp. 128-29; Terry Eastland, *Ending Affirmative Action: The Case for Colorblind Justice* (New York: Basic Books, 1996), pp. 93-98; and Peter Irons, *Brennan vs. Rehnquist: The Battle for the Constitution* (New York: Alfred A. Knopf, 1994), pp. 259-62.

45. *Fullilove* decision from Haywood Burns, "The Activism Is Not Affirmative," in Herman Schwartz, ed., *The Burger Years: Rights and Wrongs in the Supreme Court 1969-1986* (New York: Elisabeth Sifton Books/Viking, 1987), p. 103; and *The New York Times*, June 13, 1995, pp. D24-25. Boston decision in Askin and Newton, "Blood, Sweat and Steel," p. 48.

46. Tom Wicker, *Tragic Failure: Racial Integration in America* (New York, William A. Morrow and Company, Inc., 1996), especially pp. 15-16.

47. Chavez quoted in *The New York Times*, December 3, 1984, p. B10. Pendleton quoted in *The New York Times*, January 30, 1985, p. A11; and February 27, 1985, p. C7. Pendleton appointment from Robert R. Detlefsen, *Civil Rights under Reagan* (San Francisco: Institute for Contemporary Studies, 1991), pp. 140-47. For Smith appointment, *see* Elder Witt, *A Different Story: Reagan and the Supreme Court* (Washington, DC: Congressional Quarterly Inc., 1986), pp. 111, 126. For appointment of Reynolds *see* Belz, pp. 184-85.

48. For examples of this new philosophy, see the discussion of William Bradford Reynolds in Belz, *Equality Transformed*, pp. 184-85; and the discussion of Clarence Thomas in Timothy M. Phelps and Helen Winternitz, *Capitol Games: Clarence Thomas, Anita Hill, and the Story of a Supreme Court Nomination* (New York: Hyperion, 1992), p. 96.

49. Quote from Detlefsen, *Civil Rights Under Reagan*, p. 5. For examples of conflicts between EEOC and Justice, see also Phelps and

Winternitz, *Capitol Games*, pp. 97-99; and Belz, *Equality Transformed*, pp. 188-89.

50. This discussion of Thomas in the EEOC is taken largely from Phelps and Winternitz, *Capitol Games*, especially chapters 7-8. Quotes from pp. 95 & 96-97. For statistics on "patterns and practices" cases *see* Belz, *Equality Transformed*, p. 294. For a criticism of Thomas's approach, *see* Wicker, *Tragic Failure*, pp. 15-16.

51. Phelps and Winternitz, *Capitol Games*, especially pp. 97-101. See also Belz, *Equality Transformed*, pp. 188-89.

52. White quoted in *The New York Times*, June 13, 1984, p. B12. See also Belz, *Equality Transformed*, pp. 212-13; and Witt, *A Different Justice*, pp. 122-26.

53. Pendleton quoted in *The New York Times*, January 30, 1985, p. 11. JD quote from *The New York Times*, April 14, 1985, p. E4. See also Belz, *Equality Transformed*, pp. 194ff; Burns, "Activism," in Schwartz, ed., *The Burger Years*, pp. 104-5; Deborah L. Jacobs, "Reagan's War on Quotas," *Newsday*, May 18, 1985, pp. 16-17NY; *The New York Times*, January 30, 1985, p. 11; February 10, 1985, p. 28; April 14, 1985, p. E4; and June 13, 1984, pp. 1 & B12.

54. Belz, *Equality Transformed*, pp. 189-90; and Phelps and Winternitz, *Capitol Games*, pp. 104-6.

55. Belz, *Equality Transformed*, pp. 194-95; and Detlefsen, *Civil Rights under Reagan*, p. 6.

56. Brennan quoted in Irons, *Brennan vs. Rehnquist* , p. 262. For *Cleveland* decision and Justice Department response *see* also Burns, "Activism," in Schwartz, ed., *The Burger Years*, pp. 105-6.

57. *Local 28* ruling and EEOC from Belz, *Equality Transformed*, pp. 190 & 214-16.

58. Quote from Askin and Newton, "Blood, Sweat and Steel," p. 42. See also criticism in Mayor's OCIR, "Problems of Discrimination," p. 7.

59. Quotes from Detlefsen, *Civil Rights under Reagan*, p. 3; and Belz, *Equality Transformed*, p. 196.

60. For an overview of judicial appointments, see Witt, *Reagan and the Supreme Court*, Chapter 1.

61. *Wards Cove* decision from Belz, *Equality Transformed*, p. 228; Detlefsen, *Civil Rights under Reagan*, pp. 197ff; and Irons, *Brennan vs. Rehnquist*, p. 265.

62. *Croson* decision from Belz, *Equality Transformed*, pp. 229-30; and Detlefsen, *Civil Rights under Reagan*, pp. 197-200.

Epilogue

Affirmative Action in the 1990s

Affirmative action has remained a controversial issue throughout the 1990s. Philosophies and policies promoted by advocates as remedies for widespread systemic discrimination are denounced by opponents as discrimination in reverse and an attack on the merit system. Phrases such as *preferential treatment* and *quotas* appear frequently in the political dialogue and have become major targets of the conservative movement of the 1980s and 1990s.

Opponents denounce affirmative action as reverse discrimination (generally against white males), a betrayal of U.S. individualism, and a rejection of the tradition of hiring the best-qualified candidate. In the words of one critic, advocates of affirmative action "rejected equal opportunity because it did not lead to equality of condition."[1] The idea that "equality of result" has been substituted for "equality of opportunity" has become a staple of conservative criticism of affirmative action.

Another key criticism is that the civil rights leadership has substituted color-conscious for colorblind policies, thereby perpetuating the process of categorizing people by race or ethnicity. For example, in his 1975 book, *Affirmative Discrimination*, Nathan Glazer argued that by the mid-1960s the United States had made great strides against discrimination and was in the process of forging a national consensus in which race, color, religion, and national origin were no longer to be considered in determining opportunities. Just at that moment, however, advocates of controversial policies such as affirmative action and busing helped institute "the monumental restructuring of public policy to take into account the race, color, and national origins of individuals." The result was that "we entered into a period of color- and group-consciousness with a vengeance."

More than two decades later, opponents continued to level similar charges. For example, Clint Bolick of the Institute for Justice argued that in the years following the *Brown v. Board of Education* decision of 1954, the nation rejected both the actions and the policies of the proponents of racial segregation. "Americans of all colors and races and nationalities," he wrote, "were freed from racist dogma to live and work together, to attend the same schools, to marry, to stand on the ground of equality." Nevertheless, the nation remained racially divided. According to Bolick: "Much of the blame can be placed on the fact that our government continues to classify us, and to apportion opportunities, on the basis of immutable characteristics." Terry Eastland similarly charged in *Ending Affirmative Action* that affirmative action "has guaranteed the salience of race and ethnicity in the life of the nation, thus making it harder to overcome the very tendency the civil rights movement once condemned: that of regarding and judging people in terms of their racial and ethnic groups."[2]

The argument regarding colorblindness is closely associated with the long-standing assertion that color-conscious remedies violate Title VII of the 1964 Civil Rights Act. Indeed, many critics claim that they are merely attempting to restore the original intent of the architects of that law. Glazer's denunciation of group-consciousness is reflected in the philosophy of many opponents, including officials in the Reagan government discussed in the previous chapter, that legal remedies should be made available only to those individuals who can document actual cases of discrimination.

A major criticism of affirmative action is that it rejects the traditional merit system in which each individual is rewarded according to his or her abilities and the best positions are reserved for the best-qualified people. The pro-affirmative action philosophy, according to one critic, "justifies appointments not based on merit." Another critic phrased the argument this way: "Most defenders of affirmative action reject the traditional idea of individual merit as culturally biased and redefine it in terms of racial and ethnic diversity." Implicit in some of these arguments is the assumption that society as a whole will suffer if we appoint people to positions based on any criteria other than individual qualifications.[3]

Another criticism is that affirmative action demeans those whom it claims to help by raising the question of whether they could have attained success simply by their own efforts. Again quoting Eastland: "Affirmative action thus stigmatizes beneficiaries who could succeed—and have been seen to succeed—without it."[4]

Many opponents find especially questionable the practice of attributing disparities within the labor force to discrimination, either past or present. At issue here is the disparate impact theory of discrimination, in which statistics demonstrating racial or gender imbalances or exclusion can serve as *prima facie* evidence of discrimination, even when there is no concrete evidence of an intent to discriminate. Clarence Thomas expressed the discomfort of many people with this approach: "Every time there is a statistical disparity, it is presumed there is discrimination." Critics of disparate impact theory argue that underrepresentation of certain groups within specific job categories or professions can occur for many reasons other than discrimination. Clint Bolick, for example, maintains that racial disparity today is often the product of factors such as poverty and inadequate education rather than discrimination. In such cases, policies such as class-action suits and numerical formulas are inappropriate and ineffective.[5]

Affirmative action is also criticized as an undemocratic policy that lacks popular support. Indeed, many polls suggest that a majority of citizens oppose affirmative action, especially when it is presented as preferential treatment or quotas. These policies and programs survive, then, not because they reflect the popular will, but rather because of pressures by well-entrenched interest groups. As one example of this argument, Robert Detlefsen attributed the Reagan administration's failure to disassemble the federal affirmative action apparatus to opposition by "a sizable element of the American intelligentsia, particularly judges, journalists, academics, and virtually the entire organized 'civil rights community'."[6]

Other arguments directed against affirmative action are that it constitutes reverse discrimination against white people (especially white males), it heightens rather than alleviates racial animosities, and it constitutes a form of harassment against businesses, labor unions, and other institutions. In addition, the federal bureaucracy that has been created to enforce equal opportunity regulations—which total 110 pages—has contributed to the expansion of "big government," a favorite target of conservatives. For all these reasons, then, it is not surprising that conservatives (along with some former liberals) have campaigned so aggressively against affirmative action in recent years.

Proponents of affirmative action continue to defend their policies in the face of this opposition. As we have seen throughout this monograph, these individuals and groups argue that discrimination in the United States has always been a group rather than an individual phenomenon. For this reason, remedies that try to ignore race, ethnicity, and gender—however attractive they might sound in theory—would be misdirected and ultimately not very effective. In the words of Jamin Raskin: "But when we turn to the real world, we find not centuries of colorblindness and objective merit but centuries of racism, slavery, and discrimination ravaging the communities and life chances of millions of African Americans and other racial minorities." Moreover, in a society in which inequality is so deeply entrenched, colorblindness frequently "functioned as a spurious justification for maintaining the racial status quo." Put simply, women and minorities historically had been denied economic opportunities, and affirmative remedies are needed to redress this pattern.[7]

Supporters also maintain that affirmative action benefits not only women and minorities but society as a whole, by bringing qualified workers from all backgrounds into the labor force. Jesse Jackson, for example, claims that the United States now has "the strongest, most diversified work force in the world." Significantly, many corporate leaders share this view. In 1995, for example, the chairman of Mobil Corporation asserted: "I have never felt a burden from affirmative action, because it is a business necessity for us." In his view, no major corporation could attract the talent necessary to prosper if it limited its options to white males. Moreover, in our multicultural society and our increasingly globalized economy, a diverse work force was a benefit, if not a necessity. As another official observed: "We're looking purely at the business issue. We're going into diverse markets." Nor are such views limited to a few forward-looking employers. According to a 1985 survey in *Fortune*, almost 90 percent of corporations polled stated that they would retain hiring goals and targets even if they were not legally required to do so.[8]

The preceding paragraphs are not intended as a comprehensive summary of all arguments on both sides of the issue, and they do not suggest that all people on either side adhere to every argument presented. Hopefully, they illustrate the chasm between the perceptions of individuals on opposite sides of the issue, which in turn partly explains the intensity of the feelings tapped by this issue. To understand the current debate, however, we must also recognize that, in the light of political developments since the 1980s, many liberals (often Democrats) see conservative initiatives against affirmative action as part of a broader campaign that has targeted a range of policies designed to assist marginalized groups such as immigrants, racial and ethnic minorities, and lower-income people in general. Among the actions they cite are the 1996 welfare bill; a 1995 Supreme Court decision that struck down many legislative districts drawn specifically to increase minority representation; proposed restrictions on the benefits to which legal and illegal immigrants are entitled; a renewed emphasis on combating crime and drug abuse by building more prisons, lengthening prison sentences, and expanding the death penalty; and an overall effort to denigrate the term *liberalism* by associating it with "big government" and "social engineering," which in turn were often interpreted as supporting preferential treatment for ethnic and racial minorities. In the words of Partricia Ireland, president of

NOW: "Current efforts to roll back affirmative action, like the attacks on poverty programs, seem to me to be cynical attempts by congressional leaders to scapegoat women and people of color and direct attention away from the impact of their proposed tax and spending cuts that may further widen the gap between rich and poor."

Some liberals interpret these efforts as a continuation of Republican strategies dating to the 1960s and 1970s to capitalize on the feelings of disaffected white people in order to solidify their political strength. Jesse Jackson, for example, charged: "The new Republican congressional majority is using affirmative action to divide our nation for political gain." Jamin Raskin expressed a similar view: "Republicans are eager to shatter the 1996 electorate along racial and ethnic lines."[9]

The controversy concerning affirmative action, then, is often an arena for conflicts among different groups with different agendas. Moreover, on a deeper level, the affirmative action debate sometimes reflects conflicting views on the very nature of the racial issue in the United States. This topic merits more time and space than I can provide here. For now, it must suffice to examine briefly two fundamental questions that underlie much of the current controversy.

The first question is whether, and to what degree, race and sex discrimination remain major problems following three decades of antidiscrimination laws. Some—although certainly not all—critics charge that, whatever conditions might have prevailed in the past, discrimination is no longer a major obstacle in today's society. More than two decades ago, Glazer asserted that racial discrimination was no longer a major problem in the labor market. He acknowledged that the income gap between whites and blacks had not narrowed, but he attributed this failure to the rapid increase in female-headed families within black communities. Years later, an article in *National Review* lambasted "this ludicrous view of America, according to which opportunities for blacks and women have multiplied while racism and sexism have continued to run rampant." Other critics contend that discrimination still exists, but they define it in limited terms reminiscent of the early 1960s. In 1987, for example, Clarence Thomas—then still with the EEOC—claimed that discrimination consisted primarily of "individual bigots in high places." In such circumstances, class actions against large institutions were unnecessary.[10]

Proponents, in turn, deny that discrimination has disappeared. Jesse Jackson, for example, remains outspoken on this point: "We cannot fall prey to the inane notion that discrimination is an evil of the past. It is today a very painful reality." As we saw in the discussion of Eleanor Holmes Norton in

Chapter VII, many people argue that discrimination now consists not of isolated acts by highly placed individuals but, just the opposite, of deeply entrenched attitudes and practices that perpetuate past patterns of inequality. For example, citing data that indicate continued employment segregation within the U.S. economy, economist Barbara Bergmann claims that "despite the time that has elapsed since the passage of the Civil Rights Act of 1964 outlawing discrimination, thousands of American work places continue to offer jobs that seem permanently earmarked for those of a particular race or sex." To counteract this inertia, a certain amount of outside pressure—often in the form of government intervention—is necessary.[11]

The second question is whether and to what extent government can and should attempt to overcome the effects of policies practiced in past eras. Clearly, proponents feel that government, employers, and other institutions have an obligation both to traditional outgroups and to society in general to take active steps to remedy past discrimination. Many opponents challenge this view. Glazer, for one, warned that: "Compensation for the past is a dangerous principle. It can be extended indefinitely and make for endless trouble." Similarly, while serving in the Reagan Justice Department, William Bradford Reynolds asserted that Title VII was not intended to "go back and cure all the evils of past generations."[12]

That the affirmative action debate has become highly politically charged should be obvious. Since the 1980s it has also taken on a more partisan identity. Although neither party is homogeneous in its approach to affirmative action, since the Reagan presidency a general tendency has emerged for the Republican Party to call for an end to the use of numerical formulas and the Democratic Party, which is more dependent on female and minority-group voters, to defend them.

The evolution of affirmative action as a party issue can be traced throughout the 1990s. One early episode took place during the congressional elections of 1990, when Senator Jesse Helms of North Carolina was fending off a strong challenge by African-American Democrat Harvey Gantt. Late in the campaign, the Helms campaign introduced an ad that showed two white hands tearing up a rejection slip while a voice-over explained that although this individual was the most qualified candidate, the job had gone to a minority-group member to satisfy a quota requirement. This ad helped propel Helms to victory. That same year, in response to *Wards Cove* and other recent court decisions, the Democratically controlled Congress approved a bill to strengthen and clarify federal equal employment regulations. President George Bush vetoed the bill, insisting that it would "introduce the destructive force of quotas." He did, however, approve a similar measure, now known as the Civil Rights Act of 1991, the following year.[13]

In 1992, Bill Clinton became the first Democratic president in twelve years. His promise to assemble a cabinet that "looked like America" illustrated the extent to which the idea of diversity had become a part of the political lexicon. During Clinton's first two years in office, affirmative action was not a pressing issue. That reality changed in 1994, when the Republicans won control of both houses of Congress. Thus, for the first time since the passage of the Civil Rights Act, the possibility arose that Congress could assume a leading role in challenging affirmative action policies. That prospect became a reality in March 1995 when Senate Majority Leader Robert Dole, a former supporter of affirmative action and a leading contender for the Republican presidential nomination in 1996, announced that he would submit legislation to end all "preferences" for women and minorities—including goals and timetables—in federal programs. At the request of Speaker of the House Newt Gingrich, Dole later agreed to postpone introducing such legislation until the Congress had an opportunity to develop a package to assist minorities without using numerical formulas. Clinton responded to Dole's actions by ordering a comprehensive review of all federal affirmative action programs.[14]

Any hopes of either party to defuse this controversy were dashed by a highly controversial Supreme Court decision of June 1995, *Adarand Constructors v. Peña*. The case, like the *Croson* decision of 1989, involved a minority set-aside program, although unlike *Croson* the targeted program was a federal one. The case involved a highway construction program in Colorado. Although Adarand Contractors of Colorado Springs had submitted the lowest bid, the contract ultimately was awarded to the Hispanic-owned Gonzales Construction Company. Unlike Adarand, Gonzales qualified as a ôdisadvantaged business enterprise" (DBE) and thus received special consideration. The owner of Adarand, Randy Pech, challenged this arrangement in the courts. After the federal district and appeals courts in Colorado ruled against him, Pech took his case to the Supreme Court. In a 5-4 decision, the court overturned the lower court decisions and ruled in favor of Adarand.

The majority opinion, authored by Justice Sandra Day O'Connor, essentially extended her arguments in the *Croson* case to federal programs. Declaring that "all racial classifications" established by governmental agencies are "inherently suspect and presumably invalid," O'Connor ruled that "such classifications are constitutional only if they are narrowly tailored measures that further compelling governmental interests." As with state and local programs, all federal programs must be subject to "strict scrutiny." Moreover, affirmative relief was restricted to specific, provable acts of discrimination. Rather than rule on whether the Colorado arrangement passed such "strict scrutiny," the court remanded the case to the lower courts to be reconsidered on the basis on these new standards.

The *Adarand* decision was a major one, for several reasons. First, as with *Stotts* and *Croson*, the decision placed the burden on minority workers to prove discrimination, and it set strict limits on the use of numerical formulas to remedy past discrimination. *The New York Times* characterized these stipulations as a "formidable standard." Second, the decision threatened other set-aside programs, which annually channeled billions of dollars to minority contractors. Finally, the ruling highlighted the impact of the Reagan and Bush presidencies on the behavior of the Supreme Court. The four justices who joined Chief Justice Rehnquist to constitute the majority—O'Connor, Kennedy, Scalia, and Thomas—were all Reagan and Bush appointees.[15]

Although *Adarand* represented a set-back for affirmative action proponents, it was not fatal. O'Connor's ruling was actually more temperate than the accompanying opinions of justices Thomas and Scalia, who would have taken bolder steps to restrict or eliminate federal affirmative action programs. Liberals could find some consolation in O'Connor's assertion that discrimination "is an unfortunate reality, and government is not disqualified from acting in response to it." In light of the decision, Clinton ordered the Justice Department to review all federal programs to ensure that they conformed to the *Adarand* guidelines. At the end of June, the department's Office of Legal Counsel forwarded a memorandum to all cabinet agencies that contained stricter guidelines by which they were to reevaluate their affirmative action programs.[16]

In July, Clinton announced that the review of federal affirmative action programs had been completed, and he delivered a major speech on the subject. To the relief of women's and civil rights groups, the president staked out a generally pro-affirmative action position. The review, he explained, had demonstrated that: "When affirmative action is done right, it is flexible, it is fair, and it works." Declaring that "The job of ending discrimination in this country is not yet over," Clinton announced that federal programs would be modified but not drastically overhauled. He listed four criteria for all programs: (1) they would not establish quotas; (2) no unqualified individuals would be hired; (3) there would be no reverse discrimination; and (4) they would be terminated when they had achieved their goals. Clinton summarized his approach as "Mend it, but don't end it."[17]

Clinton's speech helped solidify his standing among women and minorities, and it predictably drew the ire of his Republican adversaries. Bob Dole repeated his intention to submit legislation banning affirmative action in federal programs. Dole eventually submitted what became known as the Equal Opportunity Act of 1996; the House version was submitted by Charles Canady of Florida. The Dole-Canady bill prohibited all "preferential treatment"—including goals and timetables—for women and minorities in all federal programs. In July 1996, however, Gingrich and Trent Lott, who had succeeded Dole as Senate majority leader, announced that the bill would not come up for a vote that year. They explained that with the pending election there was not enough time to consider it. Critics claimed that the Republicans lacked the votes to pass the bill, given that some moderate Republicans still supported affirmative action, and that they feared a backlash by female voters in the election.[18]

Thus, affirmative action did not become the central issue in the election that it might have. Nevertheless, it remained in the headlines. Dole's vice-presidential candidate, Jack Kemp, was a long-time supporter of affirmative action who abruptly changed his position after his selection. The issue arose in both the presidential and vice-presidential debates, with the Democratic candidates defending affirmative action (but not quotas) and the Republican candidates opposing it. While campaigning in California shortly before the election, Dole elaborated on his position regarding affirmative action. While insisting that he was opposed to all forms of discrimination, he asserted that "we believe it's wrong to use quotas, set-asides, and other preferences that serve only to pit one American against another American, or group against group." Dole conceded that he had formerly supported certain affirmative action programs that were intended to be "transitional and temporary," but he had concluded that "this was a blind alley in the search for equal justice."[19]

In the same speech Dole expressed his firm support for a state initiative popularly known as the California Civil Rights Initiative, or CCRI. Also referred to as Proposition 209, the initiative forbade the state to "discriminate against or grant preferential treatment to any individual or group on account of sex, color, ethnicity, or national origin in the operation of public employment, public education, or public contracting." With the support of Republican Governor Pete Wilson, the state Republican Party, and the Republican National Committee, supporters managed to secure the necessary votes to place the initiative on the November ballot. Dole endorsed the measure; Clinton opposed it. On November 5, 1996, California voters approved the measure by a margin of 54 percent to 46 percent.[20]

The future of affirmative action for the late 1990s remains uncertain. On the one hand, many of the practices and expectations engendered by affirmative action have become a standard part of doing business in the United States. On the other hand, affirmative action is being challenged, denounced, and reexamined by groups and institutions across the country. The final outcome of all these cross-currents is impossible to predict. Ironically, at the same time that many people in the political system are advocating an end to affirmative action, the list of groups protected by antidiscrimination laws seems to be expanding. In 1990, Congress passed and Bush signed the Americans with Disabilities Act, which extended protection from discrimination in areas such as employment, transportation, and public accommodations to an estimated 43 million people with physical or mental disabilities. Six years later, the Senate rejected by only a single vote a measure that would have prohibited employers from discriminating against gays and lesbians. It seems, therefore, that regardless of which individual or party is in office, the struggle for increased opportunities continues.[21]

The history of affirmative action is a long and complex one. Different people can review this history and arrive at differing conclusions concerning the effectiveness, appropriateness, and probable future of affirmative action programs. To conclude this monograph I will propose what I consider a few key points to be learned from the material covered in these chapters. This list is not exclusive, and other readers are free to draw their own conclusions.

> (1) Affirmative action is a much broader concept than just quotas. Based on the model from Daniel Seligman presented in the Introduction, affirmative action includes a broad spectrum of activities ranging from educational and job training programs to flexible goals and timetables to inflexible quotas. Thus, quotas are the most extreme form of affirmative action (and are often technically illegal). Of course, employers may treat goals and timetables as rigid quotas in order to meet their hiring objectives and thus avoid possible lawsuits and government intervention. In addition, most of the controversies surrounding affirmative action involve the "harder" forms of affirmative action, such as numerical objectives.

Nevertheless, the scope of possible affirmative action remedies must not be overlooked. In addition, equating affirmative action with quotas presents the philosophy in its most extreme and least popular form. Significantly, psychological studies have suggested that people are more likely to support outreach and educational programs than what they perceive as preferential treatment for women and minorities.[22]

(2) Affirmative action is not exclusively a racial policy. Although it arose out of the black struggle for economic progress, it has come to include a number of groups, including women, Latinos, and Native Americans. This statement has at least two important implications. First, the various groups eligible for affirmative action as a result of past discrimination constitute a numerical majority of the labor force. Hence, affirmative action today is intended not to advance the interests of certain select groups but to open up to all Americans opportunities that were historically reserved for one numerical minority group: white males.

Second, as we have just observed, the way that affirmative action is presented may affect the ways that people respond to it. According to a study conducted by psychologist Audrey Murrell at the University of Pittsburgh, subjects found affirmative action programs least palatable when they were applied to African Americans and most acceptable for the elderly and people with disabilities. Programs intended for women and the poor fell somewhere in between. Thus, people who equate affirmative action with preferential treatment for African Americans may be the most likely to oppose such programs.[23]

(3) As it pertains to African Americans, affirmative action has benefited individuals across different classes and backgrounds, and not just a small minority of white-collar workers. In the 1996 presidential debate, Bob Dole repeated a popular view that "nobody was really benefiting except a very small group at the top."[24] In fact,

as we have seen throughout this book, many of the beneficiaries of affirmative action programs and court decisions were blue-collar workers in the tobacco, steel, textile, and construction industries, as well as public employees such as firefighters and police officers. A detailed analysis of economic trends is beyond the scope of this book. Nevertheless, to the extent that affirmative action has helped create employment opportunities for African Americans, this has occurred throughout the economy and not just in white-collar positions.

(4) Finally, at the risk of pointing out the obvious, affirmative action has a long history. Questions about how to overcome both present and past economic discrimination have challenged concerned groups and individuals throughout most of this century and were an intrinsic feature of the civil rights movement. Issues such as proportional representation and superseniority predate by decades the passage of the 1964 Civil Rights Act. Of course, to refer to these relatively isolated cases as "prototypes" of current policies would be an extreme exaggeration. It is doubtful that as late as the early 1960s many people could have foreseen the vast equal employment opportunity apparatus that has been created since the passage of the act. Still, affirmative action as it exists today evolved from the activism of workers and civil rights groups throughout the century, as well as from the courts and the federal bureaucracy. This does not necessarily make current policies "correct" in any legal or political sense, but it does root them in activities and ideas that have been around for decades.

The future of affirmative action remains unclear. Opponents and advocates of affirmative action remain very far apart, and the issue has become both a polemical and a partisan one. At this point no mutually acceptable middle ground seems likely to present itself. Meanwhile, racial inequalities and tensions remain an everyday part of American life. Whether the nation has the resources and the will to address these issues honestly and decisively remains a major question as the United States prepares to enter the twenty-first century.

NOTES

1. Herman Belz, *Equality Transformed: A Quarter-Century of Affirmative Action* (New Brunswick, NJ: Social Philosophy and Policy Center, 1991), pp. 236-37.

2. Nathan Glazer's argument from *Affirmative Discrimination: Ethnic Inequality and Public Policy* (New York: Basic Books, Inc., 1975). Quotes from pp. 3-4, 31. Terry Eastland in *Ending Affirmative Action: The Case for Colorblind Justice* (New York: Basic Books, 1996). Quotes from pp. 7-8. Clint Bolick from *The Affirmative Action Fraud: Can We Restore the American Civil Rights Vision?* (Washington, DC: The Cato Institute, 1996). Quotes from p. 121.

3. Harvey C. Mansfield, Jr., "The Underhandedness of Affirmative Action," in Nils I. Bateman and David M. Petersen, eds., *Social Issues: Conflicting Opinions* (Upper Saddle River, NJ: Prentice Hall, 1990), p. 120; and Belz, *Equality Transformed*, p. 243.

4. Eastland, *Ending Affirmative Action*, p. 9.

5. Thomas quote from *The New York Times*, December 3, 1984, p. B10. Bolick from *Affirmative Action Fraud*, pp. 21-22. For criticisms of disparate impact theory, see relevant discussions in Belz, *Equality Transformed*; and Eastland, *Ending Affirmative Action*.

6. Eastland, *Ending Affirmative Action*, pp. 164-65; and Robert R. Detlefsen, *Civil Rights under Reagan* (San Francisco: Institute for Contemporary Studies), pp. 3-8. Quote from p. 8.

7. Quotes from Jamin B. Raskin, "Society Needs Affirmative Action to Fight Discrimination," in A.E. Sadler, ed., *Affirmative Action* (San Diego, CA: Greenhaven Press, 1996), p. 28; and Stephen Steinberg, *Turning Back: The Retreat from Racial Justice in America* (Boston: Beacon Press, 1995), p. 104.

8. Jesse Jackson quoted in "People of Color Need Affirmative Action," press release of March 1, 1995, reprinted in Sadler, ed., *Affirmative Action*, p. 10. Other quotes from *Washington Post*, March 19, 1995, p. H1. *Fortune* survey from Eastland, *Ending Affirmative Action*, p. 101.

9. Jackson quote from "People of Color" in Sadler, ed., *Affirmative Action*, p. 9. Raskin quote from "Society Needs Affirmative Action" in Sadler, p. 24. Patricia Ireland quote from *What Women Want* (New York: Dutton/Penguin, 1996), p. 300. For a comprehensive presentation of the arguments introduced in these two paragraphs, *see* Tom Wicker, *Tragic*

Failure: Racial Integration in America (New York: William A. Morrow and Company, Inc., 1996), especially Chapter 1.

10. Thomas quote from Belz, *Equality Transformed*, p. 191. Other quote from Mansfield, "Underhandedness," in Bateman and Petersen, eds., *Social Issues*, p. 119. Glazer from *Affirmative Discrimination*, pp. 41-43.

11. Jackson quote from "People of Color" in Sadler, ed., *Affirmative Action*, p. 11. See also Barbara Bergmann, *In Defense of Affirmative Action* (New York: Basic Books, 1996), p. 14 for quotes; pp. 56-57 for statistics.

12. Glazer, *Affirmative Discrimination*, p. 201; Reynolds quote from Belz, *Equality Transformed*, p. 185.

13. Helms episode from Wicker, *Tragic Failure*, pp. 99-100. Bush and civil rights bill from Jack W. Germond and Jules Witcover, *Mad As Hell: Revolt at the Ballot Box, 1992* (New York: Warner Books, 1993), pp. 41, 54-55, 132; and Bolick, *Affirmative Action Fraud*, pp. 111-113.

14. *The New York Times*, March 16, 1995, p. A1; July 19, 1995, p. A1.

15. Information and quotes from *Los Angeles Times*, January 18, 1995, p. D20; June 13, 1995, pp. A1, A13, & A15; and *The New York Times*, June 13, 1995, pp. A1, D24, & D25. See also Eastland, *Ending Affirmative Action*, pp. 127-29.

16. Court rulings and opinions from *The New York Times*, June 13, 1995, pp. A1, D24, & D25. White House review from *The New York Times*, June 29, 1995, pp. A1 & A16.

17. *The New York Times*, July 20, 1995, pp. A1 & B10. See also Elizabeth Drew, *Showdown: The Struggle between the Gingrich Congress and the Clinton White House* (New York: Simon & Schuster, 1996), pp. 289-96.

18. *Ibid.; Los Angeles Times*, March 8, 1996, p. A24; July 15, 1996, p. A18.

19. *The New York Times*, October 29, 1996, pp. A1 & A21.

20. *Los Angeles Times*, April 17, 1996, pp. A3 & A20; *The New York Times*, February 6, 1996, p. A14; November 7, 1996, p. B7.

21. Disabilities act from *The New York Times*, July 14, 1990, p. A6. Gay and lesbian vote from *The New York Times*, September 15, 1996, p. 51.

22. Studies from Tori DeAngelis, "Ignorance Plagues Affirmative Action," reprint from *APA Monitor*, May 1995.

23. *Ibid.*

24. *The New York Times*, October 17, 1996, p. B11.

Bibliography

PRIMARY

Laws and Executive Orders

Civil Rights Act of 1964. July 2, 1964. Public Law 88-352. 78 Stat. 253.
Civil Rights Act of 1968. April 11, 1968. Public Law 90-284.
Executive Order 11246. Issued by Lyndon B. Johnson, September 24, 1965. 30 *Federal Register* 12319.
National Labor Relations Act. *U.S. Code*, Title 29.
U.S. Department of Labor. Office of Federal Contract Compliance. *Revised Order #4. Code of Federal Regulations*, Part 60-2.

Court Cases

Hughes v. Superior Court of California in and for County of Contra Costa 70 S. Ct. 718 (1950)
Albemarle Paper Company v. Moody 95 S. Ct. 2362 (1975)
Louisiana v. United States 380 U.S. 145 (1965)
Griggs et al. v. Duke Power Company 401 U.S. 424 (1971)
Swann et al. v. Charlotte-Mecklenburg Board of Education et al. 402 U.S. 1 (1971)
McDonald et al. v. Santa Fe Trail Transportation Company et al. 427 U.S. 273 (1976)
Regents of the University of California v. Bakke 438 U.S. 265 (1978)
United Steelworkers of America, AFL-CIO-CLC v. Weber et al. 443 U.S. 193 (1979)
Whitfield v. United Steelworkers of America 263 F. 2d 546 (1959)
Oatis v. Crown Zellerbach Corporation 398 F. 2d 496 (1968)
Local 53 of the International Association of Heat and Frost Insulators and Asbestos Workers v. Vogler 407 F. 2d -1047 (1969)

U.S. v. Sheet Metal Workers International Association, Local Union No. 36, AFL-CIO 416 F. 2d 123 (1969)

Local 189, United Papermakers and Paperworkers, AFL-CIO v. U.S. 416 F. 2d 980 (1969)

The Contractors Association of Eastern Pennsylvania v. the Secretary of Labor 442 F. 2d 159 (1971)

United States v. Bethlehem Steel Corporation 446 F. 2d 652 (1971)

Carter v. Gallagher 452 F. 2d 315 (1971)

United States v. Local Union No. 212, International Brotherhood of Electrical Workers 472 F. 2d 634 (1973)

Head v. Timken Roller Bearing Company 486 F.2d 870 (1973)

Rios v. Enterprise Association Steamfitters Local 638 of U.A. 501 F.2d 622 (1974)

U.S. v. U.S. Steel Corporation 520 F.2d 1043 (1975)

Hall v. Werthan Bag Company 251 F.Supp. 184 (1966)

Ethridge v. Rhodes 268 F.Supp. 83 (1967)

Quarles v. Philip Morris, Inc. 279 F.Supp. 505 (1968)

Crown Zellerbach Corporation v. Wirtz 281 F.Supp. 337 (1968)

EEOC v. United Association of Journeymen and Apprentices of the Plumbing and Pipefitting Industry of the United States and Canada, Local Union No. 189 311 F.Supp. 468 (1970)

Hicks. v. Crown Zellerbach Corporation 319 F.Supp. 314 (1970)

U.S. v. U.S. Steel Corporation 371 F.Supp. 1045 (1973)

Timken Company v. Vaughan 413 F.Supp. 1183 (1976)

Crown Zellerbach Corporation v. Marshall 441 F.Supp. 1110 (1977)

Commonwealth of Pennsylvania et al. v. Local Union 542, International Union of Operating Engineers 469 F.Supp. 329 (1978)

A. S. Beck Shoe Company v. Johnson 153 Misc. 363 (1934)

Weiner v. Cuyahoga Community College District et al. 249 N.E.2d 907 (1969)

Hughes v. Superior Court in and for Contra Costa County 186 P.2d 756 (1948)

Government Documents and Publications

Bureau of National Affairs. *The Civil Rights Act of 1964.* Washington, DC: Bureau of National Affairs, 1964.

——. *The Equal Employment Opportunity Act of 1972.* Washington, DC: Bureau of National Affairs, 1973.

Code of Federal Regulations. Vols. 29 & 41. Published by the Office of the Federal Register, General Services Administration. Washington, DC: Government Printing Office, 1983.

"Civil Rights and 'FEPC'." *Congressional Digest* 43 (March, 1964): 67-96.

Congressional Quarterly. *Nixon: The First (Second, etc.) Year of His Presidency.* Washington, DC: Congressional Quarterly, Inc., 1970ff.

———. *Weekly Digest.* Washington, DC: Congressional Quarterly, Inc. Published periodically.

Congressional Record. Vols. 110; 115; and 118. Washington, DC: Government Printing Office.

Idelson, Evelyn. *Affirmative Action and Equal Employment: A Guidebook for Employers.* Vols. 1 & 2. Published for U.S. Equal Employment Opportunity Commission. Washington, DC: Government Printing Office, 1974.

Lecht, Leonard A. *Manpower Needs for National Goals in the 1970s.* New York: Frederick A. Praeger, Publishers, 1969.

Libeau, Vera A. *Minority and Female Membership in Referral Unions 1974.* Research Report No. 55. Prepared for U.S. Equal Employment Opportunity Commission. Washington, DC: Government Printing Office, 1977.

Lunden, Leon E. *Antidiscrimination Provisions in Major Contracts 1961.* U.S. Department of Labor Bulletin No. 1336. Washington, DC: Government Printing Office, 1962.

"Problems of Discrimination and Extortion in the Building Trades." Interim Report to Mayor Edward I. Koch. Prepared by the Mayor's Office of Construction Industry Relations. 2nd Ed. August, 1982.

McMillan, Kathleen A. *Minorities and Women in Private Industry 1975.* EEOC Research Report No. 54. Washington, DC: Government Printing Office, 1977.

Report of the National Advisory Commission on Civil Disorders. New York: Bantam Paperbacks, 1968.

Ruttenberg, Stanley, and Wexler, Harry J. "Recommendations for Achieving Equal Employment Opportunity Contract Compliance on City and City-Assisted Construction Protects." May 15, 1979.

Sobel, Lester A. *Civil Rights, 1960-1966.* New York: Facts on File, 1967.

———. *Quotas and Affirmative Action.* New York: Facts on File, 1980.

"Memorandum in the United States District Court for the Eastern District of Pennsylvania." *Taylor v. U.S. Department of Labor.* Civil Action #75-1437. December 7, 1982.

Ronald Taylor, et al. v. United States Department of Labor et al.. Brief of Appelants.

U.S. Commission on Civil Rights. *The Challenge Ahead: Equal Opportunity in the Referral Unions.* Washington, DC: Government Printing Office, 1976.

———. "Civil Rights under Federal Programs." CRC Special Publication #1. January, 1965.

———. "Equal Opportunity in Hospitals and Health Facilities." Special Publication #2. March, 1965.

———. "Equal Employment Opportunity under Federal Law." Special Publication #5. March, 1966.

———. "Racism in America and How to Combat It." Clearinghouse Publication #20. January, 1970.

———. "HEW and Title VI." Clearinghouse Publication #22. 1970.

———. "The System Can Work: A Case Study in Contract Compliance." Clearinghouse Publication #29. 1970.

———. "Statement on Affirmative Action for Equal Employment Opportunity." Clearinghouse Publication # 41. February, 1973.

———. *Federal Civil Rights Enforcement Efforts.* Washington, DC: Government Printing Office, 1970.

———. *The Federal Civil Rights Enforcement Effort—A Reassessment.* Washington, DC: Government Printing Office, 1973.

———. *For All the People . . . By All the People.* A Report on Equal Opportunity in State and Local Government Employment. Washington, DC: Government Printing Office, 1969.

———. *From the Highways to the Skyways: A Study of the Contract Compliance Programs of the Department of Transportation.* Washington, DC: Government Printing Office, 1973.

———. *Hearings before the U.S. Commission on Civil Rights in Cleveland, Ohio.* April 1-7, 1966. Washington, DC: Government Printing Office, 1966.

———. *Hearings before the U.S. Commission on Civil Rights, San Francisco, California.* May 1-3, 1967.

———. *Last Hired, First Fired: Layoffs and Civil Rights.* Washington, DC: Government Printing Office, 1977.

———. *Report.* Washington, DC: Government Printing Office. Published biennially beginning 1961.

——. *To Know Or Not To Know: Collection and Use of Racial and Ethnic Data in Federal Assistance Programs.* Washington, DC: Government Printing Office, 1973.

——. *Twenty Years After Brown: Equality of Economic Opportunity.* Washington, DC: Government Printing Office, 1975.

——. Ohio Advisory Committee. *Affirmative Action or Inaction?* Washington, DC: Government Printing Office, 1978.

Advisory Committees to the U.S. Commission on Civil Rights. *Reports on Apprenticeship.* Washington, DC: Government Printing Office, 1964.

U.S. Congress. House of Representatives

——. Special Subcommittee on Defense Aspects of the Equal Employment Opportunity Program of the Committee on Armed Services. 91st Congress, 2nd Session. *Defense Aspects of the EEO Program.* Washington, DC: Government Printing Office, 1970.

——. *Oversight Hearings before the Subcommittee on Equal Opportunities of the Committee on Education and Labor, 94th Congress, 1st Session.* Washington, DC: Government Printing Office, 1975.

——. *Hearings before the Subcommittee on Equal Opportunities of the Committee on Education and Labor, 93rd Congress, 2nd Session, on H.R. 15826.* Washington, DC: Government Printing Office, 1974.

——. *Hearings before Subcommittee #5 of the Committee on the Judiciary, 88th Congress, 1st Session, on Miscellaneous Proposals Regarding the Civil Rights of Persons within the Jurisdiction of the United States.* Washington, DC: Government Printing Office, 1963.

——. Hearings before the Subcommittee on Civil and Constitutional Rights of the Committee on the Judiciary. 95th Congress, 2nd Session. *GAO Report on the EEO Action Programs at the Department of Justice.* April 12 & July 12, 1978. Washington, DC: Government Printing Office, 1978.

U.S. Congress. Senate

——. *Hearing before the Committee on Labor and Public Welfare, 87th Congress, 1st Session, on the Nomination of W. Willard Wirtz to be Under Secretary of Labor.* January 25, 1961. Washington, DC: Government Printing Office, 1961.

———. *Hearings before the Subcommittee on Employment and Manpower of the Committee on Labor and Public Welfare.* 88th Congress, 1st Session. Washington, DC: Government Printing Office, 1963.

———. *Hearing before the Committee on Labor and Public Welfare, 90th Congress; 1st Session, on Clifford L. Alexander, Jr., To Be a Member of the EEOC.* July 27, 1967. Washington, DC: Government Printing Office, 1967.

———. *Hearing before the Committee on Labor and Public Welfare, 91st Congress, 1st Session, on George P. Shultz to be Secretary of Labor.* January 16, 1969. Washington, DC: Government Printing Office, 1969.

———. *Hearing before the Committee on Labor and Public Welfare, 91st Congress, 1st Session, on William Hill Brown III to be a Member of the EEOC.* April 15, 1969. Washington, DC: Government Printing Office, 1969.

———. *Hearing before the Committee on Labor and Public Welfare, 91st Congress, 1st Session, on Arthur Fletcher to be an Assistant Secretary of Labor.* April 15, 1969. Washington, DC: Government Printing Office, 1969.

———. *Hearing before the Committee on Labor and Public Welfare, 91st Congress, 2nd Session, on James D. Hodgson to be Secretary of Labor.* June 16, 1970. Washington, DC: Government Printing Office, 1970.

———. *Hearing before the Committee on Labor and Public Welfare, 91st Congress, 2nd Session, on Colston A. Lewis to be a Member of the EEOC.* June 1, 1970. Washington, DC: Government Printing Office, 1970.

———. *Hearings before the Subcommittee on Labor of the Committee on Labor and Public Welfare, 92nd Congress, 1st Session, on S.2515, S. 2617, H.R. 1746.* October 4-7, 1971. Washington, DC: Government Printing Office, 1971.

———. *Hearing before the Committee on Labor and Public Welfare, 93rd Congress, lst Session, on John H. Powell, Jr., to be a Member of the EEOC.* December 12, 1973. Washington, DC: Government Printing Office, 1974.

———. *Hearings before the Subcommittee on Administrative Practice and Procedures of the Committee on the Judiciary, 91st Congress, 1st Session, Pursuant to S. Res. 39.* March 27-28, 1963. Washington, DC: Government Printing Office, 1969.

U.S. Department of Commerce

———. Bureau of the Census. *1970 Census of the Population.* Vol. 1, Part 1. Washington, DC: Department of Commerce, 1973.
———. *County and City Data Book 1977.* Washington, DC: Government Printing Office, 1978.
———. *Census of Construction Industries.* 1972, 1977, & 1982 eds. Published by Department of Commerce.

Department of Labor

———. *Weekly News Digest.* 1963-1970. *Black News Digest.* 1970-1974.
———. Bureau of Labor Statistics. *Handbook of Labor Statistics.* Department of Labor Bulletin No. 2715. Washington, DC: Government Printing Office, 1983.
———. *The Social and Economic Status of Negroes in the United States, 1969.* Also, *1970.* Washington, DC: Government Printing Office, 1969, 1970.
———. Manpower Administration. *Negroes in Apprenticeship.* Manpower/Automation Research Monograph No. 6. Washington, DC: Government Printing Office, 1967.
———. Office of Federal Contract Compliance Programs. *Construction Compliance Program Operations Manual.* Chicago: Commerce Clearing House, Inc., 1977.

U.S. Equal Employment Opportunity Commission

———. *Annual Report.* Washington, DC: Government Printing Office. Published annually, beginning 1967.
———. *Employment Profiles of Women and Minorities in 23 Metropolitan Areas 1974.* Research Report No. 49. Washington, DC: Government Printing Office, 1976.
———. *Equal Employment Report #1: Job Patterns for Women and Minorities in Private Industry 1966.* Washington, DC: Government Printing Office, 1967.
———. *The First Decade.* Washington, DC: Government Printing Office, 1974.
———. *Hearings on Discrimination in White-Collar Employment.* New York, January 15-18, 1968. Washington, DC: Government Printing Office, 1968.

———. *Hearings on Utilization of Minority and Women Workers in Certain Major Industries.* Los Angeles, March 12-14, 1969. Washington, DC: Government Printing Office, 1969.

———. *Legislative History of Titles VII and XI of Civil Rights Act.* Washington, DC: Government Printing Office.

U.S. Fair Employment Practices Committee. *Final Report.* June 28, 1946. Washington, DC: Government Printing Office, 1947.

U.S. General Accounting Office. *The Equal Employment Opportunity Commission Has Made Limited Progress in Eliminating Employment Discrimination.* Washington, DC: Government Printing Office, 1976.

———. *Federal Efforts to Increase Minority Opportunities in Skilled Construction Craft Unions Have Had Little Success.* Washington, DC: Government Printing Office, 1979.

U.S. Library of Congress. *Affirmative Action News.* Personnel Bulletin No. 3.

The American Dream . . . Equal Opportunity. Report on the Community Leaders' Conference Sponsored by the President's Committee on Equal Employment Opportunity. Washington, DC: Government Printing Office, 1962.

Pattern for Progress. Final Report to President Eisenhower from the Committee on Government Contracts. Washington, DC: Government Office, 1961.

Walinsky, Adam, et al.. *Official Lawlessness in New York State Construction Employment, Government Inaction, and the $275 Million Annual Cost.* A study sponsored by the Committee for Efficiency in Government, 1969.

"Memorandum from Harry J. Wexler to Stanley Ruttenberg *re* Minority Hiring in the New York City Construction Trades: The City's Contract Compliance System." April 17, 1979.

Publications of Civil Rights Groups

Congress of Racial Equality. *CORE-lator.* 1956-1965.

_____. New York City. *Rights and Reviews.*

National Association for the Advancement of Colored People. Files. U.S. Library of Congress.

———. *Annual Report.* 1963-1973.

———. *The Negro Wage-Earner and Apprenticeship Training Programs.* Published 1960 by NAACP.

NAACP Legal Defense and Education Fund, Inc. *Report.* 1966-1973.
National Urban League. *The State of Black America 1976.* Published
    1976 by National Urban League.
Southern Christian Leadership Conference. *Newsletter.* 1962-1963.

Interviews, Autobiographies, Policy Statements

Abrams, Elliot. "The Quota Commission." *Commentary* 54 (October,
    1972): 54ff.
"Equal-Rights for All . . . The AFL-CIO Position." *The American
    Federationist* 71 (March, 1964): 1-5.
Interview with John H. Powell, Jr. *Black Enterprise* 4 (July, 1974):
    27-29.
Blumrosen, Alfred W. *Black Employment and the Law* New Brunswick,
    NJ: Rutgers University Press, 1971.
*Remarks by Peter J. Brennan, Secretary of Labor, before the Federal
    Committee on Apprenticeship.* Washington, DC. July 23, 1974.
"Managing Your Manpower: How Employers Are Preparing for the Civil
    Rights Act." *Duns Review* 84 (November, 1964): 57-60.
Farmer, James. *Freedom—When?* New York: Random House, 1965.
Fein, Leonard J. "Thinking About Quotas." *Midstream* 19 (March,
    1973): 13-17.
Fletcher, Arthur. *The Silent Sell-Out: Government Betrayal of Blacks to
    the Craft Unions.* New York: The Third Press, 1974.
Goodman, Walter. "The Return of the Quota System." *The New York
    Times Magazine,* September 10, 1972, pp. 28ff.
Halpern, Ben. "The Quota Issue." *Midstream* 19 (March, 1973): 3-12.
Humphrey, Hubert H. *The Education of a Public Man.* Garden City, NY:
    Doubleday and Co., Inc., 1976.
Johnson, Lyndon B. *My Hope for America.* New York: Random House,
    1964.
———. *The Johnson Presidential Press Conferences.* Vols. 1 & 2. Edited
    by Doris Kearns Goodwin. New York: Earl M. Coleman Enterprises,
    Inc., 1978.
———. *Public Papers of the Presidents. Lyndon B. Johnson.* Washington,
    DC: Government Printing Office, 1965-1969.
———. *A Time for Action: A Selection from the Speeches and Writings of
    Lyndon B. Johnson, 1953-1964.* New York: Atheneum Publishers,
    1964.

——. *The Vantage Point*. New York: Holt, Rinehart, and Winston, 1971.

Kennedy, John F. *Kennedy and the Press: The News Conferences*. Edited by Harold W. Chase and Allen H. Lerman. New York: Thomas W. Crowell, Co., 1965.

——. *Public Papers of the Presidents. John F. Kennedy.* Washington, DC: Government Printing Office, 1962-1964.

King, Martin Luther, Jr. "Birmingham, U.S.A." *New York Amsterdam News*, June 8, 1963, p. 10.

——. "The Hammer of Civil Rights." *The Nation* 198 (March 9, 1964): 230-34.

——. *Why We Can't Wait*. New York: Harper & Row, 1963, 1964.

"What the Marchers Really Want." Interviews with civil rights leaders. *The New York Times Magazine*, August 25, 1963, pp 7ff.

"Five Angry Men Speak Their Minds." Gertrude Samuels, Chair. *The New York Times Magazine*, May 17, 1964, pp. 14ff.

Nixon, Richard M. *Nixon Speaks Out*. Nixon-Agnew Campaign Committee, 1968.

——. *The Nixon Presidential Press Conferences*. Edited by Helen Thomas. New York: Earl M. Coleman Enterprises, Inc., 1978.

——. *Public Papers of the Presidents. Richard M. Nixon.* Washington, DC: Government Printing Office, 1969-1974.

——. *RN: The Memoirs of Richard Nixon*. New York: Grosset and Dunlap, 1978.

"A Conversation with Commissioner Eleanor Holmes Norton." June 29, 1979. Washington, DC: American Enterprise Institute for Public Policy Research.

Panetta, Leon E., and Gall, Peter. *Bring Us Together: The Nixon Team and the Civil Rights Retreat*. New York: J.B. Lippincott Company, 1971.

Pottinger, J. Stanley. "The Drive Toward Equality." In *Reverse Discrimination*, pp. 41-49. Edited by Barry R. Gross. Buffalo, NY: Prometheus Books, 1977.

The Presidential Campaign 1976. (Washington, DC: Government Printing Office, 1978).

Raab, Earl. "Quotas by Any Other Name." *Commentary* 53 (January, 1972): 41-45.

Rustin, Bayard. *The Meaning of Birmingham*. Glen Gardner, NJ: The Libertarian Press.

United Electrical, Radio and Machine Workers of America. *Organized Labor and the Black Worker*. Published 1967.

"Negro Leaders Tell Their Plans for '64." *U.S. News and World Report* 56 (February 24, 1964): 56ff.

Wirtz, W. Willard. "Toward Equal Opportunity." *American Child* 45 (November, 1963): 1-4.

Young, Whitney M., Jr. *To Be Equal*. New York: McGraw-Hill Book Company, 1964.

———. "The Negro Revolt." *American Child* 45 (November, 1963): 5-8.

Studies and Research

Ahart, Gregory J. "Process Evaluation of the Contract Compliance Program in Nonconstruction Industry." *Industrial and Labor Relations Review* 29 (July, 1976): 565-71.

Balmori, Diana. *Hispanic Immigrants in the Construction Industry: New York City, 1960-1982*. NYU Center for Latin American and Caribbean Studies Occasional Papers No. 38. May, 1983.

Bloom, Gordon F.; F. Marion Fletcher; and Charles R. Perry. *Negro Employment in Retail Trade*. The Racial Policies of American Industry Report #25. Philadelphia: University of Pennsylvania Press, 1972.

Caditz, Judith. *White Liberals in Transition*. New York: Spectrum Publications, Inc., 1976.

Cousens, Frances Reissman. *Public Civil Rights Agencies and Fair Employment: Promise vs. Performance*. New York: Frederick A. Praeger, Publishers, 1969.

Ferman, Louis A. *The Negro and Equal Employment Opportunities: A Review of Management Experiences in Twenty Companies*. New York: Frederick A. Praeger Publishers, 1968.

Fletcher, F. Marion. *The Negro in the Drug Manufacturing Industry*. The Racial Policies of American Industry Report #21. Philadelphia: University of Pennsylvania Press, 1970.

Marshall, F. Ray, and Vernon M. Briggs, Jr. *The Negro and Apprenticeship*. Baltimore: The John Hopkins Press, 1967.

Northrup, Herbert R. *The Negro in the Paper Industry*. The Racial Policies of American Industry Report #8. Philadelphia: University of Pennsylvania Press, 1969.

———. The Racial Policies of American Industry Report #13. Philadelphia: University of Pennsylvania Press, 1970.

———, and John A. Larson. *The Impact of the AT&T- EEO Consent Decree*. Philadelphia: University of Pennsylvania Press, 1979.

Rowan, Richard L. *The Negro in the Steel Industry*. The Racial Policies of American Industry Report #3. Philadelphia: University of Pennsylvania Press, 1968.

————. *The Negro in the Textile Industry*. The Racial Policies of American Industry Report #20. Philadelphia: University of Pennsylvania Press, 1970.

————. Shaeffer, Ruth G. *Nondiscrimination in Employment. Changing Perspectives, 1963-1972* New York: The Conference Board, Inc., 1973.

————. *Nondiscrimination in Employment: 1963-1975: A Broadening and Deepening National Effort*. New York: The Conference Board, Inc., 1975.

Newspapers

AFL-CIO News   *New York Amsterdam News*
Chicago Defender   *The New York Times*
Chicago Tribune   *St. Louis Post-Dispatch*
Cleveland Plain Dealer *Wall Street Journal*
Milwaukee Journal   *Washington Post*

Oral History Interviews—JFK Library

Lindsay, John V. April 21, 1970. Interviewed by Roberta Greene.

Marshall, Burke. Third Interview. June 13, 1964. Interviewed by Anthony Lewis.

Mitchell, Clarence, Jr. February 9 & 23, 1967. Interviewed by John Stewart.

Wilkins, Roy. August 13, 1964. Interviewed by Paul Bernhard.

Personal Interviews

Haughton, James. Director, *Fight Back!* April 4, 1984.

Hill, Herbert. Former Labor Secretary, NAACP. 1984. Telephone Conservation, December 9, 1984.

MacNamara, James. Former Special Assistant to the Commissioner of Manpower and Career Development Agency. April 12, 1984. Telephone Conversation, March 1, 1985.

Panetta, Leon. Former Director, Office of Civil Rights, Department of Health, Education, and Welfare. May 22, 1984.

Weaver, Robert C. Former Secretary, Department of Housing and Urban Development. April 25, 1984.

SECONDARY

Books

Altshuler, Alan A., ed. *The Politics of the Federal Bureaucracy.* New York: Dodd, Mead and Co., 1968.

Ambrose, Stephen E. *Nixon: Volume Two: The Triumph of a Politician, 1962-1972.* New York: Simon & Schuster, 1989.

———. *Nixon: Volume Three: Ruin and Recovery, 1973-1990.* New York: Simon & Schuster, 1991.

Aptheker, Herbert. *American Negro Slave Revolts.* New York: International Publishers, 1963.

Auerbach, Jerold S. *Unequal Justice.* New York: Oxford University Press, 1976, 1980.

Becker, Gary S. *The Economics of Discrimination.* 2d Ed. Chicago: University of Chicago Press, 1957, 1971.

Belz, Herman. *Equality Transformed: A Quarter Century of Affirmative Action.* New Brunswick, NJ: Social Philosophy and Policy Center and Transaction Publishers, 1991.

Bernstein, Irving. *Guns or Butter: The Presidency of Lyndon Johnson.* New York: Oxford University Press, 1996.

Blassingame, John W. *The Slave Community: Plantation Life in the Antebellum South.* Rev. Ed. New York: Oxford University Press, 1979.

Bolick, Clint. *The Affirmative Action Fraud: Can We Restore the American Civil Rights Vision?* Washington, DC: Cato Institute, 1996.

Bramwell, Jonathon. *Courage in Crisis: The Black Professional Today.* New York: The Bobbs-Merrill Company, Inc., 1972.

Branch, Taylor. *Parting the Waters: America in the King Years, 1954-63.* New York: Simon & Schuster, 1988.

Brauer, Carl M. *John F. Kennedy and the Second Reconstruction.* New York: Columbia University Press, 1977.

Brooks, Thomas R. *Toil and Trouble: A History of American Labor.* 2nd Ed. New York: Delacorte Press, 1971.

Brownlee, W. Elliot. *Dynamics of Ascent: A History of the American Economy.* 2nd Ed. New York: Alfred A. Knopf, 1974, 1979.

Burner, David. *Herbert Hoover: A Public Life.* New York: Alfred A. Knopf, 1979.

——, and Thomas R. West. *The Torch Is Passed: The Kennedy Brothers and American Liberalism.* St. James, NY: Brandywine Press, 1984.

Carnegie Council on Policy Studies in Higher Education. *Making Affirmative Action Work in Higher Education.* Washington, DC: Jossey-Bass Publishers, 1975.

Commerce Clearinghouse House. *New 1972 Equal Employment Opportunity Law.* Chicago: Commerce Clearing House, Inc., 1972.

Congressional Quarterly. *Almanac.* Vols. XIX; XX; XXVII. Washington, DC: Congressional Quarterly Services.

——. *Politics in America 1945-1966.* Washington, DC: Congressional Quarterly Services, 1967.

Conrad, David E. *The Forgotten Farmers.* Urbana: University of Illinois Press, 1965.

Covington, Robert N., and James E. Jones, eds. *Labor Relations and Social Problems.* 2nd Ed. Washington, DC: Bureau of National Affairs, 1971, 1973. Unit 3: *Discrimination in Employment.*

Detlefsen, Robert R. *Civil Rights under Reagan.* San Francisco: Institute for Contemporary Studies, 1991.

Derryck, Dennis A. *The Construction Industry: A Black Perspective.* Washington, DC: Joint Center for Political Studies, 1972.

Drew, Elizabeth. *Showdown: The Struggle Between the Gingrich Congress and the Clinton White House.* New York: Simon & Schuster, 1996.

Dubinsky, Irwin. *Reform in Trade Union Discrimination in the Construction Industry.* New York: Praeger Publishers, 1973.

Dulles, Foster Rhea. *The Civil Rights Commission: 1957-1965.* East Lansing: Michigan State University Press, 1968.

Eastland, Terry. *Ending Affirmative Action: The Case for Colorblind Justice.* New York: Basic Books, 1996.

——, and William J. Bennet. *Counting by Race: Equality from the Founding Fathers to Bakke and Weber.* New York: Basic Books, Inc., 1979.

Foner, Philip S. *Organized Labor and the Black Worker,* 1619-1981. New York: International Publishers, 1981.

Ford, Lee Ellen, ed. *Women's Legal Handbook.* Butler, IN: Ford Associates, 1974. Vol. 4: *Equal Pay.*

Frank, Miriam; Marilyn Ziebarth; and Connie Field. *The Life and Times of Rosie the Riveter.* Emeryville, CA: Clarity Educational Productions, 1982.

Fujita, Kuniko. *Black Workers' Struggles in Detroit's Auto Industry, 1935-1975.* Saratoga, CA: Century Twenty One Publishing, 1980.

Garrow, David J. *Bearing the Cross: Martin Luther King, Jr., and the Southern Christian Leadership Conference.* New York: Vintage Books, 1988.

———. *Protest at Selma.* New Haven, CT: Yale University Press, 1978.

Gelber, Stephen M. *Black Men and Businessmen: The Growing Awareness of a Social Responsibility.* Port Washington, NY: National University Publications, Kennikat Press, 1974.

Gelfand, Mark I. *A Nation of Cities: The Federal Government and Urban America, 1933-1965.* New York: Oxford University Press, 1975.

Genovese, Eugene D. *Roll, Jordan, Roll: The World that the Slaves Made.* New York: Vintage Books, 1974, 1976.

Germond, Jack W., and Jules Witcover. *Mad As Hell: Revolt at the Ballot Box, 1992.* New York: Warner Books, 1993.

Gill, Gerard R. *Meanness Mania.* Washington, DC: Howard University Press, 1980.

Glazer, Nathan. *Affirmative Discrimination: Ethnic Inequality and Public Policy.* New York: Basic Books, Inc., 1975.

Goodwin, Doris Kearns. *Lyndon Johnson and the American Dream.* New York: Harper and Row, 1976.

Gould, William B. *Black Workers in White Unions.* Ithaca, NY: Cornell University Press, 1977.

Goulden, Joseph C. *Meany.* New York: Atheneum, 1972.

Graham, Hugh Davis. *The Civil Rights Era: Origins and Development of National Policy.* New York: Oxford University Press, 1990.

Grant, Joanne, ed. *Black Protest.* New York: St. Martin's Press, 1968.

Hamby, Alonzo L. *Liberalism and Its Challengers: FDR to Reagan.* New York: Oxford University Press, 1985.

Harris, William H. *The Harder We Run: Black Workers since the Civil War.* New York: Oxford University Press, 1982.

Harvey, James C. *Civil Rights during the Kennedy Administration.* Hattiesburg: University and College Press of Mississippi, 1971.

Hausman, L.J.; A. Orley; B. Rustin; R.F. Schubert; and D. Slaiman, eds. *Equal Rights and Industrial Relations*. Madison: University of Wisconsin, Industrial Relations Research Association, 1977.

Heath, Jim F. *Decade of Disillusionment*. Bloomington: Indiana University Press, 1975.

Hill, Herbert. *Black Labor and the American Legal System*. Vol. 1. Washington, DC: Bureau of National Affairs, 1977.

———. *Labor Union Control of Job Training*. Howard University Institute for Urban Affairs and Research, Vol. 2, No. 1, 1974.

Hodgson, Godfrey. *America in Our Time*. Garden City, NY: Doubleday and Company Inc., 1976.

Howe, Irving, ed. *The World of the Blue-Collar Worker*. New York: Quadrangle Books, 1972.

Ireland, Patricia. *What Women Want*. New York: Dutton/Penguin, 1996.

Irons, Peter. *Brennan vs. Rehnquist: The Battle for the Constitution*. New York: Alfred A. Knopf, 1994.

Kirby, John B. *Black Americans in the Roosevelt Era*. Knoxville: University of Tennessee Press, 1980.

Kusmer, Kenneth L. *A Ghetto Takes Shape: Black Cleveland, 1870-1930*. Chicago: University of Chicago Press, 1976.

Leggett, John C. *Class, Race and Labor: Working-Class Consciousness in Detroit*. New York: Oxford University Press, 1968, 1971.

Levenstein, Harvey A. *Communism, Anticommunism and the CIO*. Westport, CT: Greenwood Press, 1981.

Levitan, Sar A., ed. *Blue-Collar Workers: A Symposium on Middle America*. New York: McGraw-Hill Book Company, 1971.

———, and William B. Johnston and Robert Taggart. *Still A Dream: The Changing Status of Blacks since 1960*. Cambridge: Harvard University Press, 1975.

Lewis, David L. *King: A Critical Biography*. Baltimore: Penguin Books, Inc., 1971.

Link, Arthur S. *Wilson: The New Frontier*. Princeton, NJ: Princeton University Press, 1956.

MacNeil, Neil. *Dirksen: Portrait of a Public Man*. New York: The World Publishing Company, 1970.

Marshall, F. Ray. *The Negro and Organized Labor*. New York: John Wiley and Sons, Inc., 1965.

———. *The Negro Worker*. New York: Random House, 1967.

Martin, John Frederick. *Civil Rights and the Crisis of Liberalism: The Democratic Party, 1945-1976*. Boulder, CO: Westview Press, 1979.

Matusow, Allen J. *The Unraveling of America: A History of Liberalism in the 1960s*. New York: Harper and Row, 1984.

McGuiness, Kevin S. *Government Memoranda on Affirmative Action Programs*. Washington, DC: Equal Employment Advisory Council, 1976.

Meier, August. *Black Detroit and the Rise of the UAW*. New York: Oxford University Press, 1979.

——. Ed. *The Transformation of Activism*. Chicago: Aldine Publishing Company, Trans-Action Books, 1970.

——, and Rudwick, Elliot. *CORE*. New York: Oxford University Press, 1973.

Mills, Daniel Quinn. *Industrial Relations and Manpower in Construction*. Cambridge, MA: MIT Press, 1972.

Morgan, Ruth P. *The President and Civil Rights: Policy-Making by Executive Order*. New York: St. Martin's Press, 1970.

Morris, Frank C., Jr. *Current Trends in the Use (and Misuse) of Statistics in Employment Discrimination Litigation.* Washington, DC: Equal Employment Advisory Council, 1977.

Murphy, Reg; and Hall Gulliver. *The Southern Strategy*. New York: Charles Scribner's Sons, 1971.

Murphy, Thomas P. *The New Politics Congress*. Lexington, MA: D.C. Heath and Company, 1974.

Murray, Robert K. *The Harding Era: Warren G. Harding and His Administration*. Minneapolis: University of Minnesota Press, 1969.

Myrdal, Gunnar. *An American Dilemma*. New York: Harper and Row, Publishers, 1944, 1962.

Nathan, Richard P. *Jobs and Civil Rights*. Washington, DC: Government Printing Office, 1969.

——. *The Plot that Failed: Nixon and the Administrative Presidency*. New York: John Wiley and Sons, Inc., 1975.

Navasky, Victor S. *Kennedy Justice*. New York: Atheneum, 1971.

Neier, Aryeh. *Only Judgment: The Limits of Litigation in Social Change*. Middletown, CT: Wesleyan University Press, 1982.

Newfield, Jack. *Robert Kennedy: A Memoir*. New York: E.P. Dutton and Company, Inc., 1969.

Newman, Dorothy K., et al.. *Protest, Politics, and Prosperity: Black Americans and White Institutions 1940-1975*. New York: Pantheon Books, 1978.

O'Neill, William. *Coming Apart*. New York: Quadrangle Books, 1971.

Osofsky, Gilbert. *Harlem: The Making of a Ghetto*. New York: Harper and Row, Publishers, 1963, 1966.

Ottley, Roi. *New World A-Coming*. Cambridge, MA: The Riverside Press, 1943.

Patterson, James T. *America's Struggle against Poverty, 1900-1980*. Cambridge, MA: Harvard University Press, 1981.

Phelps, Timothy M., and Helen Winternitz. *Capitol Games: Clarence Thomas, Anita Hill, and the Story of a Supreme Court Nomination*. New York: Hyperion, 1992.

Piven, Francis Fox, and Richard A Cloward. *Poor Peoples' Movements*. New York: Vintage Books, 1979.

Powers, Thompson, ed. *Now Hear This! Equal Employment Opportunity: Compliance and Affirmative Action*. New York: National Association of Manufacturers, 1969.

Pringle, Henry F. *Theodore Roosevelt: A Biography*. New York: Harcourt, Brace and World, 1931, 1956.

Ransom, Roger L., and Richard Sutch. *One Kind of Freedom: The Economic Consequences of Emancipation*. New York: Cambridge University Press, 1977.

Robinson, Archie. *George Meany and His Times*. New York: Simon & Schuster, 1981.

Rosenbloom, David H. *Federal Equal Employment Opportunity*. New York: Praeger Publishers, 1977.

Rowan, Richard L., and Lester Rubin. *Opening the Skilled Construction Trades to Blacks*. Philadelphia: University of Pennsylvania Press, 1972.

Ruchames, Louis. *Race, Jobs and Politics: The Story of FEPC*. New York: Columbia University Press, 1952, 1953.

Scammon, Richard M., and Wattenberg, Ben J. *The Real Majority*. New York: Coward-McCann, Inc., 1970.

Schlesinger, Arthur M., Jr. *A Thousand Days*. Boston: Houghton Mifflin Company, 1965.

Sitkoff, Harvard. *A New Deal for Blacks*. New York: Oxford University Press, 1978, 1981.

Sorenson, Theodore. *Kennedy*. New York: Harper and Row, 1965.

Sovern, Michael I. *Legal Restraints on Racial Discrimination Employment*. New York: The Twentieth Century Fund, 1966.

Spear, Allan H. *Black Chicago: The Making of a Negro Ghetto 1890-1920*. Chicago: University of Chicago Press, 1967.

Squires, Gregory D. *Affirmative Action*. Institute for Community Development, Continuing Education Service, Michigan State University, 1977.

Stasz, Clarence. *The American Nightmare: Why Inequality Exists*. New York: Schocken Books, 1981.

Steinberg, Stephen. *Turning Back: The Retreat from Racial Justice in American Thought and Policy*. Boston: Beacon Press, 1995.

Stone, Chuck. *Black Political Power in America*. New York: The Bobbs-Merrill Company, 1968.

Sundquist, James L. *Dynamics of the Party System*. Washington, DC: The Brookings Institution, 1983.

———. *Politics and Party : The Eisenhower, Kennedy, and Johnson Years*. Washington, DC: The Brookings Institution, 1968.

Toppin, Edgar A. *A Biographical History of Blacks in America since 1528*. New York: David McKay Company, Inc., 1969, 1971.

Warner, David C., ed. *Toward New Human Rights. The Social Policies of the Kennedy and Johnson Administrations*. Austin: The University of Texas, 1977.

Weaver, Robert C. *Negro Labor: A National Problem*. New York: Harcourt, Brace and Co., 1946.

Weiss, Nancy J. *The National Urban League 1910-1940*. New York: Oxford University Press, 1974.

White, Theodore H. *The Making of the President, 1972*. New York: Atheneum Publishers, 1973.

Wicker, Tom. *One of Us: Richard Nixon and the American Dream*. New York: Random House, 1991.

———. *Tragic Failure: Racial Integration in America*. New York: William A. Morrow and Company, Inc., 1996.

Witt, Elder. *A Different Justice: Reagan and the Supreme Court*. Washington, DC: Congressional Quarterly, Inc., 1986.

Wittner, Lawrence. *Cold War America*. New York: Praeger Publishers, 1974.

Wolk, Allan. *The Presidency and Black Civil Rights*. Philadelphia: Fairleigh Dickinson University Press, 1971.

Wolkinson, Benjamin W. *Blacks, Unions, and the EEOC*. Lexington, MA: D.C. Heath and Company, Lexington Books, 1973.

Wolters, Raymond. *Negroes and the Great Depression*. Westport, CT: Greenwood Publishing Corporation, 1970.

Unpublished Ph.D. Dissertations

Hubbard, Gary W. "Affirmative Action: The Law and Politics of Equality." University of Nebraska-Lincoln, 1978.

Mbatia, Oliver Lee E. "The Economic Impact of the 1964 Fair Employment Practices Act and Subsequent Executive Orders on Black Americans." Oregon State University, 1972.

Naison, Mark D. "The Communist Party in Harlem, 1928-1936." Columbia University, 1976.

Simba, Malik. "The Black Laborer, the Black Legal Experience, and the United States Supreme Court with Emphasis on the Neo-Concept of Equal Employment." 2 Vols. University of Minnesota, 1977.

Vines, Dwight D. "The Impact of Title VII of the 1964 Civil Rights Law on Personnel Policies and Practices." University of Colorado, 1967.

Articles

Adams, Arvil V. "Evaluating the Success of the EEOC Compliance Process." *Monthly Labor Review* 96 (May, 1973): 26-29.

Alleyne, Reginald. "Current Developments under Title VII of the Civil Rights Act of 1964 and Executive Order 11246." In *Current Developments in Labor Law*. Edited by Reginald Alleyne and Jan Vetter. Berkeley School of Law, University of California, 1970.

Alsop, Joseph. "The Philadelphia Plan: A Dilemma with Sharp Horns." *Los Angeles Times*, January 6, 1970, Section 11, p. 7.

Anderson, Bernard E., and Phyllis A. Wallace. "Public Policy and Black Economic Progress: A Review of the Evidence." *American Economic Review* 65 (May, 1975): 47-51.

Anderson, Roger W. "Affirmative Relief under Title VII of the Civil Rights Act of 1964." *Baylor Law Review*, Vol. 29, Part 1, 1977, pp. 373-87.

Askin, Steve, and Edmund Norton. "Blood, Sweat and Steel." *Black Enterprise* 14 (May, 1984): 40-48.

Baker, Leonard. "Compliance." *American Education* 1 (September, 1965): 24ff.

Bazell, Robert. "Sex Discrimination: Campuses Face Contract Losses over HEW Demands." *Science* 170 (November 11, 1970): 834-35.

Bell, Duran. "Occupational Discrimination As a Source of Income Differences: Lessons of the 1960s." *American Economic Review* 62 (May, 1972): 363-72.

Berg, Richard K. "Equal Employment Opportunity under the Civil Rights Act of 1964." *Brooklyn Law Review* 31 (1964-65): 62-97.

Blumrosen, Alfred W. "The Crossroads for Equal Employment Opportunity: Incisive Administration or Indecisive Bureaucracy." *Notre Dame Lawyer* 49 (October, 1973): 46-62.

———. "Labor Arbitration, EEOC Conciliation, and Discrimination in Employment." *The Arbitration Journal* 24 (1969): 88-105.

———. "Strangers in Paradise: *Griggs v. Duke Power Company* and the Concept of Employment Discrimination." *Michigan Law Review* 71 (November, 1972): 59-110.

Borosage, Robert; Barbara Brown; Paul Friedman; Paul Gerwitz; William Jeffries; and William Kelly. "The New Public Interest Lawyers." *The Yale Law Journal* 79 (May, 1970): 1069-1152.

Brauer, Carl N. "Kennedy, Johnson, and the War on Poverty." *Journal of American History* 69 (June, 1982): 98ff.

Brest, Paul. "Race Discrimination." In *The Burger Court*, pp. 113-131. Edited by Vincent Blasi. New Haven, CT: Yale University Press, 1983.

Brooks, Thomas R. "Black Upsurge in the Unions." *Dissent* (March-April, 1970): 124-34.

———. "DRUMbeats in Detroit." *Dissent* (January-February, 1970): 16-25.

Broom, Leonard, and Norval D. Glenn. "When Will America's Negroes Catch Up?" *New Society* 130 (March 25, 1965): 6-7.

Bullock, Stephen G. "The Focal Issue: Discriminatory Motivation or Adverse Impact?" *Louisiana Law Review* 34 (1974): 572-89.

Burns, Haywood. "The Action Is Not Affirmative." In *The Burger Years: Rights and Wrongs in the Supreme Court, 1969-1986,* pp. 95-108. Edited by Herman Schwartz. New York: Elisabeth Sifton Books/Viking, 1987.

"Labor Drive for LBJ Hits Own "Backlash". *Business Week*, September 12, 1964, pp. 49-54.

"Caught in the Civil Rights Crossfire." *Business Week*, August 7, 1965, pp. 102-106.

"New Drive to 'Fulfill the Rights'." *Business Week*, May 28, 1966, pp. 38-40.

"For Negroes, The Pie Cuts Too Thin." *Business Week*, August 5, 1967, pp. 26-28.

"Opening the Record on Jobs for Negroes." *Business Week*, August 12, 1967, pp. 128-30.

"Negroes Go National with Demands for Jobs." *Business Week*, August 19, 1967, pp. 37-38.

"Cram Course for Negro Apprentices." *Business Week*, November 25, 1967, pp. 88-95.

"Crafts Ease Their Stand on Bias." *Business Week*, December 9, 1967, pp. 133-34.

"Building for Peace in Construction." *Business Week*, March 16, 1968, pp. 100-103.

"Cracking Down on Job Bias." *Business Week*, June 1, 1968, pp. 34-38.

"A 'Model Employer' Fights Back on Bias." *Business Week*, October 12, 1968, pp. 122-26.

"New Secretary Leans to a Middle Course." *Business Week*, December 21, 1968, pp. 74-75.

"Not Discriminating Becomes Not Enough." *Business Week*, January 11, 1969, pp. 88-92.

"Demonstrating Again at Allen-Bradley." *Business Week*, August 16, 1969, p. 44.

"Pittsburgh Blacks Try Negotiating." *Business Week*, September 6, 1969, pp. 32-33.

"Shultz Job Plan for Blacks Hits Snag." *Business Week*, November 15, 1969, p. 109.

"The Unhappy Parent of New Hiring Rules." *Business Week*, January 24, 1970, p. 39.

"Integration Drive Fails to Overcome." *Business Week*, June 6, 1970, pp. 48-52.

"Minority Hiring under New Attack." *Business Week*, June 13, 1970, p. 10.

"Battle over Bias Charges." *Business Week*, December 19, 1970, p. 50.

"The Sit-in at A&P Was No Tea Party." *Business Week*, February 6, 1971, p. 21.

"Discrimination Suits Hit More Companies." *Business Week*, July 8, 1972, p. 20.

"Politics May Kill Quotas for Hiring." *Business Week*, September 9, 1972, pp. 36-37.

"Jesse Jackson's 13 New Targets." *Business Week*, October 7, 1972, pp. 32-33.

"Nixon's Choice." *Business Week,* August 25, 1973, p. 29.

"Acting Affirmatively to End Job Bias." *Business Week*, January 27, 1975, pp. 94-102.

"An Industry Man Takes Over A Battered EEOC." *Business Week*, June 23, 1975, pp. 113-15.

"White Business Balks at Sharing the Work." *Business Week*, November 17, 1975, p. 47.

Camejo, Peter. "The Civil Rights Movement: How It Began, What It Won." *The Militant* 38 (December 20, 1974): 5-8.

Carter, Barbara. "The Role of the Civil Rights Commission." *The Reporter* 29 (July 4, 1963): 10-14.

"White America's Recession: Black America's Depression." *Christian Science Monitor*, January 21, 1975, pp. 1 & 6.

Connolly, Harold X. "Assessing Affirmative Action." *Intellect* 106 (October, 1977): 134-36.

Converse, Philip E.; Warren E. Miller; Jerold G. Rusk; and Arthur C. Wolfe. "Continuity and Change in American Politics: Parties and Issues in the 1968 Election." *The American Political Science Review* 63 (December, 1969): 1083-1105.

Cook, Carvin. "Federal Employment Standards Legislation." *Monthly Labor Review* 96 (January, 1973): 50-51.

"Apprenticeship Test Is Upheld." *The Crisis* 74 (March, 1967): 104.

"NAACP Launches Drive for Construction Jobs." *The Crisis* 74 (July, 1967): 303.

"NAACP Sues on Building Trades Bias." *The Crisis* 76 (October, 1969): 338-39.

"Court Bans Asbestos Union Bias." *The Crisis* 77 (March, 1970): 112-13.

"New York Job Plan Opposed." *The Crisis* 77 (June-July, 1970): 234.

"Construction Job Bias Ban by Government Supported." *The Crisis* 78 (April-May, 1971): 99.

"NAACP Hails Court-Ban on Biased Job Practices." *The Crisis* 78 (September, 1971): 229.

Crotty, Phillip, and Timmons, Jeffrey. "Older Minorities Roadblocked in the Organization." *Business Horizons* 17 (June, 1974): 27-34.

Crowell, Erbin, Jr. "EEOC's Image: Remedy for Job Discrimination?" *Civil Rights Digest* 1 (Spring, 1968): 29ff.

Culhane, Charles. "Battle over Enforcement Powers for EEOC Pits Business Against Labor, Civil Rights Groups." *National Journal Reports* 3 (November 13, 1971): 2249-2259.

Current, Gloster B. "Why Nixon Lost the Negro Vote." *The Crisis* 68 (January, 1961): 5-14.

Curry, Earl M., Jr. "Employment Equality in a Color-Blind Society." *Akron Law Review* 5 (Spring, 1972): 165-201.

Day, David S. "Herbert Hoover and Racial Politics, The DePriest Incident." *The Journal of Negro History* 65 (Winter, 1980): 6-17.

DeAngelis, Tori. "Ignorance Plagues Affirmative Action." Reprint from *APA Monitor*, May 1995.

Delaney, Paul. "U.S. Is Spurring Efforts to Fight Job Prejudice." *The New York Times*, January 19, 1974, p. 43.

Dewey, Donald. "Negro Employment in Southern Industry." *The Journal of Political Economy* 60 (August, 1952): 279-93.

Donegan, Charles Edward. "The Philadelphia Plan: A Viable Means of Achieving Equal Opportunity or More Pie in the Sky?" *University of Kansas Law Review* 20 (Winter, 1972): 195-212.

Elliot, Robert M. "Reverse Discrimination: The Balancing of Human Rights." *Wake Forest Law Review* 12 (1976): 852-77.

"Outreach and OJT Programs Should Be Halted, GAO Says." *Engineering News Record*, May 11, 1978, p. 66.

Friedman, Murray. "Intergroup Relations and Tensions in the United States." *American Jewish Year Book*, Vol. 73, 1972, pp. 97-153. Published by American Jewish Committee (New York) and Jewish Publication Society of America (Philadelphia).

———. "Politics and Intergroup Relations in the United States." *American Jewish Year Book*, Vol. 74, 1973, pp. 139-93.

Grazza, Beverly A. "*Carter v. Gallagher: From Benign Classification to Reverse Discrimination.*" *University of Pittsburgh Law Review* 34 (1972): 130-44.

Gutman, Herbert G. "The Negro and the United Mine Workers of America." *In Work, Culture and Society in Industrializing America*, pp. 121-208. New York: Random House, Vintage Books, 1977.

Hacker, Sally. "Sex Stratification, Technology, and Organizational Change: A Longitudinal Case Study of AT&T." *Social Problems* 26 (June, 1979): 539-57.

Hammerman, Herbert, and Martin Rogoff. "Unions and Title VII of the Civil Rights Act of 1964." *Monthly Labor Review* 99 (April, 1976): 34ff.

Haughton, James. "The Role of the Board of Education in Perpetuating Racism in the Building Trades and Vice-Versa." In *Schools Against Children*, pp. 159-193. Edited by Annette T. Rubinstein. New York: Monthly Review Press, 1970.

Healer, Walter. "Economics of the Race Problem." *Social Research* 37 (Winter, 1970): 494-510.

Hill, Herbert. "Affirmative Action and the Quest for Job Equality." *The Review of Black Political Economy* 6 (Spring, 1976): 273-88;

——. "Black Protest and the Struggle for Union Democracy." Reprinted from *Issues in Industrial Society* 1 (1969): 19ff.

——. "The Equal Employment Opportunity Commission: Twenty Years Later." Reprinted from *The Journal of Intergroup Relations* XI (Winter, 1983): 45-72.

——. "The ILGWU Today—The Decay of A Labor Union." NAACP Reprint from *New Politics*.

——. "The New Judicial Perception of Employment Discrimination—Litigation under Title VII of the Civil Rights Act of 1964." *University of Colorado Law Review* 43 (March, 1972): 243-68.

——. "The New York City Terminal Market Controversy: A Case Study of Race, Labor, and Power." Reprinted from *Humanities in Society* 6 (Fall, 1983): 351-91.

——. "Nixon and the 'Hard Hats': 'Law and Order' v. 'Hometown' Solutions." *Social Policy* 1 (November-December, 1970): 41-43.

——. "Race and Ethnicity in Organized Labor: The Historical Sources of Resistance to Affirmative Action." Reprinted from *The Journal of Intergroup Relations* XII (Winter, 1984): 5-49.

——. "The Racial Policies of Organized Labor: The Contemporary Record." In *The Negro and the American Labor Movement*, pp. 286-357. Edited by Julius Jacobson. Garden City, NY: Anchor-Doubleday and Co., Inc., 1968.

——. "Racism within Organized Labor." Address delivered January 3, 1961. Published by NAACP.

——. "State Laws and the Negro: Social Change and the Impact of Law." *African Forum* 1 (Fall, 1965): 92-105.

Hodge, Claire C. "The Negro Job Situation: Has It Improved?" *Monthly Labor Review* 92 (January 1969): 20-28.

Hyatt, James C. "The Anti-Bias Bottleneck." *Wall Street Journal*, October 22, 1974, p. 20.

"EEOC Appointee Faces Steel Bias Decision." *Industry Week* 180 (January 14, 1974): 19-21.

"Pittsburgh Blacks Gain in Construction Trades." *Industry Week* 182 (September 9, 1974): 21-22.

"EEOC Wrestles with Backlog, Unemployment." *Industry Week* 183 (October 28, 1974): 24-25.

"United States: Equal Employment Opportunity in Apprenticeship and Training." *International Labour Review* 105 (April, 1972): 381-84.

Jackson, Jesse. "People of Color Need Affirmative Action." In *Affirmative Action*, pp. 8-13. Edited by A.E. Sadler. San Diego, CA: Greenhaven Press, 1996.

Jacobs, Deborah L. "Reagan's War on Quotas." *Newsday*, May 18, 1985, pp. 16-17NY.

Johnson, Sheila K. "It's Action, But Is It Affirmative?" *The New York Times Magazine*, May 11, 1975, pp. 18ff.

Jones, James E., Jr. "The Bugaboo of Employment Quotas." *Wisconsin Law Review*, 1970, pp. 341-403.

———. "Equal Employment Opportunities: The Promises of the '60s—The Reality of the '70s." *The Black Law Journal* 2 (Spring, 1972): 5-20.

Joyce, John T. "Construction Unions in the '70s." *The American Federationist* 80 (October, 1973): 9-15.

Kempton, Murray. "Heroes on the Right." *The New Republic* 149 (November 9, 1963): 4.

Kettlekamp, John Harold. "Reverse Discrimination." *Mississippi Law Journal* 45 (1974): 467-88.

Kruman, Mark W. "Quotas for Blacks: The Public Works Administration and the Black Construction Worker." *Labor History* 16 (Winter, 1975): 37-49.

Kuttner, Robert. "Red and Green in Civil Rights." *Commonweal* 90 (September 5, 1969): 535.

"Agreement Provides Training of Negroes As Skilled Pipefitters." *Labor* 52 (February 7, 1970): 5.

Leiken, Earl M. "Preferential Treatment in the Skilled Building Trades: An Analysis of the Philadelphia Plan." *Cornell Law Review* 56 (November, 1970): 84ff.

Lowe, Robert C. "Race Quotas As a Form of Affirmative Action." *Louisiana Law Review* 34 (1974): 552-63.

Malbin, Michael. "Agency Differences Persist over Goals and Timetables in Nondiscrimination Plans." *National Journal Reports* 5. Part I (September 22, 1973): 1400-11. Part II (September 29): 1429-34.

Mansfield, Harvey C., Jr. "The Underhandedness of Affirmative Action." In *Social Issues: Conflicting Opinions*, pp. 117-26. Edited by Nils I.

Bateman and David M. Petersen. Upper Saddle River, NJ: Prentice Hall, 1990. Reprint from *National Review*, May 4, 1984.

Milloy, Courtland, Jr. "Plan To Get More Blacks into Washington Construction Jobs Fails." *Washington Post*, March 10, 1981, pp. 1 & 10.

Monroe, William B., Jr. "Television: The Chosen Instrument of the Revolution." *In Race and the News Media*, pp. 83-97. Edited by Paul L. Fisher and Ralph L. Lowenstein. New York: Frederick A. Praeger, Publishers, 1967.

"EEOC's New Weapon." *Monthly Labor Review* 96 (February, 1973): 57-58.

"Minorities in Construction Referral Unions Revisited." *Monthly Labor Review* 96 (May, 1973): 43-46.

Moon, Henry Lee. "The Black Boycott." *The Crisis* 73 (May, 1966): 249ff.

Mounts, Gregory J. "Labor and the Supreme Court: Significant Decisions of 1976-77." *Monthly Labor Review* 101 (January, 1978): 12-17.

Nash, Peter G. "Affirmative Action under Executive Order 11246." New York University Law Review 46 (April, 1971): 225-61.

National Journal Reports. Assorted articles and news briefs, 1971-1975.

"Toothless Tiger." *New Republic* 165 (February 26, 1972): 8.

"Halleck and McCulloch." *Newsweek* 62 (November 11, 1963): 34-37.

"Gamble in the Ghetto." *Newsweek* 67 (January 31, 1966): 24-25.

"Quotas: The Sleeper Issue of '72?" *Newsweek* 80 (September 18, 1972): 36-39.

"Ma Bell Agrees To Pay Reparations." *Newsweek* 81 (January 29, 1973): 53-54.

"Tackling the Giants." *Newsweek* 82 (October 1, 1973): 84.

"HEW Sounds A Retreat." *Newsweek* 86 (July 14, 1975): 48.

"Building Trades: Controls for A Rough Industry?" *The New York Sunday Times*, September 28, 1969, p. 4E.

Niemi, Albert W., Jr. "The Impact of Recent Civil Rights Laws: Relative Improvement in Occupational Structure, Earnings and Income by Nonwhites, 1960-70." *The American Journal of Economics and Sociology* 33 (April, 1974): 137-44.

O'Hanlon, Thomas. "The Case Against the Unions." *Fortune* 77 (January, 1968): 170ff.

Oreskes, Michael, and Selwyn Raab. "Tainted Industry: Construction in New York." *The New York Times*, April 25-27, 1982.

278 *Bibliography*

Ornati, Oscar A., and Edward Gilbin. "The High Cost of Discrimination." *Business Horizons* 18 (February, 1975): 35-40.

Perry, John. "Business—Next Target for Integration." *Harvard Business Review* 41 (March-April, 1963): 104-115.

Pinkus, Edward C. "The Workers' Defense League." In *Programs To Employ the Disadvantaged*, pp. 168-203. Edited by Peter B. Doeringer. Upper Saddle River, NJ: Prentice-Hall, Inc., 1969.

Plastrik, Stanley. "Confrontation in Pittsburgh." *Dissent* (January-February, 1970): 25-31.

Potts, Georgena. "Conference on Equal Employment Opportunity." *Monthly Labor Review* 88 (November, 1965): 1320-21.

Purcell, Theodore V. "How GE Measures Managers in Fair Employment." *Harvard Business Review* 52 (November-December, 1974): 99-104.

Raskin, A.H. "Union Discrimination Is Hard To Erase." *The New York Times*, May 10, 1964, p. E5.

Reed, Merl E. "FEPC and the Federal Agencies in the South." *The Journal of Negro History* 65 (Winter, 1980): 43-56.

Reeves, Earl J. "Making Equality of Employment Opportunity A Reality in the Federal Service." *Public Administration Review* 30 (January-February, 1970): 43-49.

Remmert, James E. "Executive Order 11246: Executive Encroachment." *American Bar Association Journal* 55 (November, 1969): 1037-40.

Roberts, Lance W. "Understanding Affirmative Action." In *Discrimination, Affirmative Action and Equal Opportunity*, pp. 147-82. Edited by W.E. Block and M.A. Walker. Vancouver, British Columbia: The Fraser Institute, 1982.

Rony, Vera. "Bogalusa: The Economics of Tragedy." *Dissent* 13 (May-June, 1966): 234-42.

Rose, Stephen. "Reverse Discrimination Developments under Title VII." *Houston Law Review* 15 (October, 1977): 139-56.

Rosen, Hjalmar, and Melvin Blonsky. "Dual Standards in Employing the Hardcore." *Personnel Administration* 33 (March-April, 1970): 4ff.

Rowan, Richard L. "Discrimination and Apprenticeship Regulation in the Building Trades." *The Journal of Business* 40 (October, 1967): 435-47.

——. "Negro Employment in the Basic Steel Industry." *Industrial and Labor Relations Review* 23 (October, 1969): 29-39.

Roye, Wendell J. "The Myth of Affirmative Action." *The Journal of Intergroup Relations* VI (December, 1977): 4-22.

Russell, Joe L. "Changing Patterns in Employment of Nonwhite Workers." *Monthly Labor Review* 89 (May, 1966): 503-509.

Ryan, William F. "Uncle Sam's Betrayal." *The Progressive* 32 (May, 1968): 25-29.

Ryon, Roderick M. "An Ambiguous Legacy: Baltimore Blacks and the CIO, 1936-1941." *The Journal of Negro History* 65 (Winter, 1980): 18-33.

Schor, Willie. "Relief Under Title VII—*United States v. Bethlehem Steel Corporation,* 446 F.2d 652 (2nd Cir 1971)." *Brookyln Law Review* 38 (Spring, 1972): 993-1004.

Seabury, Paul. "HEW and the Universities." *Commentary* 53 (February, 1972): 38-44.

Seligman, Daniel. "How 'Equal Opportunity' Turned Into Employment Quotas." *Fortune* 87 (March, 1973): 160ff.

Silberman, Charles E. "The Businessman and the Negro." *Fortune* 68 (September, 1963): 97ff.

Singer, James W. "Internal Disputes Hamper EEOC Anti-Bias Efforts." *National Journal Reports* 6 (August 17, 1974): 1226-36.

Sowell, Thomas. "'Affirmative Action' Reconsidered." *The Public Interest* 42 (Winter, 1976): 47-65.

Spurlock, Delbert L., Jr. "EEOC's Compliance Process: The Problem of Selective Enforcement." *Labor Law Journal* 26 (July, 1975): 396-408.

Steel, Lewis M. "A Second 17th of May Landmark Decision." *The Crisis* 74 (June, 1967): 259-63.

———. "Nine Men In Black Who Think White." *The New York Times Magazine*, October 13, 1968, pp. 56ff.

Strauss, George, and Ingerman, Sidney. "Public Policy and Discrimination in Apprenticeship." *The Hastings Law Journal* 16 (1964-65): 285-331.

"Crossed Wires at Bell." *Time* 102 (October 22, 1973): 79.

"Caught in the Crossfire: Halleck on Civil Rights." *U.S. News and World Report* 55 (November 11, 1963): 24.

"Unions Feel Growing Pressure To Take More Negroes." *U.S. News and World Report* 56 (May 25, 1964): 86-89.

"Jobs Rights Unit Asks New Power." *U.S. News and World* Report 59 (August 2, 1965): 63.

"Now It's Whites Who Are Claiming Their Job Rights." *U.S. News and World Report* 60 (May 16, 1966): 86ff.

"Teaching People To Hold Jobs—The Philadelphia Plan." *U.S. News and World Report* 64 (January 1, 1968): 58-59.

"Job Quota Plan Survives Attack." *U.S. News and World Report* 67 (August 18, 1969): 64.

"Jobs in Building for Negroes: Agencies Split on Rules." *U.S. News and World Report* 67 (November 24, 1969): 91-92.

"Bias Suits Ask for Back Pay." *U.S. News and World Report* 71 (October 4, 1971): 96.

"Equal Employment Guidelines Expanded." *U.S. News and World Report* 72 (April 17, 1972): 88-89.

"Problems Employers Face under New Anti-Bias Rules." *U.S. News and World Report* 72 (March 13, 1972): 95.

"U.S. Orders Company: Promote More Blacks." *U.S. News and World Report* 74 (January 29, 1973): 68-69.

"Government Shifts Strategy To End Job Discrimination." *U.S. News and World Report* 75 (October 8, 1973): 104-105.

Weaver, Robert C. "An Experiment in Negro Labor." *Opportunity* XIV (October, 1936): 295-98.

Weiner, Harold M. "Negro Picketing for Employment Equality." *Howard Law Review* 13 (Spring, 1967): 271-302.

Westin, Alan F. "Ride-ins and Sit-ins of the 1870s." In *Freedom Now!*, pp. 68-74. New York: Basic Books, 1964.

Wimark, Bo. "Nonviolent Methods and the American Civil Rights Movement, 1955-1965." *Journal of Peace Research* XI (1974): 115-32.

Yeager, Dennis R. "Litigation under Title VII of the Civil Rights Act of 1964, the Construction Industry, and the Problem of the 'Unqualified' Minority Worker." *The Georgetown Law Journal* 59 (June, 1971): 1265-96.

Index